Sarbanes-Oxley and Nonprofit Management:

Skills, Techniques, and Methods

Peggy M. Jackson, DPA, CPCU

and

Toni E. Fogarty, PhD, MPH

WILEY

John Wiley & Sons, Inc.

For general information on our other products and services, or technical support, please contact our Customer Care Department within the United States at 800-762-2974, outside the United States at 317-572-3993 or fax 317-572-4002.

Wiley also publishes its books in a variety of electronic formats. Some content that appears in print may not be available in electronic books.

Library of Congress Cataloging-in-Publication Data:

ISBN-13: 978-0-471-75419-0
ISBN-10: 0-471-75419-6

Printed in the United States of America

10 9 8 7 6 5 4 3 2 1

For Paul, the love of my life.
PMJ

In loving memory
Louise Davis (Maw Maw)
TEF

Contents

Acknowledgments

Peg and Toni would like to acknowledge our editor, Susan McDermott, for her guidance and support. Thank you, thank you, thank you!

Peg is grateful for the tireless energy that Senator Charles Grassley (R–Iowa) and his staff aide, Dean Zerbe, have expended in raising public awareness of the nonprofit world's glaring need for substantive reform. Sen. Grassley's hearings in 2004 and 2005 illustrated that the American public deserves to have the same confidence in the charitable institutions to which they donate money as they have demanded of the private sector corporations in which they have invested. The staff White Paper that was produced for the 2004 hearings presents proposals that she hopes will someday become law. She fears that genuine change will not be embraced by the nonprofit world until and unless it is forced upon them. For too long nonprofits have relied upon the political capital of its "industry" lobbyists who, as recently as June 2005, produce reports to Congress claiming that the nonprofit world can regulate itself. If the private sector ever produced a report alleging that they could be trusted to regulate themselves, they would be laughed off of Capital Hill. It's time the nonprofit world was held accountable for their stewardship of donated funds. Bravo, Senator Grassley and Mr. Zerbe!

Peg would also like to acknowledge the support and encouragement she receives from friends, family, and colleagues. Paul, Rick, and Jan keep things in humorous perspective. Support from her Business Alliance colleagues at the San Francisco Chamber of Commerce and from her colleagues in the San Francisco Junior League has been steadfast and a source of inspiration.

Toni is grateful for the assistance and valuable contributions of her talented research assistants, Nataliya Lishchenko, Madeleine Mulgrew, and Archana (Archie) Rajwat—all students in the Master of Science in Health Care Administration program at California State University, East Bay. Nataliya did a great job of putting together all of the sordid details of the accounting and financial scandals, plus gave insight into Form 990 and its variants. Madeleine is now a full-fledged expert in political competence and SOX, and helped develop the overall outline of Chapter 14. Archie contributed to several chapters in the book, and was especially helpful with information regarding financial controls. She also brought a lot of enthusiasm to the project, even when working on the bibliography!

Toni has been supported by a number of friends and colleagues, all of whom help keep her on track, in life and with this project. She would like to thank Pam White, Denise Lyons, Doug Hogin, Laurie Nobilette, Frank Fulgham, Andrea Delman, Katherine Collins, and Linda Fogarty—what a great group of people! She would also like to thank her colleagues at California State University, East Bay for creating a supportive work environment—and for unlocking her office door whenever she locked her keys in. Finally, Toni would like to thank the "Ladies Who Lunch" group just for being their fabulously wonderful selves. Thanks for the support!

Preface

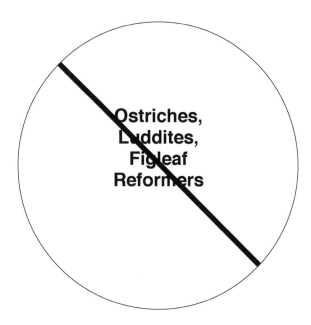

Ostriches,
Luddites,
Figleaf
Reformers

What's an ostrich, Luddite, or fig-leaf reformer? Dean Zerbe, senior aid to Senator Charles Grassley (R–Iowa) commented in an interview with the *Chronicle of Philanthropy* that he routinely encounters these three groups of nonprofit people. He defines them as "Ostriches . . . deny problems; Luddites believe there is no need for change but advocate stiffer enforcement of nonprofit laws; and fig-leaf reformers come up with ideas that appear to offer solutions but actually allow problems to persist" (Woverton, 2005, p. 38).

This book is for nonprofit board members, managers, and staff who understand that the world in general and the nonprofit world in particular have changed dramatically in the past three years. The passage of Sarbanes–Oxley (SOX) legislation introduced a new management paradigm and higher levels of accountability and transparency across all economic sectors—including the nonprofit world. From the reaction of some sectors of the nonprofit world, it would appear that resistance is still the order of the day.

Mr. Zerbe is right on all three counts. In this book, you will see examples of all three "species." The difficult truth for many nonprofits is that SOX and its best practices describe what businesses and nonprofits should have been doing all along! This book will take the reader through the history of this legislation, how SOX has influenced state legislation, and the ways in which your nonprofit can implement SOX requirements and best practices.

Here are five reasons why ostriches, Luddites, and fig-leaf reformers should become endangered species:

- The Internal Revenue Service (IRS) has committed to hold Executive Directors, CFOs, or other senior management criminally liable for veracity of financials and Form 990s.

- Banks that are publicly traded entities (which means they have to be in compliance with SOX) are requiring their clients—including nonprofits—to also be in compliance with SOX.

- SOX best practices are becoming the platinum standard for management.

- All boards (corporate and nonprofit) are being held more accountable by the federal government and its regulatory agencies such as the IRS.

- Donors, foundations, and other sources of funding will demand transparency. Being in compliance will give your nonprofit a competitive advantage.

Now, more than ever, your nonprofit needs to move to a higher level of accountability, transparency, and productivity. This book is your roadmap to the future!

CHAPTER 1

History and Legislative Background of the Sarbanes-Oxley Act of 2002

The scene is an elegant Minneapolis restaurant. Five professionals are having lunch together. Lois is the CFO of a well-known nonprofit in the Twin Cities. Shelly is an attorney with a prominent law firm. Peg is an author and consultant. Toni is a professor, author, and consultant. Virginia is a community volunteer who sits on a number of prestigious nonprofit boards. She is also the Chair of the Board of a historic Minneapolis landmark. The women met for lunch that day because they were colleagues on a pro bono project. Peg attempted, again, to convince Virginia that the conflict of interest presented by a staff member was indeed a serious issue, and the discussion turned to Sarbanes-Oxley. Virginia emphatically stated, "Sarbanes-Oxley has nothing to do with nonprofits! You don't know what you are talking about!" Both Peg and Toni attempted in vain to dissuade Virginia of this notion.

> *Yes, Virginia, Sarbanes-Oxley does apply to nonprofits!*

CHAPTER OVERVIEW

Although the Sarbanes-Oxley Act (SOX) of 2002 was passed primarily in response to wrongdoing and fiscal mismanagement in public companies, one of its effects has been to promote greater accountability within both the nonprofit and private sectors. Although the majority of management, finance, and accounting scandals in the early years of the 21st century involved public companies such as Enron, WorldCom, Adelphia Communications, and AOL Time Warner, the nonprofit world had its share of high-profile scandals, such as those involving the American Red Cross and the United Way. Recent Senate Finance Committee hearings, testimony from Mark W. Everson (Commissioner of the Internal Revenue Service), and passage of the Nonprofit Integrity Act in California all suggest a growing mistrust in the integrity of the nonprofit sector and a call for accountability. To better understand the implications of SOX on nonprofits, this chapter will review the legislation and its legislative roots, the two SOX provisions that currently apply to nonprofits, the scandals that drove passage of SOX, pertinent Senate hearings and reports, and the efforts to adopt SOX "clones," targeting nonprofit accountability.

CHAPTER OBJECTIVES

By the end of this chapter, you should be able to:

- Identify the composition requirements and responsibilities of the Public Company Accounting Oversight Board
- Outline the general requirements of SOX pertaining to auditor independence, the role of the audit committee, and the corporate responsibility for financial reports
- Define the concepts of internal controls for financial reporting and disclosure controls
- Summarize corporate accountability for document preservation and whistleblower protection
- Identify the SOX provisions that currently apply to all corporations, including nonprofits
- Discuss the testimony of relevant witnesses at the 2004 and 2005 hearings of the U.S. Senate Finance Committee
- Outline the general requirements of the Nonprofit Integrity Act of 2004 (SB 1262) in California
- Discuss the proposals made by the Panel on the Nonprofit Sector and released by the Congressional Joint Committee on Taxation in 2005

PASSAGE OF THE SARBANES-OXLEY ACT OF 2002

The Public Company Accounting Reform and Investor Protection Act of 2002 (P.L. 107–204), which typically is referred to as the Sarbanes-Oxley Act (SOX) of 2002, was signed into law by President George W. Bush on July 30, 2002. SOX has been described as the "most far-reaching reforms of American business practices since the time of Franklin Delano Roosevelt" (Office of the Press Secretary, 2002). Only the Securities Act of 1933 and the Securities Exchange Act of 1934 rival the act in its effects on public accounting, financial disclosure, and corporate governance. The act significantly broadens the authority and resources of the Securities and Exchange Commission (SEC) to monitor and regulate the securities market, and provides stiff penalties for noncompliance. In essence, the legislation complements the aim of the Securities Act of 1933 to provide "truth in securities" by improving the quality of financial reporting, independent audits, corporate accountability, and accounting services for public companies.

Compared to other legislative acts passed by Congress, SOX became law relatively quickly. On February 14, 2002, House Representative Michael G. Oxley (R-OH), the Chairperson of the House Committee on Financial Services, introduced H.R. 3763 (H.R. 3763, 2002). The purpose of the proposed legislation was "to protect investors by improving the accuracy and reliability of corporate disclosures made pursuant to the securities laws, and for other purposes." The bill had 30 House cosponsors, and was passed by the House on April 24, 2002 by a vote of 334 to 90.

On June 25, 2002, Senator Paul S. Sarbanes (D-Maryland), the Chairperson of the Senate Committee on Banking, Housing, and Urban Affairs, introduced S. 2673 (S. 2673, 2002). The purpose of this proposed legislation was "to improve quality and transparency in financial reporting and independent audits and accounting services for public companies, to create a Public Company Accounting Oversight Board, to enhance the standard setting process for accounting practices, to strengthen the independence of firms that audit public companies, to increase corporate responsibility and the usefulness of corporate financial disclosure, to protect the objectivity and independence of securities analysts, to improve Securities and Exchange Commission resources and oversight, and for other purposes." The Senate passed the bill on July 15, 2002 by a vote of 97 to 0.

Both the Senate and the House almost unanimously passed the Conference Committee Report (H.R. Rep. No. 107-610, 2002) that resolved differences in the two bills, 423 to 3 in the House and 99 to 0 in the Senate. On July 30, 2002, President George W. Bush signed the bill, and the sweeping reforms required by the act became public law (P.L. 107-204, 2002).

ANALYSIS OF THE LEGISLATIVE AND REGULATORY CONTENT OF SOX

As can be seen in Exhibit 1.1, SOX (P.L. 107-204, 2002) consists of 11 titles, with each title having multiple sections:

Title I: Public Company Accounting Oversight Board

Section 101 of Title I in SOX created the Public Company Accounting Oversight Board (PCAOB), which has extensive authority to monitor and regulate the audits and auditors of publicly held companies.

Funding Sources and Budget

The PCAOB is a nonprofit organization that is funded by public accounting firms and publicly held companies; the PCAOB is not a U.S. government agency. Partial funding for the PCAOB comes from the registration application fees and annual fees of public accounting firms that want to be authorized to provide auditing services to publicly held companies. Although the PCAOB has the authority to levy annual fees to offset the costs of reviewing annual reports submitted by the registered firms, it has not yet done so. Currently, the requirement for registered firms to submit annual reports has not been initiated. Since there are no annual reports to review, there are no reviewing costs and thus no annual fees. Once the requirement for the submission of annual reports is initiated, registered firms will be charged an annual fee. Additional funding comes from "accounting support fees" paid by companies defined as "issuers."

EXHIBIT 1.1   SOX TITLES AND SECTIONS

Title	Section
I. Public Company Accounting Oversight Board	101: Establishment, administrative provision 102: Registration with the Board 103: Auditing, quality control, and independence standards and rules 104: Inspections of registered public accounting firms 105: Investigations and disciplinary proceedings 106: Foreign public accounting firms 107: Commission oversight of the Board 108: Accounting standards 109: Funding
II. Auditor Independence	201: Services outside the scope of practice of auditors 202: Pre-approval requirements 203: Audit partner rotation 204: Auditor reports to audit committees 205: Conforming amendments 206: Conflicts of interest 207: Study of mandatory rotation of registered public accounting firms 208: Commission authority 209: Considerations by appropriate State regulatory authorities
III. Corporate Responsibility	301: Public company audit committees 302: Corporate responsibility for financial reports 303: Improper influence on conduct of audits 304: Forfeiture of certain bonuses and profits 305: Officer and director bars and penalties 306: Insider trades during pension fund blackout periods 307: Rules of professional responsibility for attorneys 308: Fair funds for investors
IV. Enhanced Financial Disclosures	401: Disclosures in periodic reports 402: Enhanced conflict of interest provisions 403: Disclosure of transactions involving management and principal stockholders 404: Management assessment of internal controls 405: Exemption 406: Code of ethics for senior financial officers

Title	Section
	407: Disclosure of audit committee financial expert
	408: Enhanced review of periodic disclosures by issuers
	409: Real-time issuer disclosures
V. Analyst Conflicts of Interest	501: Treatment of security analysts by registered securities associations and national security exchanges
VI. Commission Resources and Authority	601: Authorization of appropriations
	602: Appearance and practice before the Commission
	603: Federal court authority to impose penny stock bars
	604: Qualifications of associated persons of brokers and dealers
VII. Studies and Reports	701: GAO study and report regarding consolidation of public accounting firms
	702: Commission study and report regarding credit rating agencies
	703: Study and report on violators and violations
	704: Study of enforcement actions
	705: Study of investment banks
VIII. Corporate and Criminal Fraud Accountability	801: Short title
	802: Criminal penalties for altering documents
	803: Debts nondischargeable if incurred in violation of securities fraud laws
	804: Statute of limitations for securities fraud
	805: Review of Federal sentencing guidelines for obstruction of justice and extensive criminal fraud
	806: Protection for employees of publicly traded companies who provide evidence of fraud
	807: Criminal penalties for defrauding shareholders of publicly traded companies
IX. White Collar Crime Penalty	901: Short title
	902: Attempts and conspiracies to commit criminal fraud offenses
	903: Criminal penalties for mail and wire fraud
	904: Criminal penalties for violations of the Employee Retirement Income Security Act of 1974
	905: Amendment to sentencing guidelines relating to certain white-collar offenses
	906: Corporate responsibility for financial reports
X. Corporate Tax Returns	1001: Sense of the Senate regarding the signing of corporate tax returns by Chief Executive Officers
XI. Corporate Fraud and Accountability	1101: Short title
	1102: Tampering with a record or otherwise impeding an official proceeding
	1103: Temporary freeze authority for the Securities and Exchange Commission
	1104: Amendment to the Federal Sentencing Guidelines
	1105: Authority of the Commission to prohibit persons from serving as officers or directors
	1106: Increased criminal penalties under Securities Exchange Act of 1934
	1107: Retaliation against informants

Registration Application Fee   As can be seen in Exhibit 1.2, the amount of the application fee varies, dependent upon the number of issuer clients the applying firm audited during the year previous to the application. For firms with more than 100 clients, the fees are significantly higher than for those firms with fewer than 101 clients (Public Company Accounting Oversight Board, 2004; Public Company Accounting Oversight Board, 2005).

Accounting Support Fee   A major source of funding for the PCAOB is the "accounting support fee," which is paid by "equity issuers" and "investment company issuers." The PCAOB defines equity issuers as publicly traded companies with average monthly equity market capitalization greater than $25 million during the prior calendar year. Investment company issuers are registered investment companies and issuers that have chosen to be regulated as business development companies and had an average monthly market capitalization or net asset value greater than $250 million during the prior calendar year. The total amount of the accounting support fees is equal to the SEC-approved PCAOB budget, less the amounts collected in the previous year from registration application fees and annual fees. The basis for the accounting support fee paid by individual equity issuers and investment company issuers is the relative average monthly U.S. market capitalization. Each issuer's share is its average monthly U.S. market capitalization during the preceding calendar year, divided by the sum of the average monthly U.S. market capitalization of all equity and investment company issuers (PCAOB, 2005).

Budget   The PCAOB develops its budget and submits it to the SEC for approval. In the 2004 PCAOB budget, the net outlays were $103.297 million. The registration application fees for 2003 totaled $2.050 million, making the total accounting fee

EXHIBIT 1.2   REGISTRATION APPLICATION FEE

Number of Issuer Clients	Fee
0	$250
1–49	$500
50–100	$3,000
101–1000	$29,000
1001 and greater	$390,000

$101.247 million ($103.297 million–$2.050 million). For the 2005 PCAOB budget, the net outlays were $136.418 million. The registration application fees for 2004 totaled $308,000, making the total 2005 accounting fee $136.110 million ($136.418 million–$308 thousand).

PCAOB Membership

The PCAOB has five full-time members, each with a five-year appointment term and a two-term limit. While serving on the PCAOB, none of the members may engage in any other professional business activity or be employed. No member may share in any of the profits of a public accounting firm, nor may any member receive any payments from a public accounting firm, other than fixed continuing payments such as retirement payments. The SEC has the responsibility of appointing all five members, but it must do so in consultation with the Secretary of the Treasury and the Chair of the Federal Reserve Board. The SEC has the authority to remove any member "for good cause."

While all members of the PCAOB must be financially literate, only two of the members must be or have been certified public accounts (CPAs). The remaining three members must not and cannot have been CPAs. While the PCAOB Chair may be one of the two CPA members, he or she must not have been engaged as a practicing CPA for at least five years prior to PCAOB appointment.

PCAOB Membership   The current PCAOB members and their previous professional activities are as follows:

- **William J. McDonough, Chair**: Previously president and chief executive officer (CEO) of the Federal Reserve Bank of New York
- **Kayla J. Gillan, Member**: Previously with California Public Employees' Retirement System (CalPERS) where she served as its chief legal adviser with expertise in public pension, trust, and securities law
- **Daniel L. Goelzer, Member**: CPA, and formerly a partner at the law firm of Baker & McKenzie and general counsel to the SEC; practice focused on securities and corporate law
- **Willis D. Gradison, Jr., Member**: Previously a nine-term member of Congress (Ohio), former head of the Health Insurance Association of America, and former lobbyist at the Washington firm of Patton Boggs, LLP
- **Charles D. Niemeir, Member**: CPA, previously with the SEC where he was the co-chair of the Financial Fraud Task Force and the Chief Accountant in the Division of Enforcement

PCAOB Duties and Responsibilities

Under Section 102, only public accounting firms approved for registration with the PCAOB are authorized to prepare or issue audit reports on the financial statements of companies registered with the SEC. The application for registration requires the accounting firm to provide detailed information regarding its audit clients, internal quality control policies and procedures, accounting personnel, licensure, and financial standing. To maintain registration, approved firms must agree to undergo periodic inspections, and once the requirement for annual reports is instituted, approved firms must provide annual reports to the PCAOB. Some firms may be required to report more frequently than annually, and may be asked to supply additional information or update the initial application.

In addition to evaluating and approving firms for registration, the PCAOB has a number of other duties and responsibilities. Under Sections 103, 104, 105, 107, and 109, the PCAOB must:

- Set its budget and manage the operations of the PCAOB and its staff; funding comes from firm registration fees and accounting support fees from publicly held companies or issuers
- File an annual report with the SEC
- Establish or adopt, by rule, auditing, quality control, ethics, independence, and other standards relating to the preparation of audit reports
- Enforce compliance with SOX, PCAOB rules, professional standards, and the securities laws relating to the preparation and issuance of audit report and the related obligations and liabilities of auditors
- Conduct investigations of registered firms, replacing the traditional firm-in-firm peer review system
- Establish procedures to investigate and discipline registered firms and their personnel if suspected of rules violations
- Conduct disciplinary proceedings and impose appropriate sanctions; sanctions can include revoking or suspending a firm's registration and financial penalties up to $15 million
- Submit all disciplinary sanctions to the SEC for review; the SEC may modify or cancel sanctions

Examples of Disciplinary Proceedings and Sanctions   In a recent violations case, the PCAOB revoked the registration of Goldstein and Morris CPAs, P.C., and barred Edward B. Morris, who was the co-founder, president, and managing partner in the firm, from being an associated person of a registered public accounting firm. The PCAOB imposed these sanctions against the firm and Morris for concealing information from the PCAOB and for submitting false information during the course of a PCAOB inspection (PCAOB, 2005). As part of an inspection, the PCAOB requested information regarding the audits of two companies, New York Film Works, Inc. and RTG Ventures, Inc. One of the employees of the accounting firm had both worked on the audits of the companies and helped in the preparation of the financial statements. Auditors are prohibited from supplying accounting services, such as financial statement preparation, to their audit clients, and records regarding these services were omitted from the materials submitted to the PCAOB.

Alan J. Goldberger, CPA, and William A. Postelnik were partners at Goldstein & Morris at the time the false information was submitted and participated in discussion with Morris about concealing the records and falsifying the information, and helped to develop the plan to do so. The PCAOB censured both Goldberger and Postelnik for their misconduct. The sanctions were limited to censures because Goldberger and Postelnik voluntarily contacted the PCAOB and disclosed the violation (PCAOB, 2005).

Title II: Auditor Independence

Title II of SOX seeks to establish auditor independence from the company being audited by defining and limiting the services the auditing may provide, and by setting the engagement standards of the auditor and the company.

Prohibited Services

Under Section 201, the auditor is prohibited from providing the following services:

- Bookkeeping or other services related to the accounting records or financial statements
- Financial information systems design and implementation
- Appraisal or valuation
- Actuarial
- Expert services unrelated to the audit
- Internal audit outsourcing
- Management and human resources functions
- Investment advisor, investment banking, or broker-dealer
- Legal

Engagement Standards

In regard to the engagement standards, Sections 202, 203, and 206 require the audit committee to preapprove all services provided by the auditor before the auditor is engaged, oblige the audited firm to rotate its auditors on a regular basis, define and pro-hibit conflicts of interest between auditors and the audited company, and require the auditing committee of the audited company to be responsible for the oversight of its auditors. In addition, Section 204 identifies specific information the auditor must con-vey to the audit committee before the audit report is issued. The auditor must com-municate the following:

- All critical accounting policies and practices used in preparing the financial state-ments, including any changes to those policies and procedures
- All alternative treatments of financial information that are within generally acceptable accounting principles (GAAP) that have been discussed with management
- Any material written communications between the accounting firm and the com-pany's management

Title III: Corporate Responsibility

Title III of SOX imposes new obligations on the senior management team, the audit committee, and the attorneys of companies registered with the SEC. In addition, Title III contains provisions to guard against profiteering from issuing misleading financial information about the company to the public, to protect pension funds, and to remove individuals from management of the board for wrongdoing.

Senior Management Team Obligations

For the senior management team, Section 303 makes it unlawful for any officer or di-rector to exert improper influence on the auditor engaged in the audit of the com-pany's financial statements. Section 302 applies to public companies filing quarterly and annual reports with the SEC under either Section 13(a) or 15(d) of the Securities and Exchange Act of 1934. As part of each report, Section 302 requires the CEO, Chief Fi-nancial Officer (CFO), and others performing similar functions to certify each quarterly and annual report. In addition, the certifying officers must make disclosures in the quarterly and annual reports regarding the company's disclosure controls and proce-dures and internal controls over financial reporting.

Certification Requirements   The SEC has specified the format and wording of the certi-fication issued by the certifying officers in detail. In general, the SEC requires each cer-tifying officer to affirm the following:

- He or she has reviewed the report.
- Based on his or her knowledge and review, the report does not contain any un-true or misleading statement of material fact.

- Based on his or her knowledge and review, the report does not omit any statements of material facts necessary to make the report fair, accurate, and full.

- Based on his or her knowledge and review, the financial statements and other financial information in the report fairly present the financial condition, results of operations, and cash flows of the company.

- He or she and the other certifying officers recognize their responsibility of establishing and maintaining effective disclosure controls and procedures.

- He or she and the other certifying officers have designed the disclosure controls and procedures to ensure that they know all necessary financial and nonfinancial information in a timely manner.

- He or she and the other certifying officers have evaluated the effectiveness of the company's disclosure controls and procedures within 90 days of the filing date and have included the results of the evaluation in the report.

- He or she and the other certifying officers have reported to the auditors and to the audit committee all significant deficiencies in the design or operation of the internal controls, any weaknesses in internal controls, and any fraud in the areas of internal controls.

- He or she and the other certifying officers have included in the report any significant changes in internal controls subsequent to the evaluation, including any corrective actions.

Internal and Disclosures Controls   As part of the report certification, the certifying officers must state that they have reported any weakness in the internal controls over financial reporting. Although Section 302 requires the statement, the requirement to *actually perform* a quarterly evaluation of the effectiveness of the internal controls is in Title IV, Section 404. As part of the report certification, members of senior management also must attest to the effectiveness of the company's disclosure controls and procedures. Disclosure controls and procedures are designed to ensure that information required to be disclosed by the company in its reports to the SEC is accurately recorded, processed, summarized, and reported within the time periods required by the SEC. Disclosure controls and procedures are broader than internal controls over financial reporting. While the internal controls over financial reporting seek to ensure the accuracy and timeliness only of financial information, disclosure controls and procedures include both financial and nonfinancial information. To achieve the goal of accurate and timely SEC reports, both financial and nonfinancial information must be accumulated and communicated to the company's management in time for critical evaluation. It is especially important that members of management who are required to certify the quarterly and annual reports receive the information in a timely fashion, so they can make decisions regarding disclosure on the reports.

Audit Committee Obligations

Section 301 gives the audit committee the responsibility to appoint, compensate, and oversee the auditor, and prohibits members of the audit committee from accepting, either directly or indirectly, any compensation other than recompense directly related to their roles as members of the board of directors and its committees. Title III also requires the audit committee to develop and implement procedures to receive and resolve complaints and concerns from employees and others about accounting, internal accounting controls, and auditing matters.

Attorney Obligations

Section 307 establishes "minimum standards of professional conduct" for attorneys who provide legal services and who are in an attorney-client relationship with a public company. Both in-house attorneys and outside counsel are required to report any knowledge or evidence of a material violation of securities law or breach of fiduciary duty. The attorney first reports to the company's chief legal counsel or its CEO, but if neither responds appropriately, the attorney must then report the evidence to the audit committee, another board committee, or the board itself.

Management and Board Disincentives

Title III seeks to remove the financial incentives for misleading financial reporting through three sections (Sections 304, 305, and 306). Under Section 304, management members can no longer retain profits made from selling company stock or any bonus or other incentive-based or equity-based compensation realized during the 12-month period following the issuance of a noncompliant financial document. Section 305 gives the SEC the authority to remove any management or board member if he or she is deemed "unfit." Under Section 306, members of management and the board are now also prohibited from selling or buying any securities through the company's equity compensation plan during a pension fund blackout period.

Title IV: Enhanced Financial Disclosures

Title IV of SOX increases the financial disclosures a public company must make; prohibits personal loans to management or board members (Section 402); requires disclosure of changes in ownership by management, board members, and principal security holders (Section 403); requires management to establish and maintain adequate internal controls and procedures for financial reporting; and requires a company to disclose whether it has adopted a code of ethics for financial personnel.

Disclosure of Off-Balance-Sheet Arrangements and Non-GAAP Measures

Section 401 requires disclosure of off-balance-sheet arrangements and contractual obligations, such as long-term debt, capital lease, operating lease, or purchase obligations. Section 401 also covers publicly disclosed or released pro forma financial information, or what are termed "non-GAAP financial measures." A non-GAAP financial measure is defined as any numerical measure of a company's historical or future financial health that excludes amounts that are included in a GAAP financial measure or includes amounts that are excluded in a GAAP financial measure. An example of a non-GAAP financial measure is income before special items, such as restructuring expenses. Under the GAAP financial measure, restructuring expenses would normally be included with all other expenses that are subtracted from revenues in order to determine income. Excluding the restructuring expenses in the non-GAAP measure may mislead someone to think that the income is higher than it actually is. Section 401 currently allows the use of non-GAAP measures, but prohibits them from being misleading.

Internal Control Evaluation and Report

Under Section 404, management is required to perform quarterly evaluations of the effectiveness of the company's internal controls and procedures for financial reporting. The results of all the quarterly evaluations will be included in an internal control report that is submitted to the SEC as part of its required annual filing (Form 10-K). The annual internal control report must include the following:

- Statement of management's responsibilities to develop, implement, and maintain adequate internal controls and procedures for financial reporting
- Management's assessment of the effectiveness of the internal controls and procedures based on management's evaluation of them
- External auditor's opinion of management's evaluation of the effectiveness of internal controls and procedures

Code of Ethics Disclosure

Section 406 requires a company to disclose whether it has required the principal executive officer, principal financial officer, principal accounting officer or controller, and others performing similar functions to adopt a code of ethics. Under the SEC's definition of "code of ethics," a code of ethics must include written standards that could reasonably promote:

- Accountability for adherence to the code
- Fair, accurate, timely, full, and comprehensible disclosure in materials and documents submitted to the SEC and in other public communications

- Ethical handling of any actual or apparent conflicts of interest
- Compliance with all applicable laws, rules, and regulations
- Internal reporting of code of ethics violations

Financial Expert Disclosure

Since the effectiveness of any company's audit committee is dependent upon the committee's level of knowledge and expertise in matters related to auditing and financial issues, Section 407 requires the company to disclose annually in reports filed with the SEC whether at least one member of its audit committee has sophisticated financial expertise and can be considered an "audit financial expert." The required qualifications for being an audit financial expert include:

- Understanding of GAAP and financial statements
- Experience in preparing, auditing, analyzing, or evaluating financial statements at or beyond the level of complexity of the company's financial statements
- Understanding of internal controls and procedures for financial reporting
- Understanding of audit committee functions

Titles V, VI, VII: Analyst Conflicts of Interest, Commission Resources and Authority, Studies and Reports

Titles V, VI, and VII primarily provide details regarding security analysts, appropriations, and various studies and reports performed by the GAO and others. While these titles are important components of SOX, they are not directly relevant to the behavior of public companies, nor do they apply to nonprofits. These titles will thus not be discussed in any detail.

Title VIII: Corporate and Criminal Fraud Accountability Act of 2002

Title VIII, also referred to as the Corporate and Criminal Fraud Accountability Act of 2002, creates criminal penalties for fraud and document destruction, provides protection for whistleblowers who provide evidence of fraud, specifies that debts incurred in violation of securities fraud laws are nondischargeable (Section 803), extends the statute of limitations on securities fraud claims, and creates a new crime for defrauding shareholders of publicly traded companies (Section 807).

Document Destruction

Section 802 amends the federal obstruction of justice statute. It is now a felony to "knowingly" destroy, conceal, cover up, add to, or falsify documents or records in order to impede or obstruct any federal investigation or bankruptcy proceeding. While destruction of documents with intent to obstruct a federal investigation was already a criminal offense under the existing statute, the statute only applied to ongoing investigations. The new offense also covers contemplated investigations and provides for the imposition of fines, imprisonment for up to 20 years, or both, for the violation of the statute.

Preservation of Audit Materials

Auditors can also be charged with a felony if they fail to retain all audit and review work papers and materials for a period of five years from the end of the fiscal year in which the audit was conducted. Section 802 provides for the imposition of fines, imprisonment for up to ten years, or both, for the violation of the statute.

Whistleblower Protection

Under Section 806, employees of public companies and accounting firms who disclose private company or firm information as evidence of accounting or auditing violations or fraud to a supervisor, federal regulator, law enforcement agency, or member of Congress are extended whistleblower protection.

Under whistleblower protection, it is unlawful for the employer to discriminate against the employee in any manner if that employee engaged in the protected activity. Discrimination includes actions such as discharge, demotion, suspension, threats or harassment, blacklisting, and disciplinary actions. Under this section, whistleblowers are granted a remedy of special damages and attorney's fees. The PCAOB has established the Center for Enforcement Tips, Complaints, and Other Information to provide employees with an easy avenue for submitting evidence to the PCAOB (PCAOB, 2003).

Extended Statute of Limitations

The statute of limitations for claims of securities fraud is extended under Section 804. Previously, the statute of limitations was three years from the time the fraud was committed, or one year after the fraud was discovered. Section 804 extended the limitations to the earlier of five years from the time the fraud was committed, or two years after the fraud was discovered.

Title IX: White-Collar Crime Penalty Enhancements Act of 2002

Title IX, also referred to as the White-Collar Crime Penalty Enhancements Act of 2002, creates or enhances penalties for a variety of "white-collar" crimes. Section 902 extends the penalties for *actually committing* the crime or violation to cover individuals who only *attempt or conspire to commit* the crime or violation. Section 903 increases the penalties for wire and mail fraud from five years to 20 years; Section 904 increases the fine and penalties for violations of Section 501 of the Employee Retirement and

Security Act of 1974; and Section 905 requires the U.S. Sentencing Commission to review the Federal Sentencing Guidelines to ascertain that they reflect the serious nature of securities and accounting fraud.

Criminal Penalties under Section 906

Section 906 is one the most controversial sections of Title IX, as it creates criminal penalties for a public company's CEO and the CFO (or equivalent) in regard to certification of SEC quarterly and annual reports. Under Section 906, the CEO and CFO must certify that the quarterly and annual reports, which contain the financial statements and are submitted to the SEC as required under Section 13(a) or 15(d) of the Securities Exchange Act of 1934, comply fully with the provisions of the Securities Exchange Act. In addition, they must certify that the reports fairly present the operations and financial condition of the company. This certification is in addition to the certification that is required under Title III, Section 302. The maximum penalties for willful and knowing violations under Section 906 are a fine of not more that $5,000,000, imprisonment of up to 20 years, or both.

Title X: Corporate Tax Returns

Title X contains only one section, Section 1001, and does not require any action by any party. Section 1001 expresses Congress' belief that the corporation's CEO should sign the Federal income tax return of a corporation.

Title XI: Corporate Fraud Accountability Act of 2002

Title XI, also referred to as the Corporate Fraud Accountability Act of 2002, creates new crimes and penalties acts, and gives the SEC authority to institute additional fraud disincentives. Two sections of Title XI, Sections 1102 and 1107, apply to *all* corporations, including nonprofits.

SEC Disincentives

Two sections, Sections 1103 and 1105, give the SEC authority to institute new fraud disincentives. During the course of an investigation of possible violations of securities law, Section 1103 gives the SEC the authority to petition a Federal court to freeze the payment of any extraordinary payment to any director, officer, partner, controlling person, agent, or employee of a company for up to 45 days. This section gives the SEC the authority to prohibit, either conditionally or unconditionally, and permanently bar a person from serving as an officer or director of a public company if the person has committed securities fraud.

New Crimes and Penalties

Under Section 1104, Congress requests the U.S. Sentencing Commission to review the Federal Sentencing Guidelines and to consider changes that would enhance the sentences of officers and directors of public companies who commit acts of fraud and related offenses. Section 1106 increased the criminal penalties, both fines and prison terms, for violations of the Securities Exchange Act of 1934.

Provisions that Apply to Nonprofits

Section 1102   Section 1102 defines the tampering of any record or document to impair the object's integrity for use in an official proceeding as a crime. This section also makes obstructing, influencing, or impeding any official proceeding, or attempts to do so, a crime. The penalties for violation are a fine, imprisonment of up to 20 years, or both.

Section 1107   Section 1107 makes it a crime and imposes criminal penalties for any organization to retaliate or take any harmful action against any person who has provided any truthful information regarding the commission of any Federal offense to a law enforcement officer. This applies to an *actual* commission of an offense, and to the *possible* commission of an offense. A reasonable belief or suspicion that an offense has been committed is sufficient to create protection for the employee.

Under this section, "any harmful action" includes interference with the employment or livelihood of the employee. This thus prohibits the organization from firing, demoting, suspending, harassing, refusing to promote, or reprimanding the employee. The penalties for violations include a fine, or imprisonment up to 10 years, or both.

FACTORS THAT DROVE THE SWIFT PASSAGE OF SOX

After reviewing the legislative and regulatory content of SOX, it should be readily apparent that SOX is a major piece of legislation that brought about substantive and sweeping changes in securities law. What prompted such swift passage of such a far-reaching piece of legislation? Most public policymaking in the United States is characterized by modest modification in policy, a process aptly described as one of incrementalism (Lindblom, 1969). What factors made SOX different?

Corporate Scandals

One of the drivers of the swift passage of the legislation was the tidal wave of corporate and accounting scandals that rocked the U.S. financial markets in 2000, 2001, and 2002. The SEC, the Department of Justice, the Federal Energy Regulatory Commission, the Federal Bureau of Investigation, and U.S. Attorney Offices in New York, Denver, and Houston were all investigating a number of publicly held companies for falsifying financial statements, using questionable accounting procedures, mismanagement of assets, or otherwise misleading their shareholders and the public about their financial standing. A partial listing of the organizations under investigation included Adelphia Communications, AOL, Bristol-Myers Squibb, CMS Energy, Dynergy, Duke Energy, Enron, Global Crossing, Halliburton, Homestore.com, IMClone Systems, Mirant, Peregrine Systems, Qwest Communications International, Reliant Energy, WorldCom, and Xerox (Patsuris, 2002). The allegations included:

- **Adelphia Communications**: Gave the founding Rigas family and other executives $3.1 billion in off-the-books loans and hid the loans
- **AOL**: Inflated sales by treating barter deals and advertisements sold on behalf of others as revenues
- **Bristol-Myers Squibb**: Inflated its 2001 revenues by forcing wholesalers to accept more inventory than needed
- **CMS Energy**: Boosted trading volumes and revenues through "round-trip" trades
- **Duke Energy**: Boosted trading volumes and revenues through "round-trip" trades
- **Dynergy**: Boosted trading volumes and revenues through "round-trip" trades
- **Enron**: Boosted profits and hid debts by improperly using off-the-books partnerships, manipulated the California and Texas energy markets, and bribed foreign governments to win contracts abroad
- **Global Crossing**: Inflated revenues by engaging in network capacity "swaps" with other carriers, and shredded documents related to accounting practices
- **Halliburton**: Recorded $100 million in annual construction cost overruns before clients had agreed to pay for them
- **Homestore.com**: Inflated sales and revenues by recording barter transactions as revenue
- **ImClone**: CEO Sam Waksal engaged in insider training and improperly used ImClone assets as collateral for a personal bank loan of $44 million
- **Mirant**: Inflated revenues by $1.1 billion
- **Peregrine Systems**: Inflated sales and revenues by improperly recognizing revenues from third-party resellers
- **Qwest Communications International**: Inflated revenues by engaging in network capacity "swaps" with other carriers
- **Reliant Energy**: Boosted trading volumes and revenues through "round-trip" trades

- **WorldCom**: Recorded $3.8 billion in operating expenses as capital expenses and gave founder Bernard Ebbers $400 million in off-the-books loans
- **Xerox**: Over a five-year period, boosted income by $1.5 billion

Auditor Scandals

Certified public accounting firms also had their share of high-profile scandals. If an auditor from a public accounting firm examines the financial statements of public companies and gives an unqualified opinion regarding those statements, the shareholders and the public should have increased assurance that the statements were prepared in accordance with GAAP, that GAAP was applied on a consistent basis, and that the statements included all the information necessary to fairly present the company's financial standing. Since public companies registered with the SEC are required to have their financial statements audited by an external auditor, how were the public companies able to produce such misleading financial statements?

There are a number of reasons why the auditor's opinion does not accurately represent the condition of the financial statements. In some cases, auditors simply make errors. In other cases, however, an auditor's opinion may be biased, not objective, and not independent of the organization being audited. The auditor may have a financial incentive to misrepresent the fairness of the financial statements. If, for example, the firm performing the audit is also receiving substantial compensation for providing consulting, tax work, or other services, the accounting firm has a financial incentive to maintain a good relationship with the company being audited. The desire to maintain the relationship—and the compensation—may bias the audit report to reflect a more positive financial position than exists. Biased auditor reports can also occur if the relationship between the management of the company being audited and the auditor is too "cozy." The loyalty of the auditor may lie with management instead of with the shareholders, and the auditor's evaluation of the statements may be biased by that loyalty.

Arthur Andersen LLP and Enron

As discussed previously, one of the public companies under investigation was Enron. For several years, Enron, an energy company, participated in a number of partnership transactions that lost the company a substantial amount of money. In 2001, Enron reported that it had failed to follow GAAP in its financial statements for 1997 through 2001 by excluding these unprofitable transactions. In these erroneous financial statements, the organization reported large profits when, in fact, it had lost a total of $586 million during those years. Neither internal nor external controls detected the financial losses disguised as profits. The revelation of the erroneous financial reporting led to a collapse in the price of Enron stock. The price of Enron stock fell from $83 per share in December 2000 to less than $1 per share in December 2001. However, some of Enron's managers made millions of dollars by selling their company stock before its price plummeted. Other investors experienced substantial losses, including Enron employees who had invested a large portion of their retirement portfolios in Enron stock (Securities and Exchange Commission v. Timothy A. DeSpain, 2005; Securities and Exchange Commission v. Richard A. Causey, Jeffery K. Skilling, and Kenneth L. Lay, 2004).

The certified accounting firm of Arthur Andersen LLP, which had been one of the largest accounting firms in the world, served as Enron's auditor throughout the years of erroneous statements. The firm allegedly "overlooked" Enron's questionable accounting practices since it was making a large amount of money for providing Enron with consulting services and did not want to lose the consulting business. The firm was indicted by the U.S. Department of Justice, and in June 2002 a jury convicted the firm of obstructing justice by shredding Enron-related documents requested by the SEC. U.S. District Judge Melinda Harmon sentenced the firm to a $500,000 fine and five years' probation. The conviction, however, essentially decimated the powerful Big Five firm, and it lost most of its clients.

The 5th U.S. Circuit Court of Appeals affirmed the jury verdict, but on May 31, 2005, the U.S. Supreme Court overturned accounting firm Arthur Andersen's obstruction of justice conviction. The conviction, according to Supreme Court justices, was improper because the jury instructions during the trial were too broad and vague, and jurors couldn't correctly determine whether the company actually committed the crime. The reversal of the firm's criminal conviction is thus based entirely on a trial technicality: improper jury instructions (Arthur Anderson LLP v. United States, 2005).

Although the relationship between Enron and Arthur Andersen LLP is a dramatic example of failure in the auditing process, there were a number of other accounting firms whose auditing practices and relationships with auditing clients were under question. Examples include Deloitte Touche and Adelphia, Ernst & Young and AOL, KPMG and Xerox, and PricewaterhouseCoopers and Bristol-Myers Squibb.

Response of President Bush and the 107th Congress

As more and more scandals came to light, the public's confidence in the capital markets and in the integrity of corporate financial statements was shaken. In part in response to the lack of public confidence and the downward plummet in the stock market, both President George W. Bush and the 107th Congress responded.

On March 7, 2002, the President announced his "Ten-Point Plan to Improve Corporate Responsibility and Protect America's Shareholders," based on three core principles: information accuracy and accessibility, management accountability, and auditor independence. The points of the plan were:

• Each investor should have quarterly access to the information needed to judge a firm's financial performance, condition, and risks.

- Each investor should have prompt access to critical information.
- CEOs should personally vouch for the veracity, timeliness, and fairness of their companies' public disclosures, including their financial statements.
- CEOs or other officers should not be allowed to profit from erroneous financial statements.
- CEOs or other officers who clearly abuse their power should lose their right to serve in any corporate leadership positions.
- Corporate leaders should be required to tell the public promptly whenever they buy or sell company stock for personal gain.
- Investors should have complete confidence in the independence and integrity of companies' auditors.
- An independent regulatory board should ensure that the accounting profession is held to the highest ethical standards.
- The authors of accounting standards must be responsive to the needs of investors.
- Firms' accounting systems should be compared with best practices, not simply minimum standards.

On July 9, 2002, President Bush issued Executive Order 1371, which established the Corporate Fraud Task Force within the Department of Justice. Deputy Attorney General Larry Thompson heads the task force. The task force includes representatives from seven U.S. Attorney Offices, the FBI, and SEC to oversee the investigation and prosecution of financial fraud, accounting fraud, and other corporate criminal activity, and to provide enhanced interagency coordination of regulatory and criminal investigations. Former Deputy Attorney General Thompson explained the goal of the President's Corporate Fraud Task Force, "As we establish with ever increasing certainty the prospect that corporate criminals will lose both their fortunes and their liberty, we will have gone a long way to restoring the integrity of the market and the confidence of the nation." (Office of the Press Secretary, 2002.)

The Congress' response was the relatively quick passage of SOX, a substantial piece of legislation. It took less than six months (from February 14 to July 15) for both chambers of Congress to pass the bill and send it to President Bush for signature. The President did so on July 30, 2002.

IMPLICATIONS OF SOX FOR NONPROFITS

The nonprofit sector has recently experienced its own recent scandals of perceived wrongdoing and fiscal mismanagement. For example, the Nature Conservancy, United Way, American Red Cross, Whitney Museum of American Art, Foundation for New Era Philanthropy, and Feed the Children have all received substantial unfavorable media coverage of their apparent failures in accountability and adherence to mission (Bothwell, 2001). Incidents such as these have cast the nonprofit sector in an unfavorable light, and have damaged the public's trust in the integrity and the public benefit of nonprofits. While it is true that the majority of the SOX provisions currently only apply to publicly traded corporations and not to nonprofit organizations, nonprofits could benefit operationally from adopting some of the SOX provisions as "best practices." In addition, voluntarily adhering to the SOX standards would create greater credibility and the ability to recruit high quality board members, and attract the favorable attention of major donors, foundations, and other funding sources.

Pressure for Enhanced Nonprofit Regulation

If the nonprofit sector wants to obtain its current level of relative self-regulation, nonprofit leaders need to make a visible effort to improve organizational governance and accountability. If this does not occur, nonprofits may come under additional unwanted regulation by the government. Some members of Congress and state attorney generals have already suggested that additional provisions of SOX should be applied to nonprofits, the State of California recently passed legislation that imposes many SOX-like provisions on California nonprofits, the IRS has suggested several proposals for increased oversight and enforcement, and some nonprofit groups are developing their own set of regulatory proposals.

Senate Finance Committee

In June 2004, the Senate Finance Committee released its staff draft "White Paper" that contained a number of proposals to impose under federal law SOX-type governance requirements on the nonprofit sector (OMB Watch, 2004). The proposals were based, in part, on the findings from the June 22 hearing conducted by the State Finance Committee—"Charity Oversight and Reform: Keeping Bad Things from Happening to Good Charities." Among the proposals were the following:

- Five-year review of tax-exempt status by the Internal Revenue Service (IRS)
- Apply private foundation self-dealing rules to public charities
- Limit amounts paid for travel, meals, and accommodations
- Establish standards for acquisition and/or conversion of a nonprofit
- Improve quality and scope of Form 990 and financial statements
- Require CEO (or equivalent) to sign a declaration under penalties of perjury confirming the existence of processes and procedures ensuring that the nonprofit's Federal and state tax returns comply with the Internal Revenue Code to provide reasonable assurance of the accuracy and completeness of all material aspects of the tax return

- Establish penalties for failure to file a complete and accurate Form 990
- Establish penalty for failure to file a timely Form 990
- Require electronic filing of tax returns and financial statements
- Establish IRS standards for Form 990
- Require disclosure of performance goals, activities, and expenses in Form 990 and financial statements
- Require disclosure of investments
- Enforce governing board roles of audit and oversight
- Enforce governing board composition, terms, and liability

Nonprofit Integrity Act of 2004

California's Nonprofit Integrity Act of 2004 (Larsen, 2004) imposes many of the provisions of SOX on nonprofits operating in California. Senator Byron Sher (D–Stanford) and the bill's sponsor, Attorney General Bill Lockyer, have stated that the purpose of the legislation is to minimize nonprofit accounting scandals and incidents of abuse by some commercial fundraising outfits.

The Nonprofit Integrity Act is not the sweeping, overarching legislation that SOX is, but it is quite significant in its mandates. The new law fairly breaks into two subjects—financial reporting and governance, and charitable fundraising regulation. Some of the key provisions of the act are:

For nonprofits with gross revenues of $2 million or more, the nonprofit must:

- Conduct an external annual audit of financial statements, using GAAP
- Have an independent auditor
- Make public disclosure of audited financial statements
- Board of directors must establish an audit committee
- Board of directors must review and approve the compensation of the CEO and CFO

For all nonprofits, regardless of size, which are registered with the Attorney General, the nonprofit must:

- Make public disclosure of financial statements if they are audited
- Register with the Registry of Charitable Trusts within 30 days, changed from 6 months
- Provide notice to the Attorney General of commencement of any solicitation by a commercial fundraiser ten days before the start of the campaign
- Have all contracts with commercial fundraisers signed by an official of the nonprofit and contain a "boilerplate" of provisions

- Exert control over and assume responsibility for all fundraising activities
- Void contracts with commercial fundraisers who have not registered with the Attorney General's Registry of Charitable Trusts
- Cancel contracts with commercial fundraisers without liability if the fundraisers make material misrepresentations during solicitation, or are found to have been convicted of a crime arising from fundraising activities

Commissioner of the Internal Revenue Service—Mark W. Everson

On April 5, 2005, the Commissioner of the Internal Revenue Service, Mark W. Everson, presented a written statement before the U.S. Senate Committee on Finance hearing on "Charities and Charitable Giving: Proposals for Reform." In his statement, Everson pointed out some of the IRS' concerns regarding tax-exempt charities:

- Terrorist financing by charities
- Overcompensation of nonprofit management and staff
- Overvaluation of noncash donations
- Misuse of donor-advised fund arrangements
- Excessive political activities
- Misuse of tax shelters

In the statement, Everson requested that Congress increase IRS funding in order for it to exert more oversight over the nonprofit sector.

Panel on the Nonprofit Sector

On June 22, 2005, the Panel on the Nonprofit Sector, convened by Washington, D.C.-based Independent Sector, gave its recommendations to the U.S. Senate Finance Committee (Panel on the Nonprofit Sector, 2005; Jones, 2005). The report was in response to federal proposals aimed at improving charitable governance and accountability. The 116-page final report provided 120 suggested actions for the IRS, legislators, and charitable organizations. Some of the changes suggested to the IRS were:

- Charities with at least $2 million in total revenue and filing a Form 990 or Form 990PF would be legally required to conduct a yearly financial audit.
- Organizations with $500,000 to $2 million in total revenue would be required to have an independent public accountant review financial statements.
- Charities with less than $25,000 in revenue would face automatic suspension of tax-exempt status if they fail to file an annual notice with the IRS for three consecutive years.

- Require CEOs, CFOs, or the highest-ranking officer to sign tax and information forms.
- Suspend tax-exempt status of organizations that fail to comply with federal filing requirements for two or more consecutive years.
- Extend penalties imposed on individual and corporate tax preparers for omission or misrepresentation of information, disregard of rules and regulations to preparers of Form 990s.
- Move forward with requiring e-filing of Form 990s and allow for separate attachments.
- Coordinate federal e-filing efforts with states.
- Require e-filing of applications for tax-exempt status.

Some of the changes suggested for nonprofits were:

- Adopt and enforce conflict of interest policies.
- Include people with some financial literacy on its boards of directors.
- Create whistleblower protection policies.

Some of the changes suggested for Congress were:

- Define donor advised funds.
- Prohibit charities from making grants to private nonoperating foundations from donor advised funds.
- Enact minimum activity rules for donor advised funds.
- Prevent public charities from knowingly using donor advised funds to reimburse donors/advisers for expenses incurred by them in an advisory capacity or making grants to donors/advisers and related parties.
- Increase funding for IRS enforcement of nonprofits.

CONCLUSION

It should be clear that the current legislative environment is emphasizing greater accountability for both the private and nonprofit sectors of the economy. It should also be apparent that pressures are mounting for more SOX-like legislation directed at the nonprofit sector. While it is true that the majority of the SOX provisions currently only apply to publicly traded corporations and not to nonprofit organizations, nonprofits could benefit operationally from adopting some of the SOX provisions as "best practices." In addition, voluntarily adhering to the SOX standards would create greater credibility and the ability to recruit high-quality board members, and attract the favorable attention of major donors, foundations, and other funding sources.

WORKSHEET: SOX AND RELEVANCE TO NONPROFIT OPERATIONS

As discussed throughout this chapter, SOX and SOX-influenced legislation does have major implications for nonprofits. Exhibit 1.3, *SOX and Relevance to Nonprofit Operations*, will help a nonprofit develop a deeper understanding of those implications. For each title of SOX, review the provisions described in the chapter and develop ways in which those provisions have relevance for the nonprofit sector. For example, Title I establishes the PCAOB, which oversees public companies. Should the nonprofit sector have a similar overseeing body? Why or why not? Section 404 of SOX requires management in public companies to conduct periodic evaluation of the company's internal control system. Could this be a "best practice" for nonprofits? Why or why not?

EXHIBIT 1.3   WORKSHEET: SOX AND RELEVANCE TO NONPROFIT OPERATIONS

SOX Titles and Sections	Relevance to Nonprofit Operations
I. Public Company Accounting Oversight Board	
101: Establishment, administrative provision	
102: Registration with the Board	
103: Auditing, quality control, and independent standards and rules	
104: Inspections of registered public accounting firms	
105: Investigations and disciplinary proceedings	
106: Foreign public accounting firms	
107: Commission oversight of the Board	
108: Accounting standards	
109: Funding	
II. Auditor Independence	
201: Services outside the scope of practice of auditors	
202: Preapproval requirements	
203: Audit partner rotation	
204: Auditor reports to audit committees	
205: Conforming amendments	
206: Conflicts of interest	
207: Study of mandatory rotation of registered public accounting firms	
208: Commission authority	
209: Considerations by appropriate State regulatory authorities	
III. Corporate Responsibility	
301: Public company audit committees	
302: Corporate responsibility for financial reports	
303: Improper influence on conduct of audits	
304: Forfeiture of certain bonuses and profits	
305: Officer and director bars and penalties	
306: Insider trades during pension fund blackout periods	
307: Rules of professional responsibility for attorneys	
308: Fair funds for investors	

SOX Titles and Sections	Relevance to Nonprofit Operations

IV. Enhanced Financial Disclosures
401: Disclosures in periodic reports
402: Enhanced conflict of interest provisions
403: Disclosure of transactions involving management and
  principal stockholders
404: Management assessment of internal controls
405: Exemption
406: Code of ethics for senior financial officers
407: Disclosure of audit committee financial expert
408: Enhanced review of periodic disclosures by issuers
409: Real-time issuer disclosures

V. Analyst Conflicts of Interest
501: Treatment of security analysts by registered securities
  associations and national security exchanges

VI. Commission Resources and Authority
601: Authorization of appropriations
602: Appearance and practice before the Commission
603: Federal court authority to impose penny stock bars
604: Qualifications of associated persons of brokers and dealers

VII. Studies and Reports
701: GAO study and report regarding consolidation of public
  accounting firms
702: Commission study and report regarding credit rating agencies
703: Study and report on violators and violations
704: Study of enforcement actions
705: Study of investment banks

VIII. Corporate and Criminal Fraud Accountability
801: Short title
802: Criminal penalties for altering documents
803: Debts nondischargeable if incurred in violation of securities
  fraud laws
804: Statute of limitations for securities fraud
805: Review of Federal sentencing guidelines for obstruction of justice
  and extensive criminal fraud
806: Protection for employees of publicly traded companies who
  provide evidence of fraud
807: Criminal penalties for defrauding shareholders of publicly
  traded companies

IX. White Collar Crime Penalty
901: Short title
902: Attempts and conspiracies to commit criminal fraud offenses
903: Criminal penalties for mail and wire fraud
904: Criminal penalties for violations of the Employee Retirement
  Income Security Act of 1974
905: Amendment to sentencing guidelines relating to certain
  white-collar offenses
906: Corporate responsibility for financial reports

(continues)

EXHIBIT 1.3   WORKSHEET: SOX AND RELEVANCE TO NONPROFIT OPERATIONS (CONTINUED)

SOX Titles and Sections	Relevance to Nonprofit Operations
X. Corporate Tax Returns	
1001: Sense of the Senate regarding the signing of corporate tax returns by Chief Executive Officers	
XI. Corporate Fraud and Accountability	
1101: Short title	
1102: Tampering with a record or otherwise impeding an official proceeding	
1103: Temporary freeze authority for the Securities and Exchange Commission	
1104: Amendment to the Federal Sentencing Guidelines	
1105: Authority of the Commission to prohibit persons from serving as officers or directors	
1106: Increased criminal penalties under Securities Exchange Act of 1934	
1107: Retaliation against informants	

SOX Requirements, Best Practices, and State Legislation

The Big Bam Foundation, a breast cancer charity founded by a breast cancer survivor, has been under investigation by the California and New York Attorneys General for allegations that it misspent donations on everything from an island vacation to supernatural guidance for its founder. Fundraising revenue for the foundation was supposed to be directed toward free mammograms and to other breast cancer programs. The nonprofit's board authorized a forensic audit, which found significant errors in the 2001 and 2002 Forms 990. Allegedly, the forms indicate that 100% of the charity's revenue, which amounted to approximately $250,000 yearly, went to management and administrative expenses in 2001 and 2002. The foundation claimed that 65% of donations went to charitable programs in 2003, but some former volunteers and contractors challenged the accuracy of those figures.

Bank records, furnished to *The San Francisco Chronicle* by former volunteers, highlighted a number of questionable charges, including:

- More than $1,000 in ATM withdrawals and requests for cash back when someone used the foundation's debit card
- A $1,100 charge to a clairvoyant
- Thousands of dollars in checks that Big Bam founder and president, Janice Bonadio, wrote to herself. It's unclear whether anyone else approved the transactions

Additional allegations assert that Bam's board never formally approved Bonadio's salary. According to the *Chronicle*, Big Bam elected a new slate of board members on August 16, 2004, but didn't have any record of prior board meetings (Wallack, 2004).

CHAPTER OVERVIEW

The corporate scandals described in Chapter 1 raised the bar of accountability for all organizations—private sector and nonprofits alike. Although it may appear that SOX provisions apply strictly to publicly traded companies, the reality is that there are SOX compliance requirements that apply to all organizations, even nonprofits. Because the level of accountability and transparency has been elevated for all organizations, the best practices that emerged from the SOX legislation present an added value for nonprofits. This chapter will review the two requirements and the value that adopting the best practices will add to the nonprofit.

CHAPTER OBJECTIVES

By the end of this chapter, you should be able to:

- Describe the two SOX requirements for all organizations, including nonprofits.
- Describe SOX best practices and the benefits that these best practices provide to nonprofits.
- Describe how the legislative environment has changed public expectations of nonprofit accountability and transparency.
- Discuss the common themes and issue areas that are addressed through state legislation.

WHAT ARE NONPROFITS REQUIRED TO DO UNDER SOX?

As we learned in Chapter 1, the Public Company Accounting Reform and Investor Protection Act, commonly referred to as "Sarbanes-Oxley" and "SOX" after its sponsors, Senator Paul Sarbanes (D–MD) and Representative Michael Oxley (R–OH), was passed in 2002 in the wake of the Enron corporate scandal. Although SOX was initially intended to raise the bar for integrity and competence for publicly traded companies, its effect has been to promote greater accountability within both the nonprofit and private sectors.

SOX Requirements for All Organizations—Even Nonprofits!

Currently, only two of the provisions in SOX directly apply to nonprofit organizations. Nonprofits are required to adhere to "Whistleblower Protection" requirements, which provides protection to employees who report suspected fraud or other illegal activities. Employees or volunteers of a nonprofit are shielded from retaliation for making reports of waste, fraud, or abuse.

Nonprofits are also expected to have a fully functioning Document Preservation policy in place. The Document Preservation policy has two aspects: preservation and archiving of documents for the purpose of timely retrieval, and a prohibition against the destruction or falsification of records or documents.

Whistleblower Protection

The first obligation from SOX that applies to all organizations is the requirement for a documented Whistleblower Protection policy. SOX requires all organizations, including nonprofits, to establish a means to collect, retain, and resolve claims regarding accounting, internal accounting controls, and auditing matters. The system must allow such concerns to be submitted anonymously. SOX provides significant protections to whistleblowers, and severe penalties to those who retaliate against them.

Chapter 9 elaborates on the policies and procedures that contain at least the following aspects:

- There is a confidential avenue for reporting suspected waste, fraud, and abuse
- There is a process to thoroughly investigate any reports
- There is a process for disseminating the findings from the investigation
- The employee filing the complaint will not be subjected to termination, firing, harassment, or miss out on promotion
- Even if the findings do not support the nature of the complaint, the employee or volunteer who made the complaint will not face any repercussions

All employees and volunteers should have a copy of the whistleblower policy and it should be posted in clear view. This policy should also be covered in any orientation or training programs the organization offers for its employees and volunteers.

Document Management and Preservation Policy

Document storage and retention is another area within SOX that applies to all organizations. The language in Section 802 describes the consequences for failing to implement a Document Retention system:

> Whoever knowingly alters, destroys, mutilates, conceals, covers up, falsifies, or makes a false entry in any record, document, or tangible object with the intent to impede, obstruct, or influence the investigation or proper administration of any matter within the jurisdiction of any department or agency of the United States or any case filed under Title 11, or in relation to or contemplation of any such matter or case, shall be fined under this title, imprisoned not more than 10 years, or both.

Chapter 8 provides more insight into how this requirement needs to be tailored to address both paper files and electronic files.

SOX BEST PRACTICES

SOX best practices are designed to enhance the completeness and reliability of all aspects of the nonprofit's operations. These practices include:

- Audit committee whose role is to oversee the annual audit or financial review (for small nonprofits) and to upgrade the financial literacy of the board

- Enhanced detail and accuracy in the preparation of IRS Form 990

- Improved governance and a nonprofit board that understands its role as ultimately accountable for the actions of the nonprofit, and is willing to take steps to enhance professional development for each member

- Conflict of Interest policy and Code of Ethics that facilitate greater focus on decision-making for the good of the nonprofit

- Internal controls, particularly as these relate to financial operations, and compliance with all laws and regulations at the federal, state, and local levels

- Transparency at all levels of management

- Adherence to policies and procedures—and enforcement

The nonprofit's commitment to adopting and maintaining SOX best practices can be demonstrated in the deliverables of a review of internal controls. The process and outcomes can be used to measure the development of the platinum standard. Compliance cannot simply be a rote operation; it must be demonstrated that the commitment to excellence transcends all levels of the organization and is evident in all the operational systems and in the symbiotic relationship that exists among the various systems within the organization.

BENEFITS OF IMPLEMENTING BEST PRACTICES— ADDING VALUE TO THE NONPROFIT

- **Governance**: A more effective board whose members understand and adhere to their fiduciary obligations and recognize their responsibility in governing the company

- **Accountability**: Higher level of management and staff accountability

- **Operations**: Effective protocols to ensure the company remains in compliance with SOX and the company's "industry standards" and addresses future standards

- **Marketing**: Better competitive positioning by making known that the company adheres to the SOX gold standard in its operating practices

- **Strategic positioning**: Greater credibility and ability to attract necessary resources, be these in the form of high-quality board members, sources of capital, donors, or other fund sources

EXHIBIT 2.1	SARBANES-OXLEY REQUIREMENTS AND BEST PRACTICES CHECKLIST

- Does your nonprofit have a Whistleblower Protection policy?
- Do your staff and volunteers know how to make a confidential report of waste, fraud, or abuse? Do they know their rights under the Whistleblower Protection policy?
- Does your nonprofit have a method for storing and archiving all documents—paper, electronic, and e-mails?
- Does your nonprofit have a policy that prohibits the destruction of documents during an inquiry?
- How are board members recruited and screened for membership on the board?
- Does your nonprofit's senior management recruit board members?
- Are new and current board members required to attend orientation sessions that address their obligations and performance expectations?
- Does your nonprofit allow members of the same family to serve together on the board?
- Does your board meet at regular intervals? Is there an attendance requirement?
- Are minutes kept for all board and committee meetings? How are these minutes stored?
- Does your nonprofit have an audit committee whose role is to oversee the annual audit or financial review (for small nonprofits) and to upgrade the financial literacy of the board?
- Has your nonprofit taken steps to achieve a level of enhanced detail and accuracy in the preparation of IRS Form 990?
- Does your nonprofit have a Conflict of Interest policy and a Code of Ethics that facilitate greater focus on decision-making for the good of the nonprofit?
- Has your nonprofit reviewed and critiqued its internal controls, particularly as these relate to financial operations, and compliance with all laws and regulations at the federal, state, and local levels?

NONPROFITS: CURRENT LEGISLATIVE ENVIRONMENT

U.S. Senate Finance Committee Hearings on Nonprofit Accountability, June 2004, and Hearing on Exempt Organizations: Enforcement Problems, Accomplishments, and Future Direction, April 5, 2005

Although the features of SOX may on the surface appear to have more impact on the private sector, the public sector (i.e., government) push for greater accountability includes the independent sector (i.e., the nonprofit world) as well.

The United States Senate Finance Committee, chaired by Senator Charles Grassley (R—IA), held hearings on "Charitable Giving Problems and Best Practices" in June 2004 and April 2005. The common themes of the testimony of witnesses, documents presented, and the White Paper produced by the Committee Staff is that nonprofit organizations have, through fiscal and governance abuses, diminished public trust. Public outrage fueled these Congressional hearings on nonprofit abuses. Testimony from both of these hearings contained insights into commonly held, but nevertheless dysfunctional, belief systems that appear to populate much of the nonprofit sector. In a similar fashion, federal regulators such as Mark Everson of the IRS outline the steps the federal government is willing to take to standardize compliance within the nonprofit sector.

Internal Revenue Service Commissioner's Testimony—2004 and 2005

Mark Everson, Commissioner of the IRS, testified at both of Senator Grassley's hearings in 2004 and 2005. The IRS has been directed by the White House to more aggressively monitor the IRS filings of nonprofits, and to ensure that nonprofit Form 990s are accurate, complete, and filed in a timely manner.

IRS Commissioner's Testimony at the 2004 Grassley Hearings   As part of the Senate Finance Committee's June 2004 hearings on nonprofit accountability, Mr. Everson provided some very sobering testimony on that agency's plans for oversight and enforcement of the nonprofit sector. According to Mr. Everson, the IRS' short-term agenda for bringing about nonprofit accountability includes:

- **Addressing the Scope of the Abuses of Tax Advantages**: The approximately 3,000,000 tax-exempt entities include almost 1,000,000 Section 501(c)(3) charities and almost 1,000,000 employee plans. This sector is a vital part of our nation's economy that employs about one in every four workers in the United States. In addition, nearly one-fifth of the total U.S. securities market is held by employee plans alone . . . there are abuses of charities that principally rely on the tax advantages conferred by the deductibility of contributions to those organizations. If these abuses are left unchecked, I believe there is the risk that Americans not only will lose faith in and reduce support for charitable organizations, but that the integrity of our tax system also will be compromised. I am committed to combating abuse in this area.

- **Scope of the IRS Strategic Plan for 2005–2009**: Along with improving service and modernizing computer systems, one of the strategic goals is to enhance enforcement of the tax law . . . Historically, IRS functions regulating tax-exempt entities have not been well funded due to the lack of revenue they generated. This view is misdirected in light of the size and importance of the sector. With staffing in this area flat at best and with the number of charities increasing annually, our audit coverage has fallen to historically low levels, compromising our ability to maintain an effective enforcement presence in the exempt organizations' community. One of the plan's four specific objectives is to deter abuse within tax-exempt and governmental entities, and misuse of these entities by third parties for tax avoidance or other unintended purposes.

- **The Administration's FY 2005 Budget**: The budget contains a number of legislative proposals, originally announced by the Treasury Department in March

2002 to combat abusive transactions. These proposals include statutory changes that would create better, coordinated disclosure of abusive transactions. Although the Administration is committed to encouraging gifts to charity, it also wants to ensure that taxpayers are accurately valuing property they donate to charity.

- **Recent Nonprofit Scandals—Governance**: In recent years, there have been a number of very prominent and damaging scandals involving corporate governance of publicly traded organizations. The Sarbanes-Oxley Act has addressed major concerns about the interrelationships between a corporation, its executives, its accountants and auditors, and its legal counsel. Although Sarbanes-Oxley was not enacted to address issues in tax-exempt organizations, these entities have not been immune from leadership failures. The IRS also has seen an apparent increase in the use of tax-exempt organizations as parties to abusive transactions. All these reflect potential issues of ethics, internal oversight, and conflicts of interest.

- **Scope of Enforcement**: We have selected 50 tax-exempt credit counseling organizations for examination; the majority of these examinations are currently underway. The balance will be assigned to agents by the end of this fiscal year. To date, we have initiated and will be pursuing the use of proposed revocations of exemption of credit counseling organizations in appropriate circumstances. We also plan to seek injunctions and penalties against both individuals and companies for promoting fraudulent tax schemes. The IRS will use all tools available to ensure that these organizations act lawfully, including revoking tax-exempt status where warranted.

- **Compensation Issues**: The issues of governance and executive compensation are closely intertwined. The IRS is concerned that the governing boards of tax-exempt organizations are not, in all cases, exercising sufficient diligence as they set compensation for the leadership of the organizations. There have been numerous recent reports of executives of both private foundations and public charities who are receiving unreasonably large compensation packages. Neither a public charity nor a private foundation can provide more than reasonable compensation. In general, reasonable compensation is measured with reference to the amount that would ordinarily be paid for comparable services by comparable enterprises under comparable circumstances. This summer (2004), the IRS is launching a comprehensive enforcement project to explore the seemingly high compensation paid to individuals associated with some exempt organizations. This is an aggressive program that will include both traditional examinations and correspondence compliance checks. These organizations need to know that their decisions will be reviewed by regulatory authorities. Organizations also will be asked for details concerning the independence of the governing body that approved the compensation and details of the duties and responsibilities of these managers with respect to the organization. Other stages will follow, and will include looking at various kinds of insider transactions, such as loans or sales to executives and officers.

- **Filing of Form 990**: The IRS will be looking at organizations that failed to, or did not fully complete, compensation information on Form 990. This information will help inform the IRS about current practices of self-governance, both best practices and compliance gaps, and will help the agency focus our examination program to address specific problem areas.

- **Collaborative Enforcement Activities with Other Federal Agencies**: The IRS is working with other federal agencies in a number of areas. For example, we continue to engage in information sharing with the FTC to learn more about the credit counseling industry. We expect to continue this mutually beneficial relationship and find other ways to leverage our scarce resources.

- **Enhancing Nonprofit Governance**: Stronger governance procedures are needed for exempt organizations. The sanctions for serious lapses in governance are clear. There is the possibility of revocation of exemption, along with the various excise taxes against individuals that I mentioned before. But sanctions are a last resort. Organizations without effective governance controls are more likely to have compliance problems . . . [*The IRS will*] require disclosure of whether the organization has a conflict of interest policy or an independent audit committee, and whether additional disclosure should be required concerning certain financial transactions or insider relationships. Our Form 990 revision team is working on a comprehensive overhaul of the form to provide better compliance information about these organizations to the IRS, the states, and the public.

- **Vehicle Donations**: For a taxpayer, donating a car to a charity has definite appeal. One can help a charitable cause, dispose of the car, and take advantage of tax provisions that are designed to support the generosity of Americans. Deductions are limited to the fair market value of the property. In its recent study, the GAO estimated that about 4,300 charities have vehicle donation programs. In its review of returns for tax year 2000, the GAO estimated that about 733,000 taxpayers claimed deductions for donated vehicles they valued at $500 or more. Highly troubling is GAO's analysis of 54 specific donations, where it appears that the charity actually received less than 10% of the value claimed on the donor's return in more than half the cases, and actually lost money on some vehicles . . . we cannot ignore the clear implications of the study . . . We are educating donors and charities on what constitutes a well-run donation program . . . We will be partnering with the states to distribute the brochures to the fundraising community, as the states regulate fundraising activity. (Everson, Mark W., testimony before the U.S. Senate Finance Committee, Washington, D.C., June 2004).

IRS Commissioner's Testimony at the 2005 Grassley Hearings   In his testimony at the 2005 Grassley hearings, Mr. Everson made the following key points in his remarks:

- **The Administration strongly encourages and supports donations to our charities.** Some entities now use their privileged status to achieve ends that Congress never imagined when it conferred tax-exemption.

- **The IRS strongly supports the Eight Guiding Principles of Accountability and Governance [from the Independent Sector's report]**, and commends Independent Sector and the Panel on the Nonprofit Sector for their role in encouraging adherence to these standards of excellence. Good governance and accountability are important given the size and impact of the tax-exempt sector in our economy . . . Total assets of these organizations approximated $3.7 trillion in 2002, with revenues of $1.2 trillion. Collectively these organizations file more than 800,000 annual returns.

- **The IRS Strategic Plan for 2005–2009** recognizes the significance of this sector for tax administration. The Strategic Plan sets out four key objectives designed to enhance tax law enforcement over the next five years. One of these objectives directly addresses the charitable sector. That objective is to deter abuse within tax-exempt and governmental entities and misuse of such entities by third parties for tax avoidance and other unintended purposes.

- **Growth in IRS Budget.** Despite the importance of this sector, until recently our enforcement budget was not keeping up with its growth. By September [2005] we will see a *30 percent increase in enforcement personnel for Exempt Organizations over September 2003 levels.*

- **Nonprofit Compliance Issues.** A number of factors are impacting compliance in the tax-exempt area. As might be expected, these factors do not necessarily operate independently of one another. Taken together, however, they add up to a *culture that has become more casual about compliance and less resistant to non-compliance.* These are attitudes that we must work together to change.

- **Increase in size and complexity of the tax exempt sector.** This sector has grown . . . the number of exempt entities on our master-file has increased by almost 500,000 since 1995, to 1.8 million today. In the period from FY 1998 to FY 2002 alone, the reported value of the assets of these organizations grew from approximately $2 trillion to more than $3 trillion. Further, most recent figures show reported annual revenues for Internal Revenue Code (Code) Section 501(c)(3) organizations at $897 billion.

- **Lax attitudes toward governance.** An independent, empowered, and active board of directors is the key to insuring that a tax-exempt organization serves public purposes, and does not misuse or squander the resources in its trust.

Unfortunately, the nonprofit community has not been immune from recent trends toward bad corporate practices. Like their for-profit brethren, many charitable boards appear to be lax in certain areas. Many of the situations in which we have found otherwise law-abiding organizations to be off-track stem from the failure of fiduciaries to appropriately manage the organization . . . We have found issues relating to how executive compensation is set and reported by nonprofits. Similarly, issues exist as to whether sufficient due diligence and care is taken in filing tax and information returns.

- **Improved transparency in the tax-exempt sector.** A positive development in recent years is the improvement in "transparency" within the tax-exempt sector. "Transparency" refers to the ability of outsiders—donors, the press, and interested members of the public—to review data concerning the finances and operations of a tax-exempt organization. By creating a means by which the public may review and monitor the activities of tax-exempt organizations, we promote compliance, help preserve the integrity of the tax system, and help maintain public confidence in the charitable sector. To achieve these goals, we began in the mid-to-late 1990s to image Forms 990, the annual information returns filed by many tax-exempt organizations. We put this information on CDs, and provide it to members of the public, including a number of watchdog groups that monitor charitable organizations. These groups put the information up on their websites, where it is available to the press and to the public. This process has resulted in increased press and public scrutiny of the tax-exempt sector, which we believe is highly desirable. It has also increased the ability of the IRS and state regulators to access Form 990 data, because they are more readily available. Transparency is a lynchpin of compliance within the sector. Therefore, part of our work is to improve exempt organization transparency, including better data quality and better data availability. With our e-filing initiatives, planned changes to Form 990, expanded imaging of returns, and changes to the application process and the Form 1023, we expect substantial progress toward this goal. All exempt organizations can now file their annual returns electronically. Electronic filing was available for Form 990 and 990EZ filers in 2004, and is now available this year for private foundations, which file Form 990-PF. We want to encourage e-filing because it reduces taxpayer errors and omissions and allows us, and ultimately the public, to have ready access to the information on the return. For this reason, we have required e-filing in certain cases. Under proposed and temporary regulations, by 2007 we will require electronic filing for larger public charities and all private foundations.

- **Improving the Form 990.** The current form is not particularly "user-friendly," and does not give us all the information IRS agents need to do their jobs; the public is similarly constrained. We are at work revising the form. We anticipate that the revised form will have specific questions or even separate schedules that focus on certain problem areas. For example, filers should not be surprised to find specific schedules or detailed questions relating to credit counseling activities, supporting organizations, compensation practices, and organizational governance. The timing of the revision of the Form 990 is somewhat dependent on our partners, including the states which use the Form 990 as a state filing, and software developers. We are also expanding our Form 990 imaging capabilities. We already image the returns of public charities and private foundations. This month, for the first time, we are imaging the returns of our many categories of exempt organizations that are not section 501(c)(3) organizations. This will allow our agents immediate access to these returns, and will allow us to respond quickly to public requests for returns. While important at this time, it is our hope that imaging will become a relic of the past as electronic filing becomes the norm.

White Paper—Senate Finance Committee 2004 Hearings

Subsequent to the hearings and testimony, a staff discussion paper was released with recommendations for closer regulation of nonprofits. Presently, these are simply a series of recommendations by Congressional staff, but the tone and reach of the recommendations should be taken seriously by every nonprofit regardless of size.

The preface to the document instructs the reader that, "The document reflects proposals for reforms and best practices in the area of tax-exempt organizations based on staff investigations and research as well as proposals from practitioners, officers and directors of charities, academia, and other interested parties. This document is a work in progress and is meant to encourage and foster additional comments and suggestions as the Finance Committee continues to consider possible legislation." (Senate Finance Committee White Paper, p. 1, 2004.)

The White Paper included these proposals:

Five-year review of tax-exempt status by the IRS
The White Paper recommends that:

On every fifth anniversary of the IRS' determination of the tax-exempt status of an organization that is required to apply for such status, the organization would be required to file with the IRS such information as would enable the IRS to determine whether the organization continues to be organized and operated exclusively for exempt purposes (i.e., whether the original determination letter should remain in effect). Information to be filed would include current articles of incorporation and by-laws, conflicts of interest policies, evidence of accreditation, management policies regarding best practices, a detailed narrative about the organization's practices, and financial statements.

What would this mean for nonprofits? This recommendation would require non-profits to submit documentation every five years that proves to the IRS that the organization continues to be in compliance with its 501(c)(3) designation.

The list of documents specified here are particularly enlightening about the intent of this proposal:

Current articles of incorporation and by-laws: The nonprofit would need to be clear about how its operations and governance continue to be in harmony with its founding documents.

Conflicts of interest policies: The nonprofit would have to provide evidence of a conflict of interest policy and, most likely, proof that board members and senior management have completed annual affidavits identifying real or potential conflicts of interest.

Evidence of accreditation: This document would be based on another recommendation, which is that nonprofits be required to obtain specific accreditation.

Management policies regarding best practices: The nonprofit would be required to develop and submit written policies that demonstrate that the organization is implementing best practices in management and governance.

A detailed narrative about the organization's practices: This document would require the nonprofit to provide a detailed explanation about what the organization does, and why it is necessary/desirable in the community.

Financial statements: These financial statements would be supplemental to the Form 990 that is required on an annual basis.

Form 990s—Proposals for Reform
The White Paper recommends that:

> In a report to the Finance Committee, the General Accounting Office found significant problems in the accuracy and completeness of Form 990. Other studies, including by the General Accounting Office, have highlighted that there are no common standards for filing the Form 990, and thus similarly situated charities can have very different Form 990s. Because of the significant role played by the Form 990 in public and governmental oversight of tax-exempt organizations, some reforms are necessary to ensure accurate, complete, timely, consistent, and informative reporting by exempt organizations.

What does this mean for nonprofits? The IRS recognizes that there are no common standards for completion of a Form 990. The reform proposal seeks to identify reforms that will introduce a standardized way to submit Form 990s.

Form 990s Would Require Signature by CEO
The White Paper recommends that:

The CEO (or equivalent officer) of a tax-exempt organization sign a declaration under penalties of perjury that the CEO has put in place processes and procedures to ensure that the organization's Federal information return and tax return complies with the Internal Revenue Code, and that the CEO was provided reasonable assurance of the accuracy and completeness of all material aspects of the return. This declaration would be part of the information or tax return.

What does this mean for nonprofits? This proposal would require a nonprofit CEO to sign an affidavit that *under penalties of perjury* . . . that the organization's Form 990 complies with the Internal Revenue Code and that the CEO is providing assurance of the accuracy and completeness of all material aspects of the return. (The financials accurately reflect the financial position of the nonprofit.) This affidavit would be part of the information or tax return.

Based on recent events in the nonprofit world, if this proposal was law, there would be some very high-profile nonprofit executives going to jail. The recommendation here is clearly that nonprofit executives and board members should be held to the same criminal liability standards as those of their private sector counterparts.

Penalties for Failure to File a Complete and Accurate 990
The White Paper recommends that:

> The present law penalty for failure to file or to include required information is $20/day up to the lesser of $10,000 or 5% of gross receipts per return (increased to $100/day up to $50,000 per return for organizations with gross receipts over $1 million in a year). Under the proposal, the penalty for failure to file would be doubled, and for organizations with gross receipts over $2 million per year, the present law penalty would be tripled. Failure to file a required 990 for two consecutive years (or for three of four years) could result in loss of tax exemption, or other penalties such as loss of status as an organization to which deductible contributions may be made.

What does this mean for nonprofits? There will be severe penalties for failing to file a Form 990. The proposals recommend loss of tax exemption, or loss of status as an organization to which deductible contributions may be made. For a nonprofit, this means the organization can no longer tell donors that their contributions are tax-exempt. In other words, the "nonprofit" is out of business.

Required Disclosure of Performance Goals, Activities, and Expenses in Form 990
and in Financial Statements
The White Paper recommends that:

> Charitable organizations with over $250,000 in gross receipts would be required to include in the Form 990 a detailed description of the organization's annual performance goals and measurements for meeting those goals (to be established by the board of directors) for the past year and goals for the coming year. The purpose of this requirement

would be to assist donors to better determine an organization's accomplishments and goals in deciding whether to donate, and not as a point of review by the IRS. Charitable organizations would be required to disclose material changes in activities, operations, or structure. Charitable organizations would be required to accurately report the charity's expenses, including any joint cost allocations, in its financial statements and Form 990. Exempt organizations would be required to report how often the board of directors met and how often the board met, without the CEO (or equivalent) present.

What does this mean for nonprofits? Transparency is the predominant theme of these recommendations. The Congressional staff may have been spurred on by the volume of public complaints about nonprofit organizations that, for every donor dollar, contribute very little to programs. In recent years, the media has conducted many investigations of bogus charities, and certainly, some charities that are "household names" have also abused donor trust by misdirecting donations to exorbitant salaries, expenses, and other abuses. Note that these disclosures are required to be presented on a Form 990. The accuracy of these disclosures could carry criminal liability if the other proposal on CEO signatures is enacted into law.

Nonprofits Would Be Required to Make Certain Documents Publicly Available
The White Paper recommends that:

> Public oversight is critical to ensuring that an exempt organization continues to operate in accordance with its tax-exempt status. For charitable organizations, public oversight provides donors with vital information for determining which organizations have the programs and practices that will ensure that contributions will be spent as intended. Oversight is facilitated under present law by mandated public disclosure of information returns and applications for tax-exempt status, but more can be done. The White Paper recommends that an exempt organization would be required to disclose to the public the organization's financial statements. Exempt organizations with a website would be required to post on such site any return that is required to be made public by present law, the organization's application for tax exemption, the organization's determination letter from the IRS, and the organization's financial statements for the five most recent years.

What does this mean for nonprofits? Although the text recognizes that there are current public oversight opportunities, the authors comment that the nonprofit world could be doing more to provide transparency. The recommendations are, again, aimed at ensuring that the public has access to information that would be vital to their making a decision to make a donation. Of particular note is the recommendation that the nonprofit's website be employed to present not only those documents currently required (Form 990) but also the organization's application for tax exemption, the organization's determination letter from the IRS, and the organization's financial statements from the five most recent years.

Proposals Regarding Nonprofit Board Duties and Composition
The White Paper recommends that:

The duties of a board that are described in this paper would also be the duties of a trustee for a charitable trust. A charitable organization shall be managed by its board of directors or trustees (in the case of a charitable trust). In performing duties, a board member has to perform his or her duties in good faith; with the care an ordinarily prudent person in a like position would exercise under similar circumstances; and in a manner the director reasonably believes to be in the best interests of the mission, goals, and purposes of the corporation. An individual who has special skills or expertise has a duty to use such skills or expertise. Federal liability for breach of these duties would be established. Board composition should consist of no fewer than three members and not more than 15 members.

Any compensation consultant to the charity must be hired by and report to the board, and must be independent. Compensation for all management positions must be approved annually and in advance unless there is no change in compensation other than an inflation adjustment. Compensation arrangements must be explained and justified and publicly disclosed (with such explanation) in a manner that can be understood by an individual with a basic business background.

The board must establish basic organizational and management policies and procedures of organization and review any proposed deviations. The board must establish, review, and approve program objectives and performance measures, and review and approve significant transactions. The board must review and approve the auditing and accounting principles and practices used in preparing the organization's financial statements and must retain and replace the organization's independent auditor. An independent auditor must be hired by the board, and each such auditor may be retained only five years. The board must review and approve the organization's budget and financial objectives as well as significant investments, joint ventures, and business transactions. The board must oversee the conduct of the corporation's business and evaluate whether the business is being properly managed.

The board must establish a Conflicts of Interest policy (which would be required to be disclosed with the 990), and require a summary of conflicts determinations made during the 990 reporting year. The board must establish and oversee a compliance program to address regulatory and liability concerns.

The board must establish procedures to address complaints and prevent retaliation against whistleblowers. All of these requirements must be confirmed on the Form 990. Relaxation of certain of these rules might be appropriate for smaller tax-exempt organizations.

What does this mean for nonprofits? The proposals for reform indicate that the traditional legal standards of care, loyalty, and obedience could be incorporated into a law governing board member behavior. The proposal clearly indicates that the board is regarded as the final authority in the management of the nonprofit organization, and as such, will be held accountable for the implementation of such policies as a Conflict of Interest policy and Whistleblower Protection. Board size appears to be capped at 15, but the authors did not present clear reasons for this limitation.

The *entire* board could now be held directly accountable for the Executive Director's compensation package. Many nonprofit boards do not have access to the compensation package of the Executive Director, as this has come under the exclusive purview of the board's Executive Committee.

Proposals for Government Encouragement of Best Practices Accreditation

There would be an authorization of $10 million to the IRS to support accreditation of charities nationwide, in States, as well as accreditation of charities of particular classes (e.g., private foundations, land conservation groups, etc.). The IRS would have the authority to contract with tax-exempt organizations that would create and manage an accreditation program to establish best practices and give accreditation to members that meet best practices and review organizations on an ongoing basis for compliance. The IRS would have the authority to base charitable status or authority of a charity to accept charitable donations on whether an organization is accredited.

What does this mean for nonprofits? This proposal seeks to empower the IRS with the authority to require accreditation of nonprofits as a requisite to accepting charitable donations. The authors are seeking to empower the IRS to add another layer of compliance to the Form 990 proposals and five-year reauthorization of nonprofits.

Oversight Provisions

The White Paper recommends that:

> Exempt Organization Hotline for reporting abuses by charities and complaints by donors and beneficiaries should be established. It also recommends information sharing with State Attorneys General, the Federal Trade Commission, and the U.S. Postal Service for enforcement purposes, including referrals by the IRS and an annual report to Congress by the General Accounting Office of the results of such referrals.

What does this mean for nonprofits? This proposal would establish a hotline for anyone anywhere to file complaints about nonprofits and/or report abuses. Whether this is an anonymous hotline remains to be seen, but the authors appear to want to collect this information at a national level. How the complaints and claims would be investigated and by what agency remains to be seen.

The Independent Sector Report on Nonprofit Accountability—Presented at the Grassley Hearing in April 2005

The April 2005 Grassley Hearings heard testimony from Diana Aviv, Chair of the Independent Sector's Panel on the Nonprofit Sector. The panel was convened at the request of the Senate Finance Committee, and presents its work as seeking to help the nonprofit sector meet the highest ethical standards in governance, fundraising, and overall operations. The Panel on the Nonprofit Sector had just released an interim report for these hearings (Panel of The Nonprofit Sector, 2005).

The highlights from this report include eight principles to guide improving the accountability and governance of charitable organizations:

1. A Vibrant Nonprofit Sector Is Essential for a Vital America
2. The Nonprofit Sector's Effectiveness Depends on Its Independence
3. The Nonprofit Sector's Success Depends on Its Integrity and Credibility
4. Comprehensive and Accurate Information about the Nonprofit Sector Must Be Available to the Public
5. A Viable System of Self-Regulation Is Needed for the Nonprofit Sector
6. Government Should Ensure Effective Enforcement of the Law
7. Government Regulation Should Deter Abuse without Discouraging Legitimate Charitable Activities
8. Demonstrations of Compliance with High Standards of Ethical Conduct Should Be Commensurate with the Size, Scale, and Resources of the Organization

On June 22, 2005, the Panel on the Nonprofit Sector, convened by Washington, D.C.-based Independent Sector, gave its recommendations to the U.S. Senate Finance Committee (Panel on the Nonprofit Sector, 2005; Jones, 2005). The report is in response to federal proposals aimed at improving charitable governance and accountability. The 116-page final report provided 120 suggested actions for the IRS, legislators, and charitable organizations. Some of the changes suggested to the IRS were:

- Charities with at least $2 million in total revenue and filing a Form 990 or Form 990PF would be legally required to conduct a yearly financial audit.
- Organizations with $500,000 to $2 million in total revenue would be required to have an independent public accountant review financial statements.
- Charities with less than $25,000 in revenue would face automatic suspension of tax-exempt status if they fail to file an annual notice with the IRS for three consecutive years.
- Require CEOs, CFOs, or the highest-ranking officer to sign tax and information forms.
- Suspend tax-exempt status of organizations that fail to comply with federal filing requirements for two or more consecutive years.
- Extend penalties imposed on individual and corporate tax preparers for omission or misrepresentation of information, or disregard of rules and regulations pertaining to preparers of Form 990s.

- Move forward with requiring e-filing of Form 990s and allow for separate attachments.
- Coordinate federal e-filing efforts with states.
- Require e-filing of applications for tax-exempt status.

Some of the changes suggested for nonprofits were:

- Adopt and enforce a conflict of interest policy.
- Include people with some financial literacy on its board of directors.
- Create Whistleblower Protection policies.

Some of the changes suggested for Congress were:

- Define donor advised funds.
- Prohibit charities from making grants to private nonoperating foundations from donor advised funds.
- Enact minimum activity rules for donor advised funds.
- Prevent public charities from knowingly using donor advised funds to reimburse donors/advisers for expenses incurred by them in an advisory capacity or making grants to donors/advisers and related parties.
- Increase funding for IRS enforcement of nonprofits.

The findings and recommendations from this study will be discussed in greater detail throughout this text.

EXAMPLE OF STATE LEGISLATION—CALIFORNIA'S "NONPROFIT INTEGRITY ACT" (SB 1262)

As is shown in the previous testimony and guiding principles designed by the Panel of the Nonprofit Sector, the expectation of significantly high transparency and accountability for the nonprofit world is here to stay. In addition to federal legislation and regulatory scrutiny, nonprofits are subject to state legislation. California's *Nonprofit Integrity Act* (SB 1262) provisions appear to have influenced many of the Panel on the Nonprofit Sector's recommendations.

Provisions that Apply to Nonprofits with Budgets in Excess of $2 Million

The state of California passed a "Nonprofit Integrity Act," which imposes many of the features of Sarbanes-Oxley legislation on nonprofits with budgets in excess of $2 million operating in that state. Of particular significance is that this law also applies to *any nonprofit that solicits donation in the state of California regardless of where the nonprofit is domiciled.*
    Some of the key provisions of this law include:

- Nonprofits will be required to have an annual audit performed by a CPA who is "independent" as defined by U.S. Government auditing standards.

- The results of the audit will need to be made available to the public and the Attorney General.

- Nonprofits will be required to have an audit committee whose membership cannot include staff and must not overlap more than 50% with the finance committee; the audit committee can include members who are not on the organization's board of directors.

What does this mean for nonprofits operating in California? To ensure greater accountability in executive compensation, the law requires that the board approve the compensation, including benefits, of the corporation's President or CEO, and its Treasurer or CFO, for the purposes of assuring that these executive compensation packages are reasonable.

What does this mean for nonprofits operating in California? Requires disclosure of written contracts between commercial fundraisers and nonprofits and available for review on demand from the Attorney General's office. Fundraisers must be registered with the Attorney General's office.

The following points in the law apply to all nonprofits, regardless of size, operating in California:

a) Make their audits available to the public on the same basis as their IRS Form 990 if they prepare financial statements that are audited by a CPA.

b) Except for emergencies, notice of a solicitation campaign by a "commercial fundraiser for charitable purposes" must be filed at least ten days before the commencement of the solicitation campaign, events, or other services. Each contract must be signed by an official of the nonprofit, and include the contract provisions specified in the law.

c) Regarding fundraising activities, the law states that nonprofits must not misrepresent or mislead anyone about their purpose, or the nature, purpose, or beneficiary of a solicitation. Further, the law specifies that there be specific disclosures in any solicitation that the funds raised will be used for the charitable purpose as expressed in articles of incorporation or other governing documents. The nonprofit is expected to ensure that fundraising activities are adequately supervised to ensure that contracts and agreements are in order and that fundraising is conducted without intimidation or undue influence.

What does this mean for nonprofits operating in California? Nonprofits in California, regardless of their size, need to review their fundraising practices, particularly if some or all of their fundraising is outsourced to commercial fundraising firms. Nonprofits will be liable for abuses by vendors of fundraising services. As a practical matter, boards should insist that due diligence activities be conducted before contracting with any vendor, particularly those providing fundraising services. The California law, however, places strict parameters on third-party fundraising.

CONCLUSION

As you can see from the selected pieces of testimony and materials presented at both Grassley hearings, the government's scrutiny of the nonprofit sector is warranted, and long overdue. SOX only requires nonprofits to have a Whistleblower Protection policy and a document preservation policy. However, those two requirements plus the list of best practices have the potential for bringing about a sea change within your nonprofit's culture. These requirements and best practices are not the arbitrary and capricious musing of a bored bureaucrat; they represent practices that every nonprofit and corporation should have been doing all along!

CHAPTER 3

Anatomy of a Dysfunctional Nonprofit: Diagnosing of Organizational Dysfunction

"Your nonprofit has the absolute right to go out of business."

Fred Humphries is the Director of Social Services Funding for Crow Wing Lake County. He has seen his share of nonprofits receive large grants only to dissipate the funds and never grow their programs beyond their current status. He has a large sign on his desk that greets visitors, "Your nonprofit has the absolute right to go out of business." Fred knows that in today's more highly regulated environment, public expectations as well as those of funders have been raised significantly, particularly in terms of nonprofit boards and senior executives.

CHAPTER OVERVIEW

In this chapter we explore the "spirit" of a nonprofit—your nonprofit. Organizational dysfunction is often the catalyst for the implosion or closure of nonprofits. The sign on Fred's desk that nonprofits have the right to go out of business is contradictory to the belief that nonprofits are entitled to remain going concerns because they are part of a cause or are in business to help people. The closure or takeover of an increasing number of nonprofits is emblematic of the reality that nonprofits are not entitled to continue operations if they are not competent. This chapter describes the observable characteristics of organizational culture and presents examples of common areas of dysfunction within nonprofit organizations. The discussion will focus on why these areas are common problems, and the ways in which a nonprofit's founder might contribute to organizational dysfunction. The chapter serves as a gateway to the remaining chapters in the book by means of illustrating the anatomy of a dysfunctional nonprofit, including some common symptoms of organizational dysfunction.

CHAPTER OBJECTIVES

By the end of this chapter, you should be able to:

- Describe how a nonprofit's organizational culture and belief system can contribute to dysfunction.
- Describe some clues to observing dysfunction in each of these areas:
  - Governance
  - Mission and vision
  - Communication
  - Finance and financial management
  - Lack of internal controls
  - Information technology—use and misuse
  - Development and fundraising
  - Human resources
  - Public trust
  - Legal issues
  - Environmental scanning
- Discuss the costs of dysfunction in terms of how organizational dysfunction can affect the financial profile of the nonprofit.

ORGANIZATIONAL CULTURE

What Is Organizational Culture?

Sometimes when you walk into a nonprofit, you can just "feel" what it must be like to work there. Something about the way people talk, or dress, or act sends out signals. Other clues come from the way the offices look—are they cluttered and disheveled, or neat, but cold? Some offices exude "high class" pretension, while others have a distinctly "anti-establishment" feel.

Learning to understand a nonprofit is much like peeling an onion—there are layers upon layers to peel back. Nonprofits aren't just the people who populate them, although the people can be the "face" of a nonprofit. From deep within nonprofits come the "rules"—written and unwritten—about how things are done, how problems are solved, and what's valuable. In any new job, there is generally a person or group of people tasked with "showing the ropes" to the new hire. Often, the unwritten rules come under the rubric of "how to get along around here."

Most importantly, the unwritten rules exist because either everyone agrees with them, or everyone feels compelled to behave in compliance with them. The idea that the "way things are done around here" is a shared notion is key to understanding nonprofit culture.

Organizational culture is a system of shared basic assumptions that helps people within the organization to cope with external forces, solve problems, and pass along the learned methods for dealing with operational issues (Schein, 1992).

Organizational culture is also reflected in the way newcomers are selected to become a part of the institution, whether the newcomers are new staff, administrators, volunteers, or board members. Once the newcomers have accepted the "invitation" to join the nonprofit in whatever capacity, what they are told about the nonprofit and how they are "shown the ropes" of routine institutional life is a reflection of organizational culture. Some nonprofits are very open about how decisions are made, how ideas can bubble up, and how grievances are settled. Other nonprofits have a very hierarchical structure, and sending messages upward requires elaborate protocols. The presence of one or more bargaining units (unions) also affects the nonprofit's organizational culture.

Probably the most powerful illustration of how an organization's "culture" works is in the types of behaviors that are either rewarded or have no consequences imposed. Even more importantly, what types of behaviors are either punished or extinguished? The terms *reward* and *punishment* here are not to be taken as entirely positive or negative. Consider the two words in terms of whether negative consequences are imposed by the institution for engaging in particular behaviors. Staff who do not show up for work and have not called in sick will probably have some sort of consequences imposed for this behavior—reduction of pay for that week, assessing multiple sick days/vacation days, or a letter of reprimand. However, other destructive/negative behaviors such as failing to meet deadlines, failing to comply with new directives, or "foot-dragging" in terms of SOX best practices might have no consequences imposed.

Conversely, some behaviors are discontinued; in other words, "extinguished," because insufficient positive reinforcement has been extended. Consider the case of a staff member who worked long into the night to complete a report for the next day. If his or her supervisor does not show the requisite level of appreciation, it is unlikely that the staff member will go to those lengths in the future. Whether a behavior is repeated is often contingent on the degree of positive or negative reinforcement applied in immediate response to the behavior.

An organization's "culture" supplies the reinforcing environment, values, beliefs, and applicable resources to either reinforce or extinguish behavior. Every organization has a unique and irreplaceable "culture" that reflects its human dimension. In other words, the unique interaction of people within an organizational environment helps to perpetuate behavioral and cognitive norms that are part of the organization's culture, while punishing or extinguishing behaviors and (articulated) values that are perceived as contrary to the established norms.

Anatomy of a Dysfunctional Nonprofit

Understanding the nonprofit's organizational culture is helpful in identifying its dysfunctional attributes. Because organizational culture is intangible, the observer needs to look closely at the behavioral clues, the beliefs expressed, the stories told, and the way in which problems are solved.

Each nonprofit is a unique entity because each is populated with unique individuals. Like any other organization, nonprofits have their own ways of doing things. Dysfunction within a nonprofit can be insidious, or it can be obvious. Sometimes, dysfunction in a nonprofit is evidenced by the fact that nothing ever gets done! Other nonprofits mask their dysfunction around an aura of busyness. Yet others have highly dysfunctional boards, or management teams, or rank and file. Each of these groups can imprint their mark or malignancy on the nonprofit. Sometimes, an autocratic leader, often the founder of the organization, can be the source—and even a continuing source of dysfunction after he or she is fired. In one such instance, a charter school's board terminated the highly dysfunctional founder of the school but allowed the individual to remain on their board! Why? The board thought this person would be helpful in fundraising! Such obtuse rationale is not the stuff of fiction—it happens every day.

Often, the level of dysfunction continues to grow until it has a spillover effect on the whole organization. Exhibit 3.1 summarizes common examples of symptoms that signal organizational dysfunction.

Clues to Observing Dysfunction

Baseball great Yogi Berra was once quoted as saying, "It's amazing what you can see when you look." He also said, "Ignorance isn't what you don't know—it's what you know wrong." Most of the time, dysfunction isn't something that can be readily identified. As you observe the goings-on in a nonprofit, be aware of clues that indicate problems.

Attitudes and Beliefs

A dysfunctional belief system is often at the root of organizational dysfunction. How often have you heard people in a nonprofit say:

- We're poor, grassroots, small, not part of the "establishment," out in the boonies . . . [fill in the blank]. The litany of woes goes on forever.

EXHIBIT 3.1   SYMPTOMS OF ORGANIZATIONAL DYSFUNCTION

Symptom	Organizational Dysfunction
Senior management ignores directive of Executive Director.	Chain of command is compromised. Job descriptions and roles not clear. Failure to impose significant consequences for ignoring a superior.
Financial statements not produced on time or in a professional format.	Internal controls lacking. Staff not held accountable for failing to meet deadlines.
Staff refuse to comply with directives such as document retention policy.	Organizational culture does not support individual accountability. Management does not reinforce accountability with consequences.
Form 990s are never submitted on time—sometimes more than one year passes before they are submitted.	Board lax in holding management accountable for compliance with IRS regulations.
No policy in place to track credit card expenditures by staff and management.	Organizational culture supports naïve belief that staff and management would not misappropriate funds. Lax tracking of financials due to inattention.
Executive compensation packages are never questioned by the board.	Board does not understand its governance role. Management may have endeavored to "stack" the board with friends.
Office is untidy—papers are stacked high on desks. Trash bins are overflowing.	Organizational citizenship and morale are affected by dysfunction. Staff make no effort to make the office tidy or orderly.
Staff members are sloppy—do not present a professional appearance.	The nonprofit either does not require professional demeanor and appearance or does not enforce such standards.
Board members sporadically attend board meetings—difficult to obtain a quorum.	Board members do not understand their governance obligations, and are not required to comply with these obligations.

- No one would investigate us, sue us, or [fill in the action].
- We're a nonprofit—we don't have to do all of the things that corporations are expected to do.
- We work too long and hard as it is. We're not going to do more work.
- Our staff isn't paid very well. I can't be expected to require high performance from them.
- She's a board member. She gives us her time and money—we can't ask her to actually *do* anything!

- I'm the boss here. I started this agency and we'll do it my way. I know these clients better than anyone.
- That never works. We've tried it before.

Although the nonprofit's values are often embodied in the mission statement, not all of the values appear there. Other values and beliefs that are entrenched within the organization, but do not appear in the mission statement, are often articulated through comments such as the ones shown previously. Sometimes these beliefs and values parallel or support the mission, such as generosity, and concern for the community at large. Other beliefs and values can come into play within a nonprofit, such as not having to play by the rules because we are a nonprofit, or because we serve poor people, or because we serve rich people, or just because! The sense of entitlement, special-ness, or out-and-out adolescent rebellion on the part of people who are chronologically adults can have spectacular effects—on others and the nonprofit.

Performance and Productivity

Dysfunction within the organization can also be detected in the quality and quantity of output. How productive are staff members? Are reports and other deliverables produced on time? Are deadlines routinely missed? Documents that are produced in a haphazard and unprofessional manner do not inspire confidence in the nonprofit. More importantly, unprofessionally presented materials suggest that the content could easily be inaccurate, misleading, or simply wrong. In some instances, such as the submission of an IRS Form 990, a sloppy submission could garner unwanted scrutiny and possibly an audit.

Performance issues relate to interpersonal interactions and to preparation of documents. How are clients and/or visitors treated when they enter the nonprofit? Have clients or visitors complained that they were either ignored or treated in a callous manner? These types of complaints are not nuisance issues—take them seriously.

Appearance of Premises, Staff, and Volunteers

The old adage "you can't judge a book by its cover" does not necessarily apply to work settings and the individuals who work there. Regardless of the individual's pay status (i.e., employee or volunteer), the nonprofit's credibility is diminished by the presence of individuals whose hygiene and mode of dress suggest that they do not understand that they are working professionals. Nonprofits routinely resort to the ridiculous excuse that professionally attired staff would be upsetting to its clientele. What an insult to the clientele—as if their clients don't deserve to be served by professionals!

Similarly, the appearance of the nonprofit's interior and exterior sets the tone for clients and visitors alike. The office "housekeeping" routine—or lack thereof—can signal serious dysfunction within an organization. If papers are piled high on desks and clutter abounds, that indicates a highly stressed organizational culture—and undoubtedly, a significant number of errors based on the inability to manage documents.

Interpersonal Behavior and Distress

How do people in the nonprofit treat each other? Body language and other nonverbal cues can provide clues to the source of organizational dysfunction. When the Executive Director arrives, do people scatter? What about board members? When it is clear to the observer that the arrival of an individual prompts an exit of others, there's a problem.

How do they speak to each other? In dysfunctional organizations, there may be more overt displays of friction, such as staff shouting at each other—or at management staff. Tone of voice, use of profanity, and demeaning language are obvious clues of organizational difficulty. Whining or other adolescent-like speech patterns can hint at underlying morale problems—or can signal a previously successful method of shirking responsibility. The more the staffer whines about being overworked, having no resources, no support, no [fill in the blank], the less likely the recipient of the whining will insist on the deliverable.

More often than not, those who staff a dysfunctional organization will employ the default position of why they can't [provide the deliverable] rather than engage in meaningful discussion to develop a strategy that can deliver the goods. The more excuses, the more dysfunction.

Evidence of Dysfunction in Nonprofit Operations

Organizational dysfunction has many layers as evidenced by behavior, productivity, lack of procedures, disorder of office space, and the like. To help you better identify evidence of dysfunction within your nonprofit, consider the following examples within specific functional components.

Organizational Dysfunction and the Board

The board is the governance entity within the nonprofit. As we will see in upcoming chapters, today's expectations of nonprofit boards have ramped up significantly. Some examples of dysfunction in board structure and function include:

- Attendance at board meetings is uneven.
- Senior management runs the board meetings, and a few board members dominate discussion.

- The board meetings are highly choreographed, but the content of the agenda is superficial, including endless reports by senior management.
- Information on executive compensation packages is kept secret from all but the Executive Committee.
- Conflict is suppressed, or endless conflict is used to block business from being conducted.
- The board does not have a vision or strategic plan for moving the nonprofit ahead. Senior staff actively blocks strategic planning.
- Board members have been in place for over five years.
- Your board does not have Directors and Officers insurance and/or Employment Practices Liability insurance.

Symptom 1: Attendance at board meetings is uneven. Most meetings barely have a quorum. Having attendance issues suggests that board members either don't understand or don't care about their governance obligations to the nonprofit.

Symptom 2: Senior management runs the board meetings and discussion is dominated by a few board members. The rest of the board does not take active part in discussion and does not review materials. Effective boards are highly collaborative groups. When it is clear that one or more board members are "opting out" of the action, this should be a red flag.

Symptom 3: The board meetings are highly choreographed, but the content of the agenda is superficial, including endless reports by senior management. The meeting is a "dog and pony" show meant to convey the consistent message that "all is well—just let those of us in power handle it." This scenario is particularly dangerous because those in power are working to manipulate the agenda and the level of participation of the rest of the board. Even more troubling is that the rest of the board does not understand that, in their governance role, they are required to know what is going on, and are expected to demand to be fully informed.

Symptom 4: Does your board know how much the Executive Director makes? Does the board know what perks the Executive Director enjoys, and what his or her benefits package includes, such as pension, vacation time, and professional development time? If this data is being suppressed or withheld by the Executive Committee, your board has a problem. Board members should not tolerate the "right to privacy" claim—the Executive Director is the board's only employee. Board members have the right to know everything an employer would know about his or her employee.

Symptom 5: Conflict is suppressed, or endless conflict is used to block business from being conducted. Behind this symptom is a small group of people who are working hard to forward their own agenda by bullying, intimidating, or publicly humiliating those whose opinions differ. These individuals will create gridlock until their agenda is fulfilled.

Symptom 6: The board does not have a vision or strategic plan for moving the non-profit ahead. Senior staff actively blocks strategic planning. As Yogi Berra observed, "When you come to a fork in the road, take it." If your board and nonprofit does not know where it is headed, consider this a huge red flag.

Symptom 7: Board members have been in place for over five years. Does your board have term limits? Are the term limits enforced? It's useless to have term limits if board members are permitted to remain on or have limitless reappointments to the board. How many board members have been on the board over five years? If the number is greater than two, you need to do some serious housecleaning and board recruitment.

Symptom 8: Your board does not have Directors and Officers insurance and/or Employment Practices Liability insurance. Boards that resist purchasing adequate insurance fail to take their responsibilities of care and loyalty seriously. No one should ever join a board that is not adequately insured.

Organizational Dysfunction within the Nonprofit's Values

Just what is a nonprofit's mission? The mission statement is the rubric or overarching goal that serves to steer the organization. Nonprofits can sometimes lose sight of their mission in the quest for funding, or prestige, or real estate, or something beyond the scope of what is set out in the mission statement.

Failure to engage in meaningful strategic planning causes the nonprofit to ignore its direction for the future and become distracted by past or current conflicts or divergent approaches. Is everyone on the same page? If the board and senior management disagree on the direction of the nonprofit, one can hardly expect the rank and file to be clear about their performance expectations or to understand where the nonprofit is headed.

Organizational Dysfunction and Communication

Dysfunction in areas of communication can be observed in the way in which policies and procedures are explained, how changes in external environment are articulated, and how new policies/procedures that relate to current legislation are expected to be implemented.

Because knowledge is power, organizational leaders sometimes hoard whatever bits of information they have. Fearing that by sharing this information, their status within the organization might be compromised, these leaders do their best to ensure that only a select few have access to information. These individuals can go to great lengths to hide information that has potentially important implications. Obviously, there needs to be a reasonable method for ensuring appropriate security for confidential information, but a culture of unnecessary secrecy in a nonprofit is a huge red flag.

If the environment within the nonprofit is one of secrecy—beware. Also, beware of the gatekeepers that guard the "secrets," as these individuals are tasked with and rewarded for their unwavering attention to keeping secrets secret.

Organizational Dysfunction and Finance and Financial Management

Internal controls, the preparation and presentation of financial reports, and overall quality of financial management are important indicators of organizational function. Dysfunctional organizations have either sloppy or nonexistent policies and procedures for the management of revenues, payables, donations, and grants.

Organizational Dysfunction and the Lack of Internal Controls

Many nonprofit executives and board members believe that the concept of "internal controls" applies exclusively to finance and financial operations. Internal controls are necessary for Human Resources, IT, Operations, Crisis Communication, Governance, and Administration. The absence of internal controls is evidence not only of sloppy technique, it is also emblematic of a culture that does not have standards, or accountability. Not surprisingly, such a culture has a high probability of dysfunction if for no other reason than that of lack of accountability.

Organizational Dysfunction and Information Technology

The way in which technology is used, misused, or ignored can signal dysfunction within a nonprofit. One of the most common examples of dysfunction is the failure to stay current and to recognize that technology is an integral part of the internal control infrastructure. Sadly, many nonprofits fail to understand the degree to which they depend on technology. It isn't just computers! The term *technology* relates to other important operational tools such as software, hardware, laptops and notebooks, PDAs, cell phones, voicemail, e-mail, and Internet access. Failure to adequately manage this array of technology can indicate organizational dysfunction, and a serious risk to the nonprofit in the form of hackers, theft of confidential data, identity theft, potential for harassment of staff, donors or others, and other liability scenarios for the organization.

The current legislative environment presumes a level of competence in the use and application of appropriate technology as an integral tool in internal controls. Current expectations are that all nonprofits understand how to use and manage the types of technology that are appropriate to their organizations. Because technology reaches across all sectors of a nonprofit, dysfunction within this operational component can have far-reaching effects.

Organizational Dysfunction and Development and Fundraising

The manner in which a nonprofit chooses to raise funds for its continuing operation has the potential to show a positive or negative image to the donors and community at large. Organizational dysfunction can be evident in the manner in which a fundraising campaign is structured and executed. The quality of "customer service" that donors or patrons receive is also indicative of the degree of functioning within a nonprofit.

The quality of the overall planning and execution of a fundraising campaign can indicate levels of dysfunction within the organization. One example that became a public relations soap opera was a West Coast zoo's naming contest for two grizzly bears. The contest was initially open to the public. Then the zoo decided to auction off the naming rights and "payoff" those public entries with free tickets to the zoo. Then, the zoo's management decided that the winners of the auction really didn't get to name the bears, and then happily, the couple who won the auction had the sense to ask the zoo to open the naming contest to the public. The fiasco went full circle!

Donor privacy: If the nonprofit doesn't appear to care about its donors' privacy, or is more interested in selling donor information to obtain additional revenue, these traits should be red flags to the observer. Similarly, the degree of care the nonprofit takes to ensure the security of donor records is an indicator of the level of organizational function. Limiting access to confidential donor records is essential to the preservation of donor privacy. Staff need to be carefully screened and authorized to ensure that there is no inappropriate communication with donors.

Organizational Dysfunction and Human Resource Management

Human resource management holds many clues to the nature of organizational dysfunction. One of the most obvious indicators of organizational dysfunction is a permissive atmosphere that highlights a sense of entitlement on the part of the staff and volunteers. Staff and volunteers are habitually late, dress in an unprofessional manner, and do not produce quality work. Staff and volunteers are permitted to treat clients and visitors alike in a disinterested fashion—or even with outright hostility. Volunteers are not trained or supervised. The nonprofit fails to appropriately screen paid and volunteer staff for sensitive work and handling confidential materials.

Another sign of organizational dysfunction is the volume of complaints regarding hostile work environment, sexual harassment, or other dysfunctional behavior. Are there complaints about food or other personal items being stolen? Are office spaces orderly, or piled with paper and trash? Do staff members treat the nonprofit's furniture, equipment, and other materials with respect?

What is the "tone" of the furnishings inside staff members' workspaces? The furniture may be provided by the nonprofit, but personal items including pictures, posters, slogan buttons, and other signs can express—sometimes unmistakably—the disdain the staff member has for the organization, a boss, or other "targets" within the nonprofit.

How do staff members answer the phone? How do they greet visitors? Are staff members good organizational citizens? What sort of pride do they evidence in their nonprofit, their colleagues, and in their own work?

Although it is unrealistic to expect that everyone is happy all of the time, morale of staff is an important barometer of organizational function. Low morale should never be ignored—it is a red flag. Something is going on and further examination is indicated.

Organizational Dysfunction and Public Trust

Public trust is one of the most important assets a nonprofit has—and at the same time it is one of the most elusive. Public trust isn't something that can be shown to staff, clients, donors, or even members of the public. This fragile and subtle feature is the life breath of a nonprofit (or private sector company as well). However, like the life breath that sustains life itself, once it is compromised, the living organism either is damaged or dies. Nonprofits that experience scandals or other crises do not always return to normal operation. The nonprofits that fail to have a crisis communication plan or fail to be transparent or exhibit resentment of public inquiries about financial records are showing signs of dysfunction.

Does your nonprofit have a plan for dealing with a crisis? What if a key member of the staff dies, becomes disabled, or is under investigation? Do you have a spokesperson? Or would you sound like the interim Executive Director who commented to a reporter, "The time is not ripe to make any public statements." The local newspaper had just broken the story of fiscal mismanagement at a nonprofit organization that, ironically, was in business to help nonprofits manage their organizations more efficiently. Five months after his haughty pronouncement, the Executive Director was forced to again deal with the media—this time to announce the closure of the clearinghouse.

Organizational Dysfunction and Legal Issues

Dysfunctional organizations often either have no understanding about the significance of legal issues, or engage in games of denial to justify their ignorance. Legal issues can relate to required filings such as IRS Form 990s, workers' compensation claims, complaints to regulatory agencies regarding harassment or hostile environment claims, or even failing to understand the connection between the quality of internal controls and legal obligations.

Legal documents such as contracts, leases, filings with state and federal regulators, and licenses need to be secured in an orderly fashion. Dysfunctional organizations often fail to have a coherent filing system that provides quick access to documents when needed.

Many dysfunctional organizations do not understand how and why complaints can escalate into litigation, nor do they understand the techniques that can be employed to "de-escalate" a situation. A common reason for pursuing litigation is that the aggrieved party was either ignored, their allegations dismissed as trivial, or they were treated with disrespect. Boards and senior management can take the same ostrich-like stance because it would be "too much work" or "cost too much" to establish solid policies and procedures.

Organizational Dysfunction and the Ability to Understand the External Environment

Keeping pace with current legislative and industry trends is more important than ever. The external environment is fraught with change—and this change is unlike that ever witnessed before. In the wake of Enron and other corporate scandals, the federal government is under pressure from the public to crack down on private sector and nonprofit sector abuses. Shareholder activism has paved the way for a new type of activism, "donor" activism, which demands the same type of transparency from a nonprofit as a shareholder would expect from a corporation. The equivalence of these expectations is unprecedented. Never before have public sector expectations of nonprofits been so closely aligned with expectations of the private sector.

Organizational dysfunction is evident in the failure to stay current with legislative changes, changes in public expectations and that of important stakeholders such as funders, and failure to stay current with "industry" issues. Denial of the importance of environmental scanning results in the failure to have everyone in the nonprofit stay current on these issues and engage in routine professional development (see Exhibit 3.2).

EXHIBIT 3.2   QUESTIONNAIRE

Does Your Nonprofit Have Problems With...

- Producing accurate financial statements in a timely manner?
- Travel and other reimbursable claims that appear to be inflated or inaccurate?
- Compensation and benefits packages for executives?
- A board that isn't effective or shows evidence of dysfunction?
- Meeting deadlines for reports and documents for regulators or foundations?
- Hackers and other IT security issues?
- Employees and volunteers using the nonprofit's e-mail and Internet access for personal use?
- Fundraising, particularly as this relates to using vendors for fundraising efforts?
- Understanding how the legislative environment has changed?

What Are the Costs of Organizational Dysfunction?

The bumper-sticker slogan, "If you think education is expensive, try ignorance," rings true in dysfunctional nonprofits. Dysfunction exacts a heavy price on nonprofits. Here are some areas in which organizational dysfunction is evident in higher costs.

- **Increased insurance premiums**: A very large nonprofit was deeply in denial about their failure to adequately address risk areas within their operation. Their insurance rates more than doubled in one year's time. The underwriters were candid about the impact of their dysfunctional management on premiums. Despite its size, the nonprofit had tenuous internal controls—and engaged in virtually no oversight or due diligence on its outside projects. The underwriters were concerned that this organization presented as yet unseen risks and was taking no steps to either acknowledge these risk areas or deal with them in a coherent fashion. Insurance premiums are based on several factors, including industry trends, marketing of specialty coverage, and the insured's claims history. Insurance professionals look at nonprofits as *companies* in the same manner they look at any of their commercial insurance clients. They expect nonprofits to conduct their operations in a business-like fashion and conform to the same operational standards as organizations in the private sector.

- **Inability to obtain insurance**: If a nonprofit does not inspire confidence with their insurance professional(s), it will be difficult for them to obtain the types of insurance they need, at the limits they require, at a reasonable price. Some types of insurance such as workers' compensation can be purchased from state-supported plans, but other types of insurance such as commercial liability needs to be placed in the general market. Directors and Officers insurance can be difficult to place and very expensive. The more evidence, such as adaptation of SOX best practices, that a nonprofit can show to garner the confidence of its insurance professionals, the more likely it is to obtain the necessary portfolio of insurance.

- **Difficulty in retaining talented staff**: Good help is indeed hard to find, and it's expensive to have to continuously train new staff. Even more expensive is the loss of talented staff. Talented people bring new ideas, perspectives, creativity, and problem-solving to a nonprofit. They also know that their skills are in demand, and that whatever compensation package they have could be replicated in an organization that isn't as dysfunctional. No organization is without some type of dysfunction, but truly dysfunctional organizations exact a toll on all staff, particularly the talented ones. Sometimes, the departure of a talented staff member can be a catalyst for change, but the organization has still experienced a "brain drain."

- **Workers' compensation claims rising and associated costs**: Dysfunctional organizations often experience an increase in workers' compensation claims for emotional stress, repetitive stress injuries, or back injuries. These conditions are more difficult to prove, and often more expensive to treat because of the imprecise aspects of the injury. An insurance professional was asked by a client to review the alarming increase in repetitive stress and emotional stress claims. Upon interviewing the claimants, the insurance executive concluded that ergonomics wasn't the issue, but the client's dysfunctional management style was. The employees did whatever they could to stay out of the office.

- **HR costs—absences, sick days, lower productivity**: As was noted in the previous story, a dysfunctional environment will result in more absences, sick days, workers' compensation claims, and, ultimately, lower productivity. Staff retention is lower, which will, in turn, increase the costs of recruitment, hiring, and training.

- **Technology**: Misuse of technology is common in dysfunctional organizations. Staff surf the Net instead of working, download files and programs that can transmit viruses, and pave the way for hacker break-ins.

- **Difficulty in attracting donations, capital, or funding**: Organizational dysfunction has a way of making the nonprofit less attractive to sources of capital, major gifts, and grants. Banks, foundations, and major donors all expect the nonprofit to be able to present a professional profile in terms of governance, internal controls, and legal compliance. Several prominent philanthropists declined to give major gifts to a large nonprofit primarily because they observed that the nonprofit's chief executive and its board failed to ensure that the organization managed its money in a proficient manner. The executive had been promoted because of his scholarly accomplishments, rather than any business acumen, and board members were chosen primarily on the basis of their philanthropic "capacity." This deficiency in the executive's skill set and the board's benign disinterest had a trickle-down effect within the nonprofit's staff.

- **Difficulty in attracting board talent, collaborative ventures, and corporate partnerships**: One of the most common mantras among dysfunctional organizations is that if they demand performance, they will never be able to recruit board members. Just the opposite! People of quality generally refuse to join the governance entities of dysfunctional organizations because their skills will either be ignored or wasted.

Although no organization is perfect (i.e., without any form of dysfunction), it is important to understand the type and source of dysfunction within your own nonprofit and its impact on the financial well-being of the organization as well as on the nonprofit's standing in the community (see Exhibits 3.3 and 3.4).

EXHIBIT 3.3   COSTS OF DYSFUNCTION

What Are the Costs of Dysfunction in Your Nonprofit?

- Decision-making
  - Are decisions delayed or stymied by endless discussion, committee meetings, or other methods?
  - Are there metrics in place to establish objectives before making a decision?
  - Are the appropriate players involved in the discussion? If the discussion only entails lower-level staff who have no authority to make a decision, the process is dysfunctional.
  - How are the relevant facts and data gathered prior to making a decision?
  - How are decisions evaluated? Is there a mechanism for reviewing important decisions to determine if a course correction is needed?
- Insurance premiums and availability
  - Has the nonprofit experienced difficulty obtaining insurance at the appropriate limits for a competitive price?
  - Has the nonprofit experienced a large number of claims? Major claims? Claims in one particular area?
  - Are supervisors held accountable for the frequency and severity of on-the-job injuries? Has the nonprofit's workers' comp experience modification increased in the past three (3) years?
- Difficulty in attracting major donors, grants, and other sources of capital
  - Has your nonprofit had difficulty in securing major gifts from donors? If so, what reasons have the donors given for declining to give a major gift?
  - Has your nonprofit been turned down for grants or other project-related funding?
  - Has your nonprofit had difficulty obtaining a line of credit, mortgage, or other loan products?
- Regulators
  - Has your nonprofit received inquiries from the Internal Revenue Service and/or any state or federal regulators about your operations?
- Has your nonprofit been named in any complaints to governmental agencies?

EXHIBIT 3.4   SPILLOVER EFFECTS

Spillover Effects of Dysfunction

DYSFUNCTIONAL BOARD

- Lack of oversight and direction in governance
- Board clique or senior management making all the important decisions
- Not living up to legal obligations of care, loyalty, and obedience

DYSFUNCTIONAL SENIOR MANAGEMENT

- Potential for fraud and mismanagement of nonprofit
- Fails to provide board with accurate financial reports and other documents
- Can engage in inappropriate or illegal activities in dealing with rank and file such as sexual harassment or violation of Whistleblower Protection
- Dysfunctional behavior results in higher operating costs such as unemployment insurance, training new employees, workers' comp, and the like

CONCLUSION

As you complete the worksheets included in this chapter, consider how the types of dysfunction you have identified could act as a barrier to understanding SOX requirements and adaptation of SOX best practices. The implementation of activities to be in compliance with SOX as well as benefit from the adaptation of best practices may also involve neutralizing the areas of dysfunction within your nonprofit.

The important thing to remember is that times have changed—and the changes you need to make *are the law*. It isn't about worrying if you are going to step on toes or hurt people's feelings—your nonprofit's continued existence depends on its level of compliance. The more everyone in the nonprofit understands SOX and its requirements and best practices, the easier it will be to obtain the necessary cooperation to make changes.

CHAPTER 4

Root Cause Analysis Part I: Three Nonprofit Crises

She is a renowned cardiologist, he was an immigrant who did well in his new country, but is now serving time in a penitentiary and will probably be deported upon his release, and he was a househusband who was recently sentenced to one to three years in prison. What do these people have in common? They are all disgraced leaders of nonprofits who experienced major crises. These crises were the stuff of headlines, CNN coverage, and, in two cases, Congressional inquiry. What else do these people have in common? They operated at a stunning level of hubris, manipulating their nonprofits until time and circumstances caught up with them. They also had something else in common that was more insidious: an organizational culture that afforded them the opportunity to engage in fraudulent behavior. Board ignorance and apathy often unknowingly supported their efforts, and it was not until whistleblowers came forward and Congress began questioning that their activities were halted.

CHAPTER OVERVIEW

This chapter examines the recent crises of these three nonprofits whose good names and public image may never be fully rehabilitated. The nature of the crises will be examined for the purpose of conducting a brief root cause analysis. The common threads and the unique elements will be compared in terms of the learning that emerges from each of these crisis scenarios. Chapter 5 will examine how compliance with SOX whistleblower protection and document preservation as best practices could have averted these crises.

This chapter will examine selected nonprofit crises that have received widespread publicity. The technique of root cause analysis will be used to dissect these crises and identify the commonalities that emerge from the organizational dysfunction. The purpose of these case studies will be to present the reader with an array of "real life" factors that contributed to the disasters that took place.

A brief root cause analysis will be conducted to examine the relevant facts of the crises that affected the American Red Cross (ARC) National Headquarters and its September 11th fundraising and blood collection efforts, the United Way of the National Capital Area, and the James Beard Foundation.

The analysis of each of the crisis scenarios will include these components:

- **Source of the crisis**: What were the events, allegations, or criminal behavior that instigated the crisis scenario?
- **Who was involved**: The Board, Executive Director, or some other staff member?
- **How did they get caught?**
    - What were the clues to the dysfunction?
    - Who discovered the fraud?
    - What happened to the person(s) who discovered the fraud?
    - Where was the Board in all of this?
- **Organizational culture**: What aspects of the nonprofit's culture contributed to the events surrounding the scandal?
- **Who were the governmental or law enforcement authorities whose intervention brought the crisis to a conclusion?**
- **What was the estimated cost of the crisis?**
    - Did they lose a contract (such as the United Way and the CFC)?
    - Describe the adverse publicity.
    - Describe who lost their job and/or was prosecuted.
    - Was there a forensic audit or other review to recap the economic damages? For example, PriceWaterhouseCoopers (PWC) was engaged to conduct a forensic audit of the United Way of the National Capital Area.
- **Impact of the crisis**: What happened to the nonprofit in the aftermath of the scandal?

Each of these crises has unique aspects, but they also have common factors that contributed to the makings of the quandary. Out of each of the crisis scenarios are lessons that can serve as valuable pedagogical tools for today's practitioners. The discussion will also highlight these areas:

- What made each of these crisis scenarios unique?
- What were the common factors?
- What were the lessons learned?

- How can these lessons apply to each of these organizational components?
  - Governance and Board
  - Operations
  - Staffing
  - Relations with the public (and the media)

CHAPTER OBJECTIVES

By the end of this chapter, you will be able to:

- Trace the roots of the dysfunction in each of the three crisis scenarios presented in the chapter.
- Discuss the common factors that contributed to the crises.
- Describe the manner in which the organizational culture of each of the organizations contributed to the crises.
- Discuss the lessons learned from each one of these scenarios.

AMERICAN RED CROSS NATIONAL HEADQUARTERS AND POST-SEPTEMBER 11TH FUNDRAISING AND BLOOD COLLECTION

The first nonprofit and its crisis that will be discussed is the American Red Cross and its fundraising and blood collection activities post-September 11th.

BACKGROUND

When the United States Congress signed the Geneva Conventions in 1881, it authorized the formation of a Red Cross Society in the United States, the American Red Cross. Congress mandated that the American Red Cross would perform two primary functions. The first was to provide assistance to victims of disasters, and the second was to act as a communications liaison between the armed forces and the American public.

Clara Barton was the first president of the American Red Cross. The organization expanded its programmatic offerings in the ensuing decades, but retains its Congressional charter because it delivers the two mandated services to the public. With the introduction of blood transfusion and related technology in World War II, the American Red Cross became the primary blood collection entity in this country. Today, its biomedical services division is a multi-billion dollar business.

Source of the Crisis—What Were the Events, Allegations, or Criminal Behavior that Instigated the Crisis Scenario?

Following the September 11th attacks on New York and Washington, the American Red Cross launched a phenomenally successful fundraising and blood donor drive. In the initial hours and days after the attack, the public believed that blood donations were necessary to treat the injured, particularly those from the World Trade Center in New York. Blood donors lined up for hours to give blood at Red Cross collection sites. Monetary donations poured into the Red Cross Chapters and Headquarters.

As the days turned into weeks, it became very apparent that there were few survivors of the attack on the World Trade Center who required blood. Whole blood has a shelf life of approximately six weeks. The American Red Cross did not have sufficient refrigeration facilities to freeze and store these blood products. No alternative use for the blood was planned, such as shipping it overseas. Hence, the public watched with dismay—and often disgust—when video footage of Red Cross workers destroying the donated blood products was shown around the world six weeks after the September 11th attack.

The Red Cross claimed that all of the monetary donations were going to be used to assist the surviving families of people who were killed in the attacks. The American Red Cross President, Dr. Bernadine Healy, established the "Liberty Fund" to consolidate these donations. What the public was not aware of was a closely guarded Red Cross secret. Historically, money collected from disaster-related fundraising efforts was put into the overall budget of ARC Disaster Services. Traditionally, there was **never** any assurance to the American public that *all* of the money collected for a specific disaster would be used exclusively for that purpose. The intent was to use whatever the current "disaster" was as a means of raising funds to support future disaster scenarios. Red Cross "insiders" were outraged that Dr. Healy, who was clearly a newcomer to Red Cross and thus an "outsider," chose to segregate the enormous sums being donated as a result of the September 11th attacks. As pressure began to mount to integrate the Liberty Fund donations with the rest of the disaster relief funds, Dr. Healy delayed the payment of gifts to the victims' families. The families complained to Congress, and Senator Charles Grassley (R–Iowa), Chair of the Senate Finance Committee, began to investigate. The Red Cross changed its position and stated that all of the Liberty Fund monies would be distributed to victims' families. Dr. Healy was forced to resign as ARC President.

Who Was Involved—The Board, Executive Director, or Some Other Staff Member?

The Liberty Fund crisis scenario involved Dr. Healy and the Red Cross Board of Governors. Dr. Healy's tenure at the Red Cross had been stormy due to a variety of factors, but primarily her management style and the board's composition. This governance entity presents an interesting dichotomy. The composition is divided between political appointees (appointed by the current President of the United States) and members elected from local Red Cross Chapters. Thus, the board consists of Red Cross "insiders" whose numbers and influence far outweighed the relatively disinterested political appointees. Dr. Healy had served as head of the National Institute of Health. Her hard-charging management style and persistent questioning of board inaction were the catalyst for a fractious relationship. Immediately prior to the September 11th crisis, Dr. Healy had uncovered a $1 million fraud at a large chapter in New Jersey. She wanted to prosecute, but the board showed no interest in pursuing the matter. A more detailed discussion of the financial mismanagement that Dr. Healy uncovered will be addressed in Chapter 9.

How Did They Get Caught?

This was a crisis that was covered step by step in the media. The destruction of the blood was broadcast around the world, the families of the victims aired their complaints in the media, and Congressional inquiries were the headlines of cable and network news. The clues to the dysfunction were more carefully hidden. The composition of the board, and the fractious relationship between the board and Dr. Healy did not become apparent until she was forced to resign as President. During the televised press conference when the President of the ARC Board of Governors announced that Dr. Healy had resigned on her own, she shook her head "no" and then announced that the board forced her to resign—as the world watched.

Other clues to the dysfunction were even more difficult for outsiders to discern. The workings of the ARC Disaster Services, particularly at National Headquarters, have traditionally been intricate. Insiders in this division generally begin their Red Cross "careers" at local chapters, and because of the 19th Century Congressional mandate are viewed as having an exceptional skill set. Anyone outside of this division is an *outsider*—even other Red Cross staffers and volunteers. The Disaster Services leadership has traditionally been permitted to raise and spend funds without oversight from ARC senior management or the board.

Who Discovered the Fraud? What Happened to the Person(s) Who Discovered the Fraud?

The complaints of the September 11th victims' families raised public awareness that 1) the funds from the Liberty Fund were not being distributed as advertised, and 2) pressure was being put on Dr. Healy by Disaster Services to integrate the money into the overall Disaster Services funds. Victims' families went to the media and to Congress. Eventually, some of the families did receive cash gifts, but only after Congressional inquiry and continuing media coverage.

A CBS news story reported that some at Red Cross headquarters were afraid the National Disaster Fund was becoming a "leaky piggy bank" for chapters (Atkinson, 2002). The traditional arm's-length relationship between Red Cross National Headquarters and its chapters ensured that National would be actively discouraged from providing the level of aggressive oversight that chapter financial matters required. Red

Cross auditors were also stymied. CBS news reported that money given to the Boston chapter was "not easily traceable," according to a Red Cross audit report (Atkinson, 2002).

Rampant chapter mismanagement of donations was probably a factor in Dr. Healy's decision to establish the Liberty Fund to segregate the September 11th funds from the National Disaster Fund. The local chapters were incensed and began lobbying their associates on the Red Cross Board of Governors. The Board members from the chapters were growing impatient with Dr. Healy's relentless exposing of rampant fraud within the chapters, and the Liberty Fund appeared to be the last straw. Dr. Healy was terminated several weeks later. During the news conference, David McLaughlin, Chair of the Red Cross Board of Governors, told employees, "I don't say it's the best thing for the Red Cross, but I think Dr. Healy thinks it's the best thing." Healy shakes her head "no," and when she tries to speak, McLaughlin cuts off the news conference (Atkinson, 2002).

Where Was the Board in All of This?

The actions leading up to Dr. Healy's departure suggest that the Board of Governors took the opportunity to rid itself of Dr. Healy and her persistent pressure to address fiscal mismanagement problems in the chapters. The Board supported Disaster Services' traditional fundraising approach, but in the face of mounting public and Congressional pressure, gave in to the demands to release all of the Liberty Fund monies to the victims' families.

Organizational Culture—What Aspects of the Nonprofit's Culture Contributed to the Events Surrounding the Scandal?

The American Red Cross' organizational culture reflects the dichotomy of a national headquarters and local chapters spread out across the United States. The chapters have traditionally believed that they are the "owners" of the Red Cross name. They look at National Headquarters as meddlesome bureaucrats. The configuration of the Board of Governors has facilitated this viewpoint because the chapter representatives on the Board of Governors have considerable influence. National Headquarters does not appear to have the power or the support to provide the aggressive supervision that chapter operations require. It should come as no surprise that Dr. Healy uncovered rampant financial malfeasance at the chapter level.

Because Disaster Services was one of two Congressionally mandated services, there appears to be a culture of preeminence within the ranks. Individuals who were long-time members of Disaster Services, whether as staff or volunteers, generally had years of experience working in primitive conditions. Those common experiences further promoted the selectivity upon which this division prided itself. Dr. Healy's forging ahead with a special fund that denied this division and its affiliates in the local chapters access to the overflowing coffers from September 11th seemed to be an innovation that they did not want to implement.

Who Were the Governmental or Law Enforcement Authorities Whose Intervention Brought the Crisis to a Conclusion?

The U.S. Senate Finance Committee Chaired by Senator Charles Grassley held hearings into the matter, and forced the interim Red Cross President, Harold Decker, to agree to use all of the Liberty Fund money as cash gifts for the victims' families.

What Was the Estimated Cost of the Crisis?

The crisis surrounding the blood donations and fundraising in the wake of September 11th brought about the resignation of Dr. Healy, and subjected the American Red Cross to well deserved adverse publicity and Congressional scrutiny. Red Cross insiders believe that, of all of the Red Cross' recent crises, this was the most serious, as the Grassley inquiries possibly put the organization on a path to implode. The organization survived only by careful negotiation with Congressional authorities.

Was There a Forensic Audit or Other Review to Recap the Economic Damages?

Thanks to Senator Grassley, the Red Cross was forced to turn over all of the money in the Liberty Fund to September 11th families. Grassley also forced the Red Cross to tell the truth about the rampant financial malfeasance on the national and chapter levels. However, Senator Grassley had to insist on the truth *twice*.

Following Dr. Healy's termination, Senator Grassley sent a letter to interim President Harold Decker containing 39 questions about how the charity intended to deliver September 11th monetary relief judiciously and quickly to qualified recipients. Grassley's inquiry came after many of his constituents expressed concern over the Red Cross' delay in distributing their donations for victims' relief (Grassley, 2002).

In a follow-up letter dated August 12, 2002 to the recently installed Red Cross President, Martha Evans, a clearly infuriated Grassley concluded:

> In summary, the information that I received independent of the Red Cross leads me to conclude that the rosy picture the Red Cross sought to present does not match the reality presented in these documents. To get to the bottom of whether the Red Cross has secured all 9-11 donations in the Liberty Fund for the exclusive use of the victims and holds its chapters accountable, please provide detailed responses to the following questions: I have received information that at least one chapter has not yet turned over all donations meant for the Liberty Fund. Identify that chapter and any others that have not turned

over these donations, explain why not, and identify any penalty imposed against that chapter. For the past three years, identify any chapter that failed to provide any required financial information to any Red Cross governing body (i.e., National) in full or on time. Red Cross' answer to Question #29 is unclear as to whether there are guidelines for uniform record keeping and financial reporting by the regions and chapters ("In regard to uniform record keeping and reporting, chapters use standard charts of accounts for accounting purposes.") Please clarify this response including what is meant by "standard charts of accounts." For the past three years, identify any investigation involving allegations of mismanagement or fraud by any Red Cross officer, director, employee, or volunteer. Also, state the status of the investigation and whether any settlement or penalty resulted, and identify the settlement amount or penalty. For the past three years, identify all Red Cross officials who have left their positions under circumstances involving allegations of mismanagement or fraud. State whether any internal disciplinary proceeding was conducted or whether any lawsuit or charge was filed against the individual and the status of that action. Also, state whether he or she was allowed to retain benefits or transfer to another chapter and, if so, explain why. Identify and explain the circumstances for the "five involuntarily decharters" referenced in your response to Question #24. It is my understanding that the Red Cross has a strong policy that the chapters should be financially self-sufficient. The *CBS Evening News* reported on July 31, 2002, that the Red Cross has allowed chapters to receive money from the National Disaster Fund more than 3,000 times last year. Please list all income to and expenditures from the National Disaster Fund from Fiscal Year 2000 to the present. This list should include but not be limited to all chapter "Form 903" requests as well as chapter accruals and advances. The list should also disclose the purpose of each Form 903 request (i.e., the precise reason why the chapter requested the funds). Also, describe the method by which the Red Cross approves or denies each 903 request as well as the procedures in place to ensure, after it approves the request, that the chapters properly use the "903" funds. Information that I have received indicates that, contrary to the Red Cross' response to Question #26, the organization may receive more than 5% of its funds from federal, state, and local government sources and that in many chapters this amount frequently exceeds 30–40%. Please clarify your response and identify all chapters at which government funds (federal, state, and/or local) comprise more than 10% of the chapter budget (Grassley, 2002).

Impact of the Crisis—What Happened to the Nonprofit in the Aftermath of the Scandal?

In light of Senator Grassley's vigorous pursuit of the truth, the Red Cross has taken steps in future disasters to limit the amount of their fundraising, and in the case of the 2004 Asian Tsunami, it stopped accepting funds when the organization received as much as they could process and distribute.

There has been very little impact on the size and structure of the American Red Cross, although there were layoffs at National Headquarters, and the CFO at the time of the crisis, Jack Campbell, retired.

UNITED WAY OF THE NATIONAL CAPITAL AREA

The second nonprofit and its crisis to be analyzed is the United Way of the National Capital Area.

Background

The United Way of the National Capital Area (UWNCA) is one of the larger United Way affiliates in the United States. Prior to the scandal, the UWNCA administered the Combined Federal Campaign (CFC) in the Washington Metro Area. The CFC included all donations that came from military and federal government personnel.

Source of the Crisis—What Were the Events, Allegations, or Criminal Behavior that Instigated the Crisis Scenario?

Allegations surfaced that senior management were receiving pay in excess of their contracts, credit cards were being used inappropriately, and reimbursements were excessive and often without appropriate documentation. Individuals on the UWNCA staff who brought up questionable activities were terminated, and a board member who raised questions was removed from the board. The UWNCA's long-time auditing firm that conducted the UWNCA's audits engaged PriceWaterhouseCooper (PWC) to conduct a forensic audit. The results of the audit confirmed that Oral Suer, Executive Director of the UWNCA, embezzled over $1 million, and that at one point, UWNCA "borrowed" $3 million from the CFC funds. PWC auditors could find no evidence that the $3 million was ever returned to the CFC.

Who Was Involved—The Board, Executive Director, or Some Other Staff Member?

The PWC forensic audit implicated Oral Suer, Executive Director, and members of his senior staff. The board of the UWNCA was a large entity, but closely governed by a tightly knit Executive Committee who may have known about the financial machinations of senior management, but chose to ignore the fraud.

How Did They Get Caught?

Clues to the dysfunction began to emerge when members of the staff questioned financial records and board members began asking questions. One member of the board who persisted in asking questions was categorized as a "racist" by the board leadership. Financial records did not reconcile with receipts and other source documents. Mr. Suer and his senior management were permitted to use United Way credit cards without question, and were reimbursed for expenses without receipts or other documentation.

Who Discovered the Fraud?

The UWNCA's longtime auditor was aware of the shoddy financial management, but did not push for answers until staff and board members began to question Mr. Suer's financial dealings.

What Happened to the Person(s) Who Discovered the Fraud?

Staff and board members who either discovered the fraud or raised questions were routinely removed from the organization. The subsequent PWC forensic audit uncovered volumes of evidence.

Where Was the Board In All of This?

The board of the UWNCA was large, and met infrequently. When the board did meet, the agenda consisted of superficial topics, and the effect was a "feel good" session designed to promote cheerleading, rather than governance.

Organizational Culture—What Aspects of the Nonprofit's Culture Contributed to the Events Surrounding the Scandal?

In Mr. Suer's heyday, he was a close friend and associate to the now disgraced William Aramony, who was CEO of the United Way of America office. Mr. Suer's management of UWNCA as his own personal piggy bank presents a disturbing parallel to the charges lodged against Mr. Aramony. The appearance of the scandal suggests that UWNCA had an organizational culture in which senior managers were accountable to no one—including the board. The Executive Committee of the board enabled the dysfunctional behavior by its closed management style and culture of secrecy. Board members outside of the Executive Committee were not even permitted to have a roster of the other board members.

The UWNCA's board culture significantly contributed to the overall mismanagement of the agency primarily because they were too big and the majority too disinterested in holding management accountable. The board's decision-making appeared to be consolidated among the board leadership. Certain board members had knowledge of senior staff wrongdoing, but consistently failed to advise the rest of the board.

Interaction among board members outside of the carefully controlled meetings was virtually prohibited. Board members who requested a copy of the board roster were refused.

As a means of diverting attention from the board members who questioned financials, the board leadership subjected the questioners to harassment and public humiliation, including charges of racism. One board member who persistently raised questions and resisted board intimidation was unceremoniously removed from the board. Board members were vehemently chastised for talking to the media.

Board culture actively suppressed meaningful dialogue between membership and board officers/senior management. Board leadership abdicated their fiduciary obligations and accountability to the UWNCA's senior management. Board agendas were staff driven, and board meetings contained very little substantive discussion.

Who Were the Governmental or Law Enforcement Authorities Whose Intervention Brought the Crisis to a Conclusion?

Law enforcement arrested Mr. Suer for embezzlement. PriceWaterhouseCoopers completed an exhaustive forensic audit, which would have been even more voluminous if the auditors had been given access to the carloads of material that Mr. Suer took upon his departure from the UWNCA, and had been given access to Mr. Suer's close associates. The associates refused to cooperate with the PWC auditors on advice of counsel.

What Was the Estimated Cost of the Crisis?

The UWNCA lost their lucrative contract to handle the CFC. The organization also was the subject of Congressional inquiry, and drastically reduced its staff, replaced its entire board and senior management, and closed most of its branch locations.

Describe the Adverse Publicity

The ongoing events as the crisis unfolded were described in the *Washington Post*, *Chronicle of Philanthropy*, and other print and media outlets.

Describe Who Lost Their Job and/or Was Prosecuted

Oral Suer, former CEO, was prosecuted. His successor, Norman Taylor, was dismissed. The entire board was replaced.

Was There a Forensic Audit or Other Review to Recap the Economic Damages?

Following the crisis, PWC was engaged to conduct a forensic audit of the UWNCA's books. The PWC Executive Summary cites two issues that significantly limited their investigative ability:

- **Inability to interview all relevant key personnel**: Several of the former staff or Board members with whom we requested interviews were unavailable. Other former staff also did not return our calls, including Anthony Vallieres, former Chief Financial Officer (CFO).

- **Lack of availability of records**: As certain aspects of our FAI [Forensic Accounting Investigation] (i.e., Mr. Suer's compensation) spanned a long time period (approximately 30 years), it is natural that records prepared contemporaneously with the events under review would not have been retained in the normal course of business. Furthermore, a UWNCA staffer informed us that Mr. Suer was seen removing documents when he left UWNCA. The nature of these records is unknown. In addition, the state of organization of UWNCA's records, particularly in earlier periods, is disorganized and not optimal, as there was no index of stored records, nor was there a formal records retention policy, and some of the documents we sought were simply never located by either PWC or UWNCA.

The complete audit is a 200+ page document. The following is a sample of the PWC FAI findings:

We have found evidence that Mr. Suer apparently requested and received payments from UWNCA throughout his tenure at the organization, which appear to have been clearly above and beyond his normal Board-approved compensation. Mr. Suer's Board-approved compensation included his regular annual salary, 24 days of annual leave per year, 18 days of sick leave per year, and $10,000 per year in deferred compensation. We found that he obtained these additional amounts via a number of different methods, most authorized or approved by Mr. Suer himself without any documented outside approval/scrutiny. These apparent excess payments were made through annual leave exchanges, advances, deferred compensation payments, and other various means.

We found, according to the best available documents, that the total taxable compensation received by Mr. Suer appears to have been far greater than his Board-approved salary. We determined that this difference apparently exceeds $270,000.

We developed a listing of all manual payroll checks payable to Mr. Suer. Based on the description from the check stubs, we also assigned a category to the payment. This total was roughly $3.7 million before considering repayments.

We also found personal checks written to Mr. Suer for exchange of annual leave that were used to satisfy his personal UWNCA contribution/pledge obligation. Mr. Suer had his donations sometimes withheld from the exchange of annual leave cashed out. Two additional checks were also found relating to Oral Suer's UWNCA pledge contributions. These checks were payable to Oral Suer and total $9,000. The description on the check stubs reads, "Refund of 1988 pledge payment."

We also learned that upon Mr. Suer's retirement, UWNCA entered into a contract with him for consulting services. The terms of this contract called for a monthly payment of $6,000 to Oral Suer and up to $5,000 per month in expenses. Mr. Suer received $6,000 per month between January 2001 and January 2002 when the contract was terminated. Mr. Taylor, his successor, informed us that Mr. Suer provided little in the way of personal services to earn that amount, and Mr. Taylor believed it to be more in the manner of a not-to-compete agreement . . .

During his tenure, Mr. Suer also held six different American Express Corporate Cards. The total amount charged on these cards between 1974 and 2002 was $248,952.15. Beginning in 1997, UWNCA expense account numbers were assigned to each line item on the American Express bill.

Mr. Suer's executive calendar indicates that beginning on Friday January 25, 1991 through Sunday January 27, 1991, Mr. Suer would be attending the Super Bowl. The Super Bowl was held on January 27, 1991 in Tampa Bay, Florida. Mr. Suer submitted a receipt for $543.99 and was ultimately reimbursed for "Conference Expenses" incurred on January 26, 1991 at a hotel in Kissimmee, Florida. We have also been informed that there was no known UWNCA conference in Florida at that time.

As disclosed in the 1997–2000 OPM Audit, in March of 1999 UWNCA borrowed, on a short-term basis, $3 million from the segregated CFC [Combined Federal Campaign] accounts. In April 1999, the loan was supposed to have been repaid with interest. The repayment of the principal amount of the loan was apparently facilitated through a cash transfer of funds in the amount of $3 million. However, we could not locate evidence of an actual cash transfer made for the short-term interest portion of this amount ($13,273.91). Instead, we found UWNCA had recorded a journal entry to credit the interest to the CFC accounts. To the date of this report, we have been unable to locate a physical check or wire transfer demonstrating the movement of $13,273.91 in cash to the correct accounts. CFC policy explicitly states that UWNCA and CFC funds are not to be commingled at any time.

Impact of the Crisis—What Happened to the Nonprofit in the Aftermath of the Scandal?

Oral Suer was convicted of embezzlement. The *Washington Post* reported that at his sentencing, U.S. District Judge Gerald Bruce Lee also ordered Suer to pay $497,000 in restitution. Suer, a native of Turkey who is a permanent U.S. resident but never obtained citizenship, is likely to be deported after his sentence, defense lawyers said.

Lee gave Suer the maximum possible sentence under a federal sentencing guideline range of 21 to 27 months. He acknowledged that Suer had accomplished a great deal at the United Way but said, "At the same time, you were involved in theft. That's the only way to put it—theft." The judge agreed to recommend that Suer serve his sentence at a minimum-security prison (Markton, 2004).

The ending of the high-profile case did little to please officials at the UWNCA, which has filed a civil suit against Suer and is seeking $1.6 million, based on an audit released last summer that found he took that much. Suer has paid $94,000, which will be subtracted from the $497,000 he was ordered to hand over.

"The harm that he did to the people of this region is incalculable," said Eric Holder, an attorney for the United Way of the National Capital Area. "We don't think $497,000 adequately expresses the true nature of his crimes."

"His apologies," Holder added, "even though they may have been great in number, are way too late and have too little impact." (Markton, 2004)

In July 2005, the United Way announced that UWNCA President Charles W. Anderson, along with Resource Development and Communications staff, will operate from the new regional office at 1725 I Street, N.W. "This location puts us closer to our corporate partners and to many of the charitable agencies we serve, while enabling us our operations as inexpensively and efficiently as possible," Anderson said. Relocating the D.C. regional office was a "no-brainer" according to Ric Edelman, UWNCA Board Chair and Chairman, Edelman Financial Services. "This move is another way of showing that our United Way has become one of the most effective, responsive, and transparent nonprofit organizations in the area." Edelman added that the office relocations were supported unanimously by the United Way's board. (UWNCA press release, July 18, 2005)

JAMES BEARD FOUNDATION

The third nonprofit and its crisis discussed is the James Beard Foundation.

Background

The James Beard Foundation was created upon the death of culinary legend, James Beard. The purpose of the foundation was to serve as a launching point for up and coming chefs and to recognize excellence in the culinary world. The foundation's web page cites their mission as "To foster the appreciation and development of gastronomy by preserving and promulgating our culinary heritage, and by recognizing and promoting excellence in all aspects of the culinary arts." (www.jamesbeard.org)

Source of the Crisis—What Events, Allegations, or Criminal Behavior Instigated the Crisis Scenario?

Len Pickell ingratiated himself with the James Beard Foundation Board and became the unpaid President of the Foundation. He manufactured a "background" that presented himself as the wealthy scion of a clothing retailer, an oenophile, and a CPA who, ironically, specialized in forensic accounting. While Mr. Pickell raised the profile of the Foundation by his prolific fundraising, he also used the Foundation as an easy source of personal funding. He misused the Foundation's credit cards and arranged for the finance staff to provide him with signed blank checks for him to use to reimburse himself for expenses. He hid much of the expenditures that he felt the board would disapprove of, while using his charisma to attract donors and to curry favor with the board.

Who Was Involved—The Board, Executive Director, or Some Other Staff Member?

Mr. Pickell was the primary wrongdoer, as he embezzled almost $1 million from the Foundation. His board, however, by their lack of concern, facilitated the embezzlement by creating a culture that permitted Mr. Pickell to misuse his access to funds.

What Were the Clues to the Dysfunction?

The interaction between board members and Mr. Pickell provided the most obvious clues to the organizational dysfunction. Mr. Pickell was able to simply swindle his way into a position of high leadership in the Foundation. If anyone had bothered to check his "credentials," he or she would have discovered that he was *not* a CPA, nor was he the heir to a clothing retail fortune. He was an unemployed house husband from New Jersey. His wife held a position with a technology company. He lived in a split-level house in a middle-class suburb (Weiss, 2005).

How Did He Get Caught? Who Discovered the Fraud?

The Foundation's aging auditor finally decided to call a halt on the fraudulent behavior. Until that point, he had turned a blind eye to the activity.

What Happened to the Person(s) Who Discovered the Fraud?

The auditor turned over the evidence to the board, who contacted law enforcement.

Where Was the Board In All of This?

The board was figuratively—and possibly literally—out to lunch. The board was also in the midst of an internecine struggle with the Foundation's Advisory Board for their awards program, which is considered the "Oscars" of the culinary world.

Organizational Culture—What Aspects of the Nonprofit's Culture Contributed to the Events Surrounding the Scandal?

Because the board appeared to spend more time socializing and dining than they did governing, they fostered an organizational culture of entitlement. Board members were often the major donors of the Foundation, so in that capacity, they appeared to feel entitled to use the Foundation's money to jet to Paris to be wined and dined. The Foundation's "programs" often consisted of dinners at the Foundation's headquarters presented by chefs who were in the running for one of the awards. These pricey dinners netted the Foundation vast sums of money and visibility among the jet set. There was, however, very little in the way of funding cooking opportunities for underprivileged youth or other community outreach (Weiss, 2005).

Who Were the Governmental or Law Enforcement Authorities Whose Intervention Brought the Crisis to a Conclusion?

New York State Attorney General Eliot Spitzer's office investigated the scandal and prosecuted the case.

What Was the Estimated Cost of the Crisis?

The entire Beard Foundation board was replaced, and a separate board for the administration of the Beard Awards was installed.

Describe the Adverse Publicity

The scandal was widely reported in the print and visual media.

Describe Who Lost Their Job and/or Was Prosecuted

Mr. Pickell was sentenced to one to three years in prison and the entire board was replaced.

Was There a Forensic Audit or Other Review to Recap the Economic Damages?

A forensic audit took place, which uncovered the extent of Mr. Pickell's fraud.

Impact of the Crisis—What Happened to the Nonprofit in the Aftermath of the Scandal?

The Foundation reorganized and replaced the board while adding a separate operation with its own board to administer the Beard Foundation Awards.

Factors, Common and Unique, and Lessons Learned

The crises described in this chapter serve as rich pedagogical tools as we study the role of Sarbanes-Oxley legislation and best practices in today's nonprofit world. The publicity that each generated makes them easily recognizable—to practitioners and to Congress. The call for more aggressive regulation of the nonprofit world clearly stems from the number of crises just like these that appear almost on a daily basis.

What Made Each of These Crisis Scenarios Unique?

Each scenario reflected the unique operations of the nonprofit. In the case of the American Red Cross, the scandal emerged from a function, Disaster Services, which was mandated by Congress in 1881. Over the ensuing century, the practice of leveraging current disaster fundraising to bolster the overall disaster operations became commonplace. Dr. Healy was an outspoken leader, whose management style and unrelenting pursuit of topics they didn't want to deal with alienated powerful board members. As the Red Cross received greater scrutiny from Congress, her board appeared to choose to terminate her rather than to address the thornier and entrenched issue of corruption within the larger organization.

Conversely, it was Oral Suer's board that facilitated his looting of the UWNCA of roughly $1 million. The board of the UWNCA was so large and cumbersome that the real power rested in the hands of Suer's Executive Committee, which seemed to ignore this man's fraudulent behavior. The Executive Committee successfully ensured that the rest of the board had no knowledge of the clandestine deals and contracts that were signed. When other board members began to ask questions, they were badgered, and harassed. If that didn't silence the critics, they were removed from the board. Even the auditors of the organization were aware of the lack of internal controls, but did nothing.

The James Beard Foundation board was captivated by Mr. Pickell's charisma. They facilitated his fraud by failure to engage in even rudimentary due diligence. They simply ignored their fiduciary responsibilities. They did not insist on financial controls, nor did they provide any sort of oversight to the operations of the Foundation. Mr. Pickell was able to pass himself off as someone he wasn't purely by use of charm. The high net worth of the individual board members makes this collective naiveté even more incredible.

What Were the Common Factors?

Although the people, organizations, and actions of each of these crisis scenarios are not alike, each crisis took on a high profile, which further exacerbated the damage to the nonprofits. Although Dr. Healy was not accused of any crime, the nature of the crisis tarnished any successes during her tenure at the Red Cross. Her recovery from a malignant brain tumor prior to her becoming President of the American Red Cross led some observers to suggest her managerial problems stemmed from post-operative medical issues (Sontag, 2001).

Mr. Suer and Mr. Pickell were both individuals from very humble backgrounds whose success is the stuff of the American dream. All three leaders were energetic, self-motivated, and arrogant. It was their arrogance that led them to believe that they could prevail over boards that were either hostile or clueless. It was also their arrogance that led Messrs. Suer and Pickell to believe that their auditors would continue to ignore their fraudulent activities.

Media attention and public outrage were common factors that served to fuel the crises, and to ultimately bring the downfall of all of the leaders. Each of these crises received relentless attention in print, radio, television, and the Internet. The crises served to further solidify Congressional determination to regulate nonprofits, and were the catalyst for Senator Grassley's request for the Independent Sector to publish findings on regulation of the nonprofit sector.

What Were the Lessons Learned?

Each of these crises provides valuable lessons to the nonprofit world. Chapter 5 will discuss how compliance with Sarbanes-Oxley and the adaptation of best practices could have either diffused the crisis or reduced its impact. Exhibit 4.1 summarizes the primary lessons for each of these crises.

EXHIBIT 4.1	CRISIS COMPARISONS		
Organizational Component	ARC	UWNCA	Beard
Board	Because the ARC's Board of Governors is divided between political appointees and Red Cross "insiders," it was unwilling to deal with a dysfunctional organizational culture. Perhaps Sen. Grassley should have insisted that the entire board be replaced, along with the Disaster Services division.	The UWNCA board was replaced. The PriceWaterhouseCooper's forensic audit identified how the previous board had ignored clear signs that Mr. Suer was embezzling money. The previous board was too cumbersome to be a serious governance entity.	The board was forced to resign, and a new board was seated. A second "board" was seated to oversee the awards activities.
Operations	The public is now aware of Red Cross' disaster fundraising strategy. During the 2004 Tsunami disaster, the Red Cross stopped collecting funds when the campaign reached peak capacity for activities related to this disaster. Red Cross senior management did not want another Congressional inquiry.	The UWNCA no longer handles the Combined Federal Campaign. It closed offices in surrounding communities. The new Executive Director is hoping that time will heal wounded relations with the corporate sector. Donations from the public were down significantly in subsequent years.	The Beard Foundation is operating in two sections, the Foundation's administration and a separate division that oversees the annual awards.
Staffing	Red Cross National Headquarters laid off staff in 2002 and 2003.	UWNCA has had to lay off staff and close offices in the surrounding communities.	The James Beard Foundation website now includes a page extensively describing the Foundation's mission and commitment to ethical behavior in the workplace. The page includes discussion of the new Whistleblower Policy and Conflict of Interest policy.
Relations with the public	In the midst of the Congressional inquiry and the adverse publicity, the Red Cross changed its policy on the Liberty Fund and used it exclusively to provide cash gifts to the victims' families.	Public support of the UWNCA dropped dramatically. The Executive Director and his team are looking for ways to inspire public confidence.	The Beard Foundation's "public" is the culinary world. Despite the scandal and Mr. Pickell's trial, the Beard Foundation Awards Ceremony went on—and are scheduled to continue.

CONCLUSION

Nonprofit disasters do indeed happen. The three crisis scenarios reviewed in this chapter illustrate the price of inattention, inertia, hubris, and colossal greed. All three of the nonprofits suffered to some extent—and Senator Grassley will no doubt be monitoring the Red Cross for some time. The best outcome from these sad events is the heightened awareness of Congress, the public, and donors. The Grassley hearings in 2004 and 2005 on nonprofit accountability set the stage for real reform—even if some nonprofits will enter the 21st century kicking and screaming!

CHAPTER 5

Root Cause Analysis—Part II

In Chapter 4, we examined the recent crises at three nonprofit organizations, the American Red Cross, the United Way of the National Capital Area (UWNCA), and the James Beard Foundation. How could SOX compliance and best practices have either prevented these crises or reduced the effects of the crises?

The focus of this chapter is twofold. The first emphasis is on the ways in which compliance with SOX requirements and adaptation of SOX best practices could have helped these nonprofits avoid the damage caused by these calamities. The intent is to provide the reader with a SOX best practices template that directly addresses the common areas of dysfunction identified in these crisis scenarios.

The second focus is on the findings of the Panel on the Nonprofit Sector's Final Report to Congress and the Nonprofit Sector on Governance, Transparency, and Accountability as a means of describing the direction this collaboration of Congress and the nonprofit "industry" sees for future nonprofit practice.

CHAPTER OVERVIEW

Although hindsight is indeed 20/20, compliance with SOX and adaptation of best practices could have had a mitigating effect on the severity of the crises we examined in Chapter 4. The compliance requirements of Whistleblower Protection and Document Preservation could have provided an earlier warning that something was wrong. Best practices from SOX would have served to strengthen the nonprofit's infrastructures and ensured that their boards were awake, alert, and, most importantly, accountable.

Chapter Objectives

By the end of this chapter, you should be able to:

- Trace the factors that contributed to the crises presented in Chapter 4.

- Describe the ways in which compliance with SOX requirements could have reduced the impact of these crises.

- Explain how the implementation of SOX best practices could prevent similar crises from occurring.

Summary of Finding from Root Cause Analysis—Part I

The crises within the American Red Cross, the United Way of the National Capital Area, and the James Beard Foundation presented these common contributing factors:

- **Lack of board oversight and overall weakness of governance**: None of the boards appeared to understand its fiduciary obligations in providing oversight and governance to these nonprofits.

- **Organizational cultures**: Environments that provided opportunities for fraud, or through inaction, facilitated dysfunctional behavior.

- **Protocols for expense reimbursement**: In its forensic audit of the UWNCA, PriceWaterhouseCoopers (PWC) auditors discovered pages and pages of reimbursements without receipts. Similarly, Mr. Pickell of the James Beard Foundation was provided with signed blank checks for reimbursements that did not have supporting documentation.

- **Senior management attitudes and behavior**: In all three cases, the leaders were self-confident, autocratic, and to some degree, charismatic. They viewed their boards with either hostility or disdain. In the cases of Messrs. Suer and Pickell, they were able to charm their board leadership into compliance. Dr. Healy found herself in an adversarial role with her board because of her management style and her status as an "outsider" in the Red Cross culture.

- **Audit and/or financial review**: All three nonprofits had mechanisms that served to conceal the dysfunction within the organizations. In the cases of UWNCA and the James Beard Foundation, the auditors were complicit in preventing the discovery of the fraudulent behavior

- **Role of whistleblowers**: The individuals who were whistleblowers in these organizations came from a variety of roles and places. The victims' families and their use of media attention were the primary whistleblowers in the Red Cross scandal. Their complaints garnered Congressional attention and thus ramped up the pressure on the Red Cross. In the case of the UWNCA, several staff and board members began to question financial practices and reports. All of the whistle-blowers were terminated, including board members. As the media reported on these firings, pressure began to mount on Mr. Suer and his Executive Committee. The James Beard Foundation's auditor finally decided that enough was enough. He had seen evidence of Mr. Pickell's plundering but had kept silent to that point.

WHISTLEBLOWER PROTECTION

The boards in all three cases were deeply in denial and, to some extent, complicit in the fraud. In the cases of the UWNCA and the James Beard Foundation, whistle-blowers were the insiders who knew what was happening, but needed to transmit it to outsiders. The whistleblowers in the UWNCA were terminated for their reports and questions. Had a Whistleblower Protection policy been in effect and enforced, the reports these individuals were making may have been investigated at a much earlier stage.

In the case of the American Red Cross, the whistleblowers about the Liberty Fund were the families of the September 11th victims and, hence, outside of the organization. However, as we saw in the excerpt of Senator Grassley's letter to Marsha Evans, Dr. Healy had previously alerted the board about the widespread financial mismanagement within the local chapters. Internal memos related to the New Jersey Chapter manager's fraud suggest that the Red Cross insiders on the board found Dr. Healy's concerns an annoyance (Grassley, 2002). Although her termination was directly related to the Liberty Fund crisis and the post–September 11th blood collection, her persistence in rooting out corruption was a constant thorn in the board's side. Dr. Healy's termination might not be directly linked to her whistleblowing, but it appears that only Senator Grassley was genuinely interested in remedying the situation.

DOCUMENT PRESERVATION POLICY

In all three instances, a Document Preservation policy would have obligated the organizations to have protocols for preservation, storage, and archiving of documents. The policy would also contain a prohibition against the destruction of documents related to an inquiry. Had that policy been in place and enforced, the PWC auditors would have had access to the carloads of documents that Mr. Suer allegedly removed from the UWNCA offices upon his retirement.

A Document Preservation policy at the James Beard Foundation would have meant that the board was sufficiently engaged to actively supervise Mr. Pickell. It also could have meant that Mr. Pickell would have had to produce documentation of his professional background in the form of copies of college diplomas or transcripts—and possibly even a CPA certification. A Document Preservation policy would have also identified the appalling lack of internal controls in the Foundation's financial management.

The American Red Cross's National Headquarters had been under pressure since 1991 from the FDA's head, Dr. David Kessler, to establish and enforce a document preservation policy for its biomedical operations. In response to the FDA's increasing sanctions, the Red Cross brought in Elizabeth Dole in 1991 as president. Ms. Dole's considerable political capital seemed to keep the FDA at bay until the Clinton Administration reappointed Dr. Kessler as head of the FDA in 1992. The pressure for appropriate documentation continues to this day. The Liberty Fund crisis was, in many ways, a recurring scandal in this organization. The pattern of events includes Congressional inquiry and outrage, but the organization's charter remains intact even though crises related to fundraising and operations occur on a regular basis.

Compliance with SOX Whistleblower Protection and Document Preservation provisions would have meant a sea change in the board and organizational culture of all three of these organizations. All three boards would have had to have a level of accountability that would have facilitated their recognizing the fraud that was occurring within their organizations. They would have had to be fully present to their governance and fiduciary obligations. Most importantly, they would have had to recognize and accept that aggressive intervention was necessary to stop the fraud and change the dysfunction within their nonprofit's cultures.

SOX BEST PRACTICES

The best practices that emerge from SOX provisions and standards serve as the framework for a transparent organization. This section examines how the implementation of best practices could have averted these crises or reduced their impact.

SOX best practices include:

- Board independence and accountability
- Audit committee whose role is to oversee the annual audit or financial review (for small nonprofits) and to upgrade the financial literacy of the board
- Enhanced detail and accuracy in the preparation of IRS Form 990
- Conflict of Interest policy and Code of Ethics that facilitate greater focus on decision-making for the good of the nonprofit
- Internal controls, particularly as these relate to financial operations, and compliance with all laws and regulations at the federal, state, and local levels

Board Independence and Accountability

The board played a pivotal role in each of these crises. In all three cases, the boards were not at all independent. The Red Cross board was split between the political appointees and the Red Cross insiders whose allegiance was to an inbred organizational tradition. The UWNCA board was largely window-dressing. The Executive Committee was handpicked by Mr. Suer, who kept their allegiance firmly under his control. Similarly, Mr. Pickell, through his use of guile, ensured that his board was firmly under his control.

Because none of the boards appeared to have any understanding of its legal obligations of care, loyalty, and obedience, the implementation of board performance standards would have been a significant means of establishing accountability. Board orientations are essential in transmitting the information and protocols that board members need in order to conduct business in a transparent manner.

Board member selection and screening are important elements in ensuring board independence. The board needs to be comprised of individuals whose experience and professional credentials are in line with the governance needs of the nonprofit. Boards who are selected by the nonprofit's executive by definition lack the degree of independence needed to adhere to SOX best practices.

Audit Committee

The audits of these nonprofits present a red flag. In the cases of the UWNCA and the James Beard Foundation, the same firm and/or individual conducted the audits over many years. The auditors were aware of inappropriate dealings, but chose to keep these quiet. Best practices necessitate that auditors are rotated every three to five years. Both Messrs. Suer and Pickell had been at the helm of their organizations over five years. Had the best practices been in place, a new auditor would have also recognized the inappropriate dealings, but might have refused to stay silent.

All three boards may have had a high degree of financial literacy, but if any or all of the boards had audit committees, these committees failed to perform as they were intended. The role of the audit committee is to oversee the annual audit, which includes a frank and open discussion with the auditor without staff present. An effective audit committee would have insisted that the auditors be candid and that immediate action be taken to stop the fraudulent activity. In the case of the Red Cross, the audit committee and the auditors should have insisted that funds raised for specific disasters be spent exclusively on those disasters.

Enhanced Detail and Accuracy in the Preparation of IRS Form 990

The IRS Form 990s for all three nonprofits—the Red Cross, the UWNCA, and the James Beard Foundation—are clearly very complex. It would be very easy to obscure any misappropriation.

If the boards in each of the nonprofits had been required to review and approve the 990s, it might have been possible for them to identify problems on the amount that was spent on programs, or in the nonprofit's internal controls. There is a recommendation that 990s be signed by executives under penalty of perjury. Accuracy and transparency in the preparation of 990s are the means by which missing funds and inappropriate use of charge cards and reimbursements can be identified.

Conflict of Interest Policy and Code of Ethics

Implementation of a Conflict of Interest policy and a Code of Ethics relates to board members and to members of the executive team. The degree to which these policies are successful directly relates to the willingness of the board to be aggressive in enforcement. In the cases of the UWNCA and the Beard Foundation, the executives may not have exhibited clear conflicts of interest, but they surely violated the spirit of any code of ethics by placing their personal gain above the good of the nonprofit. Effective Conflict of Interest policies and Codes of Ethics are clear and unambiguous about what is inappropriate behavior and what are the sanctions for these behaviors.

Internal Controls

In all three cases, financial internal controls were lacking. In the case of the Red Cross, the deceitful practices in disaster fundraising had been in place for decades. The ability of the UWNCA and James Beard Foundation executives to embezzle $1 million each clearly stems from a lack of internal controls, and the board's disinterest in requiring internal controls.

The types of internal controls that would have shortened the time it took to discover the fraud could include strict requirements for furnishing appropriate documentation before a reimbursement check was issued. Obviously, the issuing of a signed blank check would never be permitted, nor would the use of a nonprofit's credit card for personal items. The auditor would have access to any and all travel claims or other instances in which reimbursement is necessary. In keeping with an effective Whistleblower Protection policy, there would be a mechanism for reporting infractions and other breeches of internal controls.

Protocols for travel claims and other reimbursements should be clearly defined and distributed among all staff and volunteers. Senior management and board members need to be held accountable for complying with these protocols. The protocols should address the types of travel expenses that are covered and are *not* covered. The policy should also specify the types of documentation that are required to be submitted before reimbursement is made.

Credit cards, particularly ATM cards, issued to the nonprofit should be carefully tracked to ensure that charges are appropriate. Each month, the bank and credit card statements should be reviewed by the Treasurer or CFO. The statements should *not* be opened by anyone prior to being routed to the reviewer. Records of all reimbursement checks should also include appropriate documentation. Any discrepancies should be reported immediately—to senior management and to the board.

Recommendations on Best Practices from Independent Sector Report to Congress and the Nonprofit Sector on Governance, Transparency, and Accountability

In the wake of numerous nonprofit scandals like the Red Cross, UWNCA, and the Beard Foundation, Senator Grassley requested that the Independent Sector's Panel on the Nonprofit Sector report on recommendations for action to be taken by Congress, the Internal Revenue Service (IRS), and nonprofits themselves. The group's final report was released in June 2005. Many of the proposals mirror the recommendations presented in the Grassley White Paper of 2004.

The Panel on the Nonprofit Sector's Recommendations for Congressional Action include:

For the IRS:

- Increase the resources allocated to the IRS for oversight and enforcement of charitable organizations and for overall tax enforcement.

- Authorize funding to be provided to all states to establish or increase oversight and education of charitable organizations. Congress should authorize additional supplemental funding for states willing to provide matching dollars for further improvements in oversight and education.

- Amend federal tax laws to allow state attorneys general and any other state officials charged by law with overseeing charitable organizations the same access to IRS information currently available by law to state revenue officers, under the same terms and restrictions.

For Congress:

- Authorize funding to enable the IRS to move forward with mandatory electronic filing of all Form 990 series returns as expeditiously as possible and to coordinate its electronic filing efforts with state filing requirements.

- Amend federal tax laws to permit the IRS to require all charitable organizations to file their Form 990 series returns electronically, with appropriate accommodations to allow charitable organizations to comply with e-filing requirements in a timely, cost-effective manner.

- Direct the IRS to require that the Form 990 series returns be signed, under penalties of perjury, by the CEO, the CFO, or the highest ranking officer of the organization, or, if it is a trust, by one of its trustees.

- Amend federal tax laws to require all organizations recognized under Section 501(c)(3) of the Internal Revenue Code that are currently excused from filing an annual information return because their annual gross receipts fall below the specified amount (currently below $25,000) to file an annual notice with the IRS with basic contact and financial information.

- Amend federal tax laws to require charitable organizations to notify the IRS if and when they cease operations and to file a final Form 990 series return within a specified period after termination.

- Amend federal tax laws to extend present-law penalties imposed on income tax preparers of personal and corporate tax returns for omission or misrepresentation of information, willful or reckless misrepresentation, or disregard of rules and regulations to preparers of Form 990 series returns.

- Direct the Secretary of the Treasury to require that Form 1023, the application for recognition as a tax-exempt organization under Section 501(c)(3) of the Internal Revenue Code, be filed electronically.

- Amend federal tax laws to require charitable organizations with at least $1 million or more in total annual revenues to conduct an audit and attach audited financial statements to their Form 990 series returns, and to require organizations with annual revenues between $250,000 and $1 million to have financial statements reviewed by an independent public accountant.

- Direct the Secretary of the Treasury to specify in regulations that the audited statements should be made available to the public on the same basis as the annual information returns.

- Direct the Secretary of the Treasury to amend the regulations regarding qualifications for recognition as a tax-exempt organization under Section 501(c)(3) of the Internal Revenue Code to require a qualifying organization, with certain exclusions, to have a minimum of three members on its governing board.

- Direct the Secretary of the Treasury to amend the regulations regarding qualifications for recognition as a public charity (and exemption from private foundation status) under Section 509(a) of the Internal Revenue Code to require that at least one-third of the members of a qualifying public charity's governing board be independent, with certain exclusions.

- Direct the Secretary of the Treasury to amend the regulations to prohibit individuals barred from service on boards of publicly traded companies or convicted of crimes directly related to breaches of fiduciary duty in their service as an employee or board member of a charitable organization from serving on the board of a charitable organization for five years following their conviction or removal.

For Nonprofits:

- Charitable organizations should encourage state legislatures to incorporate federal tax standards for charitable organizations, including prohibitions on excess benefit transactions, into state law.

- The board of a charitable organization should, as recommended practice or in accordance with the laws of its state:

- Review the Form 990 or 990-PF filed by its organization annually.

- Undertake a full review of its organizational and governing instruments, key financial transactions, and compensation policies and practices at least once every five years.

- Include individuals with some financial literacy in its membership.

- Incorporate into the organization's bylaws, articles, charter, or other appropriate governing documents a requirement that the full board must approve, annually and in advance, the compensation of the CEO.

- Adopt and enforce a Conflict of Interest policy consistent with the laws of its state and tailored to its specific organizational needs and characteristics.

- Establish policies and procedures that encourage individuals to come forward with credible information on illegal practices or violations of adopted policies of the organization. The policy should specify that the organization will protect the individual who makes such a report from retaliation.

- The charitable sector should undertake vigorous, sector-wide efforts to:

  - Educate, in partnership with the IRS and state oversight officials, charitable organizations about financial transactions that are potentially abusive tax shelters and the additional reporting requirements and risks such transactions may pose.

  - Provide information and education to organizations on the roles and responsibilities of board members and the factors that boards should consider in evaluating the appropriate size and structure needed to ensure the most effective, responsible governance.

  - Educate charitable organizations about the importance of the auditing function.

  - Educate and encourage all charitable organizations, regardless of size, to adopt and enforce policies and procedures to address possible conflicts of interest and to facilitate reporting of suspected malfeasance and misconduct by organization managers.

When Only Platinum Will Do . . . The Very Best Practices for Nonprofit Management

Senator Grassley's 2004 White Paper recommended the practices that are described in this section, but the Panel on the Nonprofit Sector did not support this position, citing its belief that the nonprofit world could regulate itself. After reviewing the three crises from Chapter 4, one might question this position. However, your nonprofit has the absolute right to establish a platinum standard of operation! Nonprofits should consider adopting the following best practices:

- Every five years, the board should conduct a full review of the nonprofit's legal documentation to ensure completeness, the nonprofit's programming to ensure that the programs are consistent with the nonprofit's mission, and a full review of the financial statements to identify trends and patterns over that time frame. The review should also examine other documentation to identify trends, such as insurance claims, newspaper reports about the nonprofit, fundraising results, HR complaints, and disciplinary action against individuals within the organization.

- Every year, the board should require senior management to present detailed reports of program and fundraising evaluations and a complete description of the metrics used to evaluate programs and fundraising.

- Every year, the board and audit committee should meet in executive session with the nonprofit's auditor. No staff should be permitted to attend this session. The auditor should be required to identify areas that he or she sees as potential problems or opportunities for fraud, or where real fraud is taking place. If the nonprofit is given a management letter by the accountant, the issues cited in the management letter should be rectified immediately, and the improvements documented.

- The board should commission the development of an organization-wide risk management plan and business continuity plan. The plans should be reviewed and updated on an annual basis.

CONCLUSION

Nonprofit crises come about because of a wide variety of factors, most of which involve lax internal controls and wide open opportunities for fraud. The SOX requirements and best practices are rapidly becoming the gold standard for management in this country—across all economic sectors. The common denominators are attention, vigilance, and accountability. Corporate and nonprofit boards alike are being held to an unprecedented level of accountability, and *that's as it should be*. Donors, clients, and the public at large deserve no less than full compliance.

CHAPTER 6

SOX Best Practices and Governance

Harry was the Executive Director of a nonprofit that provided healthcare education. He was a hard-working individual whose board largely included major donors to the nonprofit. Many of the board members felt that their donor status entitled them to treat Harry as if he was their butler. After several years of this type of abuse, Harry let it be known that he wanted his hard work acknowledged with a pay raise. The board president, one of the more arrogant board members, began the proceedings to fire Harry. In the meantime, Harry was hospitalized for quadruple bypass surgery. The board wanted to move ahead with Harry's termination despite the admonishment of one board member who insisted that a memo from her be placed in the minutes. The memo advised that what the board was doing was illegal under state laws and under the Americans with Disabilities Act.

The board pressed on with their termination of Harry, and he filed a complaint with the state labor board. The proceeds of the legal settlement permitted Harry to purchase a lovely vacation home in the country.

CHAPTER OVERVIEW

One of the hallmarks of today's emphasis on accountability is the emphasis on the board as the source of ultimate accountability in a nonprofit. Board members are held to a higher level of scrutiny and responsibility for nonprofit operations and management. Although the courts have long held nonprofit boards to the same legal standards as private sector boards, the nonprofit world has been slow to insist on board member performance. This chapter explores the role of the board, the board's legal and ethical obligations, and current trends in board accountability.

CHAPTER OBJECTIVES

By the end of the chapter, you should be able to:

- Describe the role of the board in today's nonprofit organization.
- Explain the legal standards and ethical obligations for board members.
- Describe current trends in board accountability.
- Discuss important elements in board accountability and transparency.
- Utilize various methods for ensuring independence:
  - Conflict of Interest policy
  - Code of Ethics
- Develop an effective committee system:
  - Executive
  - Audit
  - Finance
  - Nominating
  - Development and Fundraising
  - Human Resources (for employees and volunteers)

ROLE OF THE BOARD IN TODAY'S NONPROFIT

"Accountability" is an important watchword in today's nonprofit governance environment. The media is filled with examples of financial mismanagement, violation of federal employment law, and failure to conduct due diligence in outsourcing functions.

An interesting example is the San Francisco Bay Area United Way and its nonprofit subsidiary, Pipevine. Pipevine was under contract to collect and allocate corporate donations to the United Way of the San Francisco Bay Area. Pipevine allegedly skimmed millions from the donations because it had inaccurately forecasted its operating expenses and wasn't receiving sufficient revenue from the United Way to maintain solvency. Published reports indicate that this scandal has resulted in a six-year downturn in donations for this United Way affiliate. Corporations continue to be reluctant to sponsor campaigns for employee donations.

When a nonprofit encounters these dramatic crises, the board is often the first place to look for the source of the dysfunction. The first question that comes to mind in each of these sad stories is, "Where was the board?" Did the board understand what was going on? Did the board ignore or condone clearly inappropriate and often criminal behavior? Did the board even know what to look for? Today's boards and board members need to recognize that the level of scrutiny and accountability aimed at nonprofits has increased. Nonprofit boards can no longer afford to deal at arm's length with the organization—or meet on a quarterly basis as was once touted in a well-known governance model. The days of the fully accountable, fully present, "hands-on" board are here to stay.

The actions of the board and the products of governance have become central issues in SOX legislation, California legislation, and any potential clone legislation because nonprofit boards hold the ultimate accountability for what transpires within the confines of a nonprofit organization. There are *no* excuses for nonprofit board members not to understand what is going on in the organization, nor are there any excuses for board members not holding the Executive Director accountable for the actions of his or her staff.

Legal Standards and Traditional Expectations

Boards (nonprofit and private sector alike) have always had standards of behavior associated with membership. The quality of board decisions and actions are evaluated based on how board members understood their obligations to the nonprofit institution, and how carefully they deliberated before making a particular decision or taking a particular action. Board members are expected to conduct themselves and make decisions consistent with three legal standards: care, loyalty, and obedience. The three standards describe the types of consideration that should go into behavior and decisions. The basic legal standard of the "reasonably prudent person" is particularly significant, as the courts look to determine if the board took reasonable steps in decision-making or action.

EXHIBIT 6.1	LEGAL STANDS AND EXPECTED BOARD MEMBER BEHAVIOR
Legal Standard	**Expected Behavior**
Care	The director shall discharge his or her duties as a director, including his or her duties as a member of a committee in good faith and with a care that an ordinarily prudent person in a like position would exercise under similar circumstances and in a manner the director reasonably believes to be in the best interest of the organization.
Loyalty	In his or her capacity as a member of a nonprofit board, the individual is to give first priority to the institution in making financial decisions. This means that board members may not engage in activities with the nonprofit that will result in personal gain, nor are board members to use their board status as means to any personal gain—financial or otherwise
Obedience	Directors are required to act within the bounds of the law generally, and with the intent of achieving the organization's mission as expressed in its charter and bylaws.

In addition to the primary legal standards of care, loyalty, and obedience, board members have always been expected to:

- **Attend board meetings on a regular basis**: Board members who do not attend meetings regularly have only a marginal understanding of the nonprofit's operational, financial, and governance issues. These board members make poor representatives of the nonprofit, and in their lack of knowledge can make unwise decisions.

- **Understand their governance role**: Board members, by the legal standards of care, loyalty, and obedience, are expected to put the welfare of the nonprofit ahead of any personal consideration, and certainly ahead of any personal gain. Board members are not there to micromanage the nonprofit, nor are they simply "window-dressing" for senior management's agenda.

- **Read and understand (or ask questions until they obtain clarity) all materials sent in advance of a board meeting**: The operative expectation is that board members come to board meetings *prepared* to ask questions or obtain clarity because they have carefully reviewed all of the materials in advance.

- **Review financial documents carefully and provide appropriate oversight**: Board members are expected to either understand the financial documents, or seek assistance in learning how to read and interpret financial statements. In the area of financial operations, board members need to ask the difficult questions and insist on appropriate financial materials.

- **Disclose any real or potential conflicts of interest**: Board members, in order to adhere to the standard of loyalty, must disclose any real or potential conflicts of interest to the board. The rest of the board needs to know about these real or potential conflicts of interest so steps can be taken to eliminate the impact of these conflicts on board deliberations and decisions.

- **Adhere to a Code of Ethics**: Board members need to adhere to a Code of Ethics that spells out the nonprofit's values and principles. Adherence to a Code of Ethics is another way in which board members put the interest and well-being of the nonprofit ahead of their own.

New Expectations for Board Oversight and Governance

With the passage of SOX, the bar was raised on *all* organizations, not just publicly traded corporations and not just nonprofits. All organizations that conduct business within the United States are subject to greater scrutiny. Public trust is an important issue that all organizations—public, private, and independent (nonprofit)—need to address.

At issue is the level of competence and accountability within nonprofit boards. Some nonprofit boards have been collections of friends, business acquaintances, and even family members. Prior public scrutiny and expectations regarding nonprofit

EXHIBIT 6.2   BOARD MEMBER LEGAL STANDARDS CHECKLIST

Legal Standard of Care
- Are board members furnished with financial statements and other materials well in advance of the board meetings?
- Is an agenda prepared and followed for each board meeting?
- Are minutes kept for each board meeting?
- Do board members come to the meetings prepared to discuss the issues on the agenda?
- Is there a specific decision-making process; i.e., specific length of time for discussion followed by a vote?
- If a topic needs to be deferred for a vote at a later date, are there specific steps and/or information that will be gathered so the board can take a vote when the topic is revisited?

Legal Standard of Loyalty
- Are board members required to complete a Conflict of Interest letter on an annual basis?
- Does the board have specific protocols to handle conflicts of interest as they occur?
- Are board members fully briefed (usually at an orientation) about their fiduciary obligations?
- Are board members required to sign a Code of Ethics, and are they held accountable for conducting themselves in accordance with the code?

Legal Standard of Obedience
- Are board members briefed on the nonprofit's mission, and how that mission is affected by board decisions?
- Are board members briefed on the correlation between their decision-making and their fiduciary obligations as these impact the nonprofit's mission?
- Are board members briefed on the correlation between the quality of their performance and the nonprofit's mission?

boards was low—as was noted by IRS Commissioner Mark Everson at the Grassley Hearings. Federal agencies, such as the Internal Revenue Service (IRS), simply did not have the resources or the directive to pursue nonprofit compliance.

In the past, nonprofit board members were expected to provide a rubber stamp of approval for the Executive Director and raise money if necessary. Often, the members' personal checkbooks were the main source in the nonprofit's fundraising strategy. All that has changed in the past decade. The number of prominent nonprofits embroiled in financial scandals has increased dramatically. With the enactment of SOX in relation to corporate scandal, the public is demanding that the nonprofit world be held to the same level of accountability to protect the billions of voluntary donations that pour into this sector each year.

New Expectations of Board Accountability

Nonprofit boards will now be held accountable for:

- Properly preparing an annual IRS Form 990 that is submitted on time, is complete, and is accurate

- Approving compensation package(s) for senior management
- Establishing and enforcing a Code of Ethics and a Conflict of Interest Policy
- Ensuring that the nonprofit either has an annual audit or financial review
- Establishing an audit committee
- Ensuring that the auditor is independent
- Reviewing, interpreting, and questioning financial statements prepared by staff

Championing SOX Best Practices: The Board's Governance Role

The SOX best practices presume that boards are actively engaged in the operations of the nonprofit. This does not mean that boards are expected to "micromanage," but it does require that the board and senior management are highly interactive. Those 20th century board governance models that presume the board fulfills its obligations at arm's length while pondering their universal theory of governance have always been bogus and today are absolutely dangerous. Accountability is the key and will be a major component within future state laws and regulatory requirements relative to nonprofit accountability.

Board members need to understand that they are expected to fully participate in decision-making. To facilitate productive discussion and efficient use of time, board leadership can institute ground rules to control the length of time that any one person has the floor, issues related to civility of discussion, and the use of a "timed" agenda and Robert's Rules to ensure an orderly meeting. Pre-meeting preparedness is an essential element to any successful meeting. Board members need to receive materials at least one week prior to the meeting. Today's technology can streamline the process by sending the material as e-mail attachments or by fax. Regardless of the means of conveying the materials, the board members must come to the meeting prepared to deliberate and make decisions. A functional decision-making model also presumes a board culture that supports asking difficult questions and making businesslike decisions. Nonprofits can no longer afford to have a "mom and pop" mindset, nor can they afford to have competent professionals on their boards who abdicate their governance obligations.

One of the challenges in board deliberations is the tendency to engage in endless analytic exercises. Reports from standing committees or ad hoc groups should include recommendations based on solid analysis. The board should request the level of information that is necessary and sufficient for reasonable decision-making. The meeting agenda should outline the decisions that are to be made at the meeting, and allocate sufficient time for discussion and then call a vote. Board members who wish to commandeer the agenda tend to use lengthy discussion as a strategic weapon. In this way, the important issues never come up for a vote. The board leadership needs to be assertive in ensuring that the agenda is balanced and that the necessary votes are taken.

EXHIBIT 6.3   BOARD OF DIRECTORS GOVERNANCE PROFILE AND PERFORMANCE EXPECTATIONS

WORKSHEET

Identify the roles and duties of the board including the distinction between governance roles and management roles within the nonprofit.

Governance—Does your board engage in these activities?

- Policy-making and accountability—Board members recognize that they have ultimate control and authority and responsibility for the nonprofit operations.
- Supervise Executive Director or CEO of the nonprofit.

Oversight in areas of:

- Financial operations
- Internal controls
- Compliance with federal, state, and local laws and regulations

Term Limits

- Does the board have term limits?
- If so, how many consecutive terms are board members permitted to serve?
- If the board does not have term limits, is there a plan in place to introduce term limits and/or establish an advisory board?

Summary of board committees' descriptions and performance objectives

For each committee your board has, identify its function and objectives for the coming year. If the board wants to add one of these committee designations, describe its function and objectives for the coming year.

- Finance Committee
- Audit Committee
- Development and Fundraising Committee
- Personnel Committee
- Nominating Committee (for the board of directors)
- Facilities Committee
- Strategic Planning Committee
- Risk Management Committee

Board members, particularly board officers, have an obligation to the organization, its staff, clients, volunteers, donors, and the community at large to conduct themselves in a professional manner while acting in their role as board members. The good name of the organization can be enhanced or compromised depending on how they conduct themselves—in person, in print (letters or documents), and online via e-mail.

All Nonprofit Boards Should Work Toward These Ethical and Operational Principles

At the center of good governance are ethical and operational principles that guide board members in discussion, activities, and decisions that put the welfare of the nonprofit before their personal or professional gain.

The Senate Finance Committee's staff proposals and California's Nonprofit Integrity Act are based on the presumption that nonprofit boards have established policies to set goals and objectives for the organization, as well as protocols to oversee the nonprofit's operations, particularly financial operations. The Senate Finance Committee staff emphasize this belief through the proposal to impose criminal liability for the CEO to provide reasonable assurance of the accuracy and completeness of all material aspects of the return.

The board is the final authority in the nonprofit, and is obligated to closely supervise its only employee, the CEO. The Nonprofit Integrity Act further requires of nonprofits whose budgets are in excess of $2 million that the board approve the compensation packages of senior management.

Board's Overall Responsibility for the Management of the Nonprofit

In addition to the principles that have emerged from the current legislative environment, boards need to consider adopting traditional tenets that address board authority and overall responsibility for the management of the nonprofit. Boards are responsible for crafting the procedures, policies, and protocols that ensure the nonprofit is in compliance with federal, state, and local laws and is a going concern.

The board's fiduciary obligations require careful oversight of financial operations to ensure that a budget is crafted on an annual basis, to ensure that an annual audit or financial review is conducted, and that IRS Form 990s are submitted in a timely fashion. Additionally, the board is responsible for ensuring all other financial reports are generated in a timely fashion (see Exhibit 6.4).

The board should ensure that it is in compliance with relevant federal law and regulations, state law and regulations, and any local ordinances. The board should also ensure that documentation of its actions, and board minutes, are prepared in the appropriate manner and stored per the Document Retention policy.

The board should ensure that Human Resource policies are in place to safeguard the rights of employees and volunteers, and to ensure that every employee and volunteer has a job description and a method by which his or her performance is appropriately and fairly evaluated. The board should also ensure that the nonprofit publishes an employee manual and a volunteer manual that identifies and outlines policies that apply to employees and volunteers.

The board, as the ultimate authority in the nonprofit, is responsible for ensuring that the nonprofit is adequately insured, including the variety of insurance policies that are

EXHIBIT 6.4	AUDIT COMMITTEE WORKSHEET

Every nonprofit should have an audit committee no matter how small the nonprofit or its board. The purpose of the committee is to provide oversight to the annual audit, or for small nonprofits, the annual review of financials.

Composition of the committee—The committee needs to include:
- One financial professional
- Two to four members of the board who are not also members of the Finance Committee

COMMITTEE FUNCTIONS AND DELIVERABLES

Does your nonprofit's Audit Committee . . .
- Serve as a liaison between the auditor and the board to ensure that the auditing firm is appropriate for a nonprofit audit (skill set and experience) and to review the performance of the auditing firm?
- Ensure that the auditor is *only* providing auditing services and not also providing consulting services to the nonprofit, such as bookkeeping, financial information systems, HR outsource services, legal services, or other professional services that do not relate to the audit?
- Ensure that the auditing firm or partner is rotated every three to five (3–5) years? If the auditing firm is large enough, other partners or associates can rotate to provide auditing services to the nonprofit. In any event, members of the auditing firm should not be recruited to serve on the nonprofit's board or on the auditing committee.
- Ensure that the nonprofit's auditor has no financial or business connections to individual board members?
- Meet with the auditor to review the audit and make recommendations regarding board approval, or provide recommendations for modifications? The Committee makes these recommendations to the full board, which ideally, meets with the auditor to discuss the audit.
- Ensure that if the audit produces a "management letter," the issues outlined in the letter are remedied immediately?

required for the nonprofit's operations, professional liability coverage (if applicable), and Directors and Officers insurance, including Employment Practices Liability Insurance for the board. The board is also responsible for ensuring that this coverage is secured at a competitive price and that the nonprofit's insurance professional is responsive to the nonprofit's needs and requirements.

The Competent Board: Important Elements in Accountability

Current members of your nonprofit board were possibly recruited from many sources—friends, relatives, donor database, or nonprofit clearinghouses. Some of the members of the board are appropriate to the organization, and some may be above their heads in terms of understanding their role and what is expected of them. SOX best practices presumes that all members of the board are qualified to serve, that is, competent to serve in a governance role, and possess an understanding of what is expected of them as well as a skill set that serves to accomplish expected performance.

Board members should be recruited based on those specific areas of expertise, diversity, or background that the board's leadership and nominating committee have identified as significant to the nonprofit. Under no circumstances should more than one member of a family be seated on the board, nor should a family member of any staff be seated on the board. Similarly, vendors and consultants to the nonprofit should be disqualified for board membership. Those individuals who are seated on the board should also agree to sign a Conflict of Interest statement on an annual basis and should understand that they are required to disclose immediately any circumstances that could be considered a conflict of interest. In today's environment, even the appearance of a conflict of interest is unacceptable.

How do board members learn about what is expected of them? One of the best ways of offering a complete introduction to board service is through a comprehensive orientation and subsequent "in-service" training sessions. The orientation for new members should be crafted to address the important issues and expectations. The orientation should also be held at a time of day that would accommodate most members—and should be approximately 90 minutes to two hours long. The topics that are not addressed in the initial orientation can be covered in subsequent "in-service" sessions.

The primary learning objectives of any board orientation include:

- The new board members understand the nonprofit's mission, vision, and strategic plan.

- New board members have an understanding of the nonprofit's history so that they can appreciate where the organization has been and where it is headed.

- New board members understand their obligations and performance objectives.

- New board members understand the board policies on meetings, attendance, conflict of interest, and other policies that emerge from SOX best practices.

- The new board members have received their job descriptions and understand their performance expectations and fiduciary obligations as board members.

When a board member joins the board, he or she should know the length of the appointment and the rules for reappointment to the board. These rules, however, are useless unless enforced. If your board does not have term limits, it is essential that these be instituted immediately—regardless of the outcry. Responsible board members will have no objection to the enforcement of term limits. Those who protest could be offered a seat on an advisory board—but the well-being of your nonprofit is far more important than yielding to manipulative behavior.

Depending on the size of the nonprofit, the ideal board size is somewhere between 7 and 16 members. Boards smaller than 7 can become deadlocked, and those larger than 16 can become unwieldy or experience a chilling effect on discussion, dissention, and possibly the emergence of a "ruling elite" that generally takes the form of the Executive Committee.

The board should establish procedures to ensure that new members are recruited, trained, and understand their roles and obligations including term limits. Boards should ensure that the size of the board is appropriate to the size and needs of the organization. The board should also endeavor to evaluate their own performance as a governance entity, and the performance of their individual members. These performance standards should include attendance at meetings, committee work, fundraising, preparation for discussion, and participation in strategic planning, and other activities.

Committee System

The board needs to develop an effective committee system to delegate the tasks associated with managing the board and the nonprofit. Committees can be as small as three people, or much larger, although a committee greater than 15 people can be cumbersome. Committees need not be populated exclusively from the board. Inviting prospective board members to serve on a committee for a year or two can be useful to both the prospective member and the board. The individual can see how the board operates, and the board has the opportunity to see the individual in action.

Here are examples of the types of committees that support board activities:

- **Executive**: The Executive Committee generally consists of the board Chair, Vice-Chair, Secretary, Treasurer, and Senior Management Team of the nonprofit. This committee is charged with the day-to-day governance of the organization, decision-making at the executive level, and crisis management.

- **Finance**: The Finance Committee is responsible for reviewing the monthly financial reports, making decisions related to revenues and expenditures, and providing assertive oversight of all financial operations including purchase of insurance. Financial literacy for members of this committee is a must.

- **Audit**: The Audit Committee convenes for a short period of time each year. This committee must be completely independent from the Executive Committee and the Finance Committee. No staff may sit on the committee, and no members of the Executive or Finance Committee may be members of this committee. There should be at least one financial professional on the committee. The purpose of the committee is to oversee the annual audit or financial review (for small nonprofits) and to upgrade the financial literacy of the board. The roles and duties of the Audit Committee is discussed in more detail in Exhibit 6.4

- **Nominating**: The Nominating Committee is charged with recruiting, screening prospective board members, and recommending a slate of new directors for the board's approval.

- **Development and Fundraising**: The Development Committee is charged with oversight into development and fundraising activities for the nonprofit. Often, members of the Development Committee are expected to conduct development activities for the board itself. State laws, such as California's Nonprofit Integrity Act, require the board to provide active oversight into any and all contracts for fundraising vendors and activities.

The committee system within a board can provide an effective means of distributing the work that is needed to ensure SOX compliance and adaptation of best practices. Having a conflict of interest policy and procedures in place will help make the board and its committees more effective. Exhibit 6.5 provides materials that will be helpful in developing the policy and procedures

EXHIBIT 6.5   CONFLICT OF INTEREST POLICY AND PROCEDURES WORKSHEET

Does Your Board Have a Conflict of Interest Policy? If So, Does It Contain These Talking Points?

- Legal standard of loyalty requires board members to put the financial interests of the nonprofit ahead of any personal gain. One way to achieve this is to identify those relationships and/or business dealings that either present a conflict of interest or have the potential for being a conflict of interest.

- By signing a letter indicating real or potential conflicts of interest, or stating that the individual has none, the nonprofit has a record of those areas that may pose a conflict of interest for individual board members. The nonprofit can then take steps to ensure that the individual board member does not take part in discussions or votes related to those areas.

- Transparency and full disclosure are very important in today's nonprofit environment.

- Explain the procedures for dealing with conflict of interest:

  - Conflict of Interest letters are signed on an annual basis.

  - When a board discussion addresses an area that has been identified as a conflict of interest, the individual involved is excused from the discussion and not permitted to vote. This is recorded in the minutes of the meeting.

  - The board reserves the right to ask an individual who presents a very serious conflict of interest to resign from the board, or be placed in a capacity that neutralizes a conflict of interest.

Every board member should be required to sign a Conflict of Interest Disclosure letter on an annual basis. The text of the letter should include these points:

I, [Name of Board member], state that I have/do not have the following personal, business, or professional relationships that may present a conflict of interest:
[circle here] I do not have any conflicts of interest.
[circle here] I have the following relationships or business interests that may pose a conflict of interest:

List those relationships and businesses that might pose as conflict of interest.

As a member of the [Name of the Nonprofit] Board, I commit to placing the Agency's interest and gain ahead of my own, and will further commit to excusing myself from any discussion or votes related to those areas in which I may have a conflict of interest.

Signed,

Date

Another way of improving the effectiveness of the board and its committees is to have a Code of Ethics for both the board and senior management team. Exhibit 6.6 provides materials that will be helpful in developing the Code of Ethics.

EXHIBIT 6.6 CODE OF ETHICS FOR BOARD AND SENIOR MANAGEMENT WORKSHEET

The Code of Ethics needs to describe:

- The types of behavioral expectations that relate to the roles of board members and members of senior management
- How employees or volunteers can raise ethical concerns. One provision that is particularly significant is the prohibition against any type of loan or financial gift by the nonprofit to a board member or member of the staff at any level.
- Note: Board, staff, and volunteers should be required to read/sign the code of ethics.
- How the nonprofit commits to being in compliance with laws and regulations, being accountable to the public, and responsibly handling resources.

TALKING POINTS:

What the organizational values are that are present or expressed in the nonprofit's mission and other supporting documents such as strategic plans.

- Mission
- Governance
- Conflicts of interest
- Legal compliance
- Responsible stewardship of resources and financial oversight
- Openness and disclosure
- Professional integrity as related to all aspects of services rendered and in the process of development/fundraising
- Other issues that relate to how your nonprofit operates

SAMPLE CODE OF ETHICS FOR A NONPROFIT BOARD MEMBER

As a member of the [Name of the nonprofit] Board, I will:

- Endeavor at all times to place the interest of the [Name of Your Nonprofit] above my own personal interests.
- Be diligent in the performance of my duties, come prepared to all board meetings, and fulfill my obligations as a board member.
- Not seek or accept any personal financial gain from my membership on the board of the [Name of Your Nonprofit].
- Seek to continually improve my knowledge of the [Name of Your Nonprofit] and the nonprofit sector.
- Strive to establish and maintain dignified and honorable relationships with my fellow board members, the [Name of Your Nonprofit] staff, clients, and donors.
- Strive to improve the public understanding of the mission and vision of the [Name of Your Nonprofit].
- Obey all laws and regulations and avoid any conduct or activity that would cause harm to the [Name of Your Nonprofit].

The Time for SOX Compliance and Implementation of Best Practices Is Now . . . But Is Your Board Ready?

The time has come to embrace SOX compliance and adopt the best practices, but is your board *on board*? Does your board exhibit any of the behaviors described in Exhibit 6.7?

EXHIBIT 6.7   BOARD DYSFUNCTION

Example of Board Dysfunction	Description of Board Culture
Dominated by leadership who bully and dominate members.	Board is a collection of primarily passive individuals who choose, for whatever reasons, to tolerate being forced into accepting the current leadership.
The board consists of passive board members who have no term limits or obligations, and who deal with the organization at an arm's length.	Board members do not understand their responsibilities and legal obligations. Board attitudes are consistent Yogi Berra's definition of ignorance, "Ignorance isn't what you don't know; it's what you know wrong."
The Executive Director of the nonprofit fields at least six phone calls a day from board members who wish to be updated on operational matters.	The board is micromanaging. The culture of this board is distrust of the senior management. Board members and their leadership do not understand the governance role.
Board president, who has been the president for 20 years, is the nonprofit's biggest donor.	Board culture is one of inertia. Some of the board members have long-term social ties with each other and see their positions of power on the board as appropriate "payback" for their level of financial contribution.
Board has two tiers of membership. The upper tier consists of socially prominent individuals with money and connections, and the lower tier consists of members who are expected to be "worker bees."	This board's culture emerges from an organization that is socially prominent, but has a constituency that demands to be represented despite the fact that there are few socially prominent individuals within that constituency. The lower tier is expected to "pay their way" for being allowed on the board by contributing or raising a stipulated sum each year, sitting on multiple committees, and being assigned to projects that are time and labor intensive.
	The upper tier of the board is recruited from that city's "high society," and these board members generally have no committee or project obligations. They are simply expected to lend their name to the organization and make significant financial contributions.
The board's committee system produces no results. The board leadership is visibly passive and allows the senior staff to run the board.	This is the classic "rubber stamp" board. The culture in this board is one that defers all power to the senior management. Board members view their role on the board as "feel good."

Example of Board Dysfunction	Description of Board Culture
Artistic director is the board chair, and his volunteer assistant is the second most powerful person in the organization. The board chair routinely keeps information that he refused to share with the other board members. Board is window-dressing.	This board is a variation on the classic "rubber stamp" board. In this example, the board is a "checkbook" and "rubber stamp" board. The difference here is that board members were expected to be passive, and expected to make significant financial contributions.

What Are the Factors that Contribute to Board Dysfunction?

Board dysfunction is not simply the result of one issue or even one person. Generally, dysfunction reflects the confluence of a number of dysfunctional factors:

- The board does not understand its governance and fiduciary role in the nonprofit. Board members have not been briefed regarding the legal standards of care, loyalty, and obedience. Their fiduciary obligations are not clear, nor do they understand what "governance" means in terms of role and deliverables.

- Board members come to meetings unprepared to engage in meaningful discussion or decision-making. The board's working paradigm could be one of passive acceptance of staff reports, or like the United Way in Washington D.C., a cheerleading squad.

- The nonprofit's organizational culture suppresses board participation because the board tolerates this behavior. Conversely, a board can attempt to micromanage a nonprofit for many reasons, the most damaging being due to a past organizational crisis. The board feels obligated to direct operations because it still does not have confidence in the management team.

- Board members are recruited for their social status and financial resources. This type of "means testing" as a prerequisite for board membership gives board members a sense of entitlement. Consequently, these board members believe that making significant financial contributions is sufficient to meet board requirements.

- Board members have leveraged their donor status to secure a leadership role on the board. In some, but not all, situations, this can prove to be damaging to the board. Conversely, some board members become interested in serving on the board because they have donated generously to a nonprofit. These individuals can prove to be good additions to the board.

- Nonprofit management intentionally recruits passive individuals to establish a "window-dressing" board, but do not orient the board on issues that might establish an assertive board. The level of dysfunction comes from management expectations that the board members will do as they are instructed. The board never fully understands its governance role, nor does it understand that in today's environment it can be held criminally liable for the nonprofit's actions.

Strategies for Introducing Change in the Board Culture

Any type of organizational change can benefit from a "jump start." Here are some recommendations to move your board toward a higher level of productivity:

- Talk with your auditor and your insurance professional. These advisors can provide you with information on new laws, regulations, and industry standards that can serve as a catalyst for change.

- Recruit at least three to five top-notch board members in the next six months. These individuals should present the types of skill sets that are currently missing from the board. These individuals should be fully aware that they have been recruited to assist you in the transformation of the board.

- Introduce term limits or a plan to enforce current term limits. Establish an advisory council and board emeritus group without voting power. Eliminate dead wood or dysfunctional board members.

- Develop an agenda of "deliverables" based on traditional expectations and SOX best practices to establish priority areas for immediate action. Establish a core group within the board to develop a strategy to achieve the deliverables. Institute performance expectations, such as attendance, financial support, funding, voting, and other behavioral norms.

- Begin the process to ensure that term limits are adopted or enforced. Transition those members whose time and welcome have run out to the advisory council and/or board emeritus group.

- Institute a Conflict of Interest policy that includes an educational component. The educational component defines conflicts of interest, how to disclose a conflict of interest, and how to address conflicts of interest in an appropriate manner—policy, protocols, and annual conflict of interest statements.

- Take steps to ensure that board meetings are run in a business-like fashion—with a timed agenda, rules for discussion, and, if necessary, limited discussion time prior to taking a vote. Conversation is not permitted to run on and thus obstruct the business that is slated for that meeting.

- Board leadership and/or senior management should consider assertiveness training to actively deal with the dysfunctional board members and/or situations that arise.

Achieving Current Board Expectations: Putting SOX Best Practices in Motion

The SOX legislation ushered in a new accountability based on a set of expected outcomes. The discussion in this section outlines the types of best practices that emerged from the SOX legislation and how these would work for your nonprofit board:

- **Board recruitment and retention**: Today's nonprofit boards cannot afford to be populated with individuals who are passive and/or lack the requisite skills— and assertiveness—to provide appropriate governance and oversight to the nonprofit.

- **Audit Committee**: Nonprofit boards need to have a separate Audit Committee that includes at least one board member who is a financial expert. The Audit Committee must ensure that auditors are not also engaging in additional services, such as consulting, for the nonprofit. The committee is also responsible for ensuring that either the auditing firm is rotated every three to five years, or that the lead auditor is rotated off the nonprofit's audit every three to five years. The members of the Audit Committee need to be independent board members in other words, not also members of Senior Management.

- **Financial literacy**: More rigorous review of financial statements and transactions. Financial literacy for all board members means that the nonprofit may need to establish a training program to ensure that all members of the board understand how to read and interpret financial reports. The Executive Director and CFO need to be able to certify the accuracy of financial documents and other submissions such as Form 990s. All members of the board are fully aware of the financial condition of the organization, and senior executives such as the Executive Director and the CFO are able to sign without hesitation.

- **Code of Ethics for board and senior management—prohibition of inside dealings**: The board needs to adopt a policy strictly prohibiting personal loans to any director, or officer, and a Human Resources policy that prohibits lending money to the CEO, ED, CFO, or other staff. This policy describes the types of behavioral expectations that relate to the roles of board member and member of senior management. One provision that is particularly significant is the prohibition against any type of loan or financial gift by the nonprofit to a board member or member of the staff at any level. No exceptions should *ever* be made to these policies.

- **Conflict of Interest policy**: Why is not disclosing a conflict of interest a violation of this legal standard? Contrary to what many nonprofit board members believe, disclosing that you may have a potential conflict of interest is not a crime against humanity! A conflict of interest is simply that—the situation can, if ignored, establish conflicting interests between the board member and the nonprofit. The individual board member is not "guilty" of anything by disclosing that he or she has a potential conflict of interest. Actually, this type of disclosure is something to be applauded! The important next step is to have the potential conflict of interest documented via a "Conflict of Interest Statement" that all board members—and senior staff—should submit on an annual basis or in the event the board member learns of a potential conflict of interest. Once the conflict of interest is documented, the individual should be excused from the conversation/vote whenever his or her participation would be inappropriate. The minutes should reflect that Ms. or Mr. X was excused from the discussion on the nonprofit's insurance coverage because he or she is a member of the insurance company's board.

- **Whistleblower Protection (SOX Requirement)**: It is important that the nonprofit have a Whistleblower Protection policy for all staff and volunteers and enforce it without exception. Board members are willing to blow the whistle on inappropriate behavior and will be supported by other board members and board leadership.

- **Document Preservation policy (SOX Requirement)**: This policy was also discussed in detail in Chapter 5. Establish a system that documents the policies that are in place and the methods for enforcement and enforce it.

- **Adequate insurance**: The nonprofit and the board need to be adequately protected. It is essential that the nonprofit purchase Directors and Officers liability insurance, general liability, business interruption, automobile, property and casualty, and other important insurance coverage. The nonprofit's insurance professional is a key player on this team. He or she can provide advice on the types of policies that are right for your organization.

- **Keep informed about current regulatory practices**: The proceedings of the Grassley Hearings, the report of the Independent Sector's Panel on the Nonprofit Sector, and agencies such as the IRS provide materials to keep abreast of current developments in the legislative environment.

CONCLUSION

The board is the rudder that guides the nonprofit through the rough waters of its competitive environment. The board is also the compass that aids the nonprofit in being steadfast in its mission. In today's legal environment, the board is the ultimate authority in a nonprofit and is the collective entity that will be held accountable for what transpires in a nonprofit. These expectations are not new—but they haven't been enforced to the degree that they are today. Sitting on a nonprofit board is no longer a hobby, it's serious work and demands complete attention to the task.

CHAPTER 7

SOX Best Practices and the Nonprofit Executive Team

He was a "sincere and dedicated employee and a charming person. He was very pious. He was the most religious guy I have ever met." Who is this man? He's the former CFO of a community clinic that saw its beginnings in San Francisco's famous "Summer of Love" in the late 1960s. He's also a man who may have embezzled close to $1 million. He used a government requirement in an ingenious manner. The federal government requires that nonprofits receiving federal grants return any unspent money at the end of the fiscal year. The CFO was supposed to be remitting the unspent money directly to a government office, but instead he created a bank account in Sacramento under a name that was similar to that of the agency where he was supposed to send the money. For two years, he had the clinic staff give him the checks, which he deposited in the bogus account. The CEO noticed some irregularities and the board authorized an investigation before the CFO was fired and the clinic went to the authorities (Van Derbeken, 2004).

CHAPTER OVERVIEW

This chapter examines the role of the executive and his or her team in introducing compliance with SOX provisions and best practices. In the introductory story, the CEO did not spot the financial irregularities until almost $1 million went missing. Although the community clinic instituted new controls in an attempt to prevent future fraud, the clinic is still responsible for reimbursing the federal government, and attempting to recoup the embezzled money. As incidents of fraud in nonprofits become more commonplace, Congress and state legislatures seek to change the laissez-faire culture in which nonprofits have traditionally operated. The expectations of the public sector reflect the expectations of the public at large.

CHAPTER OBJECTIVES

By the end of this chapter, you should be able to:

- Discuss how recent state and federal legislation and proposals, such as the Grassley White Paper, have changed the public's expectations of CEO and CFO behavior.

- Explain why the Executive Team is a crucial link between the board and nonprofit operations.

- Describe the role of the Executive Team in coordinating SOX compliance and best practices.

- Trace the connection among the supporting factors that contribute to fraud in a nonprofit.

- Provide an outline of an effective crisis communication plan.

- Identify the ways in which the executive team can provide oversight to important components of SOX compliance and best practices within the nonprofit.

SOX Expectations of Management Team

The history of the events leading up to the passage of SOX pointed to the common factor of corruption in the board and the executive team. Since then public expectations of Executive Team accountability have been raised across all economic sectors. The two requirements of SOX and its best practices reflect these public expectations for nonprofits:

- **Accountability**: The Executive Team will support the board in its role as ultimate authority in the nonprofit.

- **Transparency**: Financial and other operational transactions will be open for review and fully transparent.

- **Disclosure**: Nonprofit management will ensure that transactions will take place under the mantle of full disclosure. Examples of this include:

  - Sign the IRS Form 990s and other financial statements under penalty of perjury.

  - Responsible for ensuring that protocols exist to ensure full disclosure and organizational transparency.

  - Responsible for ensuring that the SOX requirements of Whistleblower Protection and Document Preservation are in place and enforced.

  - Responsible for implementing SOX best practices throughout the organization.

  - Responsible for facilitating change in the board's culture and in the organization's culture.

Today's legislative tone has made this mandate for change permanent. There's no turning back. As we saw in Chapter 4, media attention and donor reaction to nonprofit scandals leave permanent scars on the nonprofit's ability to raise money and enjoy the level of public trust that they had before the scandal. The executive team needs to lead the way in changing the nonprofit's current methods to introduce permanent change.

The Executive Team Is Vital in Facilitating Organizational Change

The benefits of SOX requirements and best practices can be translated into higher performance through meaningful change in the nonprofit's culture and operations. The Executive Team gains nothing from just minimal compliance with SOX. In order to achieve a higher level of performance, the executive team needs to work closely with the nonprofit board, staff, and volunteers to introduce these change agents.

The executive team needs to:

- **Communicate the deeper meaning of Sarbanes–Oxley legislation**: Donors, clients, and the public deserve a nonprofit that provides services in a transparent fashion in their community. Many nonprofits would prefer to whine about the unflinching provisions of this law and the expectations of its best practices. Introducing meaningful change requires a steadfast adherence to these requirements and best practices. In other words, *no whining* from anyone! The SOX requirements and best practices are protocols that every organization—private sector or nonprofit—should have been doing all along!

- **Establish the intention for change**: Central to setting a resolute tone is the expectation that governance and accountability will be taken to a higher level in your nonprofit. Implementing SOX requirements and best practices without fully expecting a higher level of efficiency and performance is a waste of everyone's time. You're just dabbling. Minimum compliance is almost as bad as not complying at all.

- **Talk openly about fraud:** One of the most difficult topics for an Executive Team to address or even talk about is fraud. No one likes to believe that people in their organization (particularly nonprofits) would ever steal or use resources in inappropriate ways. If you believe that there's no chance of fraud in your nonprofit, please stop reading this chapter, reread Chapter 4, and then come back to this paragraph. Executive Team needs to candidly address the issue of fraud before internal controls can be strengthened and before the rest of the organization understands why "business as usual" is not an option.

Talking to Staff and Volunteers about Fraud

Studies have shown that many of the cases involving fraud first involved the CEO and/or the CFO (COSO, 1999). The fraud began, literally, at the top. This means that the Executive Team needs to first model the behavior they expect from the rest of the nonprofit. Executives need to adopt a Code of Ethics that includes prohibitions against loans and gifts to management, stringent procedures for travel claims and management of expense accounts, and transparency in their dealings. Modeling the behavior is the most effective method of communicating that SOX compliance is not a fad. Before the Executive Team can talk to the organization about fraud, they need to either augment their current ethical standards or design standards that will address common areas of executive fraud.

Some of the more troublesome areas for nonprofits have been:

- **Loans and gifts to executives**: Nonprofit boards often agree to loans and gifts to executives as incentives or as rewards for performance.

- **Bonuses and perks:** CEOs and members of the Executive Team either are rewarded bonuses and perks by the board, or they institute such practices either overtly or covertly with implicit board approval.

- **Excessive Compensation and Benefits packages:** Congress and state legislatures have taken up the issue of executive compensation because excessive compensation has been a recurring factor in nonprofit scandals.

- **Expense accounts and travel claims:** Financial misappropriation often is hidden in transactions involving expense accounts and travel claims.

- **Lack of an enforceable Code of Ethics:** Having a Code of Ethics is not just for show. Members of the board and the Executive Team are *obligated* to conduct themselves accordingly—and need to be subject to disciplinary measures including termination for unethical conduct.

- **Lack of an enforceable Conflict of Interest policy:** Similarly, a Conflict of Interest policy should apply to the board and Executive Team alike.

At the very minimum, the preceding issues should be addressed in the nonprofit's HR policies. The Executive Team leads the way in changing the nonprofit's culture by adopting ethical practices and ensuring that they set the example by their business dealings. Do not expect the rest of the nonprofit's staff and volunteers to change their behavior unless they see that the Executive Team has adopted these measures as part of daily operations, and that the Executive Team is willing to hold themselves accountable.

How to Talk to Your Nonprofit about Fraud

The Executive Team needs to be candid about the factors that support fraud, and why the implementation of SOX requirements and best practices will help the nonprofit reduce the potential for fraud within the organization. The team also needs to be resolute in its approach. Don't be sidetracked by the long-time staff person or volunteer whose "feelings will be hurt" if protocols and expectations are changed. The well-being of your nonprofit comes first. These individuals will just have to get over their "hurt" if they want to remain part of the nonprofit. Management needs to be very clear about their message to all staff and volunteers.

Change is not negotiable. Our nonprofit will change with or without you.

Framework for Fraud

There are supporting factors within a nonprofit or any organization that facilitate opportunities for fraud:

- **Motivation**: People have to want to engage in fraudulent activities—and believe that there will be few if any consequences if they are ever caught.

- **The occasion for the fraud to take place**: In other words, there is an open door or opportunity to engage in fraudulent activities.

- **Sloppy or nonexistent internal controls**: It's easier to cover one's tracks when there are no protocols or records kept.

- **Access to electronic databases and online checking**: Often, electronic records will need to be altered to cover the fraud. Individuals who have access to sensitive databases are in a position to set up sham accounts and issue checks to themselves.

- **Organizational culture**: The environment either denies the possibility of anyone committing fraud, or even more insidious, a culture that transforms staff and volunteers into martyrs. How many times have you heard people say, "We work so hard here for so little money." Even more serious is the Executive Team's enabling of this dysfunctional attitude. "We pay these people so little, we really can't expect them to agree to these requirements."

- **A board of directors that is asleep at the wheel**: How often do we hear stories about fraud committed at nonprofit organizations only to learn that the board knew nothing about it and suspected nothing?

SOX requirements will provide individuals with the opportunity to report waste, fraud, or abuse without fear of retaliation. Document preservation will facilitate more efficient record keeping and provide auditors (external and internal) with better data for their review. The overall strengthening of the internal controls that comes with the implementation of best practices will further reduce the opportunities for fraud, and will introduce a change in the organizational culture.

The Executive Team's Role in Setting the Organization's Values and Shaping its Culture

In Chapter 3, we discussed the elements of organizational culture and how this invisible element shapes the profile of a nonprofit. We examined how an organization's culture can contribute to its dysfunction. Organizational culture is not set in stone—it can be changed—and in order to implement Sarbanes-Oxley requirements and best practices, often the essence of a nonprofit's culture needs to change. The primary change agents are the board and the Executive Team. These leaders begin the process and use strategies along the way that bring about a sea change in the way in which a nonprofit does business, looks at its programs, its clients, its donors, its staff, and its future.

The nonprofit's culture is reflected in its values and its belief system, the way in which experiences are translated into lessons learned, and the ways in which new methods are introduced. The Executive Team has a number of tools that can be applied to bring about attention and reinforcement to the changes that have been announced. Some of the ways in which the Executive Team can highlight the changes that they expect to see, and the consequences for failure to change, include:

- Change what they articulate as measures of success. The Executive Team controls the metrics for quality. Staff and volunteers will need to adopt a new understanding of quality within the nonprofit. The Executive Team needs to present the new standards.

- Allocate financial and other resources directly in support of the necessary changes. This may require budgetary changes or reordering of priorities, but the advice to "follow the money" is necessary. Other resource reallocation can take the form of changing staff workstations or offices. Office "real estate" conveys powerful messages.

- Change how rewards and consequences are distributed. It is important to reward the desired behavior and have swift consequences for foot-dragging or outright refusal to comply. It is equally important to document performance expectations and actual performance.

- Change the way in which staff members are promoted, assigned to plum projects, or awarded special recognition.

Staff and volunteers need to be able to clearly see the connection between the desired behavior and the positive reinforcement. Their behavior will need to change, but equally important is that they also see that the behavior of the board and the Executive Team has changed as well.

How Implementation of SOX Requirements and Best Practices Facilitates Change

The Executive Team's important duties in coordinating SOX compliance and best practices center on coordinating and providing oversight for the Whistleblower Protection policy, including the design of a confidential reporting mechanism and investigation protocols, for the design of an internal controls review, and for the implementation of a Document Preservation policy and prohibitions against destroying documents during an investigation.

Whistleblower Protection

The first obligation from SOX that applies to all organizations is the requirement for a documented "whistleblower protection" policy. SOX requires all organizations, including nonprofits, to establish a means to collect, retain, and resolve claims regarding accounting, internal accounting controls, and auditing matters. The system must allow for such concerns to be submitted anonymously. SOX provides significant protections to whistleblowers, and severe penalties to those who retaliate against them.

The board and Executive Team should direct the Human Resources division to either create a Whistleblower Protection policy, or augment your nonprofit's current policy to articulate these standards. Additionally, HR needs to be instructed to create a mechanism to make confidential reports, and to design training so that all staff and volunteers know how to make a report, know their rights, and understand how the investigation will take place and results reported. This is a federal law, so your nonprofit needs to be in compliance now. Chapter 9 provides more detail on the design and talking points of a Whistleblower Protection policy.

Document Preservation Policy

Document storage and retention is another area within SOX that applies to all organizations. The language in Section 802 describes the consequences for failing to implement a Document Retention system:

> Whoever knowingly alters, destroys, mutilates, conceals, covers up, falsifies, or makes a false entry in any record, document, or tangible object with the intent to impede, obstruct, or influence the investigation or proper executive team of any matter within the jurisdiction of any department or agency of the United States or any case filed under Title XI, or in relation to or contemplation of any such matter or case, shall be fined under this title, imprisoned not more than 10 years, or both.

Although Chapter 8 addresses the design of a Document Retention policy in more detail, some key areas for consideration include:

- What documents and records should be preserved and why?
- Are the documents paper only or are electronic files included? Which ones?
- What about e-mail and instant messaging?
- What are the expectations about the way in which documents are stored or archived and the ability to retrieve documents?
- How long are you supposed to keep these documents?
- Is there a protocol for disposing of documents once their storage time has elapsed?
- When should you *not* destroy materials?
- How can you make sure that everyone in the nonprofit—staff and volunteers— understands and adheres to these requirements?
- What happens if your nonprofit is in violation?

There needs to be a statement developed by the Executive Team that contains the following talking points:

- What the Document Retention policy is and why it is required by law. It is important that the staff and volunteers understand that document preservation is a component of SOX that applies to all organizations.
- What the new procedures are that emerge from the policy. Staff and volunteers need to understand how to be in compliance, and what specific actions are required.
- What are the obligations of individuals to ensure that your nonprofit is in compliance. Requirements for individual staff and volunteers should be presented in writing. Because this is probably a very new requirement in your organization, the more user-friendly the guidelines, the better.
- What is expected in terms of new behaviors and procedures, and what are the consequences for individual employees and volunteers for failing to adhere to the new procedures. It is particularly important that the Executive Team be prepared to carry out unpleasant consequences swiftly to send a strong message throughout the organization.

The Executive Team needs to coordinate the activities in the implementation of a Document Preservation policy. Since most of today's documents are stored in electronic format, the details of the design of the policy are addressed in Chapter 8. The system you design for document storage, archives, and retrieval must be logical and user friendly. If staff can't understand what it's about, what's expected of them, and why they are being asked to do this, the probability of compliance is low.

The Executive Team would need to create a cross-functional team representing each division within the nonprofit. Each member of the team would be tasked with being that functional area's Document Manager. The individual's performance expectations would be altered to reflect the new responsibilities. This individual would be tasked with coordinating the Document Preservation policy components that apply to his or her department. It is essential that these individuals all have the same training and knowledge of organizational systems and any technology such as scanners, software, and the like, to ensure that documents are selected, preserved, archived, and able to be retrieved in a consistent, standardized manner.

Establish rules for appropriate and secure electronic transmission of sensitive materials. Work with IT and legal professionals to ensure that these rules are comprehensive and appropriate to your nonprofit.

The Executive Team will oversee the development of retention rules (based on legal requirements and the operational needs of your nonprofit) and ensure that these rules are clearly disseminated to all staff and volunteers. There needs to be a security classification system (develop a simple one) that allows for documents to be classified as "confidential," "private," or other designation that precludes them from general access.

The Executive Team needs to ensure that a directive against destruction of documents that are part of an investigation is written and distributed throughout the organization. The team also needs to review and approve rules for managing, storing, preserving, and archiving electronic messages or other electronic data. The rules should address the important issues, including listing the types of documents that are to be retained and how these documents are to be stored.

Lastly, the Executive Team needs to conduct routine audits of the Document Retention system—generally on an unannounced basis. The findings of these audits will provide the team with valuable insight into the quality of the current protocols, the degree to which staff members are in compliance, and what midcourse corrections would be necessary to achieve full compliance.

The days of the "Mom and Pop" nonprofit are over—you have an obligation to your donors, your clients, your board, and your staff to ensure that your organization is in compliance with this component of SOX legislation. It's not just a "best practice," it's the *law* and it applies to all organizations in this country, including your nonprofit. Exhibit 7.1 provides a SOX best practices checklist to help the Executive Team assess and improve its practices

Technology Policy

An important add-on to a Document Preservation policy is a Technology policy. The Executive Team needs to design the policy to address the use of all types of technology that are present within the nonprofit, including e-mail, Internet access, voice mail, cell phones, laptops, PDAs, faxes, and other equipment owned by the nonprofit.

EXHIBIT 7.1	EXECUTIVE TEAM COORDINATION OF SOX COMPLIANCE AND BEST PRACTICES CHECKLIST

- The executive team has regular meetings with the board's Executive Committee.
- The executive team reviews the nonprofit's Whistleblower Protection policy to ensure it is written in compliance with SOX requirements.
- The executive team reviewed the mechanism for whistleblower complaints to be filed to ensure the rights of whistleblowers are preserved.
- The nonprofit has a Document Preservation policy in place.
- The executive team has reviewed and approved a policy prohibiting the destruction of documents during an inquiry or legal action.
- The executive team has conducted (or is planning to conduct in the near future) a review of the nonprofit's internal controls.
- The executive team has developed a crisis communication plan for the nonprofit.
- The executive team has ensured that the procedures for all SOX requirements and best practices have been shared with everyone, staff and volunteers alike.
- The executive team has taken responsibility for conducting unannounced reviews of procedures and protocols to ensure compliance.

Although Chapter 8 examines the design of this policy in greater detail, the policy needs to include these talking points:

- Clearly state that all aspects of the nonprofit's technology belong to the nonprofit. There are *no* expectations of personal privacy when using the nonprofit's technology.

- Identify all of the nonprofit's technology: hardware and software including laptop computers, desktop computers, hand-held devices such as PDAs and Blackberry, cell phones, Internet access, e-mail, and all software programs purchased through the nonprofit. Be aware that when electronic devices such as laptops or PDAs are "recycled" to another staff member, the "hard drive" of the device may still contain data, documents, or transactions from the previous employee. It is important to institute a procedure to erase the hard drive once all of the documents have been extracted and stored according to your nonprofit's Document Retention policy.

- Develop a policy on the storage and transportation of sensitive information out of your nonprofit's facilities. Published reports routinely describe scenarios of laptops being stolen that contained sensitive data. The same thing could happen to your nonprofit if you store sensitive information about donors, clients, or staff on laptops that leave your premises.

Staff and volunteers who are entrusted with the nonprofit's cell phones, laptops, PDAs, or other electronics need to understand that they will be held personally accountable for the safety of the equipment, the safe use of the equipment, and the security of the data that is stored within these electronics.

Crisis Communication and Public Trust

Why is it important to plan for a crisis? From the moment your organization experiences the onset of a crisis until services are returned to normal, you must be prepared to act. Crisis planning will facilitate the development of a *rational response* to a crisis. A crisis is defined as "an unstable or crucial time or state of affairs in which a decisive change is impending; especially one with the distinct possibility of a highly undesirable outcome" (Merriam-Webster http://www.m-w.com).

Examples of crisis scenarios would include:

- Fire, earthquake, or flood destroys nonprofit's offices
- Key executive resigns, dies, or accepts another job
- Client accuses nonprofit of wrongdoing
- Nonprofit vehicle involved in serious auto accident
- Larger implications of a crisis
- Loss of public trust
- Loss of donations

- Loss of public sector/private sector contracts or other collaborative ventures
- Adverse publicity and its effects on observers; for example, pictures on *CNN* of ARC destroying blood products two months after 9/11

Developing a Crisis Communication Plan

The Executive Team needs to develop a crisis management plan well in advance of any incident. The plan should include these components:

- Communication and media relations plan
- Supporting staff, volunteers, and clients
- Positioning the nonprofit to resume operations
- Accepting and acknowledging emergency donations

Communication and Media Relations Plan

Develop a Crisis Communication plan that includes a designated spokesperson and a backup spokesperson. These individuals need to be skilled in communicating with media representatives. Additionally, everyone in the nonprofit should have contact information to reach key staff 24/7. The Executive Team needs to develop materials that can be drafted in advance and available at all times to the designated spokespersons.

Media relations are particularly important, as the way in which your nonprofit interacts with the media can send a message that either reinforces your nonprofit's good name, or sends a message of disorganization and incompetence. The Team needs to ensure that there are written protocols for interacting with media representatives. These protocols should include these directives:

- All media inquiries must be directed to the designated spokesperson—no exceptions.
- Consequences must be imposed, including termination, for violating the preceding rule. These consequences need to apply to volunteers as well.
- Before speaking with the media, the spokesperson should prepare a summary statement based on *confirmed* facts—always tell the truth.
- Determine the most appropriate way to brief board members, staff, volunteers, and clients.
- Update the media as the situation evolves.

Supporting Staff, Volunteers, and Clients

Staff, volunteers, and clients may not be directly involved in the crisis, but need to have access to necessary and sufficient information. If the crisis involves a community-wide disaster such as a flood, earthquake, or tornado, then staff, volunteers, and clients could be directly affected.

If the crisis is confined to your nonprofit, staff, volunteers, and clients will be seeking information. It is important for the Executive Team to determine the level of detail that is appropriate for a variety of constituencies. The Executive Team should consider how staff, volunteers, and clients might be able to access the nonprofit's website or voice mail to obtain information.

It is essential that the Executive Team develop a written directive that all staff and volunteers are required to sign that instructs them to direct all media inquiries to the nonprofit's designated spokesperson. Staff and volunteers need to understand that the nonprofit's spokesperson is the *only* individual authorized to speak with the media because that person has the latest and best information on the situation. Staff and volunteers should understand that failing to comply with this directive will result in termination.

Positioning the Nonprofit to Resume Operations

In the event of an emergency or crisis, the plan should address this sequence of events:

1. **Alert the designated spokesperson that an incident has occurred.** There should be a designated spokesperson and at least one backup spokesperson to ensure that the plan can be activated immediately.

2. **Confirm the facts and determine the level of detail needed for each of these stakeholder groups.** Staff, volunteers, and clients will all want to know about what happened. It is up to the Executive Team to ensure that stakeholder groups have the level of detail that is appropriate. Board members need to have the most detail; other constituencies need to have the quality of information that is necessary and sufficient for their role in the nonprofit.

3. **Disseminate the information to each stakeholder group via phone, e-mail, or media coverage.** There should be a defined sequence for information dissemination. The board needs to be informed first, then staff and volunteers, and then clients and other stakeholders.

4. **Positioning the nonprofit to resume operations.** The sooner the nonprofit can access electronic data and files, the sooner operations can resume. The Executive Team should include designing redundancies as part of their work on internal controls. Keep copies of important account numbers, files, and documents stored offsite.

5. **Form an effective crisis team to develop plans that meet the needs of your nonprofit.** Before any crisis strikes, it is important that the Executive Team appoint a crisis management team. Everyone in the nonprofit needs to know who these individuals are, what they will be doing in the event of a crisis, and how to contact them, particularly after hours.

6. **Tell the truth, always**: The test of a crisis communication plan is how it preserves the nonprofit's integrity and public trust. Telling the truth is absolutely essential. Understanding and managing media relations is an important aspect of a good crisis communication plan. If the Executive Team does not have this skill set, it is important that they obtain training and work with a public relations professional to ensure that the crisis communications plan is effective.

Accepting and Acknowledging Emergency Donations

We live in a very generous society. In the event of a crisis, your nonprofit could very well be besieged by kindhearted citizens who want to help. There should be plans in place to accept emergency donation of time, talent, and money. As we saw in Chapter 4, however, the mismanagement of emergency donations brought down the senior executive of the American Red Cross. Donors to your nonprofit need to understand where and how their money will be spent. If emergency donations to your nonprofit will be spent for a particular program or facility, donors should be advised of this *before* they make the donation. Donors have the right to be fully informed before they make a donation.

Consider developing protocols to accept emergency cash donations through a variety of venues such as your nonprofit's website, via media coverage, and through correspondence sent to your nonprofit's current donor base. In-kind donations are usually offered during a crisis, and the Executive Team, in conjunction with the board, need to decide if the nonprofit will accept these types of donations. The Executive Team in conjunction with the nonprofit's development division must establish a procedure to acknowledge these donations in a timely manner.

By developing an efficient crisis communication plan, the Executive Team can ensure that the nonprofit's public "image" will remain strong and that its covenant of trust with the community at large will not be damaged. Exhibit 7.2 will help the Executive Team develop an effective communication plan.

EXHIBIT 7.2   CRISIS COMMUNICATION PLAN WORKSHEET

Does your nonprofit's crisis communication plan have these components?
Communication and media relations plan

- A designated spokesperson and a backup spokesperson who are trained in communications and media relations.
  - Important! All staff and volunteers should understand that *all* media inquiries are to be directed to the designated spokesperson. This is to ensure that all information given to the media is accurate and up to date. Staff and volunteers also need to know that there are severe consequences for breaching this protocol.
- A prepared statement that can be used in the event of a crisis—the statement is prepared in advance and has these talking points:

(continues)

EXHIBIT 7.2   CRISIS COMMUNICATION PLAN WORKSHEET (CONTINUED)

- Give basic facts—name of the nonprofit, location, and brief description of the nonprofit's mission.
- The statement should have a section (that would be filled in when a crisis occurs) that describes (there should not be any detail until facts and circumstances can be *verified*):
  - What happened in very general terms
  - Who was involved
  - When the crisis occurred
  - Where the crisis occurred
- Information on how to contact the nonprofit—solicit emergency donations
- The nonprofit's commitment to the community and its clients

Supporting staff, volunteers, and clients

- In the event of a crisis, staff and volunteers need to know how to obtain information on the situation and what is expected of them in terms of service.
- Clients will need to know how to obtain services and what programs might be temporarily curtailed.

Accepting and acknowledging emergency donations

- Spokespersons and supporting staff should have a listing of key media outlets to provide press releases and other information on the crisis.
- There should be a protocol for accepting emergency donations, obtaining donor information, and acknowledging the donations. If emergency donations can be made on the nonprofit's website, there should be a special icon that directs the reader to the emergency donations link.

CONCLUSION

The Executive Team are the leaders within the operations of the nonprofit. Their primary role is to ensure that SOX requirements and best practices are put into place, and monitored for compliance. Although fraud is a difficult topic to discuss, particularly in a nonprofit setting, the times demand that the Executive Team be resolute in confronting this issue. Today's business environment also demands that the Executive Team model ethical behavior and accountability.

The Executive Team is the "face" of the nonprofit in the event of a crisis. The design of a solid crisis communication plan is crucial in weathering a type of business interruption or community-wide disaster that the nonprofit might face.

CHAPTER 8

Sarbanes-Oxley Best Practices and Information Technology

The nonprofit is a household name because of its environmental work. Its website led the viewer through all the various programs and services it had to offer. It even had a link for individuals to make donations. The development director and the technology director were shocked to discover that a porn site was soliciting donations for the nonprofit through a link in the porn site's web page. Viewers of the porn site were also directed to the environmental group's site. How did the environmentalists ever find out? The owners of the porn site proudly sent the environmental group a check for the donations they had collected! The environmentalists' attorney sent the porn site a cease and desist letter and returned the check.

CHAPTER OVERVIEW

The use of technology has permeated all aspects of the business and nonprofit worlds. While technology has helped to bring donors, volunteers, and the nonprofit closer together, the potential for hackers to infiltrate and loot the nonprofit's databases and files has dramatically increased. This chapter presents the who, what, why, and how of SOX best practices in the information technology (IT) division.

CHAPTER OBJECTIVES

By the end of this chapter, you should be able to:

- Describe the role of technology in SOX compliance and best practices.
- Produce a sample design of a Document Management program.
- Develop a technology policy for your nonprofit.
- Identify the ways in which your nonprofit's website can show the SOX compliance and best practices that your nonprofit has implemented.

BENEFITS OF IMPLEMENTING SARBANES-OXLEY BEST PRACTICES

Implementation of SOX best practices in the area of IT and electronic Document Management compliance can serve to strengthen internal controls, raise awareness of cyber-risks throughout the organization, produce a higher level of efficiency and productivity, and maintain public trust by keeping electronic access to websites, databases, and confidential information safe.

SOX best practices have some additional benefits as well for IT. Public expectations such as putting the Form 990s on the website can be achieved without compromising sensitive data on the page with the major donors. The way in which SOX best practices are implemented can serve as the beginning of a sea change within the organization. As we have seen in the passage of California SOX-clone legislation, it is only a matter of time before many of these best practices become law, or are codified in the regulatory requirements of federal agencies such as the IRS. As always, the issue of technology can be something of a hot button for employees and volunteers who are either not technology conversant, or are reluctant to model new behavior.

The board and Executive Team set the tone in IT as well as in the adaptation of all of the SOX best practices. As one private sector executive pronounced, "Noncompliance is *not* an option." The same message must be communicated to everyone in the nonprofit.

Role of IT in Overall SOX Compliance and in Adaptation of SOX Best Practices

Technology and its application have become the backbone of nonprofit operations. Virtually all nonprofit organizations use technology to some degree, whether in the use of computers, databases, Internet access, websites, PDAs, laptops, notebooks, cell phones, pagers, or voice mail. The proliferation of technology is a double-edged sword. While technology can facilitate higher and more efficient levels of productivity, it is also an integral part of SOX compliance and adaptation of best practices. The bar has been raised permanently in terms of degree of compliance and using technology to strengthen the nonprofit's internal controls. There's no going back!

Applying the Lessons Learned From the Private Sector

The private sector is an important source of learning about the adaptation of best practices. Although private companies, like nonprofits, are not required to comply with all of the Sarbanes-Oxley legislation, they have learned that adaptation of best practices that closely approximate full compliance are considered essential for their financial viability and competitive positioning.

The private sector understands that:

- SOX is not going to go away.
- SOX addresses practices that should have been in place for all organizations, publicly traded, private, and nonprofit.

    IT is an essential component in the implementation of SOX Document Management compliance. The preservation and proper storage of electronic documents including e-mail, instant messages and voice mail are critical elements in the nonprofit's overall Document Management compliance plan. Compliance is based on preservation of all vital records and the ability to retrieve important documents when needed.

Benefits of Having a Solid Document Management Program

The benefits of having a solid document management program in place provide value to organizations in the form of:

- **Ability to manage institutional knowledge**: Executives, managers, and employees know *where* documents and records are stored. There is a method that facilitates immediate access, in addition to a set of protocols for archiving documents, and, at the appointed time, the destruction of documents.
- **Compliance with SOX**: Compliance is assured by means of a policy prohibiting destruction of documents during an investigation or discovery. Everyone on the staff knows what the policy is, and knows that consequences for noncompliance will be vigorously enforced.
- **Opportunities for continuous improvement**: Change and continuous improvement are accepted parts of the technology applications. The document management program needs to grow, expand, and improve with new technology and methods.
- **Implementing a document management program is one of the methods for communicating management's commitment to change within an organization**: Because document management is required under Sarbanes-Oxley, the enforcement of this policy is an important signal that the organization *will* be in compliance.
- **Make compliance part of the employees' performance reviews**: If an employee is not managing his or her documents per SOX requirements, this is reflected in performance reviews. The employee's future salary adjustments, or even continued employment can be contingent upon the degree of compliance.
- **Auditors expectations and observations**: The nonprofit's auditors will be examining the way in which documents (electronic and otherwise) are managed, and the way in which technology is used to facilitate SOX compliance.

- **Raises performance levels**: The ability to access files instantly saves time and energy for everyone on the staff. Further, it brings about an efficiency of scale that translates into higher levels of productivity (Davis, 2005).

SOX compliance standards reflect what organizations should have been doing all along! Having an integrated document management system ensures that important documents are stored in safe, accessible locations and backed up on a daily basis. The core of any document management system is access and accountability. Having a solid document management program in place will introduce a higher level of efficiency, and accountability. Each division will have individuals who are responsible for document preservation and whose performance review reflects how well they carry out these responsibilities.

New IT Role—Document Management Program: Establishing a Framework

As business operations have become increasingly dependent on technology applications and products, the role of IT has emerged as one of the key operational units within any company or nonprofit. The Executive Team is tasked with ensuring that SOX compliance and best practices are implemented, but it is the IT division that will execute the assignment.

Tone at the Top—Board and Management Team

Because your nonprofit's document management program is required for Sarbanes-Oxley compliance, the board and senior management need to announce its implementation and emphasize that it is not a fad. Compliance with your nonprofit's document preservation policy is a condition of continued employment. Delegation of responsibilities and accountability is essential in the design of any document management program, but constant communication up and down the organization is also essential. The reason people believe management innovations are fads is because they are not constantly reminded of the change, nor is there sufficient training or personalization of the change. In other words, staff and volunteers do not understand that they have an individual responsibility for compliance, and that the quality of their compliance will be assessed at their next performance evaluation. Enforcement of document management compliance needs to be consistent and a condition of employment. Consequences for failing to comply need to be swift and well publicized.

Overview of the Program: Designing an Method for Managing Electronic Documents

Does your nonprofit have document management protocols? Some nonprofits have a set of procedures for handling and storing documents. Many nonprofits have never embarked on such a plan.

For example, do you know:

- Whom to contact when looking for a specific type of record?
- Who is the "go to" person for document preservation and to locate records in every department of your nonprofit? Does every department in your nonprofit even have such a person?
- How vendors handle your files? If you outsource a function such as payroll, the vendors need to manage your nonprofit's documents *in the manner the nonprofit expects*. Do not allow any divergence from the way documents are managed in your nonprofit.

Basic Components of a Document Preservation Policy

Implementing a document management program need not be overwhelming. Consider how the following components might be applied in your nonprofit:

- **Policies and procedures**: The policies and procedures serve as a framework for the document management system. These policies and procedures need to address what is *necessary and sufficient*. The requirements need to be easily understood and user friendly in terms of performance.
- **Communication and training**: The quality of the training in document management is the second key to its success only behind the policies and procedures needed to establish the program.
- **Auditing and monitoring**: Auditing and monitoring of the program will need to be an ongoing process. There are three primary elements:
  - **External audit**: An external consultant assesses program. This means that the nonprofit brings in an individual from outside of the nonprofit to review and assess the current program.
  - **Internal audit**: The management team or their representatives do a spot check of individuals to see if their records are in compliance. If these records are not in compliance, it is documented and included in the employee's performance review. The employee can be subject to consequences for his or her noncompliance.
    - **Record categories**: As part of the spot check, the reviewer should determine where particular records should be located and check to see if the documents are where they should be.
- **Consistent enforcement**: The results of the ongoing auditing and monitoring should be reviewed to determine if further enforcement is necessary to bring about standardized results.
- **Continuous Improvement**: The program should also contain a continuous improvement aspect to ensure that new processes are adapted to capture further efficiencies and effectiveness (Kahn, 2004).

The following documents should be retained:

- *Financial documents*, reports, analysis, and forecasts
- *Donor records*, history and correspondence
- *Human Resources Records*, including volunteer and board files and contracts with your nonprofit's management, staff, and volunteers (if applicable)
- Documents that reflect the *sale of property, merchandise*, or any tangible or intangible assets
- *Documents that a regulatory agency or the law requires* you to retain, such as tax returns, business license document, professional licenses, vehicle registration forms, and *correspondence* regarding these documents or about your nonprofit's operations
- Documents containing information that *an auditor or regulator would need to review*
- *Contracts with vendors* for services, including insurance policies, auditor contracts (particularly to demonstrate that the auditing firm is not providing any other services to your nonprofit)
- *Contracts with external clients* (such as public sector agencies) to provide services to these external clients
- *Client files* and correspondence, including any contracts for services
- *Donor files* and correspondence with donors
- *Proposals* in response to Requests for Proposals (RFPs)
- *Documents* related to your nonprofit's operations or documents that have historical, legal, or programmatic significance
- *Instant Message or e-mail that contains negotiations for a contract* or other legal agreement
- *Business transactions*, including any document that would provide evidence that your nonprofit took action in a business, contractual, or legal matter

Policies on Document Preservation

Policies on document preservation should be developed by the board and senior management. There needs to be a statement developed by senior management that contains the following talking points:

- What the Document Retention policy is and why it is required by law. It is important that the staff and volunteers understand that document preservation is a component of SOX that applies to all organizations.
- What are the new procedures that emerge from the policy? What are the deliverables that the board expects?
- What does this legal requirement mean for your nonprofit?
- What are the obligations of individual employees to ensure that your nonprofit is in compliance?

- What is expected in terms of new behaviors and procedures, and what are the consequences (for individual employees and volunteers) for failing to adhere to the new procedures. (Note: Understand that middle and senior management must be prepared to carry out the consequences swiftly to send a strong message throughout the organization.)

How to Build a Document Retention System that Is in Compliance with SOX

The system you design for document storage, archives, and retrieval must be logical and user-friendly. If staff can't understand what it's about, what's expected of them, and why they are being asked to do this, the probability of success is low.

Step 1: Consider what types of documents your nonprofit would need to store/archive and be able to retrieve. Some examples of documents that need to be stored include: grant documents, tax and other financial documents, and copies of policies. Be sure to build in the requirements of any third-party reviewers such as auditors or regulatory agencies, so your system will satisfy the expectations of these reviewers.

Step 2: Inventory the nonprofit's current record system to determine what records are in use, what records are in storage, and what records are archived. This step should also include a review of the types of e-mail messages and instant messages that are routinely transmitted along with attachments.

Step 3: Develop retention rules (based on legal requirements and the operational needs of your nonprofit) and ensure that these rules are clearly disseminated to all staff and volunteers. There needs to be a classification system (develop a simple one) that allows for documents to be classified as "confidential," "private," or other designation that precludes them from general access. As part of this step, it is essential that a training program be developed for staff to ensure that they understand what is expected of them, what the procedures are, and what records they are expected to retain.

Step 4: Develop a process for finding and preserving documents that either will be or are part of an investigation or legal action. There must also be a mechanism for announcing that no documents are to be destroyed until an "all clear" notice is given—and stiff consequences for failing to adhere to this directive.

Step 5: Develop rules for managing, storing, preserving, and archiving electronic messages or other electronic data. The rules should address the important issues, including listing the types of documents that are to be retained and how these documents are to be stored. The process need not be complicated, but the rules need to be standardized—there is no room for "doing your own thing." Staff and volunteers need to understand that they are obligated to adhere to the rules—or face the consequences. The rules should also include steps to be taken to ensure that the documents cannot be tampered with, such as using PDF files or passwords. It is particularly important to store financial records in such a way as to ensure that they represent a true and honest picture of the nonprofit's financial profile and/or other financial description. Regulators will expect to be able to rely on the accuracy of all of your electronic records—no exceptions.

Specific employees within each division of your nonprofit should be assigned the responsibility and the requisite power and resources for Document Retention within their division. It is essential that these individuals all have the same training and knowledge of organizational systems and any technology such as scanners, software, and the like, to ensure that documents are selected, preserved, archived, and able to be retrieved in a consistent, standardized manner.

Establish rules for appropriate and secure electronic transmission of sensitive materials. Work with IT and legal professionals to ensure that these rules are comprehensive and appropriate to your nonprofit.

Step 6: Develop a means by which the Document Retention system will be audited on a regular basis to ensure that all staff are in compliance with the provisions. Board and staff should understand that the audits will be random and unannounced. Consequences for noncompliance should be meted out quickly to send a message to the entire organization. Please understand that your nonprofit is a *business*, and you need to conduct operations in a businesslike fashion. The days of the "Mom and Pop" nonprofit are over; you have an obligation to your donors, your clients, your board, and your staff to ensure that your organization is in compliance with this component of SOX legislation. It's not just a "best practice," it's the *law*, and it applies to all organizations in this country, including your nonprofit.

Exhibit 8.1 will help your organization develop an effective document retention and storage policy, along with the needed protocols and procedures.

Special Designations for Sensitive Documents

Design a *simple* classification system that allows for some of the documents to be classified as "confidential," "private," or other designation that precludes them from general access. *The fewer documents that need a special classification, the better.* You don't want to have to invoke the Freedom of Information Act to access your own files.

Staff should be screened before receiving clearance to handle sensitive documents. Password protection can be a means by which sensitive electronic documents are secured. Access to varying degrees of sensitive material should always be on a "need to know" basis, which reduces the potential for individuals browsing through confidential materials.

Exhibit 8.1	DOCUMENT RETENTION POLICY AND STORAGE PROTOCOLS WORKSHEET

Document Retention Policy—Talking Points

Key areas for explanation in a document retention policy include:

- Why does [your nonprofit] need a document retention and storage policy?
    - It's required by the Public Company Accounting Reform and Investor Protection Act of 2002 (Sarbanes-Oxley).
- What documents and records should be preserved and why?
    - See list of documents below.
- Why is there a rule against document destruction? When should you not destroy materials?
    - If an official investigation is underway or even suspected, nonprofit management must stop any document purging in order to avoid criminal obstruction charges.

Writing the Policy—Talking Points

What the Document Retention and Storage Policy is—and why it is required by law. It's not just a "best practice"—it's the law and it applies to all organizations in this country. Your nonprofit has an obligation to your donors, your clients, your board, and your staff to ensure your organization is in compliance with this component of Sarbanes-Oxley legislation.

How does it work? In this section of the policy, provide your staff and volunteers with some clear guidelines. (Just emphasize the important issues—the guidelines should not be voluminous. If your guidelines are over ten pages, consider if all of the information is necessary and sufficient.)

The guidelines should answer the questions:

- How do I start?
- What should my files look like when I'm finished?
- How long do I have to do this?
- What files should I ensure are retained and stored (this will be discussed in the next section)?
- When should I *not* destroy files? When an instruction is sent to everyone at the [your nonprofit] to stop document destruction. You are expected to stop destroying documents until you receive an instruction stating that document destruction can resume.
- How to maintain files and determine which are sent to storage? Also discuss when files can be destroyed (after X number of years—depending on the type of file—and not when a moratorium is in place).
- Documents—Not all of these document categories are applicable to your nonprofit, so only include the ones that are and add those special document categories your nonprofit needs (but might not have been on the list). Be sure to include a brief description of these documents that would be meaningful to the staff and volunteers at your nonprofit.

Types of documents your nonprofit would need to store/archive and be able to retrieve:
Financial documents, reports, analysis, and forecasts:

- Donor records, history, and correspondence.
- HR records, including volunteer and board files and contracts with your nonprofit's management, staff, and volunteers (if applicable).
- Documents that reflect the sale of property, merchandise, or any tangible or intangible assets.
- Documents that a regulatory agency or the law requires you to retain, such as tax returns, business license documents, professional licenses, vehicle registration forms, and correspondence regarding these documents or about your nonprofit's operations.

(continues)

EXHIBIT 8.1	DOCUMENT RETENTION POLICY AND STORAGE PROTOCOLS WORKSHEET (CONT.)

- Documents containing information that an auditor or regulator would need to review.
- Contracts with vendors for services, including insurance policies, auditor contracts (particularly to demonstrate that the auditing firm is not providing any other services to your nonprofit).
- Contracts with external clients (such as public sector agencies) to provide services to these external clients.
- Client files and correspondence.
- Donor files and correspondence with donors.
- Proposals in response to Requests for Proposals (RFPs).
- Documents related to your nonprofit's operations.
- Instant Message or e-mail that contains negotiations for a contract or other legal agreement.
- Business transactions—Any document that would provide proof that your nonprofit took action in a business, contractual or legal matter.
- Special designations for sensitive documents.

Design a *simple* classification system that allows for some of the documents to be classified as "confidential," "private," or other designation that precludes them from general access.

Storing and archiving the documents
The rules for managing, storing, preserving, and archiving electronic messages or other electronic data should address the important issues, including listing the types of documents that are to be retained and how these documents are to be stored. The rules should also include steps to be taken to ensure the documents cannot be tampered with—such as using PDF files or passwords. It is particularly important to store financial records in such a way as to ensure that they represent a true and honest picture of the nonprofit's financial profile and/or other financial description. Regulators will expect to be able to rely on the accuracy of all of your electronic records—no exceptions.

Testing the System
Develop a means by which the Document Retention system will be tested on a regular basis to ensure that documents are stored properly, and, more importantly, can be retrieved quickly. Staff and volunteers should understand that the audits will be random and unannounced. Consequences for noncooperation should be meted out quickly to send a message to the entire organization.

Storing and Archiving the Documents

Develop rules for managing, storing, preserving, and archiving electronic messages or other electronic data. The rules should address the important issues, including listing the types of documents that are to be retained and how these documents are to be stored. The process need not be complicated, but the rules need to be standardized—there is no room for "doing your own thing." Staff and volunteers need to understand that they are obligated to adhere to the rules—or face the consequences. The rules should also include steps to be taken to ensure that the documents cannot be tampered with, such as using PDF files or passwords. It is particularly important to store financial records in such a way as to ensure that they represent a true and honest picture of the nonprofit's financial profile and/or other financial description. Regulators will expect to be able to rely on the accuracy of all of your electronic records—no exceptions.

Testing the System Develop a means by which the Document Retention system will be tested on a regular basis to ensure that documents are stored properly, *and, more importantly, can be retrieved quickly*. Staff and volunteers should understand that the audits will be random and unannounced. There should be consequences for noncooperation that should be meted out quickly to send a message to the entire organization.

Policy on Prohibition of Destruction of Documents

Why is there a rule against document destruction? When should you not destroy materials?

If an official investigation is underway or even suspected, nonprofit management must stop any document purging to avoid criminal obstruction charges. Sarbanes-Oxley legislation is clear about the requirement to provide investigators with any and all documents necessary for the investigation. This means that the nonprofit, and its IT division, need to be able to retrieve documents in a timely fashion.

Draft a *brief* policy with simple language that is easily understood that prohibits the destruction of documents while the nonprofit is part of an investigation or other crisis scenarios. The policy need not be lengthy, just a statement that in the event of an investigation or crisis, there will be a general order circulated that prohibits the destruction of any documents. Failure to comply can result in termination. Important! It is essential that your nonprofit be prepared to execute the consequences that it states in a policy like this. If your nonprofit is not prepared to terminate someone for violation of this policy, don't include language to that effect. Exhibit 8.2 will help you develop an effective document destruction statement.

EXHIBIT 8.2   PROHIBITION AGAINST DESTROYING DOCUMENTS WORKSHEET

The nonprofit's document preservation policy needs to include a policy that prohibits destruction of documents during a regulatory or legal investigation.

Talking Points:
- When are staff and volunteers prohibited from destroying files?
- When an instruction is sent to everyone to stop document destruction.
- Staff and volunteers are expected to stop destroying documents until such time that they receive an instruction stating that document destruction can resume.
- Staff and volunteers must always receive permission before documents in any of the document preservation categories are destroyed.

Privacy Issues and Document Preservation

Does your nonprofit have a privacy policy that relates to donor information? Information about clients, staff, and volunteers? If not, you need to develop and disseminate the policy(ies) to the various constituencies, such as staff, volunteers, donors, and other stakeholders. For example, if your nonprofit has a website, do you list the names of donors? If you list these names, have each of the donors signed a consent document? In today's world of identity theft and Internet hacking, it is particularly important to emphasize the need for privacy to protect donors, staff, and board members.

In today's business environment, virtually all of the sensitive information kept on staff, volunteers, donors, clients, and other stakeholders is stored in databases or electronic files. As part of the privacy policy, nonprofits should commit to maintaining the confidentiality of these documents, and to ensuring that the records are secure. As part of the policy, the nonprofit should specify how staff are limited in their access to secure records, and the protocols that are in place to preserve the confidentiality of the documents.

Staff, volunteers, clients, and donors should be provided with information on how your nonprofit is taking steps to guard their privacy, and contact information if they need assistance in ensuring privacy.

Designing a Technology Policy

The use of technology has permeated all aspects of the business and nonprofit worlds. While technology has helped to bring donors, volunteers, and the nonprofit closer together, the potential for hackers to infiltrate and loot the nonprofit's databases and files has increased dramatically.

An important component of IT implementation of SOX Best Practices is the design of a technology policy or the revision of your current technology policy.

Your nonprofit's technology policy should have these talking points:

- Clearly state that all aspects of the nonprofit's technology belong to the nonprofit. *There are no expectations of personal privacy when using the nonprofit's technology.* Staff and volunteers need to understand that they may *not* use the nonprofit's e-mail for personal business or to send inappropriate messages to other staff, volunteers, donors, or anyone. All staff and volunteers should also understand that the nonprofit's Internet access belongs to the nonprofit. Web surfing, access to porn sites, or other inappropriate sites is strictly prohibited. Failure to comply should result in strict penalties including possible termination.

- Identify all of the nonprofit's technology, hardware and software, including laptop computers, desktop computers, handheld devices such as PDAs and Blackberry, cell phones, Internet access, e-mail, and all software programs purchased through the nonprofit. Be aware that when electronic devices such as laptops or PDAs are "recycled" to another staff member, the "hard drive" of the device may still contain data, documents, or transactions from the previous employee. It is important to institute a procedure to erase the hard drive once all of the documents have been extracted and stored according to your nonprofit's Document Retention policy.

- Develop a policy on the storage and transportation of sensitive information out of your nonprofit's facilities. Published reports describe multiple scenarios of laptops of bank employees being stolen that contained client financial data. The same thing could happen to your nonprofit if you store sensitive information about donors, clients, or staff on laptops that leave your premises.

- The policy should also have provisions on appropriate use of portable technology such as PDAs, cell phones, and laptops. Safety and security issues need to be spelled out particularly as these apply to:
  - Using cell phones while driving
  - Discussing confidential information via cell phone
  - Using the cell phone for personal business, or illegal uses such as crank calls or harassing another person
  - Logging of numbers on the cell phone memory

All staff and volunteers who have access to any of the nonprofit's technology should be required to read and sign the Technology policy. Each person who signs the policy should have a copy of it to keep for his or her reference. Exhibit 8.3 will help you to develop an effective Technology policy

Your Nonprofit's Website

Your nonprofit's website is the electronic "face" of your organization. The way in which it is designed, its features (which make it user-friendly, or not), and the content say important things about your organization. Some nonprofits use their websites to collect donations, sell merchandise, or respond to a global disaster. The nonprofit's Document Preservation policy should also include those "documents" that can be pages on the website, such as:

- Your nonprofit's 990s for the past three years; these documents are on www.guidestar.org anyway, so there's no point in hiding them
- Documents that demonstrate SOX compliance and best practices, such as your nonprofit's Whistleblower Protection policy and Document Preservation policy
- Reports, information about board members, programs, annual reports, and financial reports

---

EXHIBIT 8.3   TECHNOLOGY POLICY CHECKLIST

- All aspects of the nonprofit's technology belong to the nonprofit. There are *no* expectations of personal privacy when using the nonprofit's technology.
- E-mail and web access belong to the nonprofit.
- Examples of inappropriate e-mail messages:
  - Jokes
  - Harassment
  - Political commentary, particularly hate messages
  - Anything you wouldn't want to read on the front page of your local newspaper, or have CNN broadcast
- The policy covers all of the nonprofit's technology—hardware and software, including laptop computers, desktop computers, handheld devices such as PDAs and Blackberry, cell phones, Internet access, e-mail and all software programs purchased through the nonprofit.
- Requires returning of all electronic devices such as laptops or PDAs when leaving the employ or volunteer assignment of the nonprofit.
- Policy on the storage and transportation of sensitive information on laptops that leave your premises.
- Staff and volunteers who are entrusted with the nonprofit's cell phones, laptops, PDAs, or other electronics need to understand that they will be held personally accountable for the safety of the equipment, the safe use of the equipment, and the security of the data that is stored within these electronics.

Security is rapidly becoming one of the most significant challenges to websites—any website—nonprofit or private sector. Nonprofit websites need to have firewalls and encryption software to protect donor information and to ensure that transactions online with donors are secure. When donors put a credit card number on your website, they and you need to feel confident that this sensitive information is properly encrypted and transported to the correct location. You should also consider including recommendations for safety in online transactions, such as using a credit card, rather than a debit card, checking credit card statements to ensure that all the transactions are accurate, and, if possible, include a link to your local Better Business Bureau, Chamber of Commerce, or nonprofit clearinghouse to verify that you are a member in good standing.

Who Owns Your Website?

This may appear to be a nonsensical question, but consider the case of the small dance company. The company had a volunteer who spent a significant amount of time working on projects. In fact, this volunteer seemed to be everywhere at all times. The volunteer offered to design the dance company's website, and his efforts were lauded. One board member, however, found this individual's activities, and his whole demeanor, suspicious. The board member went to the website www.whois.com and looked up the dance company. Guess who owned the dance company's website? That's right, the volunteer. Judging from his reaction when confronted, he never thought anyone from the board would ever think to check. The board had to request that the phone company hosting the website take it down until the matter was settled. The volunteer was paid an undisclosed sum to surrender the rights to the website.

Jump-start the Process!

Implementing a "compliance" project can seem daunting, but that doesn't have to be the case. A fresh perspective can bring life to the planning.

Consider these steps:

1. Board and Senior Management announce that the changes are permanent, there are rewards for compliance, and the plan for putting the Document Preservation policy in place. There's no turning back—and the stakeholders need to understand that. The policy and the plan need to be *user-friendly*. If staff and volunteers are confronted with a document in legalese, there will be a revolt and not compliance.

2. The board and Senior Management need to create a team to design policies that are relevant to the whole organization. Be sure that the team consists of star players representing all of your nonprofit's functions. Membership on this team should be high status and include perks such as assistance in completing their regular work.

3. Build the plan to address what you are already doing (so you don't have to reinvent the wheel), and include those areas of improvement you wanted to acquire. Conduct a *brief* assessment and review—it will be worth the time. Don't engage in "paralysis by analysis"—keep it moving. Emphasize the processes that create efficiency, and ultimately, *less work!*

4. Use the tools that you already have—document the process using technology and ensure that copies of the Document Preservation policy are widely disseminated. Also, consider developing a one-page "shortcut" list to highlight the ways documents should be handled, and preserved, on a daily basis. The faster the staff and volunteers can assimilate the desired behaviors into their daily routine, the faster the plan will solidify.

5. Have an outside expert review the plan and process once it is in place to ensure that it would make sense to a regulator or other stakeholder.

It's important to recognize that the first draft of a compliance plan does not need to be perfect, it just needs to incorporate the important elements. The plan will be refined over time, particularly if regular updates are scheduled into the process.

CONCLUSION

With the growth of technology, nonprofits and businesses have become highly dependent on computers, laptops, cell phones, PDAs, databases, and software applications. IT has emerged as a primary operational building block within nonprofits. Sarbanes-Oxley compliance and best practices are highly dependent on the effective use of technology.

CHAPTER 9

Human Resource Management— Sarbanes-Oxley Requirements and Best Practices

Dr. Bernadine Healy headed the American Red Cross for two years. In her short but stormy tenure, she discovered rampant financial irregularities within the local offices of the organization. She even discovered that a local manager had embezzled $1 million. Her board did not appear to be interested in pursuing these matters, but Senator Charles Grassley (R–Iowa) was. In an angry letter to Martha Evans, the woman who replaced Dr. Healy as Red Cross President, Senator Grassley asserted that the Red Cross board had ignored:

- The embezzlement of $1 million by Hudson County, New Jersey, chapter officials. [Dr. Healy] states that information about this crime "demonstrates that many of the controls presumed by you [the Board] and senior management to be in place are not there."

- Dr. Healy's assertion that the Red Cross is in need of institutional reform: "Compensation information from chapters is voluntarily reported to headquarters. Headquarters does not have direct access to a complete record of this information. Therefore, we cannot assure the accuracy of the Form 990 (annual Return of Organization Exempt from Income Tax) provided to the Internal Revenue Service . . . Other issues that have been festering and are widely known include the lack of accountability of chapters for annual performance; a reluctance of Headquarters to exercise hiring and firing authority over chapter executives; and a tendency of Headquarters to relegate its authority to an advisory role as it relates to chapters. We have limited organization-wide systems to ensure compliance."

Senator Grassley's letter continues by reviewing an August 2001 internal document prepared at Dr. Healy's request, entitled "Emerging Trends in the FY 2001 Operations of Chapters." This report details findings based on 80 audits at Red Cross chapters nationwide to reveal serious financial mismanagement.

The examples he cites are:

- "National disaster contributions are not remitted to national headquarters or are not remitted timely (classified as a 'Critical Issue')."
- "Bank reconciliations are not completed, or not completed timely, reviewed, or tested by someone with no cash-related responsibilities and/or signed and dated by the reviewer (classified as a 'Major Issue')."
- "Endowment moneys are not appropriately maintained, e.g., maintained locally (classified as a 'Critical Issue')."
- "Investments (e.g., stocks, corporate bonds, and collateralized mortgage obligations) are not in compliance with corporate policy (classified as a 'Critical Issue')."
- "Financial reports to the board are not prepared or reviewed regularly and/or do not contain adequate information (e.g., comparison to the budget, a balance sheet, or year-to-date figures), and/or are not accurate (classified as a 'Critical Issue')." (Grassley, August 12, 2002)

Although her work in uncovering what appears to be long-standing corruption within the Red Cross was laudable, she was forced by her board to resign later in 2002 because of the organization's post-September 11th fundraising and blood collection crisis.

CHAPTER OVERVIEW

Two common areas of dysfunction within nonprofit organizations are the management of reports of waste, fraud, or abuse commonly known as "whistle-blowing" and the protocols for reimbursement of travel and other types of expenses. Whistleblower Protection is a SOX requirement while protocols for travel claims and other reimbursement issues is an important best practice. Policies need to be in place to ensure reimbursements are handled in a consistent manner regardless of the status of the staff or volunteer. As we saw in Chapter 4, two of the three crisis scenarios involved CEOs embezzling money from their nonprofits mainly through travel claims and other reimbursements that were either bogus or not related to the nonprofit's business.

CHAPTER OBJECTIVES

By the end of this chapter, you should be able to:

- Discuss the function of a Whistleblower Protection policy and the features that must be included in this policy to be in compliance with SOX.
- Compare the means by which employees are distinct from independent contractors and the regulatory implications.

- Explain why nonprofits need to establish protocols for exit interviews, including turning in electronic devices and ensuring that the hard drives of these devices are properly cleaned.
- Provide examples of protocols for handling travel expenses, credit cards, and other credit accounts.

WHISTLEBLOWER PROTECTION

The first obligation from SOX that applies to all organizations is the requirement for a documented Whistleblower Protection policy. SOX requires all organizations, including nonprofits, to establish a means to collect, retain, and resolve claims regarding accounting, internal accounting controls, and auditing matters. The system must allow for these reports to be submitted anonymously and for the individuals filing the reports to be shielded from retaliation.

If not, policies and procedures should be developed that contain, at the minimum, the following features:

- **There is a confidential means for reporting suspected waste, fraud, and abuse**: Staff and volunteers need to know how to go about filing the report and what types of evidence they should provide to substantiate their claims.
- **There is a process to thoroughly investigate any reports**: Volunteers and staff should also know how investigations are conducted and what will be expected of them in terms of providing a statement or answering questions.
- **There is a process for disseminating the findings from the investigation**: The whistleblower should also know how the findings of the report will be disseminated.
- **The employee filing the complaint will not be subjected to termination, firing, harassment, or miss out on promotion**: This is the most important part of the policy. All staff and volunteers should know what their rights are under the Whistleblower Protection policy.
- **Even if the findings do not support the nature of the complaint, the employee or volunteer who made the complaint will not face any repercussions**: Staff and volunteers also need to understand that if they file a report and the findings don't support their claim, there will not be any repercussions.

Communication is key in ensuring that all employees and volunteers understand why reporting waste, fraud, and abuse is expected, what their rights are, and how investigations are conducted and findings presented. Every employee and volunteer should have a copy of the Whistleblower policy, and it should be readily available for review in hard copy and online. This policy should also be covered in any orientation or training programs the organization offers for its employees and volunteers. The nonprofit's legal counsel should review the wording of the Whistleblower Protection policy and provide advice whenever "whistleblower" reports are filed.

The Nonprofit Times reports that a "survey found only 16 percent of nonprofits have whistleblower policies in place . . . [compared with previous year's survey] that found 21 percent of respondents were considering such policies . . . having a whistleblower protection policy shows an organization's constituents, membership, or funders that it is taking internal control seriously . . . 'Having a policy is important' the Senate Finance Committee staffer said. 'It's even more important to listen to what they're saying and act on it.' The staffer said whistleblowers are an important part of the government's oversight of the sector. 'We benefit mightily,' the staffer said. 'Invariably, we have whistleblowers who talk to us,' regarding nonprofit investigations (Sinclair, 2004).

Exhibit 9.1 will help you develop an effective Whistleblower policy.

EXHIBIT 9.1   WHISTLEBLOWER PROTECTION POLICY WORKSHEET

Your nonprofit needs to have:

- A Whistleblower Protection policy
- A method for reporting waste, fraud, or abuse
- Procedures for conducting investigations
- Protocols for disseminating findings (in conjunction with your legal counsel)

Whistleblower Protection Policy

- The Whistleblower Protection policy is being implemented at [your nonprofit] to comply with the Public Company Accounting Reform and Investor Protection Act of 2002 (Sarbanes-Oxley).
- At [your nonprofit], any staff member or volunteer who reports waste, fraud, or abuse will not be fired or otherwise retaliated against for making the report.
- The report will be investigated, and even if determined not to be waste, fraud, or abuse, the individual making the report will not be retaliated against. There will be no punishment for reporting problems—including firing, demotion, suspension, harassment, failure to consider the employee for promotion, or any other kind of discrimination.

Methods for Reporting Waste, Fraud, or Abuse

There are several ways in which your staff and volunteers can report suspected waste, fraud, or abuse:

- Contact the nonprofit's ombudsman.
- Call the designated hotline that your nonprofit has set up for this purpose.
- Send an e-mail to a designated address that your nonprofit has established for these types of reports.
- Make the report in writing.

Investigating the Report

Your nonprofit would list the steps it would take to:

- Investigate the allegation.
- Disseminate the report on your findings, including providing the person filing a report with a summary of the findings.
- Take steps to deal with the issue addressed, including making operational or personnel changes.
- If warranted, contact law enforcement to deal with any criminal activities.

WHY INDIVIDUALS ARE RELUCTANT TO "BLOW THE WHISTLE" ON WASTE, FRAUD, AND ABUSE

As we saw in the introductory story, whistle-blowing can be a career-limiting gesture. Despite the pervasive financial irregularities that Dr. Healy discovered, she received virtually no support from her board to remedy the situation and hold people accountable. Her story is a highly visible example, but the types of response within nonprofits to whistle-blowing can be more subtle, but just as effective in silencing or discrediting the whistleblower.

Whistleblowers are not universally embraced by management in any organization, private or nonprofit. Often, they are described as "not a team player" or are categorized as troublemakers. Management can use tactics such as rumor and innuendo to make the whistleblower look bad. Other tactics include the silent treatment by supervisors or colleagues, or even changing the location of the person's office or the type of equipment that is assigned to him or her. The organizational displeasure is intended to be obvious to the whistleblower and to everyone else. (Sinclair 2001)

The Whistleblower Protection requirement of SOX is clear about the prohibition against retribution of any kind—even the subtle acts. Having an effective Whistleblower Protection policy is important because of the SOX legal requirements, and to provide a mechanism to protect the nonprofit's integrity and future viability. The crises that are described in Chapter 4 exacted heavy damage on the affected nonprofits. Many people lost their jobs, and the previously good names of the organizations were tarnished by relentless adverse publicity.

CREATING A CONFIDENTIAL REPORTING SYSTEM

Confidentiality is the key in developing a process whereby employees and volunteers feel safe in reporting waste, fraud, and abuse. One way a confidential reporting system can be established is to use an ombudsman. Another way would be to use a third-party reporting system that is not connected to the organization.

Ombudsman

For many years, organizations in Europe and long-term care facilities in the United States have used ombudsmen as a way to provide a safe avenue for employees and clients to report fraud and abuse. In the U.S., a long-term care ombudsman is an advocate for residents of nursing homes, board and care homes, and assisted living facilities. Ombudsmen are trained to resolve problems and can address complaints brought to them. A long-term care ombudsman can be a confidential ear for complaints and concerns, can help resolve complaints and concerns, educate residents about their rights, and help long-term care facilities develop more effective practices. Nonprofit organizations can use the role of the long-term care ombudsman as a guideline for creating their own confidential reporting system. To be effective, an ombudsman is independent of the organization and is someone whose position as ombudsman cannot be terminated for reasons other than failure to perform. Having this type of program in place can go a long way to correct problems as they arise and to meet the SOX requirements.

Third-Party Reporting Systems

Third-party anonymous hotlines are a risk-free way to report unethical or illegal activity. With a third-party anonymous hotline, an employee or volunteer can report questionable activities any time of day or night. The hotlines can handle a variety of reporting issues, such as:

- Accounting irregularities
- Violations of governmental regulations
- Fraud
- Falsification or destruction of organizational records
- Workplace violence
- Substance abuse
- Discrimination
- Sexual harassment
- Conflicts of interest
- Release of proprietary information

Employees and volunteers who feel uncomfortable coming forward via internal reporting processes might feel more comfortable reporting issues via a third-party hotline. Reports filed in an anonymous fashion still obligate the nonprofit to conduct an investigation. However, if the caller does not identify himself or herself and provides only sketchy details, the investigation may be hampered.

Conducting an Investigation

Once a staff member or volunteer has reported waste, fraud, and abuse, it is of paramount importance to conduct an investigation that is balanced and designed to get to the bottom of the problem reported. How the report is handled and the way in which everyone involved is treated can be the difference between a professional approach and a further invitation to disagreement.

Before a complaint is even lodged, the nonprofit should have an established protocol for conducting an investigation. When an individual makes a report, he or she should be advised on how the investigation will be conducted, how confidential information will be handled, and how the findings will be disseminated. The individual making the complaint should also be reminded of his or her rights under the Whistleblower Protection policy and should be assured that the nonprofit takes these protections seriously.

An individual should be appointed to handle the investigation who has been trained in how to conduct an investigation and deal with conflict management. The individual conducting the investigation should also present:

- **An unbiased attitude toward the individuals involved**: It is important that the individual conducting the investigation is not a superior or a subordinate of any of the individuals involved. If the nonprofit is so small that this would be impossible, a board member should be enlisted to conduct the investigation.

- **Impartial approach that puts the best interest of the nonprofit first**: The individual conducting the investigation should not have any real or potential conflicts of interest in the outcome of the investigation.

- **The individual's workload and other obligations should be such that he or she can devote sufficient time to conduct the investigation**: This is an important aspect of a successful investigation. If the staff member or board member is swamped with other work, his or her commitment to an impartial investigation will suffer (Kastl, Avitabile, Kleiner, 2005).

The structure of the investigation should emphasize gathering of facts and interviews with the parties involved. The interviews should facilitate the presentation of facts, but can also be opportunities to determine the variety of perceptions and viewpoints. The interviewer should also be aware of the clues given by body language and verbal cues.

As the facts are gathered and individuals interviewed, the individual conducting the investigation must make a recommendation to the nonprofit's management. Decisions about action or discipline need to be consistent with organizational policy and applicable law. The findings should be communicated to the involved parties, taking into consideration privacy issues. If an individual is disciplined, the person filing the complaint should not be privy to the specifics, but should be told the matter has been resolved. As with any personnel issue, consultation with the nonprofit's legal counsel is essential in crafting the presentation of the findings.

TRAVEL CLAIMS AND REIMBURSEMENT POLICIES

One of the most problematic areas in terms of financial internal controls is that of protocols for reimbursement of travel expenses. Reimbursement issues are among the most common sources of fraud and financial misappropriation evident in the crisis scenarios reviewed in Chapter 4.

The Independent Sector's Report to Congress presents the following recommendations for the IRS and for nonprofits on travel expenses policies:

The Internal Revenue Service should:

- Require charitable organizations to disclose on their annual information returns (Forms 990 or 990-PF) whether or not they have a travel policy.

- Provide specific information in the instructions to the Forms 990 and 990-PF regarding travel costs that are not permitted or that should be reported as taxable income (including reference to IRS Publication 463: *Travel, Entertainment, Gift and Car Expenses*).

Recommendations for Charitable Organization Action:

- Charitable organizations that pay for or reimburse travel expenses of board members, officers, employees, consultants, volunteers, or others traveling to conduct the business of the organization should establish and implement policies that provide clear guidance on their travel rules, including the types of expenses that can be reimbursed and the documentation required to receive reimbursement. Such policies should require that travel on behalf of the charitable organization is to be undertaken in a cost-effective manner. The travel policy should be provided to and adhered to by anyone traveling on behalf of the organization.

- Charitable organizations should not pay for nor reimburse travel expenditures (not including de minimis expenses of those attending an activity such as a meal function of the organization) for spouses, dependents, or others who are accompanying individuals conducting business for the organization unless they, too, are conducting business for the organization.

The Independent Sector Report also includes these points on travel policies:

- The same standards for reimbursement of travel expenditures should be applied to the organization's board members, officers, staff, consultants, volunteers, and others traveling on behalf of the organization. Decisions on travel expenditures should be based on how to best further the organization's charitable purposes, rather than on the title or position of the person traveling. (Independent Sector, Report to Congress and the Nonprofit Sector, 2005)

Crafting a Travel Expenses Policy

Nonprofits can look to the Independent Sector's full report for guidance on the crafting of an effective Travel Expenses policy. Important components of a Travel Expenses policy include:

- **Who is covered by the policy and who is *not* eligible**: The Travel Expenses policy should apply to all board, staff, and volunteers who are obligated to travel for business purposes. The authorization to travel needs to be documented and approved. In other words, the ED's travel should be reviewed and approved by either the Board Chair or another member of the Executive Committee. Travel by members of the board should also be approved by the Executive Committee. The policy should clearly specify that spouses, dependents, or others who are accompanying individuals conducting business for the nonprofit are not covered unless they are conducting business for the nonprofit too (Independent Sector, 2005).

- **The types of expenses that are reimbursable**: The nonprofit needs to clearly identify the types of expenses that are covered and the types of expenses that are not covered. Some nonprofits will reimburse for the cost of an entire meal, others will not reimburse for any alcohol that is purchased as part of the meal. If this is the case with your nonprofit, it needs to be clearly stated, and the documentation (i.e., restaurant receipt) must be required to show that the request for reimbursement is for food only.

- Similarly, the policy on reimbursement for travel to and from the airport or train station must be clearly stated, as well as the policy on payment for parking fees. If these expenses are not eligible for reimbursement, the policy must be specific.

- **Protocols for submitting a travel claim including the required documentation**: Although the exhortation to require documentation as part of a travel claim may appear to be rudimentary, the escapades of two Executive Directors in Chapter 4 will provide ample evidence that not everyone is paying attention. The real issue is how regimented this obligation will be in your nonprofit. It *should be* an absolute requirement for everyone—no exceptions. Rank does not have any privileges in this area.

Exhibit 9.2 will help you to develop an effective travel claim policy.

Training on Protocols for Submitting Travel Claims

If protocols for travel claims are a new venture within your nonprofit, it is important to offer training and user-friendly resources for staff/volunteers and board members to use. The training can either be in person or online and should include a discussion of why travel claims protocols are being standardized and how to submit a travel claim. Be sure to include examples of forms and how various types of travel claims are documented. It is particularly important for those individuals who must review and approve the travel claims for payment to understand that incorrectly completed forms, or forms lacking proper documentation, *must* be returned to the individual with a clear explanation on what modifications are necessary. Standardization is the key—no one should be permitted to receive payment for claims that are improperly prepared.

EXHIBIT 9.2   TRAVEL CLAIMS POLICY CHECKLIST

- Travel claims are submitted on a specific form designed by the nonprofit. The form needs to capture the name of the staff/volunteer/board member, dates traveled, purpose of travel, listing of expenses and documentation attached (original documentation should be required).

- The travel claim indicates the purpose of the trip, who authorized the travel, and a copy of the documentation.

- If the travel claim includes reimbursement for meals, the purpose of the meal and the names of the guests are included. For example, if the meal was a business lunch as part of attending a conference, the receipt for the meal needs to be included, and any guests or clients should be listed.

- If parking or transportation to the airport is an authorized expenditure, the travel claim also needs to have either a receipt for parking or a mileage listing.

- The nonprofit should specify the time frame when a travel claim needs to be filed; for example, within ten (10) business days of returning to the office.

- The travel expense policy includes a list of authorized expenditures. Any expenditures that are not included as authorized expenditures on the list must be approved by the CFO or Treasurer before they can be reimbursed.

- Travel claims will not be paid unless the form is completed correctly and there is supporting documentation for all expenses.

- The executive team and/or the board's executive committee will make random and unannounced examinations of travel claims within a specific time frame to ensure compliance.

EMPLOYEES OR INDEPENDENT CONTRACTORS? WHY THE IRS WANTS TO KNOW

An important but thorny issue in nonprofits is the accurate classification of paid staff. If a paid staff person is classified as an independent contractor, the nonprofit is not liable for payroll taxes, workers compensation, or unemployment insurance. If your non-profit is found to be improperly classifying employees as independent contractors, the IRS can exact sanctions against your organization in the form of unpaid employment taxes and insurance—and, of course, stiff penalties.

In this era of heightened IRS scrutiny, it is important for nonprofits to classify their paid staff correctly. Exhibit 9.3 details which factors the IRS considers in determining whether the paid staff is an employee or independent contractor.

PROTECTING THE PRIVACY OF STAFF AND VOLUNTEERS

When a nonprofit hires an individual as an employee or permits an individual to volunteer, the organization requires that the individual provide certain types of personal information. Employees are generally required to provide sensitive information such as

Factor	Employee	Independent Contractor
Supervision	The worker must follow specific instructions on where, when, and how to perform the work.	The worker must produce a specified result, but is permitted to work at another location.
Schedule	Worker works full-time for one employer.	The worker works for more than one employer.
Workday	Employer defines how long the worker works per day.	The worker sets his or her own hours unless otherwise specified by engagement contract.
Location of work	Worker works exclusively on employer's premises.	Worker completes tasks at locations of his or her choice.
Assistants	Employer assigns assistants to worker.	Worker hires and supervises his or her own assistants.

(Allbusiness.com: The Advisor, 2005)

their social security number, names and contact information for next of kin or other family members, and possibly document numbers that reflect a particular immigration status.

Privacy issues have become more complex because of the proliferation of cell phones, PDAs, laptops, and other electronics. Additionally, Internet access and e-mail have also contributed to privacy infringement. Although privacy concerns apply to other areas within the nonprofit such as client services and fundraising, the Human Resources division is responsible for maintaining the privacy and security of personnel records of staff and volunteers.

Privacy and Document Preservation: Access to HR Records

Human Resources' document preservation guidelines need to ensure that steps are taken to protect confidential records and sensitive information. Because today's personnel records are most likely kept on databases, it is important to work collaboratively with the nonprofit's IT division to ensure that access to sensitive information is restricted. Individuals who have access to these records should be carefully screened, including background and credit checks, and should be closely supervised.

Identity theft is one of the fastest growing crimes in the United States. The Federal Trade Commission estimates that over 10 million Americans have become the victims of identity theft, and the FDIC reports that the collective impact on the financial sector of the economy was over $50 billion in 2003.

Identity Theft

In today's world of identity theft, databases and electronic files can be fertile sources of information for thieves. The problem is that the identity thieves can be located in the same workplace as the victims. How easy does your nonprofit make it for identity theft?

Personnel files should be treated as highly confidential, particularly if these files are stored electronically. All databases should be password-protected, and protocols should be in place to ensure that staff do not leave their workstations with a confidential file on the screen. Similarly, if personnel files are in paper files, these files should never be permitted to be left unattended on a desk or in an unlocked file cabinet. Salary spreadsheets, benefits documents, and the like need to be similarly secured.

Trashcans and recycle bins are goldmines to identity thieves. The HR department should invest in several sturdy shredders. All paper that is disposed from this department should first be shredded. The trashcan is for waste other than paper.

Knowledge is power! Talk to staff and volunteers about how to protect themselves from identity theft and how to routinely check their credit card invoices and credit reports for evidence of improper charges or the creation of new accounts. The more that staff and volunteers are informed, the better they will understand and comply with the precautions your nonprofit has implemented.

Electronics and Privacy

The use of laptops, PDAs, cell phones, pagers, and other electronic devices is so widespread that almost no one notices anymore. The difficulty is that employers sometimes forget that these devices have been issued to staff. When a staff member or volunteer resigns, the exit interview does not always include procedures such as turning in electronic devices. Even if these devices are returned, they can be recycled to new staff without first taking the proper precautions to ensure that the hard drives of these devices are properly cleaned. Laptops aren't the only electronic devices with hard drives. PDAs have hard drives, and cell phones have memories. If your nonprofit chooses to recycle these devices to new staff, it is imperative that IT cleanses the hard drive to ensure that any confidential material is permanently deleted.

CONCLUSION

Whistleblower protection is essential to maintaining the nonprofit's integrity. Staff and volunteers need to know that they will be safe when reporting waste, fraud, or abuse. Opportunities for fraud, such as the misuse of travel and reimbursement claims and identity theft, need to be dramatically reduced if not eliminated. The longer these problems fester or are covered up, the greater the damage from the fallout of the inevitable crisis. Sarbanes-Oxley requirements and best practices can serve to make your nonprofit's HR function more secure and more productive.

CHAPTER 10

SOX Best Practices
and Fundraising

The AIDS support organization was a shadow of itself following one of the most damaging scandals the community had ever seen. The organization, which became one of the oldest AIDS service providers in the country, grew rapidly in the early 1980s from its roots as a volunteer-based support service for terminally ill people. As the AIDS pandemic hit San Francisco, the nonprofit began to focus its energies on serving people who were living with AIDS. At the time, this was a pioneering effort, as AIDS was a highly feared and misunderstood disease. The nonprofit grew rapidly in size, stature, and revenues. Volunteers flocked to help, donations poured in, and Ryan White funds were awarded to support its endeavors. The organization entered into a contract with the city/county government to manage residences for people with HIV/AIDS.

In addition to the funds, volunteers, and contracts, the organization also attracted charlatans on the board and on the management team. The board turned a blind eye to financial reports that failed to track statistics and produce reports in a manner that was required by the city/county government. One day, an internal whistleblower went to the city/county to report that funds were being commingled and misused. In the subsequent scandal, the nonprofit lost the contract, and saw donations fall from $1 million per year to $10,000. It took eight years and four Executive Directors before the nonprofit was able to regain its good name.

CHAPTER OVERVIEW

Fundraising is often the primary method of revenue generation for nonprofit organizations. Aside from this important aspect of revenue generation, fundraising is an integral part of the nonprofit's "face" in the community, a fragile aspect of the nonprofit's public trust. The nonprofit exists because it has taken the steps necessary to obtain a 501(c)(3) designation from the IRS, and has filed the necessary paperwork with its state government. What keeps a nonprofit a viable entity is the continued trust the public has in the good work and integrity of the organization. When that trust is broken, it may take years to repair. The introductory story is an all too common illustration of a nonprofit that has found an important niche, grown quickly, and in the process, almost destroyed itself.

CHAPTER OBJECTIVES

By the end of this chapter, you should be able to:

- Discuss the changing federal and state legislative environment and its impact on fundraising practices.
- Describe the role of the board and Executive Team in providing oversight and guidance to a nonprofit's fundraising.
- Explain how internal controls are essential in combating fraud in nonprofit fundraising.
- Identify red flags for fundraising fraud, and methods for ensuring the security of donor records and other confidential information.

THE CHANGING LEGISLATIVE ENVIRONMENT'S IMPACT ON FUNDRAISING PRACTICES

Although the features of the Sarbanes-Oxley legislation may on the surface appear to have more impact on the private sector, the public sector (i.e., government) push for greater accountability includes the independent sector; in other words, the nonprofit world as well. This section presents the summary of findings of the United States Senate Finance Committee June 2004 and April 2005 hearings on Charitable Giving Problems and Best Practices, along with the highlights of recent California "Sarbanes-Oxley clone" legislation (SB 1262) signed into law on September 29, 2004. The common theme of the testimony of witnesses, the Congressional staff papers, and the California "Nonprofit Integrity Act" (SB 1262) is that nonprofit organizations have, through fiscal and governance abuses, *particularly as these relate to fundraising*, diminished public trust. Public outcry for reform served as the catalyst for these Congressional hearings on nonprofit abuses.

Fundraising and the U.S. Senate Hearings on Nonprofit Accountability

As discussed in Chapter 2, Senator Charles Grassley (R–Iowa) held hearings on nonprofit accountability in June of 2004 and April 2005. Senator Grassley had long been a champion of nonprofit transparency, particularly as this relates to ensuring that donor funds are appropriately spent. The June 2004 hearings featured confidential witnesses, one of whom was "Mr. Car," who testified about the abuses that are rampant in car donations. In the April 2005 hearings, Senator Grassley invited Art Taylor, president and CEO of the Better Business Bureau's Wise Giving Alliance, to testify about a donor expectations survey the Alliance had recently conducted.

Summary of Mr. Car's Testimony before the U.S. Senate Finance Committee—June 2004

"Mr. Car" is the pseudonym of a confidential witness testifying at the 2004 Grassley hearing on nonprofit accountability. This witness had firsthand knowledge of the methods used by fundraising vendors who specialize in managing automobile donations for nonprofits. In his testimony, he outlines in great detail the process for car donations. The following summary describes several processes used in these transactions.

The Process of Auto Donation Using a "Broker"

- Potential donors see an advertisement in their local newspaper proposing fair market value as a tax deduction. The donors are usually are looking at donating an older vehicle they do not use, but in some cases the cars are nearly new.

- Donors call a toll-free number, at which point either the charity will answer the call or the call is forwarded to a third-party broker. The potential donor provides a description of the vehicle to the broker, year, make, and model. The broker will verify if the vehicle has a clean title. The broker will then tell the donor to refer to *Kelly Blue Book* to determine the amount of his or her tax deduction.

- Next, the broker will tell the donor that a local towing company will pick up the car in five to ten working days. In most cases, the towing company is owned by either an auto auction or used car dealer.

- After the car is picked up, it goes to auction. The standard commission for the auto auction house is 25% of the sale price of the vehicle. If the car goes to a used car dealer, there is usually flat rate pricing. Flat rate pricing will typically be $75 a car and $125 for trucks. These are the rates for cars produced between 1985 and today. In addition, the broker at the beginning gets a sliding scale reimbursement between 30% and 45% of the check value he or she receives for performing the following duties: advertising, operating the toll-free hotline, title work, and assigning auctions to pick up the cars. Check value is *not* what the car sold for. For example, if a car sells at auction for $1,000, the auto auction receives 25%, or $250. The broker will receive 30%–45% of the $750 remaining. However, the auto auction double dips by charging a buyer's fee to the purchaser and will thus make close to $350. However, this unfortunately is the best-case scenario.

The Process of Auto Donation Using Flat Rate Sales

Flat rate sales are the way for insiders to cheat the charities. Again, these are cases that I know firsthand. We received a vehicle donation for a charity of a 1999 Ford Contour. We received a fax for the pickup order and it was a $75 unit. This meant that the car was already assigned to be sold at the used car lot and, regardless of sale price, the most the broker would get is $75, and the charity would only get a percentage of that; for example, $30–$40. The car actually sold for $3,500. Thus, the intermediaries got well over $3,000 profit and the charity received pennies. This is common industry practice across the board and is known as "flat rate sales" fees.

The Process of Auto Donation Using "Fixing Cars"

Another example of an even more terrible practice is what is known as "fixing cars." Involves intermediaries purposely disabling vehicles that were prescreened as running vehicles—and therefore worth more—so when the vehicle arrives at the auto auction or used car dealership, they can call the broker and inform them the car was misrepresented, and the broker 99% of the time does not contact the donor to reconfirm the vehicle's condition. Again, "fixing cars" is a common practice in the industry. For example, a 1996 Ford Crown Victoria was picked up in running condition. However, two days prior to auction, the vehicle was disabled by turning the distributor cap to offset the timing. In this case, the auto auction disabled the vehicle and then sold it to them through their used car license. That car, the Ford Crown, went for $275 dollars, and it was then after the auction that the insiders took a timing light to reset the distributor and drove the car away. The intermediaries later sold the car for probably about $3,700. Another technique is to simply pull out the fuse block or blow the fuse and then put it back in after they've purchased the car themselves for less than its actual value. This, again, is very common. In fact, I personally was approached by a couple who donated their vehicle because their son died. They wanted to donate their vehicle to the charity to try and make a difference. The car was sold at auction for $4,200. Once all the percentages were taken out that charity received less than $300. There has to be something that can be done about this. So many people out there donate their cars to make a difference for research, treatment, and transplants. However, the truth is, there wouldn't be enough money from that car donation to buy my mother's medication for one month, let alone help the progress of research and treatment.

The following exchange took place following "Mr. Car's" testimony:

Senator Grassley: Mr. Car, why are charities getting pennies on the dollar for the cars that are donated?

Mr. Car. Because the charities are not paying attention to what options they are using to get the highest market value for the vehicle, and they are overlooking the flat sale fee of $75 and $125 that I mentioned earlier. They are basically not minding the store. If they did, the charities would see the cars going for much more money than they are.

Senator Grassley: Ms. MacNab . . . (Ms. J. J. MacNab of Insurance Barometer LLC) I would ask your views on why these abuses are happening, why charities are willing to participate, and, finally, your thoughts and views on how widespread is the trend of abuses involving charities.

Ms. MacNab: I see it happening right now because regulatory supervision is almost nonexistent. Whereas, in the financial world, you have State and Federal agencies fighting a turf war over who gets to take care of the bad guys, when it comes to charities, it is kind of a reverse turf war. Everybody assumes that someone else will handle it. Even though there are several agencies that can take over the regulatory spanking, no one is stepping up to the plate. Also, audits are nonexistent. If you talk to a handful of charities, no one can remember the last time anybody lost their tax-exempt status. If you are going to have a voluntary compliance system, there has to be some expectation that you can get caught if you do something wrong.

The second thing that is going on, why charities are participating in these plans, is right now charities are having a couple of hard years. Fundraising is down, corporate donations are down. They have lost money on their own portfolios in the market, and they are looking for money anywhere they can get it. (Senate Finance Committee Hearings, June 2004)

Better Business Bureau Wise Giving Alliance Testimony

Similarly, evidence of donor apprehension is seen in the testimony by BBB of America—Art Taylor, president and CEO of the BBB Wise Giving Alliance. In 2001, the Alliance commissioned Princeton Survey Research Associates International to conduct a major donor expectations survey, the results of which are available on the www.give.org website.

Among the key findings of the Wise Giving Alliance survey were:

- 70% of respondents say it is difficult to know whether a charity is legitimate.

- 44% say it is difficult to find the information they want in making a giving decision.

- 50% say they would be "very likely" to get information they wanted from the charity itself, although only 50% think the charities provide enough information about their activities to help them decide about giving.

- Donors are not sure what information they need or where they should get it, or in some cases, how to assess the information they have. They are looking for help in finding accountable charities.

- The Alliance produces reports on national charities that specify whether an organization meets or does not meet the Standards for Charity Accountability.

- Our reports do not rank or grade charities, but rather seek to assist donors in making informed judgments about charities soliciting their support.

- In addition, the Alliance goes beyond standards to issue special alerts and advisories for individuals on topics related to giving. These include tips on donating cars, as well as tips on charity telemarketing, police and firefighter appeals, and charitable responses to disasters.

Testimony of Brian Gallagher—CEO of United Way of America

Other testimony on fundraising and nonprofit accountability at the 2005 Grassley hearings included comments from Brian Gallagher, CEO of the United Way of America. Mr. Gallagher commented [that]:

> The number one reason that people don't have faith or trust in the nonprofit sector is that donors don't know how charities spend their money. It's overwhelming—71% of respondents that don't trust charities said that their trust in nonprofits would be greater if they knew how the money was spent.
>
> To address that concern, I respectfully suggest that nonprofit organizations be asked to report concrete results annually that are tied directly to their missions, not just the level of activity. Perhaps a results section such as that can be added to the annual Form 990. We should be asked to report concrete results that are tied directly to our missions, not just the level of activity we produce. When you're asking people to contribute, you're asking for an investment in your mission. And like a for-profit business, you are then accountable to your investors, not just for keeping good books, but for creating value and offering a concrete return (Gallagher, 2005).

The Grassley hearings in 2004 and 2005 continue to emphasize that the board is now held ultimately accountable for the actions of the nonprofit staff. This means that the board must provide active oversight to development and fundraising efforts. This expectation is further codified in California's Nonprofit Integrity Act (SB 1262), which obligates the board to review all contracts with fundraising vendors. The testimony from "Mr. Car" at the 2004 Grassley hearings was particularly chilling in terms of how little nonprofits actually received from these endeavors.

EXAMPLE OF STATE LAW RELATIVE TO FUNDRAISING: PROVISIONS OF CALIFORNIA'S SB 1262 NONPROFIT INTEGRITY ACT TO FUNDRAISING ACTIVITIES

The California Nonprofit Integrity Act (SB 1262) is the first of what might be many other Sarbanes-Oxley "clone" laws dealing with nonprofits. As other states adopt these types of "clone" laws, the topic of fundraising will surely be a common theme. As was codified in the new California law on nonprofit integrity, the board has an obligation to ensure that fundraising activities are conducted with integrity, with attention to donor privacy. Further, the board has an obligation to perform due diligence before signing contracts with third-party fundraising vendors. The California law also placed the burden of closer supervision of all fundraising activities on the shoulders of the nonprofit (i.e., the board). Of particular note should be the provision in the law *that the Act applies to all corporations formed under the laws of other states that do business in California or hold property in California. By "doing business," this includes soliciting donations in California by mail, by advertisements in publications, or by any other means from outside California." (Cal-*

ifornia Dept. of Justice webpage.) This means that if a nonprofit is domiciled outside of California, yet solicits donations in California, the provisions of the Nonprofit Integrity Act of 2004 apply to that charity.

The activities targeted by the California law were fundraising practices that involved coercion or undue influence. Under this new law, nonprofits would be held accountable for the fundraising abuses of their vendors. This provision presents similar themes to the testimony of witnesses at the Senate Finance Committee hearings in June 2004 and April 2005.

THE ROLE OF THE BOARD AND EXECUTIVE TEAM IN PROVIDING OVERSIGHT AND GUIDANCE TO A NONPROFIT'S FUNDRAISING

Establishing the "tone at the top" is essential in ensuring that development and fundraising practices are consistent with federal and state laws. As we have seen in the discussion points on the Grassley hearings, speaker after speaker described the types of abuses that stem from inadequate oversight from the board and a management team that is asleep at the wheel—or at least takes a benign neglect approach. Essential in setting the tone is the connection between the nonprofit's mission, vision, and fundraising objectives. The testimony at the Grassley hearings in 2004 and 2005 carried a common theme that a primary factor in fiscal mismanagement is that nonprofits are pressured to chase after money. The failure of the nonprofit's board and Executive Team to genuinely connect the mission/vision with the fundraising objectives often results in a development department that chases after money from whatever source— and seeks to have the board/executives rubber-stamp whatever needs to be done to secure funding. Before long, the mission and vision are twisted to suit the requirements of the funder.

Establishing Fundraising Policies and Ethical Standards

The board and Executive Team, in conjunction with the Development Director, need to establish a framework for fundraising policies and ethical standards. These policies and standards need to be simple, clear, and most importantly, promulgated throughout the entire organization—volunteers, too. Everyone in the nonprofit needs to know what activities are appropriate for fundraising, what types of activities are not appropriate, and the ethical standards from which fundraising plans will be developed. The issues addressed in ethical standards can include behavioral norms such as keeping donor information confidential, interaction with donors, and conflict of interest.

Fundraising needs to be done in an organized, coherent fashion. The board, Executive Team, and the Development Director need to design a plan that is appropriate for the needs of the nonprofit, is achievable, and is approved by the board. Essential to building an annual fundraising plan is the design of its framework, the goals, objectives, and strategies that will carry the plan to fruition.

Communication strategies are an essential element of the fundraising policies and ethical considerations, and should be crafted with two general constituencies in mind. The first constituency is the nonprofit itself. Everyone in the nonprofit should understand why fundraising projects are being conducted, particularly if there are special projects or activities. Everyone in the nonprofit should understand why the nonprofit is committed to conducting its fundraising in an ethical manner—and what each staff member or volunteer's role is in ensuring ethical fundraising.

The public, including all donors, should have access to information about the nonprofit and its programs. The nonprofit needs to scrupulously ensure that all materials and statements honestly represent the nonprofit and the purpose of the donation/solicitation. This means that any and all financial information is accurate, particularly if the solicitation is being made in person.

The Chair of the Development Committee of a large nonprofit was asked to call upon a major donor. In preparation for the meeting, the board member asked for financial information relating to what percentage of every donated dollar went to programs versus administration. Because the nonprofit was between Executive Directors, the Board Chair provided this information along with other financial reports. Shortly after the meeting, the organization's new Executive Director was hired. At the Executive Director's first board meeting, he announced that he had begun a comprehensive review of the financials only to find that virtually all of the financial information was inaccurate—including the information on the ratio of funding for programs versus funding for administration! The Chair of the Development Committee was livid, and the major donor gave his money to another charity.

Exhibit 10.1 describes ten red flags that signal possible fundraising fraud.

BEST PRACTICES AND INDUSTRY STANDARDS FOR FUNDRAISING AND DEVELOPMENT

Example of Industry Standards—BBB Wise Giving Alliance

The BBB Wise Giving Alliance was formed in 2001 with the merger of the National Charities Information Bureau and the Council of Better Business Bureaus Foundation and its Philanthropic Advisory Service. The BBB Wise Giving Alliance is a 501(c)(3) charitable organization, affiliated with the Council of Better Business Bureaus. The overarching principle of the BBB Wise Giving Alliance *Standards for Charity Accountability* is full disclosure to donors and potential donors at the time of solicitation and thereafter. However, where indicated, the standards recommend ethical practices beyond the act of disclosure to ensure public confidence and encourage giving. The standards address a wide range of issues, but standards 15–18 are focused on ensuring that a charity's representations to the public are accurate and complete. (BBB Wise Giving Alliance)

EXHIBIT 10.1   RED FLAGS FOR FUNDRAISING FRAUD

Fundraising Administration

- Donations received for a designated project or program are commingled with the nonprofit's general funds.
- Donations are not appropriately entered into financial records in a timely fashion.
- Donations of cash and checks are not in locked storage.
- No accurate accounting of the amount of donations or if the donations are restricted.
- Restricted donations used for purposes other than what was designated.
- Expenses incurred for specific fundraising campaigns are not tracked against the revenues from the campaigns.
- Staff and volunteers have access to petty cash and/or are not required to adhere to specific reimbursement protocols.

During Fundraising Events:

- Lockboxes are not counted on a regular basis, nor are the contents moved to a secure location daily.
- No oversight of the handling of cash or other valuables.
- For weekend events, cash receipts or checks are taken offsite and stored in the home of a staff member or volunteer.
- Large amounts of cash and/or checks are stored in the nonprofit's office following a fundraiser.
- Staff and volunteers assigned to handle money at fundraising events are not screened, trained, or supervised.
- There are no protocols for receiving and/or acknowledging donations during a fundraising event.

Listed here is a summary of BBB Wise Giving Alliance Standards 15–18:

- Design and distribute solicitations and informational materials that are accurate, truthful, and not misleading.

- A charity should also be able to appropriately document the timing and nature of its expenditures in a manner consistent with the charity's solicitations.

- The charity must provide samples of its solicitations and informational materials, including direct mail appeals, telephone appeals, invitations to fundraising events, print advertisements (newspapers, magazines, etc), scripts of television and radio appeals, grant proposals, and Internet appeals.

- If the charity's appeals state or imply that donations will be used during a certain time period (e.g., immediate disaster response) and/or for a specified purpose (e.g., to assist disaster victims), the charity should be able to substantiate that it has followed through on these commitments.

- The charity needs to clearly describe the program activities and/or problem that will benefit from donations. If the appeal describes a problem (e.g., a recent disaster or missing children) without a description of how the charity plans to address it, the charity does not meet this standard.

- Charities are expected to produce an annual report available to all, on request, that includes at least the following:
  - The organization's mission statement.
  - A summary of the past year's program service accomplishments.
  - A roster of the officers and members of the board of directors.
  - Financial information that includes (i) total income in the past fiscal year, (ii) expenses in the same program, fundraising and administrative categories as in the financial statements, and (iii) ending net assets.
- The roster of the board of directors that appears in the annual report should identify the officers of the organization (i.e., chair, treasurer, and secretary).
- Include on any charity websites that solicit contributions, the same information that is recommended for annual reports, as well as the mailing address of the charity and electronic access to its most recent IRS Form 990.
- Donors should be provided with a means (e.g., such as a check-off box) for both new and continuing donors to inform the charity if they do not want their name and address shared outside the organization.
- Donors should also have easy access to the charity's privacy policy. The policy should include information on:
  - What information, if any, is being collected about them by the charity and how this information will be used.
  - How to contact the charity to review personal information collected and request corrections.
  - How to inform the charity (e.g., a check-off box) that the visitor does not wish his or her personal information to be shared outside the organization.
  - What security measures the charity has in place to protect personal information. (BBB Wise Giving Alliance webpage)

These standards can serve as a framework for developing effective internal controls for fundraising and development. As your nonprofit begins to adopt SOX best practices, it is important to consider adopting "industry" standards that are recommended by respected organizations such as the Better Business Bureau.

INTERNAL CONTROLS AND ETHICAL CONSIDERATIONS FOR FUNDRAISING

Ethics and internal controls go hand in hand. Grassroots organizations often tend to deemphasize organizational infrastructure and the need for instituting good internal controls because their entire focus is on programs or fundraising. Some have even reached the point where fundraising is the most important venture, as the organization is living hand to mouth. Frequently, the boards of these organizations are donors or members of the community who have been associated for decades with the organization. A stunning example of such a quandary comes in the form of a financial scandal at a West Coast police watchdog group. Published reports indicated that independent auditors determined that $500,000 was unaccounted for primarily through "poor bookkeeping, administrative failure or theft . . ." At the heart of the financial irregularities was the practice of making questionable loans to employees and board members, including the board treasurer. Virtually none of these loans was repaid. The newspaper account indicated that making loans of this type was a longtime practice. In defense of this loan practice, the ousted Executive Director claimed, "In organizations that work with poverty, there is often the need to take these types of emergency measures." Clearly, there is no justification for loans to employees or board members under any circumstances. Using the spurious claim that his organization was "working with poverty," the former ED insinuates that a "poverty mentality" is justification for subverting donor funds (Johnson, 2004).

An effective review of internal controls begins with a critical review of the way in which fundraising is conducted in your nonprofit. Documents related to donor files and donor history—document retention, storage, and security—are important SOX best practices. Access to donor records should be carefully considered. All employees and volunteers who have access to donor records need to be briefed on security and confidentiality issues. Strict guidelines need to be enforced to ensure donor privacy and ensure that sensitive information is not compromised.

Donor privacy is one of the most important elements of the development and fundraising function. Documents related to donor privacy include correspondence to and from donors, and documents such as those providing or declining authorization to use the donor's name. Mailing lists are also confidential and should have limited access. Exhibit 10.2 provides materials that will be helpful to develop policies and procedures to protect your donors' privacy.

Does your nonprofit have contracts with vendors such as telemarketing vendors, or vendors who process donated vehicles? If so, then review the contract and other materials to ensure that your nonprofit has conducted a due diligence review of the vendor. If your nonprofit is in California, you will need to ensure that the vendor is properly registered with the State.

The Review of Internal Controls Should Determine If the Following Protocols Are in Place

Internal controls are not only a measure used to combat waste, fraud, and abuse, but also a method for implementing SOX best practices and ensuring that the nonprofit's activities meet today's exacting standards of transparency and accountability. Are these protocols present in your nonprofit's fundraising?

- Donor databases should include information on the amount of the gift, the date of the gift, and any restrictions. Donor information should be limited to names, address, phone numbers, and other information that is necessary and sufficient. Asking donors for information such as driver's license number, social security numbers, and dates of birth is inappropriate.

EXHIBIT 10.2   DONOR PRIVACY CHECKLIST

Do your donors know . . .

- They have the right to "opt out" of future mailings and phone calls?
- How to indicate that they do not want to receive mailings (paper or e-mail) and phone calls?
- That they must give your nonprofit permission to list their name in a brochure, program, or other material?
- That your nonprofit might sell their donor information to another nonprofit or a vendor?
- That they are under no obligation to give your nonprofit any information it requests?
- That your nonprofit has a Donor Privacy Statement that is available for their review?

Donor Privacy Statement—Talking Points

- Your nonprofit is committed to maintaining donor privacy. To that end, donors to your nonprofit should expect:
  - That their information will be held in the strictest confidence. *If your nonprofit plans to sell donor information, you must disclose this to potential donors.* If you don't want them to know, don't sell their information!
  - That they will be given information regarding "opt out" features. Donors will be able to "opt out" of paper mailings, e-mails, telephone calls, or other types of solicitations.
  - That they can opt to have their names and information not listed in a brochure, program, or other material.
  - That they are under no obligation to provide information such as telephone numbers, addresses, and names of family members.
  - Your nonprofit will not ask for sensitive information such as social security numbers or driver's license numbers.
  - That information such as credit card numbers is stored and encrypted to ensure security. If any breech of security takes place, your nonprofit should commit to advising donors in a timely fashion.

- Donor files should be secured at all times. Electronic databases need to be password protected. Only authorized individuals should have access to donor files. Staff who have access to donor databases should be required to follow special protocols, such as closing donor files before leaving a workstation.

- Donor files and databases should be backed up on a daily basis. The backup should ideally be uploaded to a secure website, or taken to a secure off-site location for safekeeping.

- All staff associated with development or fundraising should be screened and trained to ensure that donor privacy is maintained.

- Fundraising vendors should be carefully investigated to ensure that your nonprofit's interests are preserved, and that your nonprofit receives the percentage of the proceeds specified in the contract.

- Develop a comprehensive and understandable Donor Privacy policy. Donors have the right to know if your nonprofit is selling your donor lists. If you don't' want to disclose this, you shouldn't be selling the list! Donors should be asked to give permission to print their names on your nonprofit's materials and should be offered the option to "opt out" of mailings, telephone solicitations, and e-mails.

- There should be internal controls to ensure that donors are promptly thanked for their donations and are provided with documentation of the donation for tax purposes.

- The fundraising department in any nonprofit needs to meticulously adhere to the nonprofit's document preservation policy. The donor database is an essential element within this collection of documents, along with solicitation letters to major donors, contracts with vendors, specific e-mail messages to donors, particularly as these relate to specific gifts, and other essential correspondence.

Exhibit 10.3 will help you develop effective fundraising and development internal controls.

EXHIBIT 10.3 **DEVELOPMENT AND FUNDRAISING INTERNAL CONTROLS WORKSHEET**

For each of the items below, provide examples that prove your nonprofit's controls are in place.

Donor Records—ensuring privacy and security
- Donor records are stored in a secure facility, either a locked file cabinet, or if in electronic form with password protection.
- Protocols are in place for retrieving donor records, working on the records, and returning the records to the proper storage.
  - Staff are screened and trained before they are permitted to have access to donor records.
  - Staff are held accountable for the confidentiality of the donor records. Consequences for breach of confidentiality are swift, and documentation of such infractions are included in the staff or volunteer's personnel file.
  - Staff are not permitted to leave donor records on the desk or open on a computer screen if the staff member is not actively working on the files.
  - Data entry for donor records is done only by staff who have been screened and trained.
- Direct communication with donors is done only by individuals who have been screened and trained. Content of written communications is reviewed by supervisory staff.

Special Events and Campaigns—Fundraising
- Staff and volunteers are screened and trained before they are assigned to tasks involving the handling of money.
- If the nonprofit can accept credit cards, are staff and volunteers trained in how to process the credit cards? Are supervisors readily available to assist?
- If the event involves handling of cash, are the funds handled by at least two (2) individuals at a time, with a supervisor observing?
- Do patrons of fundraising events receive receipts for their cash donations?
- If the fundraising is for a special project, do potential donors know what the money will be used for? Are donors aware of the percentage of their donation that is actually going to that project?
- If the event involves using vendors for fundraising services, such as telemarketers, does your nonprofit have a contract for the services and proof of insurance from the vendor?

CONCLUSION

Development and fundraising are generally the nonprofit's sole means of generating revenue. The success of these important functions is also highly contingent upon the level of public trust that the nonprofit enjoys. Donors are the nonprofit's primary stakeholders. They donate their funds and sometimes lend their names to support the nonprofit's functions. They expect that their privacy will be respected and that the nonprofit will manage their donations in a responsible manner. The implementation of Sarbanes-Oxley best practices establishes a context for responsible fundraising and preserving public trust.

CHAPTER 11

SOX Best Practices and Internal Controls

Two members of a small investment club are meeting for coffee to discuss the presentation they were going to make to the club that evening about the two companies they had researched. "Paul, isn't the Whitney Museum of American Art one of the museums you donate money to every year?" asked Rita. "Yes," said Paul, "I've been a donor for about the last five years or so. Why?" "Have you heard about how much money the museum lost due to employee theft?" "What are you talking about?" said Paul. "I haven't heard anything about that." "Two employees, the manager of visitor services and one of her staff members, allegedly had a scam going where they stole nearly $900,000 by voiding ticket sales and keeping the cash." "Nine hundred thousand!" exclaimed Paul. "I wouldn't think the museum even had that much in ticket sales. Twenty thousand per day is more in line with what the cash ticket sales would be. They must have been taking more than just the cash from ticket sales." "Well, the scam apparently began over two and a half years ago," said Rita. "It wasn't just a short-term operation and I can see how they could have stolen $900,000 over that length of time." "Two and a half years!" said Paul. "I can't believe it would take that long for the finance managers or the auditors to find the discrepancy in the financial statements. Surely, they monitored the number of visitors to the museum and matched the ticket receipts with admission. That's just common sense." "That's not how they were caught," said Rita. "I think one of the staff talked with the museum officials about his suspicion that his boss was stealing from the ticket sales. The museum secretly installed cameras and videotaped *both* of them voiding tickets and pocketing the cash. Who knows how long the scam could have gone on if one of them hadn't tried to cover up by pointing a finger at the other one?"

CHAPTER OVERVIEW

Many of the provisions in SOX, particularly Sections 302 and 404, require public organizations to develop, implement, and conduct on-going assessment of an internal control system. Although the SOX requirements currently only pertain to public companies, the increased demand for accountability in nonprofits creates a need for nonprofits to incorporate such a control system. In addition, an internal control system has the potential to increase the overall performance of all aspects of the nonprofit, allowing it to better meet its mission. This chapter provides an overall examination of the internal control system, discusses the value of an internal control system, describes a widely used framework for developing an internal control system, and provides examples for each of the five components of the system. In addition, internal financial controls are explored in more detail, including examples of activity-level controls.

CHAPTER OBJECTIVES

By the end of this chapter, you should be able to:

- Discuss the function of an effective internal control system
- Define the five components in an effective internal control system and provide examples of each.
- Trace the connection between the development of SOX and the Committee of Sponsoring Organizations and the National Commission on Fraudulent Financial Reporting.
- Identify the primary objectives of the internal control system.
- Use a widely used framework to develop an internal control system.
- Provide examples of activity-level controls.
- Discuss the roles of the board of directors, management, and staff in developing and maintaining an effective internal control system.
- Create an effective internal control system.

NEED FOR AN INTERNAL CONTROL SYSTEM

The incident at the Whitney Museum of America Art is a classic example of how an inefficient internal control system can hurt an organization. The two cashiers at the museum's ticket counter allegedly used a rather unsophisticated method to steal the museum's money without being caught. They would sell the tickets to visitors, collect the sold tickets at the museum's entry checkpoint, and then void them after the visitors left, showing them as ticket cancellations. This continued for over two and a half years, resulting in a total loss to the museum of $880,000 (Pogrebin, 2004; Siegel, 2005).

Despite such a large discrepancy between the number of visitors to the museum and the amount of receipts collected, neither the museum's board of directors nor any of the accounting or finance staff were aware of the discrepancy. Due to the museum's apparently ineffective accounting and internal control system, it is doubtful that the system would have ever detected the embezzlement. If there had been an effective internal control system in place, it is doubtful that the two employees could have embezzled such a large amount or that their activities could have continued for two and a half years.

Evidence of Fraud and Abuse within Organizations

The accounting and financial scandals discussed in Chapter 1 certainly provide compelling evidence of fraud and abuse at individual public companies. However, the prevalence of fraud and abuse across the U.S. is fairly high, and is present in all sectors. The 1996 *Report to the Nation on Occupational Fraud and Abuse*, published by the Association of Certified Fraud Examiners, was based on 2,608 cases of fraud and abuse collected from Certified Fraud Examiners during a ten-year period (Association of Certified Fraud Examiners, 1996). The report defined occupation fraud and abuse as "the use of one's occupation for personal enrichment through the deliberate misuse or misapplication of the employing organization's resources or assets." The primary findings from the study were:

- Fraud and abuse costs U.S. organizations more than $400 billion annually.
- Fraud and abuse costs employers an average of $9 a day per employee.
- The average organization loses about 6% of its total annual revenue to fraud and abuse.
- The most costly abuses occurred in organizations with less than 100 employees.
- Losses from fraud caused by managers and executives were 16 times greater than those caused by nonmanagerial employees.

The 1999 report, *Fraudulent Financial Reporting: 1987–1997—An Analysis of U.S. Public Companies* (COSO, 1999) reported the findings from a study that examined 200 randomly selected cases of alleged financial fraud investigated by the SEC between 1987 and 1997. The primary findings regarding fraudulent reporting were:

- Most fraud was not limited to a single fiscal period; the fraud was on-going, perpetrated over several fiscal periods, with an average fraud period of 23.7 months.
- The majority of the fraud schemes involved the overstatement of revenues and assets.
- Assets were inflated by recording nonexistent assets, overstating the value of tangible assets, or understating allowances for receivables.

- Revenues were inflated by recording revenues prematurely or fictitiously.

- Most fraud occurred in smaller companies (assets < $100 million), but the average amount of fraud was relatively large ($25 million).

- Senior managers were frequently involved; in 83% of the cases, the CEO, the CFO, or both, were associated with the financial statement fraud.

- The boards of directors of these companies were dominated by directors with significant equity ownership, directors with limited board experience, or directors who were insiders.

- Most audit committees met once a year or the company had no audit committee.

ADVANTAGES OF ADOPTING SOX BEST PRACTICES REGARDING INTERNAL CONTROLS

Based on the findings in the two reports regarding fraud and abuse, and the embezzlement example of the Whitney Museum of American Art, it is not unreasonable to assume that similar types of theft, fraud, and poor management of organizational assets are occurring in a significant number of nonprofits. As discussed in Chapter 1, the nonprofit sector has recently experienced a number of incidents of perceived wrongdoing and fiscal mismanagement. The Nature Conservancy, United Way, American Red Cross, Foundation for New Era Philanthropy, and Feed the Children, for example, have all received substantial unfavorable media coverage of their apparent failures in accountability and asset management (Bothwell, 2001). In many of these incidents, the lack of an effective internal control system was at the heart of the problem. Nonprofit organizations may be especially vulnerable to employee fraud because they tend to place more trust in employees who have access to organizational assets, and they generally have fewer financial and security controls in place.

What keeps an organization functioning efficiently is an inbuilt "internal control" system—a system that closes the authentication loop in any business function. The internal control system is the backbone of every organization. Proper internal controls provide a check on the workings of the organization and prevent fraud and other organizational failures, or at least detect them in a timely fashion. As discussed in Chapter 1, many of the provisions in SOX relate to internal controls, especially the internal controls over financial reporting. SOX requires senior management of public companies to develop, implement, and periodically evaluate the organization's internal control system. In addition, SOX requires that management report the results of the system evaluation and any corrective modifications made as a result of the evaluation to the SEC, board of directors, stockholders, and the external auditor. By adopting some of the SOX provisions regarding internal control, a nonprofit could improve its accountability, and its credibility, with its donors, funding foundations, regulators, and the public at large.

WHAT IS AN EFFECTIVE INTERNAL CONTROL SYSTEM?

Many people erroneously believe that internal controls are only financial controls. Although one of the primary goals of an internal control system is to provide reasonable assurance for the prevention and timely detection of fraud and unauthorized acquisition or disposition of an organization's assets, financial controls are only a subset of the overall internal control system. Limiting the concept of internal controls to financial controls can lead to a nonfinancial crisis that could have been avoided through a broader understanding.

Internal controls are an integral part of any organization's financial and business policies and procedures. Internal controls consist of all the measures taken by the organization for the purpose of protecting its resources against waste, fraud, and inefficiency; ensuring accuracy and reliability in accounting and operating data; securing compliance with the policies of the organization; and evaluating the level of performance in all organizational units of the organization. Simply put, internal controls are good business practices, and a nonprofit has an effective system if the board of directors and management have reasonable assurance that:

- They have an evidence-based and accurate understanding regarding the extent to which the nonprofit's operational objectives are being met.
- The financial statements and all other financial data reported publicly are prepared reliably and properly within GAAP.
- The nonprofit is complying with all applicable laws and regulations at the federal, state, and local level.

Policies, Procedures, and Processes

An internal control system consists of a number of organizational policies, procedures, and processes. The majority of the chapters in this book describe examples of policies, procedures, and processes a nonprofit should have, under the designation of "best practices." For example, Chapter 8 discusses some of the policies and procedures that should be in place regarding information technology. In essence, these best practices are part of the overall internal control system. A small sample of policies, procedures, and processes that should be a part of an effective control system include:

- Risk assessment procedures
- Check signing procedures
- Reimbursement authorization process
- Whistleblower policy
- Bank statement reconciliation process

- Volunteer background check procedures
- Segregation of Duties policy
- Business interruption and disaster mitigation procedures
- Employee vacation approval process
- Discrimination policy
- Staff termination procedures
- Internal control system assessment
- Bookkeeping and accounting procedures
- Sexual harassment report process
- Cash disbursement authorization procedures
- Information Technology policy
- Internal communications procedures
- Document and Record Preservation policy
- Staff recruitment procedures
- Code of Ethics policy

An effective internal control system provides for the prevention and timely detection of material errors, omissions, or irregularities in the nonprofit's operations, allowing it to more effectively meet its mission.

COMMITTEE OF SPONSORING ORGANIZATIONS

To some degree, everyone in the nonprofit is responsible for ensuring that the internal control system is effective, however, the greatest responsibility rests with the management and the board of directors. In general, the board of directors is responsible for the overall control process in the nonprofit, providing direction and oversight. Management typically designs and implements the control system, and is responsible for the evaluation and modification of the system. One model of internal controls that is widely used is the one developed by the Committee of Sponsoring Organizations (COSO). Using the COSO framework as a guideline would increase a nonprofit's likelihood of developing an effective system.

COSO is a voluntary private sector organization that was originally formed in 1985 to sponsor the National Commission on Fraudulent Financial Reporting (Commission). The Commission was jointly supported by the American Accounting Association, the American Institute of Certified Public Accountants, Financial Executives International, the Institute of Internal Auditors, and the National Association of Accountants, and is frequently referred to as the "Treadway Commission," reflecting the name of its first chairperson, James C. Treadway, Jr. The purpose of the Commission was to identify the factors that can lead to fraudulent financial reporting and to develop recommendations to address these factors. The Commission was independent of each of its supporting organizations, and consisted of representatives from industry, public accounting, investment firms, and the New York Stock Exchange.

Report of the National Commission of Fraudulent Financial Reporting

In 1987, the Commission published its findings in the *Report of the National Commission of Fraudulent Financial Reporting* (COSO, 1987). The report indicated that fraud occurs as "the result of certain environmental, institutional, or individual forces and opportunities." Examples of these forces include:

- Weak or nonexistent internal controls
- Weak ethical climate
- Desire to earn a higher price from a stock or debt offering
- Attempts to meet shareholder expectations
- Desire to postpone dealing with financial difficulties
- Personal gain, such as additional compensation, promotion, escape from penalty for poor performance
- Unrealistic budget pressures, particularly for short-term results
- Absence of a board of directors or audit committee that properly oversees the financial reporting process
- Ineffective internal audit staff

As can be seen in the analysis of the legislative and regulatory content of SOX in Chapter 1, many of the findings and recommendations from the Commission were incorporated into SOX. Among factors that drove the swift passage of SOX discussed in Chapter 1, one should include the *Report of the National Commission of Fraudulent Financial Reporting* and additional COSO publications as among the most powerful drivers.

Internal Controls—Integrated Framework

In 1992, COSO published *Internal Controls—Integrated Framework*, a framework for developing an effective internal control system. The COSO *Internal Controls—Integrated Framework* (Framework) can provide direction to any nonprofit that wishes to establish an effective internal control system. The Framework breaks effective internal control into five interrelated components: control environment, risk assessment, control activities, information/communication, and monitoring.

Control Environment

The board of directors and senior management establish the organizational-level control environment. It sets the tone of the nonprofit and influences the control consciousness of the organizational members. Leaders of an area, function, or activity establish an activity-level control environment, which influences the control consciousness of the staff within that span of control. The control environment is the foundation for the other four components of internal control as it provides the discipline and structure context. Control environment factors include:

- Integrity and ethical values
- Attention and involvement of board of directors
- Commitment to competence
- Management philosophy and operating style
- Adherence to authority and responsibility

Due to the diversity of boards and senior management teams, the control environment varies among nonprofits. A nonprofit whose Executive Director demonstrates a commitment to ethics and expects others in the organization to also do so will have a different control environment from the nonprofit whose Executive Director sets a tone of deceit and greed. Given the importance of the control environment as a component of the internal control system, it is not surprising that SOX contains provisions regarding a code of ethics.

Risk Assessment

Every nonprofit faces a variety of external and internal risks that can threaten the achievement of the nonprofit's objectives. Risk assessment is the identification of the risks and the potential severity the risks have. Once the risks have been identified, the nonprofit can take steps to manage the risk, eliminate it, or mitigate its effects.

Obviously, before the nonprofit can assess and take the necessary steps to manage risks, the objectives must first be established, both at the organizational level and at the activity or process level. The three broad categories of objectives are operations, financial reporting, and compliance. Operations objectives relate to effectiveness and efficiency of the operations, including performance and financial goals and safeguarding resources against loss. Financial reporting objectives pertain to the proper preparation of reliable financial statements, including prevention of fraudulent financial reporting. Compliance objectives pertain to meeting the requirements of laws and regulations at the federal, state, and local levels. Within the three broad categories of objectives, there are multiple levels of subobjectives of narrowing focus. For example, within the category of financial reporting are the subobjectives of proper preparation of the balance sheet, proper preparation of the statement of operations, and proper preparation of the statement of cash flows. Within the subobjective of proper preparation of the balance sheet is the subobjective of accurate valuation of assets. At each level, the focus becomes narrower and more specific.

Due to the diversity of nonprofits, the level and type of risk varies among them. For example, a nonprofit that has many daily cash transactions might face a more severe risk to operational objectives than a nonprofit that rarely has many cash transactions. A nonprofit that has inadequate staffing in its accounting function might face a more severe risk to financial reporting objectives than a nonprofit that has an adequately staffed accounting department that provides extensive training for its staff. A large nonprofit that frequently conducts major fundraising campaigns might face a more severe risk to compliance objectives than a small nonprofit that engages in relatively infrequent or small campaigns.

Control Activities

Control activities are the policies, procedures, and processes that help ensure management directives are carried out properly and in a timely manner. They help ensure that necessary actions are taken to address risks to achievement of the organizational objectives. Control activities occur throughout the organization, at all levels, and in all functions. They include a range of activities as diverse as approvals, authorizations, verifications, reconciliations, reviews of operating performance, security of assets, and segregation of duties. Examples of specific control activities can be seen in Exhibits 11.1, 11.2, 11.3, and 11.4.

Information and Communication

Pertinent information must be identified, captured, and communicated in a form and time frame that enables the board, managers, and staff to carry out their responsibilities. Effective communication must occur in a broad sense, flowing down, across, and up the organization. Information, both internal and external, must be effectively communicated to management in a timely manner to enable the board and senior management to make informed business and reporting decisions. All personnel must receive a clear message from top management that information and communication responsibilities must be taken seriously. They must have a means of communicating significant information upstream. The importance of having effective information and communication is reflected in the SOX's requirements regarding disclosure controls.

Monitoring

Internal control systems need to be monitored—a process that assesses the quality of the system's performance over time. Monitoring is an ongoing process and leads to refinement of the internal control system. Ongoing monitoring occurs in the ordinary course

EXHIBIT 11.1   ACCOUNTS RECEIVABLES PROCESS

Step	Days from Date of Charge	Action
1	30	Send first statement to customer.
2	60	Send second statement to customer.
3	75	Send a letter to customer requesting immediate payment.
4	90	Telephone or send a second letter to customer.
5	105	Send a letter informing the customer that unless the past due payment of $ _____ is received within the next 15 days, it will be necessary to refer the account to a collection agency.
6	120	Send a Delinquent Account Data form to the Controller's Office (an original and one copy) for each account that has been processed through the above steps. The Controller's Office will forward the original Delinquent Account Form to the collection agency and file the duplicate.
7	360	If the account has been at the collection agency for at least 6 months without any collections, the Controller's Office will request that the collection agency return the delinquent account.
8	360	When the account has been returned from the collection agency, the Controller's Office will notify the department to submit a Department Write-off Request.

EXHIBIT 11.2   DISCRIMINATION AND HARASSMENT POLICY

The company will maintain work environments that are free of discrimination, racial/ethnic harassment, sexual harassment, and retaliation for filing a complaint under this policy. Discrimination based on race, ethnic or national origin, sex, sexual orientation, religion, age, ancestry, disability, military status, or veteran status is prohibited. Retaliation against a person for reporting or objecting to discrimination or harassment is a violation of this policy whether or not discrimination, racial/ethnic harassment, or sexual harassment occurred. Persons who violate this policy are subject to disciplinary action, up to and including dismissal from employment. Managers and supervisors are obligated to report complaints to Human Resources, to keep complaints confidential, to protect the privacy of all parties involved in a complaint, and to prevent or eliminate discrimination, harassment, or retaliation; failure to do so is a violation of this policy. Appropriate sanctions and remedial actions will be taken.

Complaints must be filed within one year of the alleged behavior, are confidential, and will not be disclosed to anyone who does not have a need to know. The company cannot guarantee complainants, respondents, or witnesses absolute confidentiality because the company is obligated to investigate complaints. A Human Resources manager will evaluate each complaint and, if necessary, conduct a prompt, thorough, and fair review. The time required for reviews may vary, but the goal is to complete reviews as expeditiously as possible.

Any person who knowingly files a false complaint, or who knowingly provides false or misleading information is subject to disciplinary action. No action will be taken against an individual who makes a good faith complaint, even if the allegations are not substantiated.

EXHIBIT 11.3   NEW EMPLOYEE ORIENTATION PROCEDURES

Check each activity once you have completed it. Once all activities are completed, sign and date the form and return to HR.

Introductions and Interpersonal Relations

_____ Introduce the new employee to fellow workers.

_____ Give the employee a current organizational chart.

_____ Explain the mission of the work unit.

_____ Show location of coatroom, restrooms, official bulletin boards, etc.

_____ Suggest places available for breaks and lunches.

_____ Explain any security, confidentiality, or privacy issues related to the work area.

General Information

_____ Tell where and how to enter premises; arrange for necessary keys.

_____ Cover starting and quitting time, lunch period, and breaks.

_____ Show how to report time worked and leave taken.

_____ Explain overtime policy, if applicable.

_____ Explain safety policy and emergency exits.

_____ Instruct concerning the reporting of all accidents and injuries.

_____ Discuss communications (telephone, voice mail, e-mail, or pagers).

_____ Tell when and whom to call when absence is necessary.

_____ Determine how to contact the employee during non-working hours.

_____ Arrange for employee to obtain parking permit.

_____ Take or send to get an I.D. card and explain uses of I.D. card.

Work Assignment

_____ Review position description with employee and give him or her a copy.

_____ Explain performance review system: priority outcomes, performance review sheets, and probationary period. Give employee a copy.

_____ Arrange for work assignment and step-by-step introduction to the job.

_____ Schedule on-the-job training and any required training.

_____ Designate a person to whom the new employee should go for help.

_____ Cover departmental standards and requirements (licensing, dress, travel).

_____ Explain equipment and supplies available and how to obtain additional ones.

_____   _____

Signature   Date

EXHIBIT 11.4   CALLING CARD USAGE PROCESS

Within the U.S., using your company calling card, you may place a call at any time to any company number or any regular number in the 50 states or internationally, but different processes apply to different circumstances, as follows:

I. When calling to a U.S. number from any touch-tone telephone:
    1. Dial 1-800-XXX-XXXX; listen for the prompt.
    2. At the prompt, dial the 14-digit authorization code; listen for the prompt.
    3. At the prompt, dial the 10-digit number you wish to call; do not dial "0" or "1" before dialing the area code.

II. When calling to a U.S. from any rotary dial or pulse dial telephone:
    1. Dial 1-800-XXX-XXXX; a company operator will answer.
    2. Give the operator your 14-digit authorization number.
    3. Give the operator the number you wish to call.
    4. The operator will complete the call.

III. When calling to a number outside of the U.S.:
    1. Dial 1-800-XXX-XXXX; listen for the prompt.
    2. At the prompt, enter your authorization number; listen for the prompt.
    3. At the prompt, enter "011", the country code, city code, and the telephone number.

---

of operations, and includes regular management and supervisory activities, and other actions personnel take in performing their duties that assess the quality of internal control system performance.

The scope and frequency of separate evaluations depend primarily on an assessment of risks and the effectiveness of ongoing monitoring procedures. Internal control deficiencies should be reported upstream, with serious matters reported immediately to senior management and the board of directors.

Designing the internal control system is just one-half of the equation. Testing, assessment, and modification of the system comprise the other half. Procedures that were once effective may become less effective due to the arrival of new personnel, varying effectiveness of training and supervision, time and resources constraints, or additional pressures. Furthermore, circumstances for which the internal control system was originally designed also may change. Because of changing conditions, system monitoring must be conducted to determine whether the internal control system continues to be effective. The value of ongoing monitoring is reflected in the SOX's requirements of periodic assessment and assessment reports.

In monitoring the internal control system, it must be stressed that simply evaluating the control activities component of the system leaves out the other components. The monitoring system itself needs to be evaluated, as do the control environment component, information and communication component, the risk assessment component. If the effectiveness of the internal control system is based on fewer than all five of the system's components, the effectiveness rating may be higher or lower than the actual rating.

Roles within the Framework   Everyone within the nonprofit has some role in developing and implementing an internal control system. The roles vary depending on the level of responsibility and the nature of involvement by the individual. The responsibility of the board of directors is to provide guidance to and oversight of the Executive Director and senior management, especially through the audit committee. The Executive Director has the responsibility to "set the tone at the top" that has an overall effect on integrity and ethics, and he or she must provide leadership to senior management. The senior management team provides leadership to department or unit managers and assigns responsibility for the development and implementation of department or unit-specific internal controls. Managers and supervisory personnel are responsible for executing control policies and procedures at the detail level within their specific unit. Each individual within a unit has the responsibility to be cognizant of proper internal control procedures associated with his or her specific job responsibilities. The importance of the roles of management and the board of directors in the internal control system is reflected in several of the SOX requirements. The CEO and members of the senior management team must attest to their creation, implementation, and on-going evaluation of the internal control system. The board of directors, particularly the audit committee, also has specific internal control system responsibilities under SOX.

IMPORTANCE OF INTERNAL FINANCIAL CONTROLS

The importance of internal financial controls is so great that many people believe that the financial controls *are* the internal control system. While this is not true, financial controls are key controls required for an effective internal control system and form the basis of a safe and sound organization. The challenge of designing financial controls is greater for nonprofits, as their financial reporting is not as minutely scrutinized as that of public organizations. While the overall internal control system is important, this section focuses on financial controls.

Financial controls are internal controls to protect the assets and assure accurate financial reporting. These are standards established by management to ensure accuracy, timeliness, and completeness of financial data as well as compliance with internal and external policies and regulations. A properly designed and consistently enforced system of financial controls helps management and the board of directors to safeguard and ascertain that assets and financial records are not stolen, misused, or accidentally destroyed. In addition, accurate financial reporting provides useful and reliable information for sound decision-making. Implementing and maintaining internal financial controls are important aspects of running a successful business.

Financial controls are important, since financial fraud easily happens in the absence of effective financial controls. The Whitney Museum of American Art experience is an example of how easily fraud can occur within, and many other examples exist.

In New York City, a paralegal at Honeywell International allegedly embezzled nearly $600,000 by submitting fake bills, forging her boss' approval, and then depositing the checks into an account she set up. Between January and March 2003, the paralegal submitted seven phony invoices, totaling $595,682. The invoices were made to look as if they were from Fish & Neave, a well-known patent law firm that had done work for Honeywell International in the past. The paralegal then forged her boss' approval and persuaded the company's accounts payable department to send the checks to her for delivery instead of mailing them to the law firm.

Posing as a lawyer, the paralegal allegedly obtained a business certificate from the Westchester County Clerk using "Fish Neave" as her name. She used the certificate to set up a bank account in Westchester, deposited the checks made out to "Fish & Neave" into the "Fish Neave" bank account, and then quickly withdrew them for personal use (Ventures, 2005).

Such examples make it clear that all organizations, including nonprofits, should examine their operational processes and identify any gaps in the system. Other than theft, money can disappear due to improper spending controls. For example, if there is no financial control that limits spending or scrutinizes expenses, an employee might choose to travel in business class instead of economy class, resulting in much higher travel expenses for the nonprofit. All concerned organizations, including nonprofits, should welcome internal financial control. A good control system should cover all individual elements of the nonprofit's financial administration.

Key Areas of Financial Controls

The following are key areas of financial controls that help to detect and prevent erroneous or inappropriate transactions.

Cash Receipts

Cash receipts relates to issuance of receipts, acceptance of cash, deposits, and recording of cash in any form. It includes currency and checks. Financial control helps to ensure that all cash intended for the organization is received, promptly deposited, properly recorded, reconciled, and kept under adequate security.

Cash Disbursement

For an effective financial control of any cash disbursements, it is essential to develop policies so different people authorize payments, sign checks and record payments in books, and reconcile the bank statements. It is important to ensure that the cash disbursement is made under proper authorization and for valid business reasons. All disbursements are recorded properly.

Accounts Receivable

Accounts receivables are amounts owed to the nonprofit from sales or delivery of services to its clientele made on credit. A good financial control to handle accounts receivable is to properly record and arrange for quick recoveries. Recovery efforts should escalate if there is any delay in the recovery process. Parties with continued issues with recoveries should be tracked and flagged and corrective action should be taken.

Accounts Payable

Accounts payable are amounts due to suppliers or others from whom the nonprofit has received goods or services on credit. A proper financial control of accounts payable ensures that all invoices are legitimate and accurate, they are properly recorded, and payment is made to the right supplier.

Petty Cash

Petty cash is a cash fund maintained for payment of small incidental purchases or reimbursements. Dealing in cash represents an extra degree of risk, so a greater degree of care needs to be exercised. Proper controls of petty cash could include the following governing rules:

- Petty cash should always be kept under lock and key.
- There should be tabs on the minimum and the maximum amount to be kept in the fund.
- There is a limit on the amount of petty cash that can be used for a single disbursement.
- The fund should be enough to cover petty cash expenditures for a month.
- There must be a process for petty cash disbursement.

An example of a petty cash disbursement for reimbursement process includes:

1. The payee first completes a reimbursement form, attaching all relevant receipts and documentation.
2. The payee submits the reimbursement form to the authority for approval.
3. The authority reviews the reimbursement form and either approves or disapproves.
4. Upon approval, the form goes to the cashier who makes the payment after proper identity verification of the payee.
5. The cashier records the transaction and notes the remaining balance in petty cash fund. The cashier's supervisor then reviews the records and rechecks the balance in the petty cash fund.

Segregation of Duties

Financial control includes written policies that an organizational structure should design to ensure appropriate segregation of responsibilities. It reduces a person's opportunity to commit and conceal fraud or errors. It also includes rotation of duties. Duties should be divided between staff to reduce the opportunity for errors and frauds. Segregation means that no one person handles any financial transaction from beginning to the end. For example, in the case of paying invoices, one person should authorize the payment, another should draw the checks and record the payment in proper books of accounts, a third person should sign the checks, and a fourth person should reconcile the bank statements. Since each individual is given the ownership of that particular task, any break in the flow immediately flags the person who committed the fraud.

Check Signing

A simple control regarding check signing requires checks to be signed by at least two different people if the amounts of purchases go above a certain level. The purpose of this is to create a check and balance on check signing and give the decisions of whom to pay, how much to pay, why to pay, and when to pay to multiple individuals. This makes misappropriation of funds difficult.

Payment Documentation

Every payment should be supported by the original invoice, with receipts and other documentation attached to the invoice. When the payment is made by check, the entry should be recorded, name of the person or firm to whom payment is made should be recorded, and the check number, check date, and check amount should also be noted. The names of the check signing authorities should also be recorded and their signatures obtained.

Inventory

Internal controls to manage inventories of goods for sale or in stock recommend that all items in inventory should be properly documented. All deliveries should record the vendor name, product name and stockkeeping unit number, delivery date, shipment number, delivery quantity, and also document the shipment notice signed by the vendor. Beginning stock and ending stock should be computed every day and reconciled with sales numbers to identify any difference. The warehouse should be responsible for inventory numbers at the warehouse, if there is one, while a store manager should be responsible for sales and on-shelf inventories. Product returns should be tracked separately and authorized by a manager.

Employee Advances

Employee advances for expected expenses should have guidelines defining the maximum cash advance that can be given to an employee, documentation of the cash advance request, and approval of the request before the cash advance is made. The loop does not close until final documentation regarding the use of the cash is received and verified. For example, an employee might receive a cash advance to purchase an office printer based on a quote. The transaction closes only after submission of final original receipts from the vendor to make sure there are no differences in the quote and final invoice, as well as safeguard that the employee does not return the purchase using the original receipt and exchange the item for something less costly.

Employee Travel

Control guidelines for employee travel include specified modes of travel, travel notice, travel approvals from employee's managers, and documented justification of the need to travel. If the employee makes the travel arrangements, the employee must provide proper documentation in terms of original receipts and a manager-approved form for reimbursement.

Payroll

It is necessary to ensure that payments are made only to bona fide employees for authorized amounts. The employees should be issued pay-slips showing their gross salary, all deductions including tax and insurance, and the net salary. A separate payroll bank account should be maintained, and reconciliation of the net amounts of the pay-slips and the actual amounts paid by checks should be done every month by the payroll department to avoid fraud or misuse of organization's funds. Payroll should also keep salary and expense reimbursement accounts separate for clarity.

Fixed Assets

Fixed assets are those that are not easily converted into cash in the short term (i.e., within one year). They are long-term assets whose value extends beyond the accounting period. Fixed assets are both tangible and intangible assets. Land, building, furniture and fixtures, and vehicles are examples of tangible assets, and goodwill, copyrights, licenses, and patents are examples of intangible fixed assets. Tangible fixed assets are recorded at their original cost and are depreciated proportionately every year, while intangible fixed assets are recorded at their original cost and are amortized proportionately every year. The procedure of recording fixed assets includes proper tracking and control of the assets. Financial controls ensure that fixed assets are acquired and disposed of only on proper authorization and with adequate safeguard, and also that the transactions are properly recorded. Also, due diligence should be performed and documented before any fixed asset is purchased to ensure that the purchase amount paid is as per expectation.

Bank Statement Reconciliation

Bank statement reconciliation is the process of systematically comparing the cash balance as reported by the bank with the cash balance on the company's books and explaining any differences between them. Reconciliation makes sure that the balance of the bank statement, checkbook balance, and the balance in the accounting book (i.e., the ledger and the journal) all tally/agree with each other.

There frequently are differences in the balances of the checkbook and the bank statements. The reasons are many:

- Checks may be issued by the nonprofit in one month, but might not be processed by the payee in the same month.
- Interest may be credited or debited to the nonprofit's bank account, but it might not be recorded in the nonprofit's books.
- The amount of the check may have been altered by the payee.
- Transfers might be recorded in the books of accounts in a particular month, but not recorded in the same month in the bank account.
- Checks could have been stolen from the nonprofit and forged.
- There may be some arithmetic mistakes or other recording errors made by the nonprofit or by the bank.

Whatever the reason for differences between the amounts in the nonprofit's books and the bank statement, reconciliation of the statement should find it and prompt any necessary corrective action.

Fund Management or Funding

Without good financial controls, an organization might consume its funding faster than anticipated. It is therefore important to keep a close watch on how the funds are raised, and on how, where, and why are they used.

CONCLUSION

It should be readily apparent that nonprofits should use the Framework to develop internal control systems. First, having such a system gives the nonprofit a greater opportunity to meet its mission effectively. The internal control system can help to safeguard the financial and nonfinancial resources of the organization, which will enable it to more efficiently deliver its services. Having an effective system can also give the nonprofit more credibility with potential donors and funders, as well as with regulators.

WORKSHEET I: CONDUCTING AN INTERNAL CONTROL SYSTEM REVIEW

The first step in conducting an internal control system review is to convey to all members of the organization the importance and purpose of an internal control system, the importance and purpose of the internal control system review, and the importance of the review to management and the board of directors. Senior management will be critical in "setting the tone" of the review, and must demonstrate strong leadership in the review process. If it appears that management thinks the review is a waste of time, then staff will not effectively participate in the review.

The next steps include the following:

1. Review the current controls that are in place, both at the organizational level and the nonprofit's functional areas.

2. Determine the priority level of each control, including missing controls.

3. Evaluate the effectiveness of each existing control.

4. Make appropriate assignments to management and staff to address any deficiencies in the existing controls and in missing controls.

5. Establish a realistic timeline for developing corrective actions for each control, keeping in mind the priority level of the control and the level of correction needed.

6. Evaluate the proposed corrective actions for "doability" and completeness, and make revisions if necessary.

7. Establish a realistic timeline for implementing the corrective actions for each of the controls.

8. Implement the corrective actions for each control, according to the timeline.

9. Establish a realistic timeline for evaluating the effectiveness of the implemented corrective actions for each control.

10. Evaluate the effectiveness of the implemented corrective actions for each control, according to the timeline.

11. Write a report for senior management and the board of directors.

12. Senior management and the board of directors respond to the report, suggesting areas of improvement, reconsiderations of priority levels, and suggested corrective actions.

13. Establish a realistic timeline to implement the recommendations of senior management and the board of directors.

14. Implement the recommendations, according to the timeline.

15. Establish a realistic timeline for evaluating the effectiveness of the implemented recommendations.

16. Evaluate the effectiveness of the implemented recommendations.

17. Write a report for senior management and the board of directors.

18. Begin again

It should be readily apparent that the internal control review is not a "quick fix," and, as evidenced by the last step, it is an on-going process. The internal review process must become a part of the nonprofit's culture, with internal controls and continuous improvement of the controls being the norm.

Not every nonprofit will have the resources necessary to complete every step in the review, and provide corrective actions for all existing and missing controls. That is why establishing the priority level for each control is important. In addition, establishing realistic timelines should take organizational resources into account and avoid "organizational overload." The important key to improving internal controls is simply to start. As operations, financial reporting, and compliance with laws and regulations begin to improve as a result of the internal controls and the internal control system review, the nonprofit will have first hand experience with the value of the review. Senior management and the board of directors will have to leverage that sense of value into more commitment to an internal control system and its review. With each cycle of review, there should be increased improvement and increased commitment.

One tool that will be helpful to start the internal control review process can be seen in Exhibit 11.5, the Internal Control System Review Worksheet. The worksheet contains a number of commonly used internal controls, which will help to determine which controls are in place and which are missing. For each control, a priority level is assigned, and each control can be identified as being met or as needing work. The worksheet also prompts for a realistic timeline for completion. This worksheet will help in moving through the first steps in the review process.

Exhibit 11.5   WORKSHEET 1: INTERNAL CONTROL SYSTEM REVIEW

Priority Level	Indicator	Met	Needs Work	N/A	Timeline
	The nonprofit follows accounting practices that conform to generally accepted accounting principals (GAAP).				
	The nonprofit has communication systems in place to provide accurate and timely financial information to management and the board to make sound financial decisions.				
	The nonprofit prepares financial statements (Balance Sheet, Statement of Operations, Statement of Changes in Net Assets, Statement of Cash Flows) in a timely manner and the board reviews them.				

Priority Level	Indicator	Met	Needs Work	N/A	Timeline
	The nonprofit prepares an in-depth variance analysis of the budget, analyzing the variance between the budgeted revenues/expenses and the actual revenues/expenses.				
	The nonprofit develops an annual comprehensive operating budget that is reviewed and approved by the board.				
	The nonprofit has established a code of ethics or conduct to which all board members, management, and staff are accountable.				
	The nonprofit monitors unit costs of programs and services.				
	The nonprofit prepares cash flow projections.				
	The nonprofit periodically forecasts year-end revenues and expenses to assist in making sound management decisions during the year.				
	The nonprofit reconciles all cash accounts monthly.				
	The nonprofit conducts an annual internal audit to assess the accuracy of financial information.				
	The nonprofit has control activities for invoicing, follow-up and collections of accounts, and writing off of bad debt.				
	The nonprofit monitors compliance with all laws, regulations, and conditions regarding government contracts and grant agreements.				
	The nonprofit's payroll procedures comply with applicable federal, state, and local regulations.				
	The nonprofit has a nondiscrimination policy.				
	The nonprofit takes periodic inventories to monitor the inventory against theft, to reconcile general ledger inventory information, and to maintain an adequate inventory level.				
	The nonprofit has a written fiscal policy and procedures manual and follows it.				
	The nonprofit has documented a set of financial controls, including the handling of cash and deposits, approval over spending and disbursements, and segregation of duties.				

(continues)

Exhibit 11.5   WORKSHEET 1: INTERNAL CONTROL SYSTEM
REVIEW (CONTINUED)

Priority Level	Indicator	Needs Met	Work	N/A	Timeline
	The nonprofit has a policy identifying authorized check signers and the number of signatures required on checks in excess of specified dollar amounts.				
	The nonprofit has and follows petty cash control activities.				
	The nonprofit has a written Whistleblower policy.				
	The nonprofit conducts periodic risk assessment regarding its operations, financial reporting, and compliance objectives.				
	The nonprofit has a business interruption and disaster mitigation plan.				
	The nonprofit has control activities for check writing.				
	The nonprofit has a Document Retention policy.				
	The nonprofit has suitable insurance coverage that is periodically reviewed to ensure the appropriate levels and types of coverage are in place.				
	The nonprofit has an information technology policy, which covers e-mail, intranet, Internet, cell phones, PDAs, desktop computers, and laptops.				
	The nonprofit has payment documentation control activities in place.				
	The nonprofit has employee travel control activities.				
	The nonprofit's board has an audit committee.				
	The nonprofit has control activities regarding telephone usage.				
	The nonprofit files IRS Form 990s in a timely basis within prescribed time lines.				
	The nonprofit has established control activities to protect the nonprofit's fixed assets.				
	The nonprofit reviews income annually to determine and report unrelated business income to the IRS.				
	The nonprofit has an annual, independent audit of its financial statements, prepared by a certified public accountant.				

Priority Level	Indicator	Met	Needs Work	N/A	Timeline
	The nonprofit has cash receipt control activities.				
	The nonprofit receives a management letter from the external auditor containing recommendations for improvements in the financial operations of the nonprofit.				
	The nonprofit's board, management, staff, and volunteers know and understand their roles in the internal control system.				
	The nonprofit has human resources control activities regarding hiring, supervision, and termination.				
	The nonprofit has control activities protecting donor files and databases.				
	The nonprofit has control activities regarding fundraising vendors, such as proper state registration, fundraising tactics, and nonprofit compensation.				
	The nonprofit has a Conflict of Interest policy.				
	The nonprofit has procedures for client complaint and grievance.				
	The nonprofit has staff orientation procedures that convey the nonprofit's code of ethics.				
	The nonprofit has human resources control activities regarding the Family and Medical Leave Act, Workers Compensation claims and legislation, and HIPPA.				
	The nonprofit has a transportation policy.				
	The nonprofit's board, or an appropriate board committee, is responsible for soliciting bids, interviewing auditors, and hiring an auditor for the nonprofit.				
	The nonprofit performs thorough background checks for all board members, management, staff, and volunteers.				
	The nonprofit has a public relations policy.				
	The nonprofit has control activities regarding data entry, data verification, data backup, and data recovery.				
	The nonprofit's computers, computer network, and website are protected against viruses, worms, unauthorized access, and other dangers.				

(continues)

EXHIBIT 11.5	WORKSHEET 1: INTERNAL CONTROL SYSTEM REVIEW (CONTINUED)

Priority Level	Indicator	Needs Met	Work	N/A	Timeline
	The nonprofit has implemented a political competence strategic plan, which includes monitoring relevant external policies such as legislation and regulations.				
	The nonprofit has established control activities for fundraising.				
	The nonprofit has an information policy, which covers Internet and e-mail usage.				
	The nonprofit has established control activities regarding illness and injury prevention.				
	The nonprofit has control activities regarding the disposal of unneeded paper records and other paper waste, such as shredding requirements.				
	The nonprofit's internal policies are widely disseminated throughout the nonprofit.				
	The nonprofit has instituted privacy protection control activities, including those for electronic data.				
	The nonprofit's audit committee is financially literate, and at least one of the members is a financial expert.				
	The nonprofit's board, or an appropriate committee, reviews and approves the audit report and management letter, and institutes any necessary changes.				
	The nonprofit rotates its auditors every five years.				
	The nonprofit's Form 990, including the audited financial statements, is readily available to service recipients, volunteers, contributors, funders, and any other interested parties.				
	The nonprofit's board understands its fiduciary duties.				
	The nonprofit's policies, procedures, and processes regarding finance are all documented, and have adequate enforcement control activities.				
	The nonprofit has control activities regarding lobbying and other types of political activity.				

Priority Level	Indicator	Needs Met	Work	N/A	Timeline
	The nonprofit's policies, procedures, and processes regarding information technology are all documented, and have adequate enforcement control activities.				
	The nonprofit's policies, procedures, and processes regarding program operations are all documented, and have adequate enforcement control activities.				
	The nonprofit has identified its objectives and subobjectives in the areas of operations, financial reporting, and compliance.				
	The nonprofit has familiarized itself with the SOX requirements and has adopted the SOX best practices.				
	The nonprofit's policies, procedures, and processes regarding human resources are all documented, and have adequate enforcement control activities.				
	The nonprofit conducts various training opportunities for the board and appropriate staff on relevant accounting and finance topics.				

WORKSHEET 2: QUESTIONS FOR THE SENIOR MANAGEMENT AND THE BOARD OF DIRECTORS

An effective internal control system helps to identify and manage risk, monitor the integrity of financial and operating information, and ensures that the audit committee is effective. COSO designed the questions in Exhibit 11.6 to help senior management and the board of directors gain a better understanding of what comprises an effective internal control system. Working through these questions will give direction to senior management and the board as to how to begin to establish a culture of internal control in the nonprofit,

Although these questions were designed by COSO with public companies in mind, most of the questions are relevant for nonprofit boards of directors.

EXHIBIT 11.6	WORKSHEET 2: QUESTIONS FOR SENIOR MANAGEMENT AND THE BOARD OF DIRECTORS

Ethical Environment

- Do board members and senior executives set a day-in, day-out example of high integrity and ethical behavior?
- Is there a written code of conduct for employees? Is it reinforced by training, top-down communications, and periodic written statements of compliance from key employees?
- Are performance and incentive compensation targets reasonable and realistic, or do they create undue pressure for short-term results?
- Is it clear that fraudulent financial reporting at any level and in any form will not be tolerated?
- Are ethics woven into criteria used to evaluate individual and business unit performance?
- Does management react appropriately when receiving bad news from subordinates and business units?
- Does a process exist to resolve close ethical calls?
- Are business risks identified and candidly discussed with the board of directors?

Risk Assessment and Control Activities

- Is relevant, reliable, internal and external information timely identified, compiled, and communicated to those positioned to act?
- Are risks identified and analyzed and actions taken to mitigate them?
- Are controls in place to ensure management decisions are properly carried out?
- Does management routinely monitor controls in the process of running the organization's operations?
- Are periodic, systematic evaluations of control systems conducted and documented?

Audit Committee Effectiveness

- Has the board recently reviewed the audit committee's written charter?
- Are audit committee members functioning independently of management?
- Do committee members possess an appropriate mix of operating and financial control expertise?
- Does the committee understand and monitor the broad organizational control environment?
- Does the committee oversee appropriateness, relevance, and reliability of operational and financial reporting to the board, as well as to investors and other external users?
- Does the committee oversee existence of and compliance with ethical standards?
- Does the committee or full board have a meaningful but challenging relationship with independent and internal auditors, senior financial control executives, and key corporate and business unit operating executives?

Source: *Internal Control—Integrated Framework by the Committee of Sponsoring Organizations (COSO) of the Treadway Commission, 1993.*

CHAPTER 12

The Financially Literate Board

Phil and Francis, two board members of a small nonprofit, were discussing the latest meeting of the nominations committee. "I just don't understand why Archana and Nataliya objected to nominating Jing for board membership," said Phil. "I understand that it would be nice to have someone on the board with a background in finance, but Jing had a lot of great qualities. I just don't see why they are both so dead-set on requiring that all new board nominees have some financial expertise." "I know," said Francis, "and it's not just Archana and Nataliya who want people with financial expertise. The new Executive Director also seems to be pushing the board to recruit people who know finance. Every person she has invited to board functions since she arrived is somehow in the field of accounting or finance." "Well," said Phil. "I think it's a mistake to focus so heavily on people with money smarts. I think we should be more concerned with meeting our mission than tracking money!"

CHAPTER OVERVIEW

Although nonprofits and their boards should certainly be concerned with meeting their missions, recent scandals of nonprofit fiscal mismanagement have cast the nonprofit sector in an unfavorable light, and have damaged the public's trust in the integrity and public benefit of nonprofits. As discussed in Chapter 1, Congress and the IRS are considering a number of proposals that would create increased financial accountability for nonprofits and their boards. Some states, such as California, are starting to adopt SOX-influenced legislation and regulations regarding increasing board responsibility for financial oversight. Unfortunately, many nonprofit board members lack the necessary financial expertise to exert the required financial oversight. This chapter presents topics that should be included in training sessions for board members to increase their competence in financial matters. The format of the training sessions and the effect of different learning styles, especially those of adult learners, are examined. The chapter also discusses the nonprofit's audit committee composition and duties, and how the audit committee can deal effectively and efficiently with financial issues.

CHAPTER OBJECTIVES

By the end of this chapter, you should be able to:

- Diagnose the level of financial competence of the board of directors.
- Differentiate the needs of adult learners from those of "traditional" learners.
- Discuss the different types of learning styles and modalities to address them.
- Identify the accounting and finance terms, concepts, and techniques that board members should understand in order to be financially literate.
- Describe how board members can use budget analysis to analyze budget performance.
- Identify methods that board members can use to analyze financial statements for trends and red flags.
- Summarize the organization, functions, and duties of an audit committee.
- Develop a series of training sessions designed to increase board financial competence.

NEED FOR A FINANCIALLY LITERATE BOARD OF DIRECTORS

Unlike a for-profit organization that is responsible primarily to its shareholders, a non-profit organization is responsible to a number of stakeholders. The stakeholders have an interest in a nonprofit meeting its mission, and the nonprofit is accountable to its stakeholders for doing so. A nonprofit's stakeholders include the clientele it serves, its donors and funders, its employees, taxpayers, and society at large. While it may be easily understandable that nonprofits are accountable to their clientele, donors and funders, and employees, nonprofits' accountability to taxpayers and society at large may not be as clear. As part of obtaining its status as a nonprofit, the organization must provide services that are recognized to have societal value, and the organization must operate for the benefit of society and not for the benefit of private individuals. The societal value of the services and the societal benefit of the nonprofit form the basis of society at large as a nonprofit stakeholder.

One of the advantages of nonprofit status under the Internal Revenue Code Section 501(c)(3) is federal income tax exemption. Another advantage is that contributions to the nonprofit are deemed deductible for federal income, estate, and gift tax purposes for the donor. As such, all taxpayers underwrite nonprofits and thus become stakeholders in nonprofits.

Issues Caused by Financial Illiteracy

Given that nonprofits are responsible to a large number of stakeholders, financial accountability is a critical requirement for nonprofits. Without financial accountability, the nonprofit may not be able to efficiently provide the services its clientele requires, or effectively use the resources gained from donors and funders, which will decrease the nonprofit's benefit to the taxpayers and society at large. Unfortunately, however, many members of nonprofit boards of directors lack the requisite skills and expertise necessary to provide the needed financial oversight. This lack of financial expertise is so prevalent in the nonprofit sector that some have called it "the dirty little secret of nonprofit boards" (Gottlieb, 2003). Not having the requisite financial skills on the board of directors creates a number of serious issues:

- The board may face increased potential personal legal liabilities for not competently meeting its fiduciary duties.
- The board may not be able to participate competently in the development of the budget or competently evaluate the nonprofit's actual performance against its budgeted performance.
- The board may not be able to gauge the need for fundraising correctly, and may not be able to evaluate the effectiveness of external fundraisers quantitatively.
- The board may not be able to help in the development or in the evaluation of the nonprofit's internal control system.
- The board might review and approve financial statements that it may not be able to comprehend or interpret fully.
- The board may lack a clear understanding of the financial standing of the nonprofit.
- The board may not be able to fulfill its "check and balance" role with management in terms of asset preservation, possibly exposing the nonprofit to management fraud and malfeasance.
- The board may not be able to evaluate the competency of the external auditor, may not be able to devise an effective audit plan, and may not clearly understand the ramifications of the auditor's report.

It should be readily apparent that having a financially illiterate board of directors does not bode well for the effective functioning of the nonprofit. The SOX requirements for increased board competence in providing financial oversight, the creation of an audit committee, the presence of a "financial expert" on the audit committee, and the increased role of the board to provide constructive financial oversight certainly have relevance for nonprofits and would increase effectiveness of nonprofit operations and functioning. As such, it is critical that the board receives any training in relevant financial topics and concepts that is necessary for the board to be financially literate.

DETERMINING BOARD COMPETENCE IN FINANCIAL MATTERS

The first step in designing and implementing effective financial training for the board is to determine the level of competence that currently exists with the overall board and with its individual members. One way of determining competence is to use the attributes identified in Section 407 of SOX (P.L. 107–204, 2002) as being those of a financial expert:

- An understanding of GAAP and financial statements
- The ability to assess the general application of GAAP
- Experience preparing, auditing, analyzing, or evaluating financial statements
- Experience supervising one or more persons who are preparing, auditing, analyzing, or evaluating financial statements
- An understanding of internal controls and procedures for financial reporting
- An understanding of audit committee functions

An individual can be judged as having the aforementioned attributes if he or she has relevant education and experience in the area of financial management, auditing, accounting, and financial statement preparation. If a substantial number of the board members do not have the SOX required attributes, the overall board has low financial competence, and training is required.

Accounting and Finance Terms and Concepts

Another way of determining the level of board competence is to have an in-depth and frank discussion with the board, outlining the attributes a financially competent board should have. The board members could be surveyed to determine which attributes, if any, the board does not have. As part of the discussion, the board could be asked if it has a good level of understanding of a variety of accounting and finance terms and concepts, and if the board understands its financial oversight role. At a minimum, the board should have a working understanding of the following:

- Difference between the cash basis of accounting and the accrual basis of accounting
- Definition of assets, including the difference between current and non-current assets
- Types of assets and liabilities (e.g., cash, long-term debt, short-term investments, supplies, prepaid expenses, accounts payable, wages and salaries payable, assets limited as to use)
- Definition of liabilities, including the difference between current and non-current assets

- Definition of net assets, including the difference among permanently restricted net assets, temporarily restricted net assets, and unrestricted net assets
- How the basic accounting equation (Assets = Liabilities + Net Assets) is affected by financial and operational transactions
- Difference between gross accounts receivable and net accounts receivable
- Difference between gross property and equipment and net property and equipment
- Purpose of the four basic financial statements (Balance Sheet, Statement of Operations, Statement of Changes in Net Assets, Statement of Cash Flows)
- Definition of the items that typically appear on the Statement of Operations (e.g., expenses, operating income, nonoperating income, donor contributions, change in net unrealized gains and losses, increase in unrestricted net assets, below the line items, and excess of revenues, gains, and other expenses over expenses)
- Definition of the items that typically appear on the Statement of Changes in Net Assets (e.g., increase or decrease in unrestricted net assets, increase or decrease in permanently restricted net assets, total increase or decrease in net assets, net assets released from restrictions for operations)
- Definition of the items that typically appear on the Statement of Cash Flows (e.g., adjustments to reconcile changes in net assets to net cash provided by operating activities, cash flows from investing activities, cash flows from financing activities, and cash and cash equivalents at end of year)
- Difference between the financial statements for nonprofits and those for for-profits
- Financial statement analysis, using common financial ratios
- Purpose of the annual budget
- Budget variance analysis
- Purpose of an internal control system
- Components of an internal control system
- Role of the board regarding the development and evaluation of the internal control system
- Role and composition of the audit committee

Understanding what the board does and does not understand in terms of accounting, finance, and the board's financial oversight role will indicate the topics that should be covered in the board training sessions. In essence, to be considered financially literate, the board should be able to evaluate and interpret the four basic financial statements (balance sheet, statement of revenues and expenses, statement of changes in net assets, and statement of cash flows), should understand the budget process and how to evaluate budget performance, and should comprehend the components of an effective internal control system and the board's role in developing and evaluating the system.

ADULT LEARNERS AND LEARNING STYLES

After determining the topics that should be included in the training sessions, some thought should be given to the topic of adult learners and learning styles. As can be seen in Exhibit 12.1, adult learners and child learners are different in a number of ways, not just in age (Knowles, 1984; Knowles, 1995). Unlike children, adult learners tend

EXHIBIT 12.1   COMPARISON OF ADULT LEARNERS WITH CHILD LEARNERS

Childhood	Adulthood
Children depend on adults for material support, psychological support, and life management. They are other-directed.	Adults depend on themselves for material support and life management. Although they must still meet many psychological needs through others, they are largely self-directed.
Children perceive one of their major roles in life to be that of learner.	Adults perceive themselves to be doers; using previous learning to achieve success as workers, parents, etc.
Children, to a large degree, learn what they are told to learn.	Adults learn best when they perceive the outcomes of the learning process as valuable—contributing to their own development, work success, etc.
Children view the established learning content as important because adults tell them it is important.	Adults often have very different ideas about what is important to learn.
Children, as a group within educational settings, are much alike. They're approximately the same age, have similar education levels, etc.	Adults are very different from each other. Adult learning groups are likely to be composed of persons of many different ages, backgrounds, education levels, etc.
Children actually perceive time differently than older people do. Our perception of time changes as we age—time seems to pass more quickly as we get older.	Adults, in addition to perceiving time itself differently than children do, are more concerned about the effective use of time.
Children have a limited experience base.	Adults have a broad, rich experience base to which to relate new learning.
Children generally learn quickly.	Adults, for the most part, learn more slowly than children, but they learn just as well.
Children are open to new information and will readily adjust their views.	Adults are much more likely to reject or explain away new information that contradicts their beliefs.
Children's readiness to learn is linked to both academic development and biological development.	Adults' readiness to learn is more directly linked to need—needs related to fulfilling their roles as workers, spouses, parents, etc. and coping with life changes (divorce, death of a loved one, retirement, etc.).
Children learn (at least in part) because learning will be of use in the future.	Adults are more concerned about the immediate applicability of learning.

Childhood	Adulthood
Children are often externally motivated (by the promise of good grades, praise from teachers and parents, etc.).	Adults are more often internally motivated (by the potential for feelings of worth, self-esteem, achievement, etc.).
Children have less well-formed sets of expectations in terms of formal learning experiences. Their "filter" of past experience is smaller than that of adults.	Adults have well-formed expectations, which, unfortunately, are sometimes negative because they are based on unpleasant past formal learning experiences.

Source: The National Center for Research in Vocational Education. (1987). "*Plan instruction for adults, Module N-4,*" Ohio State University, Columbus, OH.

to reject new information if it does not fit in with their current belief system, are concerned about the use of their time, and their readiness to learn is linked to fulfilling specific needs; for example, the need to fulfill their professional or work role.

Preferences of Adult Learners

When designing the financial literacy training for the board, it is important to incorporate the characteristics of adult learners into the plan. The structure of the learning experience, the learning climate, the focus of learning, and the training strategies should all be based on the preferences of adult learners. Adult learners tend to have clear expectations about how the learning experience should be conducted, and expect instructors to accommodate those expectations. In regard to the structure of learning, adult learners tend to prefer flexible schedules that respond to their own time constraints and prefer interactive activities to more passive activities. The preferred learning climate for adult learners is one in which they are invited to express their views and experiences, and there is an atmosphere of mutual helpfulness and peer support. Since adults learn more readily when they perceive what they are learning as contributing to their professional success and as having immediate applicability, they prefer the focus of learning to be practical "how-to" learning that increases their autonomy.

Learning Style Considerations

When designing the financial literacy training for the board, in addition to considering the characteristics and preferences of adult learners, differences in adult learning styles should be considered. What is a learning style? A learning style is the primary method by which an individual best learns (Kolb, 1984; Kolb, 1985; Smith, 2001). Individuals perceive and take in information in different ways, and training that works well for one learning style may be unsuccessful for other styles. To be successful, training must incorporate modalities that are successful with a variety of training styles (Stroot, et al. 1998).

VAK Learning Style

Although there is a variety of widely-accepted learning style theories, some research indicates that learners fall into one or more of three different styles or categories: visual, auditory, and kinesthetic. This approach to learning is the VAK Learning Style (Clark, 2000; MacRae, 2004).

Visual Learning Style

Some individuals are visual learners, meaning that they learn best by seeing. If an individual with a visual learning style sees a particular task being done, he or she is more likely to learn the task than if he or she is "told how" to accomplish the task. For this type of learner, using reading materials, taking notes, drawing diagrams, or creating reference cards are the preferred methods of learning. If they see it, they can learn it.

Auditory Learning Style

Other individuals are auditory learners, meaning they learn best by hearing. This type of learner can listen to a lecture or presentation and process the information well, meaning they can easily recall what they have heard. For this type of learner, hearing lectures and presentations or listening to tapes are their preferred methods of learning. If they hear it, they can learn it.

Tactile Learning Style

The third learning style is the tactile learner, learners who learn by doing. These individuals are "hands-on" learning. They learn best in labs, in workshops, by typing, and by doing something creative. If they do it, they can learn it.

Tactics to Reinforce Particular Learning Styles

Although individuals tend to learn best by either seeing, hearing, or doing, information that is presented in a way that doesn't suit the primary learning style is not necessarily ineffective. For example, if an individual is primarily a visual learner but listens to a trainer who writes on the chalkboard or whiteboard while he or she is talking, the learner benefits primarily from the "seeing," but the "hearing" can reinforce that learning. Using training tactics that integrate all three of the learning styles is more effective than trying to sort the learners into learning styles and teaching only to that style. Training tactics that address visual learners would include:

- Use graphs, charts, illustrations, or other visual aids.
- Use videos, movies, slides, or PowerPoint presentations.
- Write notes on the chalkboard or whiteboard.
- Distribute copies of the visual materials for future examination.

- Distribute handouts that include plenty of content to reread after the learning session.
- Use flip charts to show what will come and what has been presented.

To integrate the auditory learning style, the following tactics would be helpful:

- Begin material with a brief explanation of what is coming and conclude with a summary of what has been covered (in other words, "tell them what they are going to learn, teach them, and then tell them what they have learned").
- Include auditory activities, such as brainstorming, small discussion groups, and oral quizzes.
- Use the Socratic method of lecturing by questioning learners to draw as much information from them as possible and then fill in the gaps.
- Leave time to "debrief" each training session, summarizing what was covered and the key points.

Kinesthetic learners learn best by touching, moving, or doing. To integrate this style into the training session:

- Distribute highlighters, colored pens, or pencils so learners can highlight the written material.
- Use activities that get the learners up and moving, such as moving to a different area of the room.
- Give frequent stretch breaks and have everyone move about in the room.
- Have learners transfer information from one medium to another; for example, have learners transfer some of the text in the written materials to a computer file.

CONTENT THAT SHOULD BE COVERED

As discussed previously, it is important that the board of directors understands what an internal control system is and what their role is in designing and evaluating the system. Much of the material presented in Chapter 11 can be used to educate the board about the internal control system. Understanding the role and importance of the audit committee is also required for the board to be financially literate; the audit committee is covered in Chapter 13. The rest of this chapter covers accounting and finance content that can be used in training sessions with the board regarding the financial statements and analyzing the budget.

Financial Statements

This section discusses the four basic financial documents and the analyses that can provide the board with an indicator of the nonprofit's current fiscal "health." The four basic statements include the balance sheet, the statement of operations, the statement of changes in net assets, and the statements of cash flows. What should a financially literate audit know about the financial statements? Knowing the basic components of each of the statements and being able to analyze the statements through horizontal, vertical, and ratio analysis will give the board the ability to better evaluate and interpret the financial statements. This will allow the board to judge the competency of analyses performed by others, including the staff and management members of the organization, the external auditors, and any other outside financial consultants.

Accrual Basis of Accounting

Before beginning the examination of the four basic financial statements, the accrual basis of accounting must be understood. Two types of accounting may be used for financial reporting—cash basis and accrual basis. In the cash basis of accounting, what is tracked is the flow of cash into and out of the nonprofit. Transactions are not recognized as occurring until cash is received by the organization or paid out by the organization. For example, a nonprofit would recognize revenues only when the payment, or cash, was received for delivering the good or service. Expenses are recognized as occurring only when the nonprofit actually pays for the resources used in its operations. This approach to accounting is similar to how people keep their personal checkbooks and is fairly straightforward.

In the accrual basis of accounting, revenues are recognized when they are earned, not when payment is received. Expenses are recognized as expenses when assets are used in the process of creating and delivering a service or good, not when the costs of the assets are paid. This is not as straightforward as the cash basis of accounting, but the accrual basis of accounting is the more generally accepted method, and provides more information about a nonprofit's fiscal health than does the cash basis of accounting. For example, let's assume that a nonprofit is using the cash basis of accounting and has a very large invoice due in December. Let's also assume that what is owed is a very large amount, so large that it is doubtful that the nonprofit will be able to pay it in full. If you were a creditor trying to make a decision about whether you should extend credit to the nonprofit, you would want to know that the organization was close to defaulting on a debt. However, if you were examining the financial statements from September, October, and November, this debt would not even appear, and you might think the nonprofit was in better financial health than it actually is. Since the cash basis of accounting only reports cash when cash flows into or out of the organization, it only reports what *has happened*, not what is *going to happen* in the future, even in the very near future. It wouldn't notify you that the nonprofit has debt that it is not going to be able to pay.

As well as not reflecting what debt an organization has, the cash basis of accounting also doesn't reflect the amount of money that is owed to the nonprofit. For example, the nonprofit may have extended credit to a number of its clients and is expecting to receive the payments within the 30 days, in the month of December. If you were a donor trying to make a decision about whether you should make a donation to the nonprofit, you would want to know that the nonprofit has this money due to it. However, if you were examining the financial statements from September, October, and November, you would not know that the organization expects to receive payments in December. Your opinion about the financial standing of the nonprofit would be faulty and you might make an incorrect donation decision. Since the accrual basis of accounting is the more generally accepted form of accounting and provides more information about an organization's fiscal health, the financial statements presented in this chapter are based on the accrual basis of accounting, not the cash basis.

Balance Sheet

The balance sheet presents the assets, liabilities, and the net assets of the nonprofit. In other words, the balance sheet presents the resources the nonprofit owns, the debt it must pay, and the nonprofit's net worth. The balance sheet provides a snapshot of the nonprofit, as it captures what the nonprofit looks like at a particular point of time, generally the last day of the accounting period. Typical accounting periods are monthly, quarterly, half-yearly, and yearly. The basis of the balance sheet is the basic accounting equation:

$$\text{Assets} = \text{Liabilities} + \text{Net Assets}$$

Since the total of what the nonprofit owns equals the combined total of the nonprofit's debt and the nonprofit's worth (net assets), there must be a balance between the total assets and the total liabilities plus the net assets. In the for-profit world, net assets would be the same as owners' equity or shareholders' equity.

Assets

Assets of the nonprofit are the resources it owns, both current and noncurrent. Examples of current assets include cash and cash equivalents, accounts receivables, and investments that have a life of one year or less. For example, if a nonprofit owns a six-month certificate of deposit, the certificate of deposit is considered a current investment. Examples of "cash equivalents" would be a savings account or a money market account, where the funds are easily available. Noncurrent assets include assets with a life greater than one year, such as property and equipment. For example, the building owned by the nonprofit is a noncurrent asset, as the nonprofit expects to be able to use the building for more than one year. Computer equipment is also a good example of a noncurrent asset. The IRS views most computer equipment as having a "life" of greater than one year, and most nonprofits use their computer equipment for several years. A term that is used interchangeably for *noncurrent* is *long-term*. Likewise, the term *short-term* can be used instead of *current*.

Liabilities

Liabilities are the obligations of the nonprofit to pay its creditors. As with assets, liabilities are divided into two categories: current and noncurrent. Examples of current liabilities include accounts payable, the current portion of long-term debt, and accrued expenses. Accrued expenses are the expenses that the organization generates as a result of "doing business," and these expenses must be paid for on a periodic basis. A good example of an accrued expense would be salaries or wages. The organization "uses up" the labor provided by its employees and once it has used it, it has incurred an expense that must be paid. As in the case of current assets, "current" for liabilities are liabilities that should be paid in one year or less; conversely, noncurrent liabilities are liabilities that have a payment life of more than one year. Examples of noncurrent liabilities are mortgages payable and bonds payable. These liabilities can have a life of 15 to 30 years.

Net Assets

In a nonprofit organization, the organization is exempt from taxes. In exchange for this exemption, the nonprofit is not owned by "investors," but rather by the community in which the nonprofits resides and by the clientele it serves. The net assets are the community's interest, or ownership, of the assets of the nonprofit. In a for-profit nonprofit, this portion of the nonprofit is referred to as "owners' equity" or "shareholders' equity." In the past, "fund balance" was used in nonprofits to indicate the net assets; however, that is rarely used now. In a nonprofit, the community "owns" the assets of the nonprofit, and net assets are the quantifiable reflection of that ownership. Net assets are equal to the value of all assets minus any liabilities:

$$\text{Net Assets} = \text{Assets} - \text{Liabilities}$$

This equation is simply a restatement of the basic accounting equation. The net assets are generally categorized into three classifications:

- Unrestricted net assets
- Temporarily restricted net assets
- Permanently restricted net assets

Unrestricted net assets are the dollar value of net assets where there is no restriction on how the net asset can be used. For example, if a donor contributes $10,000 to the nonprofit and does not specify how the donation must be used, that donation would be a part of unrestricted net assets. Unrestricted net assets do not have any stipulations or restrictions for their use, other than legal or ethical considerations. Temporarily restricted net assets reflect the dollar value of net assets that have a restriction on their use, but that restriction has a time limit. For example, a donor may give land to the nonprofit with the stipulation, or restriction, that the land cannot be sold for five years.

Since the land has a temporary restriction on its use, it is a part of temporarily restricted net assets. Permanently restricted net assets are net assets that have restrictions on their use, and that restriction does not have a time limit. An example of a permanently restricted net asset is an endowment that allows the nonprofit to spend the interest, but never any of the principal.

A sample nonprofit balance sheet can be seen in Exhibit 12.2.

EXHIBIT 12.2   SAMPLE NONPROFIT BALANCE SHEET FOR THE PERIOD ENDING DECEMBER 31, 20x0

ASSETS	
Current Assets	
Cash and Cash Equivalents	4,258
Short-Term Investments	9,136
Net Accounts Receivable	15,020
Supplies	1,997
Prepaid Expenses	670
Other	783
Total Current Assets	31,864
Noncurrent Assets	
Net Property and Equipment	49,358
Long-Term Investments	16,979
Assets Limited as to Use	10,470
Other	6,375
Total Non-Current Assets	83,182
TOTAL ASSETS	115,046
LIABILITIES	
Current Liabilities	
Long-Term Debt, Current	1,470
Accounts Payable	2,817
Wages and Salaries Payable	3,001
Supplies Payable	2,143
Utilities Payable	1,969
Total Current Liabilities	11,400
Noncurrent Assets	
Long-Term Debt, Net	20,100
Other	6,997
Total Noncurrent Assets	27,097
TOTAL LIABILITIES	38,497
NET ASSETS	
Unrestricted	67,720
Temporarily Restricted	3,216
Permanently Restricted	5,613
TOTAL NET ASSETS	76,549
TOTAL LIABILITIES AND NET ASSETS	115,046

Statement of Operations

The statement of operations is primarily a summary of the nonprofit's expenses and revenue, gains, and other support over a period of time. In the for-profit world, this statement is typically called the "income statement," "profit and loss statement," or "P & L statement." Revenues refer to any amounts earned by the nonprofit by selling a product or providing a service. For example, if the nonprofit is a hospital, it would earn revenues whenever it delivered hospital services to its patients. Gains occur when assets are sold for more than their book value. For example, if the nonprofit owns property and sells that property for an amount greater than the property's original purchase or donation value, the nonprofit has incurred a gain. Other support includes unrestricted donations, donations released from restriction, and appropriations from governmental nonprofits or other grant-making nonprofits. The basic formula for the statement of operations is:

Revenues, Gains and Other Support – Expenses = Excess of Revenues, Gains and Other Support over Expenses

A positive difference between revenues, gains, and other support and expenses is not considered profit, but rather an increase in the net assets. In the for-profit world, profits are distributed to the owners of the for-profit; in a nonprofit, the excess of revenues, gains, and other support over expenses should be used to generate more programs or services for the nonprofit's clientele. If they are not used to generate more programs or services, they become a part of the net assets of the nonprofit, and increase the nonprofit's overall net worth.

Below the Line Items

The statement of operations may also contain information on what are known as "below the line items." For example, donations that are made specifically to acquire capital assets are not considered a part of revenues, gains, and other support because their use is restricted to the purchase of capital assets. Another example of a below the line item are transfers to the parent nonprofit (assuming there is one). The effect of these below the line items appears on the statement of operations, below the value of excess of revenues, gains, and other support (hence the phrase "below the line item"). Below the line items directly affect the value of net assets, either positively or negatively. The effect is positive if the below the line item reflects an inflow of value to the nonprofit and, conversely, the effect on the net assets is negative if the below the line item reflects an outflow of value.

A sample nonprofit statement of operations can be seen in Exhibit 12.3.

Exhibit 12.3	SAMPLE STATEMENT OF OPERATIONS FOR THE PERIOD ENDING DECEMBER 31, 20x0

Unrestricted Revenues, Gains, and Other Support	
Net Program A Revenue	30,421
Net Program B Revenue	33,620
Net Program C Revenue	10,555
Other Revenues	3,576
Donor Contributions	20,735
Net Assets Released from Restrictions for Operations	300
Total Revenues, Gains, and Other Support	99,207
Expenses	
Wages and Salaries	59,751
Supplies	10,635
Utilities	8,059
Transportation	14,985
Depreciation	2,572
Bad Debt	1,035
Other Expenses	1,018
Total Expenses	98,055
Total Operating Income	1,152
Non-Operating Income (Investment)	975
Excess of Revenues over Expenses	2,127
Change in Net Unrealized Gains and Losses	105
Net Assets Released from Restrictions Used for Equipment Purchase	437
Increase in Unrestricted Net Assets	2,669

Statement of Changes in Net Assets

The purpose of the statement of changes in net assets is to account for any changes in the net assets of the balance sheet from one accounting period to the next. There are two reasons why the value of net assets would change:

- Changes in unrestricted net assets
- Changes in restricted net assets

Changes in unrestricted net assets flow directly from the statement of operations. If the excess of revenues, gains, and other support is positive, unrestricted net assets are increased. A positive change reflects that the nonprofit's revenues, gains, and other support are greater than its expenses, and the amount of the unrestricted net assets is increased by that amount. In this case, the nonprofit is making a "profit." Conversely, if the nonprofit's expenses are greater than its revenues, gains, and other support, the amount of the unrestricted net assets is decreased by that amount. In this case, the nonprofit is experiencing a "loss."

As discussed previously, the statement of operations contains information in addition to the value of the excess of revenues, gains, and other support over expenses. These below the items directly affect the value of the unrestricted net assets, by either increasing or decreasing them. Changes in restricted net assets, through either a temporarily restricted or a permanently restricted donation, directly affect the value of the net assets. However, not all changes in restricted net assets change the value of net assets. For example, temporarily restricted assets are only restricted for a specific period of time. If the restriction period for any of the temporarily restricted net assets expires, the value of that net asset "moves" to unrestricted net assets. Although the value of restricted net assets is reduced, the value of net assets is not changed since the reduction is offset by the increase in unrestricted net assets.

A sample nonprofit statement of changes in net assets can be seen in Exhibit 12.4.

Statement of Cash Flows

The fourth basic financial statement is the statement of cash flows. This statement answers the following two questions:

- Where did the cash come from?
- Where did the cash go?

Exhibit 12.4   SAMPLE STATEMENT OF CHANGES IN NET ASSETS FOR THE PERIOD ENDING DECEMBER 31, 20x0

Unrestricted Net Assets	
Excess of Revenues over Expenses	2,127
Change in Net Unrealized Gains and Losses	105
Net Assets Released from Restrictions Used for Equipment Purchase	437
Increase (Decrease) in Unrestricted Net Assets	2,669
Temporarily Restricted Net Assets	
Net Assets Released from Restrictions to be Used for Equipment Purchase	(437)
Net Assets Released from Restrictions for Operations	(300)
Net Unrealized Gains and Losses	575
Increase (Decrease) in Temporarily Restricted Net Assets	(162)
Permanently Restricted Net Assets	
Net Unrealized Gains and Losses	289
Contributions for Endowment Funds	1,500
Increase (Decrease) in Permanently Restricted Net Assets	1,789
Total Increase (Decrease) in Net Assets	4,296
Net Assets, Beginning of Month	72,253
Net Assets, End of Month	76,549

The statement of cash flows tracks cash flows from operating activities, cash flows from investing activities, and cash flows from financing activities. Operating activities are the normal business activities in which the nonprofit engages to generate revenues. Examples of operating activities are the selling of products or the provision of services. Investing activities include activities such as the purchasing and selling of investments, transfers to the parent nonprofit (if there is one), and capital expenditures. The statement of cash flows tracks the cash inflows and outflows from these activities and reports the net increase (or decrease) in cash and cash equivalents as the result of these activities.

A sample nonprofit statement of cash flows can be seen in Exhibit 12.5.

Financial Statement Analysis

Now that the components of each of the financial statements have been discussed, learning how to analyze the information contained in the statements is the next step. The real

EXHIBIT 12.5	SAMPLE STATEMENT OF CASH FLOW FOR THE PERIOD ENDING DECEMBER 31, 20X0

Cash Flows from Operating Activities	
Change in Net Assets	
Adjustments to Reconcile Changes in Net Assets to	
Net Cash Provided by Operating Activities:	4,896
Depreciation	2,572
Net Unrealized Gains and Losses	(971)
Bad Debt	1,035
Restricted Contributions Received	(1,500)
Increase (Decrease) in:	
Net Accounts Receivable	(6,544)
Accounts Payable	2,000
Wages and Salaries Payable	13,350
Supplies Payable	1,477
Utilities Payable	2,478
Long-Term Debt, Current	500
Net Cash Provided by Operating Activities	19,293
Cash Flows from Investing Activities	
Purchases of Investment	(5,175)
Capital Expenditures	(12,996)
Net Cash Flows Used in Investing Activities	(18,171)
Cash Flows from Financing Activities	
Increase in Long-Term Debt	5,100
Payments on Long-Term Debt	(3,512)
Net Cash Used in Financing Activities	1,588
Net Increase in Cash and Cash Equivalents	2,710
Cash and Cash Equivalent at Beginning of Year	1,548
Cash and Cash Equivalents at End of Year	4,258

value of financial statements lies in the fact that they can be used to help predict the nonprofit's future financial condition, and provide a view of the nonprofit's current condition. Analyzing the financial statements can help to answer the following questions:

- Is the nonprofit profitable? Why or why not? Compared to other similar nonprofits, how well is this nonprofit faring in profitability?

- How effective is the nonprofit in collecting what is owed to it? How does the nonprofit compare to other similar nonprofits?

- Will the nonprofit be able to meet its debts in a timely manner? Compared to other similar nonprofits, is this nonprofit doing better or worse?

- How efficiently is the nonprofit using its assets? Compared to other similar nonprofits, is improvement needed? If the nonprofit is using its assets inefficiently, it is using more resources than are necessary to produce and deliver its programs and services.

- Are the nonprofit's facility and equipment in need of replacement? Does the nonprofit meet the standard for facility and equipment replacement? If all of the nonprofit's computer equipment is more than five years old, the nonprofit will soon have to replace that equipment. That could be a large expense for the nonprofit, and the board and management should be aware of this upcoming expense.

- Is the nonprofit in a good position to take on additional debt, or is it overextended? Compared to other similar nonprofits, does the nonprofit have too much or too little debt? Having too much debt can cause repayment problems for a nonprofit, but having too little debt means that the nonprofit isn't taking advantage of the leverage that debt can give.

Financial Ratios

Financial ratios express the relationship between two numbers and basically pull together two elements of the financial statements: one expressed as the numerator and one as the denominator. There are almost an unlimited number of financial ratios that can be calculated, and we will not, of course, be able to cover each possible ratio here. However, if the board member is able to calculate and interpret some ratios from each of the four common classifications of ratios, the job of analyzing the financial statements can more thoroughly be accomplished. There are four general classifications of financial ratios: liquidity, profitability, asset management or activity, and capital structure. The following section describes the components of each and explains what board members should look for in terms of "red flags."

- Liquidity ratios measure a nonprofit's ability to meet short-term obligations, collect receivables, and maintain sufficient cash on hand. Liquidity ratios help to answer the question, "How able is the nonprofit to meet its short-term obligations and debt?"

- Profitability ratios help to answer the question, "Is the nonprofit profitable?"

- Asset management or activity ratios help to answer two questions, "How efficiently is the nonprofit using its assets to produce revenues?" and, "In view of current and projected revenues, is the amount of each type of asset reasonable, too high, or too low?"

- Debt management or capital structure ratios help to determine the extent to which a nonprofit uses debt to finance its assets. These ratios help to answer the questions, "How are the nonprofit's assets financed?" and, "How able is the nonprofit to take on new debt?"

Since ratio analysis can best be interpreted relative to a standard, ratio analysis should thus be a comparative analysis. The standard may be the nonprofit's past performance, a goal set by the nonprofit, or the average performance level in the industry or a group of equivalent nonprofits. Trade associations frequently publish the financial ratios standards, or benchmarks, for the nonprofits in the industry.

Liquidity Ratios

Liquidity ratios reflect the ability of the nonprofit to meet its current obligations, to pay bills that are due. If the nonprofit does not has enough cash on hand to pay its obligations when they come due, the nonprofit's credit rating may be adversely affected, which could result in a loss of credit, loss of vendor relationships, and loss of trade discounts. Frequently used liquidity ratios include:

- Current ratio
- Quick ratio
- Days receivables ratio
- Days cash on hand
- Average payment period

Current Ratio

The current ratio reflects the short-term solvency of the nonprofit. The current ratio equals current assets divided by current liabilities. Both of these values can be found on the balance sheet.

$$\frac{\text{Current Assets}}{\text{Current Liabilities}} = \text{Current Ratio}$$

RED FLAG:

If the current ratio = 1 or more, the nonprofit has sufficient current assets to meet its current liabilities. If the current ratio is less than 1, the nonprofit may experience difficulty in meeting its short-term obligations. For example, if the current ratio = .45, for every $1 owed in short-term obligations the nonprofit only has 45 cents to cover those obligations. In general, a nonprofit would like to be equal to or above the current ratio standard. If the current ratio is substantially greater than the standard, however, the nonprofit may be holding too much cash on hand and should investigate longer-term investments. If the nonprofit finds itself in a nonliquid position, it should develop and implement plans to either improve the flow of cash into the nonprofit or reduce its short-term obligations.

Quick Ratio

The quick ratio is a more stringent indicator of liquidity as it only uses the most liquid current assets in its formula. Assets that are current but are not immediately liquid are excluded. Examples of current assets that are excluded include accounts receivables and product inventory. The quick ratio equals cash plus short-term investments (also known as cash equivalents) plus net accounts receivables divided by current liabilities. The values of these four accounts can be found on the balance sheet.

$$\frac{\text{Cash} + \text{Cash Equivalents} + \text{Net Accounts Receivables}}{\text{Current Liabilities}} = \text{Quick Ratio}$$

RED FLAG:

As in the case with the current ration, in general a nonprofit would like to be equal to or above the quick ratio standard, but not substantially above the standard. An organization does not want to be short of cash, but it also does not want to have a lot of cash that is "sitting around and not working" for the nonprofit.

Days Receivables Ratio

The days receivables ratio is a measure of how long the average client or customer takes to pay the invoice for services or products sold. The quicker clients or customers pay their invoices, the quicker the nonprofit is converting its receivables into cash. The days receivables equals net accounts receivables divided by net revenues divided by

365. The value of net accounts receivables can be found on the balance sheet, and the value for net revenues can be found on the statement of operations.

$$\frac{\text{Net Accounts Receivables}}{\text{Net Revenues} / 365} = \text{Days Receivable}$$

RED FLAG:

The days receivables ratio should be equal to or below the standard. If the non-profit is not at least meeting the standard, it may be experiencing some liquidity problems. Developing and implementing a plan to improve the collections of receivables may improve the nonprofit's liquidity position by bringing cash more quickly into the nonprofit.

Days Cash On Hand

Days cash on hand is a measure of how long the nonprofit could meet its obligations if cash receipts were discontinued. Days cash on hand equals unrestricted cash and cash equivalents divided by expenses minus depreciation expense divided by 365. The values of these two accounts can be found on the balance sheet.

$$\frac{\text{Unrestricted Cash} + \text{Cash Equivalents}}{\text{Expenses} - \text{Depreciation Expense} / 365} = \text{Days Cash on Hand Ratio}$$

RED FLAG:

In general, a nonprofit would like to be equal to or above the days cash on hand ratio, but not substantially above the standard. The days cash on hand ratio can be improved by either increasing the inflow of cash or decreasing the expenses.

Average Payment Period

The average payment period is a measure of how long it takes the nonprofit to pay its bills. Developing and keeping a good credit relationship with vendors and suppliers is critical to the financial well being of the nonprofit, and the nonprofit should thus attempt to pay its bills on time. The average payment period equals current liabilities divided by expenses minus depreciation expense divided by 365. The value of current liabilities can be found on the balance sheet, and the values of expenses and depreciation expense can be found on the statement of operations.

$$\frac{\text{Current Liabilities}}{\text{Expenses} - \text{Depreciation Expense} / 365} = \text{Average Payment Period}$$

RED FLAG:

In general, the average payment period should be equal to or less than the standard. If the average payment period is substantially below the standard or is substantially less than 30 days (the typical number of days allowed to pay an invoice), however, the nonprofit may be paying its bills too quickly and may be missing opportunities for short-term investment. It may also be that the nonprofit is paying its bills in less than 30 days to earn trade discounts, a reduction in the amount paid in exchange for early payment. One has to investigate the cause of the ratio value before one can decide what action, if any, needs to be taken.

Profitability Ratios

The profitability ratios are all measures of the ability of the nonprofit to produce a profit, or to generate excess revenues, gains, and other support over expenses. A nonprofit that is only "breaking even" or, worse, suffering a loss, will not be able to expand its delivery of services. If the nonprofit experiences continued losses, it may not even be able to survive. Frequently used profitability ratios include:

- Operating margin
- Return on total assets

Operating Margin

The operating margin measures the proportion of excess revenues, gains, and other support over expenses earned for each dollar of revenues, gains, and other support. The operating margin equals excess of revenues, gains, and other support over expenses divided by revenues, gains, and other support. Both of these account values can be found on the statement of operations.

$$\frac{\text{Excess of Revenues, Gains, and Other Support over Expenses}}{\text{Revenues, Gains, and Other Support}} = \text{Operating Margin}$$

RED FLAG:

In general, a nonprofit would like to operate at or slightly above the standard. Although the mission of the nonprofit is not to generate a profit or excess revenues, gains, and other support over expenses, having a good operating margin gives the nonprofit the financial ability to expand its delivery of services. If the operating margin were substantially higher than the standard, however, the nonprofit may be charging too much for its services and products, and not meeting the needs of the community.

Return on Total Assets

The return on total assets is a measure of how much "profit" is earned for each dollar invested in assets. The return on total assets equals the excess of revenues, gains, and other support over expenses divided by total assets. The value of revenues, gains, and other support can be found on the statement of operations, while the value of total assets can be found on the balance sheet.

$$\frac{\text{Excess of Revenues, Gains, and Other Support over Expenses}}{\text{Total Assets}} = \text{Return on Total Assets}$$

RED FLAG:

In general, a nonprofit would like to have a return on assets at or slightly above the standard. If the nonprofit is below the standard, it is not using its assets effectively, or it doesn't have the right "mix" of assets to effectively deliver services and generate excess revenues, gains and other support.

Asset Management Ratios

The asset management ratios provide a measure of how much in revenues, gain, and other support is generated for each dollar invested in assets.

Asset management ratios include:

- Total asset turnover ratio
- Fixed assets turnover ratio
- Age of facility ratio

Total Asset Turnover Ratio

The total asset turnover ratio measures the overall efficiency of the nonprofit's assets to produce revenues, gains, and other support. The total asset turnover ratio equals revenues, gains, and other support divided by total assets. The value of the revenues, gains, and other support can be found on the statement of operations, and the value of total assets can be found on the balance sheet.

$$\frac{\text{Revenues, Gains, and Other Support}}{\text{Total Assets}} = \text{Total Asset Turnover Ratio}$$

In general, a nonprofit would like to have a total asset turnover ratio equal to or greater than the standard. The higher the ratio, the more efficient the nonprofit is in its use of its assets.

Fixed Assets Turnover Ratio

The fixed assets turnover ratio is a measure of the nonprofit's efficiency in using its fixed assets of facility and equipment to produce revenues, gains, and other support. The fixed assets turnover ratio equals revenues, gains, and other support divided by facility and equipment minus accumulated depreciation. The value of the revenues, gains, and other support can be found on the statement of operations, and the values of facility, equipment, and accumulated depreciation can be found on the balance sheet.

$$\frac{\text{Revenues, Gains, and Other Support}}{\text{Facility} + \text{Equipment} - \text{Accumulated Depreciation}} = \text{Fixed Assets Turnover Ratio}$$

In general, a nonprofit would like to have a fixed assets turnover ratio equal to or higher than the standard. If the ratio is substantially higher than the standard, however, it may be an indication that the nonprofit has not invested enough in fixed assets and will need to upgrade its facility or equipment in the near future.

Age of Facility Ratio

The age of facility ratio provides a measure of the average age of a nonprofit's facility and equipment. The age of facility ratio equals accumulated depreciation divided by depreciation expense. The value of accumulated depreciation can be found on the balance sheet, and the value of depreciation expense can be found on the statement of operations.

$$\frac{\text{Accumulated Depreciation}}{\text{Depreciation Expense}} = \text{Age of Facility Ratio}$$

In general, a nonprofit would like to be equal to or below the standard. If the ratio is substantially higher than the standard, it may indicate that the nonprofit needs to replace its equipment or facility soon.

Debt Management Ratios

Debt management ratios reflect the nonprofit's long-term liquidity by quantifying the relationship between the nonprofit's assets and its long-term debt. Debt management ratios also give an indication of a nonprofit's ability to cover its long-term debt and its ability to take on more long-term debt. Debt management ratios include:

- Long-term debt to net assets ratio
- Times interest earned ratio
- Debt service coverage ratio

Long-Term Debt to Net Assets Ratio

The long-term debt to net assets ratio is a measure of the relationship between long-term debt and the assets owned by the nonprofit. It is a reflection of the proportion of net assets that were financed through long-term debt. The long-term debt to net assets ratio equals the long-term debt divided by the net assets. The value of both long-term debt and net assets can be found on the balance sheet.

$$\frac{\text{Long-Term Debt}}{\text{Net Assets}} = \text{Long-Term Debt to Net Assets Ratio}$$

In general, a nonprofit would like to have a long-term debt to net assets ratio equal to or lower than the standard. Although all nonprofits should take advantage of the leveraging power of long-term debt, taking on too much debt may place the nonprofit in the risky position of not being able to easily repay the debt. In addition, having too much debt may put the nonprofit in the position of not being able to take on additional debt when it is needed.

Times Interest Earned Ratio

The times interest earned ratio is a measure of the nonprofit's ability to meet its interest payment for long-term debt. The times interest earned ratio equals the excess of revenues, gains, and other support over expenses plus interest expense divided by the interest expense. The value of both excess of revenues, gains, and other support over expenses and the interest expense can be found on the statement of operations.

$$\frac{\text{Excess of Revenues, Gains, and Other Support Over Expenses} + \text{Interest Expense}}{\text{Interest Expense}} = \text{Times Interest Earned Ratio}$$

In general, a nonprofit would like to have a times interest earned ratio equal to or greater than the standard. The value of the times interest earned ratio is especially important if the nonprofit wishes to take on more long-term debt in the near future. Creditors and lenders use the times interest earned ratio to evaluate a nonprofit's ability to repay debt.

Debt Service Coverage Ratio

The debt service coverage ratio is a more stringent measure of a nonprofit's ability to repay its long-term debt. Unlike the times interest earned ratio, the debt service coverage ratio does not just measure the nonprofit's ability to cover its interest expense. Instead, this ratio measures a nonprofit's ability to meet its entire loan requirements, principal plus interest. The debt service coverage ratio equals the excess of revenues, gains, and other support over expenses plus interest expense plus depreciation expense divided by the interest expense plus the principal payment. The value off the interest expense, depreciation expense, and the excess of revenues, gains, and other support over expenses can be found on the statement of operations.

$$\frac{\text{Excess of Revenues, Gains, and Other Support Over Expenses} + \text{Interest Expense} + \text{Depreciation Expense}}{\text{Interest Expense} + \text{Principal Payment}} = \text{Debt Service Coverage Ratio}$$

In general, a nonprofit would like to have a debt service coverage ratio equal to or greater than the standard. The greater the debt service coverage ratio, the better able the nonprofit is to handle additional long-term debt.

ANNUAL BUDGET

What is a budget? In essence, the annual budget is about the nonprofit's future. For the upcoming year, it represents the nonprofit's mission and objectives, the priorities of the board and management, expectations about the services the nonprofit will provide, the sources of funding and revenues, and the costs of providing the services. The budget indicates what the nonprofit is trying to achieve in the coming year, how much the nonprofit expects it will cost to achieve those goals, and how the nonprofit expects to pay those costs. In addition, the budget serves as a "control document" since it allows management and the board to analyze what actually happened against what was planned in terms of funding and revenues, services, and costs.

Three Stages of Budget Planning

In essence, the budget is the end product of the budget planning process, which consists of environmental assessment, programming, and budget preparation.

Environmental Assessment

For all organizations, and in particular for nonprofits, the future is uncertain. Organizational success rests in part on how well the nonprofit anticipates the future events that may affect the nonprofit's ability to survive and deliver services. Since the environment is constantly changing, before a nonprofit can begin to plan for the upcoming year, it first has to assess what kind of environment it will be operating in for the next year. The environment can be viewed according to the nonprofit's external environment and its internal environment.

External Environment

The nonprofit's external environment is comprised of the factors that are outside of the jurisdiction or control of the nonprofit. Examples of factors in the external environment that can affect the nonprofit include:

- Governmental and regulatory policies, such as SOX and SOX-influenced legislation or changes in IRS regulations
- Local and national economy, such as changes in unemployment, average income, value of the stock market, inflation, or interest rates
- Competition for funding and donors, such as an increase in the number of non-profits that offer similar services or donor/funder interest shifting to nonprofits delivering a different type of service
- Need and demand for the nonprofit's services, such as changes in the number of clients, the intensity level of required services, or in the client population

The nonprofit must take its external environment into account when it is planning for next year's activities; otherwise, the plan won't accurately reflect reality. For example, a severe economic turndown may have a negative effect on the nonprofit's level of donor contributions. If the nonprofit anticipates the economic downturn, it can include steps in its plan to mitigate the impact of reduced donor contributions. If it doesn't anticipate the economic turndown, the nonprofit may have erroneously planned to receive donor contributions that won't materialize.

Internal Environment

In addition to its external environment, the nonprofit must assess its internal environment, which consists of the nonprofit's management, staff, board of directors, mission, past performance, culture, and policies and procedures. All of these factors combine to become both resources and constraints in regard to plans for the future. For example, does the level of staffing correspond with the nonprofit's plan for the next year, or should the level of staffing be increased or decreased? Will the nonprofit have higher salary costs if it needs to have more technical skills to implement its plan? What is the nonprofit's mission and how will it be reflected in plans for next year? Does the nonprofit have the policies and procedures in place that mesh with the planning for the coming year, or do they need revision or development?

Programming

The second stage of the budget planning process is programming. In this stage, the nonprofit translates its assumptions about the future into the steps to achieve its mission. Based on the environmental analysis, what are the goals, objectives, and activities for the next year? What type of programs and services will the nonprofit offer and who are the potential clients? What resources does the nonprofit need to carry out its goals? What labor, materials, supplies, capital resources are needed?

Budget Preparation

Once the goals, objectives, and resource requirements have been identified in the programming stage, the actual preparation of the budget can begin. Budget preparation translates the goals, objectives, and activities into a forecast of the anticipated volume of services to be delivered, of the resources needed to provide the services and the costs of these resources. Typically, the annual budget consists of the operating, cash, and capital budgets.

Operating Budget

The operating budget consists of two subbudgets—the expense budget and the revenues budget. The expense budget is a dollar estimate of the amount of resources needed to provide services during the coming year. Common types of expenses include:

- Labor—salary or wages plus fringe benefits
- Telephone
- Insurance
- Travel
- Cleaning
- Utilities
- Depreciation
- Interest
- Equipment maintenance
- Other administrative and general expenses

   The revenue budget is the dollar estimate of two sources of revenue—revenue from the delivery of services and revenue from nonservice related activities such as donor contributions or grants. It is important to specify the sources of revenue so that decisions regarding fundraising and grant writing can be made.

Cash Budget

The operating budget is prepared on the accrual basis of accounting and does not indicate the expected flow of cash into and out of the nonprofit. The cash budget converts the operating budget from the accrual basis of accounting and reflects the nonprofit's cash inflows and outflows. It also details when it is necessary to borrow to cover cash shortages and when excess cash is available to invest.

Capital Budget

The capital budget reflects the expected expenses related to the purchase of major capital items such as plant and equipment. These items require major expenditures that must be anticipated and financed.

Budget Analysis

Many nonprofits, especially the smaller ones, ignore or forget the other half of the budgeting. Budgets are too often proposed, discussed, accepted, and then forgotten. Variance analysis looks "after the fact" at what caused a difference between the planned and the actual fiscal performance. One way for the board to evaluate the nonprofit's fiscal performance is to conduct a budget analysis, looking for variance in net income (revenues – expenses). A budget variance is the difference between what was budgeted and what actually occurred, and its effect on net income. Variance in net income can be caused by variance in either revenues or expenses, or variance in both. Variance in revenues can be caused by two sources:

- Variance in the volume, or quantity, of goods, or services sold
- Variance in the unit price of the goods or services sold

Revenue Volume Variance = (Actual Volume – Budgeted Volume) × Budgeted Unit Price
Revenue Unit Price Variance = (Actual Unit Price – Budgeted Unit Price) × Actual Volume

   As with the revenues variance, the variance in expenses can be caused by two sources:

- Variance in the volume, or quantity, of goods or services sold
- Variance in the cost of the resources used to produce the services

Expense Volume Variance = (Actual Volume – Budgeted Volume) × Budgeted Unit Price
Expense Cost Variance = (Actual Unit Cost – Budgeted Unit Cost) × Actual Volume

Variances are either positive or negative, depending on the type of variance and the direction of the variance. For the revenue variance, if the amount of the actual revenues is higher than the budgeted revenues, then the revenue variance is positive, or favorable. For the expense variance, if the difference between the actual expenses is higher than the budgeted expenses, then the expense variance is negative, or unfavorable. Every variance should stimulate questions. Why did one project cost more or less? Were objectives met? Is a positive variance a cost saving or a failure to implement? Is a negative variance a change in plans, a management failure, or an unrealistic budget?

Once the sources of the total budget variance are identified, the board can identify the causes in the difference between the nonprofit's budgeted performance and its actual performance and can take the steps necessary to improve the nonprofit's operations and budget planning.

CONCLUSION

SOX's requirements for increased board involvement in financial oversight certainly have implications for nonprofits. A nonprofit's financial health depends on board financial oversight. For nonprofit boards to competently exercise their financial oversight role, the board must be financially literate. Finance literacy requires that the board be able to understand and fulfill its role in developing and evaluating the internal control system, understand and fulfill the role of the audit committee, read and interpret the nonprofit's financial statements, and competently participate in budget development and evaluation. For the financially illiterate board, the corrective training sessions must incorporate the preferences of adult learners and a variety of training tactics that will appeal to different learning styles.

WORKSHEET: DEVELOPING A FINANCIAL LITERACY TRAINING PLAN

Board development can be a sensitive subject in many nonprofits. Conducting effective training is critical; most board members won't appreciate or respond well to training that isn't well planned and executed. Exhibit 12.6 outlines an eight-step process to develop effective training. Working through this process will help a nonprofit efficiently develop a financially literate board.

EXHIBIT 12.6	DEVELOPING A FINANCIAL LITERACY TRAINING PLAN

Steps	Actions
Step 1 Identify the learning objectives.	The goal of this training is to develop a financially literate board. To achieve that goal, the training must include specific learning objectives. What concepts, skills, techniques should the board learn? The learning objectives should be based on the diagnosis of the level of board financial literacy. Examples: • The board should be able to discuss the purpose of each of the four basic financial statements. • The board should be able to perform a budget variance analysis.
Step 2 Sequence the learning objectives.	Many of the learning objectives will depend on other learning objectives. It is important to determine the proper sequencing of the learning objectives for effective training. For example, the board would not be able to understand the basic accounting equation without first understanding the concepts of assets, liabilities, and net assets. How many training sessions are required to cover all of the learning objectives but not overwhelm or exhaust the board? Should there be multiple training sessions or an all-day retreat?
Step 3 Pick the training method or tactic for each of the learning objectives	The training methods should incorporate the adult learner preferences and the different learning styles discussed in the chapter. What tactics (lecture, video, discussion, real-life problem solving, on-line information, group work, written handouts, case study analysis, etc.) will be used for each learning objective? There should also be a backup training tactic in case the primary tactic isn't successful during the actual training. Examples: • Use a PowerPoint presentation to demonstrate how changes in assets affect the other elements of the balance sheet. • Break the group into groups of three, and have each group conduct a budget analysis on last year's budget and present their findings.

(continues)

Exhibit 12.6	Developing a Financial Literacy Training Plan (continued)

Steps	Actions
Step 4 Develop any needed training materials.	What materials are needed to implement the training methods developed in Step 3? Are audio-visual aids, textbooks, PowerPoint presentations, hand-outs, list of websites, sample financial statements, workbooks, real-life problems, paper copies of PowerPoint presentation, etc. going to be used as training methods? These materials must be developed before training can begin. Is there a training budget to cover the costs of developing appropriate materials?
Step 5 Develop learner assessment tactics.	Now that the sequence of learning objectives is in place, the training tactics selected for each objective, and the training materials have been developed, it is time to develop tactics to assess learning. How will the trainer know if the board is understanding the material? Will he or she solicit group feedback, have short tests, use real-life materials to judge the board's performance, or talk one-on-one with each board member?
Step 6 Schedule facilities.	Is the trainer scheduled to conduct the sessions? Is the training schedule compatible with the board members' personal schedules? Have all board members confirmed that they can and will attend the training? Where will the training be conducted? Are all needed technology resources available? How large is the training area? Does the site have comfortable chairs and tables? Is there a map with written directions for the board? Are there sufficient restroom and break facilities at the training site?
Step 7 Conduct the training.	Use all of the steps above to conduct the training, but the trainer has to be flexible if the training tactics developed in Step 4 aren't working. Use the backup training tactics if necessary.
Step 8 Post-training follow-up.	Are the board members able to successfully use what they learned in the training? Is the board more financially literate? At an acceptable level of literacy? If not, additional training is probably necessary. Go back to Step 1.

CHAPTER 13

SOX Best Practices
and Legal Compliance

"I don't know why Gwen is so hysterical about this year's audit," said Jeff. "We've had our books audited every year for the past 15 years, we've used the same auditor, and every year he has given us a clean bill of health. I don't see why she thinks the board has to be so involved in the audit. We've always let the Executive Director and the auditor work out what needs to be done, and it's been fine every year." "I know," said Jacob. "Every time we get one of those new gung-ho board members, we have to hear about the UWA, Foundation for New Era Philanthropy and UWNCA horror stories. I'm frankly tired of hearing about it. Yes, I know that they had some auditing problems, and yes, I know that the boards were criticized for not being more vigilant, but we're just a small nonprofit. We're not even in the same league with those guys! I don't think our board needs to get so involved in the audit, and if I hear the words 'board financial oversight responsibilities' one more time from her, I'm going to have to set her straight. And if I hear 'Form 990' again, well, I just won't be responsible for what I say!" "Good," said Jeff. "I think with Gwen, we're just going to have to nip all of her pushing for us to do more work on the audit and the Form 990 in the bud. If we don't, the next thing she might start talking about is forming an audit committee. That's the last thing we need—another committee."

CHAPTER OVERVIEW

In the past, nonprofits were not subjected to as much public scrutiny as for-profit organizations, and did not have the same level of regulation. Primarily, nonprofits were regulated by the state in which they were incorporated and by the IRS rules pertaining to tax-exemption status. Partially as a result of SOX and the factors that drove SOX, nonprofits must now exert legal compliance with a number of rules, regulations, and laws. This chapter reviews some of the newer IRS rules for nonprofits, discusses how nonprofits can work with their external auditors and attorneys to ensure compliance, reviews the legal requirements for filing Form 990, and outlines the role and duties of the audit committee. The chapter also briefly covers two of the recent scandals in the nonprofit sector that served, or will serve, as driving factors for more SOX-influenced legislation.

Chapter Objectives

By the end of this chapter, you should be able to:

- Define the composition and duties of an effective audit committee.
- Evaluate the suitability of potential external auditors.
- Trace the connections between recent changes in IRS regulations and nonprofit scandals.
- Design an "up the ladder" reporting plan for a nonprofit's attorney.
- Outline the process of procuring tax-exemption status.
- Summarize the new IRS public disclosure regulations.
- Identify the requirements of Section 4958 of the Internal Revenue Code.

Need for Board Oversight

The nonprofit sector has experienced several scandals involving management fiscal mismanagement and the apparent inability of boards of directors to competently provide managerial oversight. For example, in February 1992, William Aramony, president and CEO of United Way of America (UWA) resigned under allegations that he conspired to defraud UWA and its spin-off companies. During the investigation that followed, it was revealed that Aramony received an annual salary of $390,000, plus $73,000 in other compensation. He incurred very high travel and entertainment expenses, including the overuse of taxis and limousines, luxury condominiums, and made several questionable supersonic Concorde jet flights. On April 3, 1995, Aramony was convicted in the U.S. District Court for the Eastern District of Virginia on various counts of conspiracy, fraud, and filling false tax returns. He served 84 months in prison, and was released in October 2001.

In 2003, a forensic audit at the United Way National Capital Area (UWNCA) revealed that the former CEO of 27 years, Oral Suer, had allegedly stolen roughly $1.6 million from the organization. In 2004, in the Alexandria Federal District Court, Suer pled guilty to transporting $403,000 in stolen money across state lines and to taking $94,279 more than he was entitled to from the UWNCA's pension plan. Suer falsified expenses, billed personal trips to Las Vegas to UWNCA, and took cash advances that were never repaid. In addition, he ordered the UWNCA auditor, the firm of Councilor, Buchanan & Mitchell, to withhold information regarding his misconduct from the board of directors. U.S. District Judge Gerald Bruce Lee sentenced Suer to 27 months in prison and required him to pay $497,000 in restitution (Chronicle of Philanthropy, 2004; Johnston, 2004).

The main question is, "Who was watching the store?" It doesn't appear that anyone was.

THREE DUTIES OF THE BOARD OF DIRECTORS

The primary functions of the board of directors are governance and fiduciary management. The board of directors is tasked with providing financial oversight and establishing polices that will keep the nonprofit viable. Board members are expected to conduct themselves and make decisions consistent with three legal standards—care, loyalty, and obedience (Herman, et al., 2004). The duty of care refers to the responsibility of conducting the affairs of the nonprofit with competence, and with the care an ordinarily prudent person in a like position would exercise. To exercise the duty of care, board members should:

- Actively participate in the management of the organization including attending meetings of the board, evaluating reports, reading minutes, reviewing the performance and compensation of the Executive Director, etc.
- Establish committees having the authority of the board and who operate subject to the direction and control of the board.
- Maintain written minutes for board meeting that accurately reflect board discussions as well as actions taken at meetings.
- Assure that the nonprofit's records and accounts are accurate.
- Be aware of what the financial records disclose and take appropriate action to make sure there are proper internal controls.
- Protect, preserve, invest, and manage the nonprofit's property and do so consistent with donor restrictions and legal requirements.
- Assist the organization in obtaining adequate resources to enable it to further its mission.
- Investigate warnings or reports of officer or employee theft or mismanagement. In some situations, a director may have to report misconduct to the appropriate authorities, such as the police or the Attorney General.

The duty of loyalty requires that board members put the interests of the nonprofit above their personal interests when making decisions and taking actions on the nonprofit's behalf.

To exercise the duty of loyalty, board members should:

- Establish and adhere to a written policy on avoiding conflicts of interest.
- Not seek loans or accept loans from the nonprofit.
- Not engage in or benefit from a business opportunity that is available to and suitable for the nonprofit.
- Avoid self-dealing.

The third duty, obedience, requires board members to conduct themselves in accordance with the nonprofit's mission. Decision-making and policymaking should be consistent with the mission and values of the organization.

To exercise the duty of obedience, board members should:

- Be familiar with state and federal statutes and laws relating to nonprofit corporations, charitable solicitations, sales and use taxes, FICA and income tax withholding, and unemployment and workers' compensation obligations.
- Be familiar with the requirements of the IRS.
- Protect their nonprofit's tax-exempt status with federal and state agencies.
- Comply with deadlines for tax and financial reporting, for registering with the Attorney General, for making social security payments, for income tax withholding, etc.
- Be familiar with their nonprofit's governing documents and follow the provisions of those documents.
- Ensure that proper notice is given for meetings, regular meetings are held, and directors are properly appointed.

To meet these duties, the board must work with professionals to ensure compliance with the federal, state, and local laws, and rules and regulations that relate to nonprofits. In particular, the board should have an audit committee that establishes the relationship with the external auditor, should keep abreast of changes in the Internal Revenue Code that affects the nonprofit's tax-exempt status, and establish an "up the ladder" reporting plan for its attorney.

Role of the Audit Committee

Although members of the management team typically prepare the financial statements, it is the board's responsibility to review and evaluate the statements. Most boards delegate this oversight responsibility to a committee within the board. In public organizations, this responsibility is given to the audit committee whose major task is to monitor the preparation and auditing of financial statements.

In nonprofit organizations, these responsibilities typically fall to the finance committee, which has a broader charge. Since preserving the integrity of the financial statements is such an important responsibility, a nonprofit organization should form a separate audit committee that can focus on the nonprofit's financial reporting practices, work directly with the external auditor, and develop policies to enhance the organization's internal control system. The audit committee can help the board meet its financial oversight financial responsibilities by serving as a liaison among the board, the internal and external auditors, and management. Having a well-functioning audit committee can demonstrate the nonprofit's commitment to exercise due diligence regarding the review and evaluation of any financial information that is to be released to the organization's stakeholders and the general public.

Based on these new responsibilities and requirements, what should a nonprofit audit committee do? Who should serve on the audit committee? What skills and competencies should the audit committee members have? How involved should the audit committee be with the organization's internal accounting system? While each nonprofit must answer these questions for itself, the following information provides some direction.

The nonprofit audit committee should be organized as a standing committee of the board, and should only be comprised of board members, not any members of management. Of course, members of management will work and frequently meet with the audit committee, but management should not be a part of the committee itself. An audit committee should be large enough to have a sufficient amount of financial expertise in the audit committee, but not too large as to create paralysis. As discussed in Chapter 12, all of the board members should be financially literate, but at least one member of the audit committee should have a very high level of financial expertise, someone who would qualify as a financial expert. To qualify as a financial expert, the individual should have:

- A clear understanding of GAAP and financial statements.
- Experience in applying GAAP in connection with preparing or auditing financial statements.
- Familiarity with developing and implementing internal financial controls and procedures.

In addition, no audit committee member may accept any consulting, advisory, or other compensatory fee from the nonprofit, except in his or her capacity as a board or board committee member.

The value of having an audit committee is also reflected in the number of SOX provisions regarding the composition of the audit committee and its financial oversight duties in public companies. An effective audit committee should be responsible for the following tasks:

- Providing oversight of the internal control system
- Recommending an independent auditor to the board of directors

- Reviewing the overall of plan of the audit
- Reviewing the results of the audit with the external auditor
- Reporting the audit findings to the full board

In essence, the role of the nonprofit audit committee is to oversee, monitor, and work collaboratively with management to prepare financial statements and conduct internal audits of those statements. The committee also must oversee, monitor, and work collaboratively with external auditors in conducting audits. In light of the many corporate and nonprofit financial scandals, the audit committee must perform this role in a proactive manner. The audit committee needs to safeguard the overall objectivity of the financial statements, financial reporting, and the internal controls process. To do so, the audit committee should ensure that effective internal control processes have been developed and fully implemented by management and staff. In addition, the audit committee should ascertain that all employees and managers involved in the financial reporting and internal controls process understand their roles, and that they are fulfilling those roles. The audit committee also should work closely with external auditors to identify and analyze financial reporting problems, and then use that information to make policy recommendations to management and the rest of the board.

The role of the audit committee in regard to the internal control system was covered in Chapter 11. This chapter will thus focus on the other four responsibilities.

Selecting the External Auditor

Evaluating potential external auditors to be retained to examine the financial statements is one of the primary responsibilities of the audit committee. A number of factors must be considered:

- Does the potential auditor have strong experience in the nonprofit sector; does he or she understand the specific accounting requirements for nonprofits?
- Does the potential auditor have a strong tax specialty in the nonprofit sector; maintaining its tax-exempt status is critical for a nonprofit, is the auditor well-versed in the requirements for tax-exempt status?
- Does the potential auditor use information technology that is compatible with that of the nonprofit; will the auditor be able to access the nonprofit's electronic data with limited disruption?
- Does the potential auditor already provide accounting, consulting, or other services to the nonprofit, giving him or her a financial incentive to maintain the relationship at the expense of the audit?
- Does the potential auditor indicate that he or she will be able to work compatibly, but independently with the nonprofit's management team?

- Does the potential auditor understand that he or she will report directly to the audit committee, and not to management?
- Does the potential auditing firm have effective internal control policies, and how are they periodically evaluated?
- Does the potential auditing firm have effective recruitment, hiring, and staff training policies, and how are they periodically evaluated?
- Does the potential auditing firm have sufficient personnel?
- Are the fees proposed reasonable?

In addition to making an auditor recommendation to the full board, once the auditor is selected, the audit committee has additional duties. The committee should have the authority and responsibility to:

- Approve any significant nonaudit engagements, keeping in mind that the more services an auditor provides to the nonprofit, the greater the potential loss of objectivity.
- Develop the auditor's loyalty to the audit committee and the board, while at the same time encouraging an open and collaborative relationship between the auditor and management.
- Develop an overall audit plan with the auditor, including a timetable and the scope of the examination.

Developing the Overall Audit Plan

In essence, the audit plan specifies the auditor's strategy for conducting the audit. It is a description of the expected scope and conduct of the audit with sufficient detail to guide the development of the necessary audit programs. An audit program describes what and how much evidence is required to be gathered and evaluated, and how, when, and by whom it is to be gathered and evaluated during the auditor visits. An audit program details the nature, timing, and extent of the planned audit procedures relating to a particular account balance. Simply put, the audit plan details what the auditor plans to do, the financial areas that will receive the most scrutiny, the methods he or she will use, the documents and records the auditor will need to examine, the number of auditing staff that will be needed, and how long the audit will take. A well-thought-out audit plan is at the heart of a properly executed audit.

As discussed in Chapter 1, there have been some spectacular audit failures in both the public and nonprofit sectors, with Enron and Arthur Andersen LLP being among the most notable. Audits fail for a number of reasons. As can be seen in Exhibit 13.1, in a study of the 45 audits of fraud-related SEC cases that occurred between 1987 and 1997 the most common auditor deficiency, 80% of the cases, was failing to gather suf-

Exhibit 13.1   Top 10 SEC Audit Deficiencies: 1987–1997

Problem Area	Number of Cases	Percentage
Gathering sufficient audit evidence	36	80%
Exercising due professional care	32	71%
Demonstrating appropriate level of professional skepticism	27	60%
Applying or interpreting GAAP requirements	22	49%
Designing audit programs and planning engagement	20	44%
Relying too heavily on inquiry as form of evidence	18	40%
Failing to obtain adequate evidence related to the evaluation of management estimates	16	36%
Confirming accounts receivable	13	29%
Failing to recognize and/or disclose key related parties	12	27%
Relying too much on weak internal controls	11	24%

Source: Beasley, M.S., Carcello, J.V., and Hermanson, D.R. (2001). *"Lessons from Fraud-Related SEC Cases: Top 10 Audit Deficiencies,"* *Journal of Accountancy, On-Line Issues*, retrieved June 5, 2005 from http://www.aicpa.org/pubs/jofa/apr2001/beasley.htm.

ficient evidence. Audit program design was the deficiency found in 44% of the cases, and in 24% of the cases, relying on internal controls that were weak or nonexistent was the deficiency.

Given the importance of the audit plan, the audit committee should review the audit plan with the auditor, being sure that the audit plan addresses any concerns the committee might have about the nonprofit's internal control system or other financial areas. Reviewing the audit plan should also entail raising questions about the cost of the audit. Are there any steps the nonprofit can take to help control the cost of the audit, without affecting the overall quality of the audit? If any additional work is required by the audit committee, what would the costs be?

After any questions or issues regarding the audit plan are resolved, the audit committee should request the auditor to summarize his or her understanding of the services to be rendered and the cost of those services in an engagement letter. Only after reviewing that the document accurately reflects the expected services and costs should the audit committee engage the auditor.

The quality of the auditor selected and the overall audit plan is critical due to the importance of conducting a thorough audit of the internal control system and the financial statements.

The Importance of an Audit

Having a thorough audit of the nonprofit's financial statements increases the likelihood that the financial statements will accurately portray the nonprofit's financial standing. Potential lenders, donors, funding organizations, and other stakeholders use the financial statements to make decisions about a nonprofit's financial health, so it is essential that the statements present an accurate representation of the nonprofit's financial status. Otherwise, the stakeholders of the nonprofit may make poor decisions about making loans, giving contributions, or providing funding.

An *audit* is the examination of the financial statements by an independent public accounting firm in order to form an opinion regarding the statements' adherence to GAAP. This type of audit is an external audit, as the individual performing the audit should not be directly connected with the nonprofit being audited. Once the audit is complete, the auditor prepares the auditor's report, which contains the auditor's opinion regarding the financial statements. The auditor's report is also known as the "Report of Independent Accountants."

What Are the Types of Opinions and What Do They Mean?

The auditor's opinion can be one of five different opinions: unqualified, unqualified with explanatory language, qualified, adverse, or disclaimer of opinion. The unqualified opinion is regarded as a clean bill of health, where the auditor makes no exceptions and does not include qualifications in the report. An unqualified opinion should only be made when the independent auditor deems that the financial statements were made in accordance with GAAP, that GAAP were applied in a consistent basis, and that the statements include all of the information necessary to make the statements accurate. If circumstances require an auditor to add clarifying language to the standard report, the opinion is not considered qualified, but rather unqualified with explanatory language. Adding the additional language is not regarded as a qualification since the inclusion of explanatory language serves to advise the readers or users of the statements.

Auditors add explanatory language to an unqualified opinion for the following reasons:

- To emphasize a particular matter or circumstance
- To justify a departure from GAAP
- To highlight an uncertainty that could have a significant effect on the financial statements

For example, the auditor may want to draw attention to the fact that the nonprofit is facing significant litigation, or has a trend of losing money from operations. The auditor may include explanatory language if there is a question about the quality of the records or supporting documentation.

Qualified opinions may be broadly classified into two categories—qualifications that relate to a limitation of the examination, and qualifications with respect to the exceptions in presentation in accordance with GAAP. The limitation or exception must be significant, but not so much material as to overshadow an overall opinion of the financial statements. The qualified reports include a separate explanatory paragraph before the opinion paragraph disclosing the reasons for the qualification. The qualified opinion should be viewed as a warning or alert to individuals using the financial statements.

An adverse opinion is the opposite of an unqualified opinion; it is an opinion that the financial statements do not present fairly the financial position, results of operations, and cash flow of the company in conformity with GAAP. An auditor should express an adverse opinion if the statements are so lacking in fairness that a qualified opinion would not be enough warning.

A disclaimer of opinion is basically the same as no opinion. This type of report results from very significant limitations in the scope of the auditor's examination or limitations that are imposed by the client. If the auditor cannot evaluate the fairness of the statements, he or she should issue a disclaimer of opinion.

Reviewing the Results of the Audit with the Auditor

The audit committee has several post-audit duties and responsibilities. One of those duties is to meet with the external auditor to review the financial statements and the audit results. In reviewing the audit results with the external auditor, the committee's primary concern is the level of fairness in the financial statements. Do the statements present fairly the nonprofit's status in conformity with GAAP? Assuming that the statements are fair and in conformity with GAAP, the committee should next try to ascertain the auditor's opinion about the effectiveness of the nonprofit's internal control processes and the overall accounting system. Some questions the committee might want to ask the auditor include:

- Do you have any suggestions for improvements in accounting, reporting, or operating procedures?

- Was the management team cooperative and forthcoming with requested information and documentation?

- Were there any significant disagreements between you and management regarding accounting principles, financial reporting practices and policies, or other auditing matters?

- How do our accounting policies and procedures compare with those of other comparable nonprofits?

- What adjustments or additional disclosures, if any, did you propose?

- Are there any items that might be disputed by the IRS? If yes, what documentation should be on hand to bolster the item?

- Assuming that the auditor performed the last year's audit, did the management team follow the auditor's suggestions in correcting weaknesses in the internal accounting system?
- Did you encounter anything that would jeopardize our tax-exempt status?
- Is there anything regarding the financial statements or the internal control system that you believe should be brought to the board's attention?

Prepare a Report of the Audit Findings

After meeting with the auditor and reviewing the final auditor report, the audit committee should prepare a report to the full board on the status of the financial statements, the results of the audit, and any policy recommendations the board should consider.

WORKING WITH THE IRS

Having IRS tax-exempt status under Section 501(c)(3) of the Internal Revenue Code is among the most valuable resources a nonprofit has. However, as a result of perceived abuse of tax-exempt organizations, both the federal and state governments have increased their monitoring of the nonprofit sector. Recently, the IRS revoked the tax-exempt status for four credit-counseling agencies after a number of consumer complaints about deceptive and fraudulent marketing practices (Mayer, 2005). In addition, the "Dirty Dozen," the IRS 2005 list of notorious tax scams, include scams that either manipulate laws governing charitable groups or abuse nonprofit credit counseling services. A number of new IRS rules, regulations, and enforcement efforts that attempt to limit abuse of tax-exempt status have recently been instituted.

Section 4958

In 1996, in part responding to the UWA and William Aramony scandal, Congress adopted Section 4958 of the Internal Revenue Code. These provisions, known as the "intermediate sanctions" legislation, were intended to give the IRS an additional weapon to fight corruption in the charitable sector. Previously, the IRS could only revoke tax-exempt status, which was deemed draconian. The new rules impose "intermediate sanction," that do not punish the organization itself, but rather the individuals in the organization who used their influence to obtain "excess benefits."

Section 4958 allows for the imposition of an excise "tax" as a penalty on those who receive an "excess benefit" from transactions with a tax-exempt organization. Excess benefit occurs whenever "the value of the economic benefit provided exceeds the value of the consideration received for providing the benefit," without regard to motive or intent. Excess benefit can occur only when the transaction involves what is termed a "disqualified person." A disqualified person is anyone in the organization who was in a position to exercise influence over the organization's affairs. Examples of a disqualified person include:

- The CFO
- Voting member on the board of directors
- A family member of a disqualified person, such as a spouse, children, siblings

Under the new law, the organization is not penalized, but rather the disqualified person who participated in the transaction that generated the excess benefit. The penalties are tiered; if the disqualified person returns the excess benefit within 90 days of receiving an IRS notice, he or she pays a penalty of 25% of the excess amount. If the penalty is not paid within 90 days or the excess amount is not returned, the penalty increases to 200% of the excess amount. In addition, if the nonprofit's manager who participated in the transaction did so knowing that it would result in excess benefit, he or she is fined 10% of the excess benefit, up to $10,000.

It should be noted that while Section 4958 does not levy a penalty on the organization, under other sections of the Internal Revenue Code the organization could lose its tax-exempt status for "private inurement." Private inurement occurs when the nonprofit's assets are used for the benefit of disqualified persons. Embezzlement, theft, disproportionately high compensation, excessive travel, or entertainment expenses are all examples of private inurement. Section 4958 creates *more* IRS remedies; it does not *replace* all existing remedies.

Exhibit 13.2 provides an example of the application of Section 4958.

EXHIBIT 13.2   SECTION 4958—EXCESSIVE BENEFIT

In 1999, Grant Simpkins, Ph.D. was hired as a senior finance manager with a fairly large nonprofit organization. He received $500,000 in total annual compensation, including fringe benefits. In 2000, the IRS determined that "reasonable" total compensation for a senior finance manager with Dr. Simpkins' qualifications, experience, and responsibilities should only have been $250,000.

Dr. Simpkins has received $250,000 of excess benefit (the actual compensation amount of $500,000—the reasonable amount of $250,000). Section 4958 imposes a 25% excise tax of $62,500 (25% of the $250,000 excess benefit). If Dr. Simpkins returns the $250,000 excess benefit, plus interest, to the nonprofit, within 90 days, he will only owe the 25% tax of $62,500. If Dr. Simpkins does not return the excess amount within 90 days, he will be liable for a tax penalty of 200% of the excess benefit, an excise tax totaling $500,000.

If any of the nonprofit managers who participated in setting the compensation did so knowing that it would result in excess benefit to Dr. Simpkins, he or she would be liable for $25,000, a 10% tax on the excess benefit of $250,000.

The nonprofit itself is not liable for any excise tax under Section 4958 for the excess benefit. Its tax-exempt status, however, may be revoked under other IRS rules due to the private inurement, disproportionately high compensation.

Tax Exempt Compensation Enforcement Project

In 2004, the IRS announced a new enforcement effort to identify and halt abuses by tax-exempt organizations that pay excessive compensation and benefits to their officers and other insiders. As part of the Tax Exempt Compensation Enforcement Project, the IRS will contact nearly 2,000 charities and foundations to seek more information about their compensation practices and procedures. Because part of the project's objective is to gather information regarding current practices, contact by the IRS should not necessarily imply improper activity by an organization (Flynn, 2004; Stamer, 2004).

The purposes of the enforcement effort are to:

- Address the compensation of specific individuals or instances of questionable compensation practices.
- Increase awareness of tax issues as organizations set compensation in the future.
- Learn more about the practices organizations are following as they set compensation and report it to the IRS and the public on their annual Form 990 returns.

The initiative is focused on particular areas, including the compensation of specific officers and various kinds of insider transactions, such as loans and the sale, exchange, or leasing of property to officers and others. The IRS will also focus on Form 990 reporting.

Complying with Excessive Compensation Requirements

The key to compliance with IRS regulations regarding executive compensation is to set "reasonable" compensation levels. Reasonable in this instance means comparable to the value that would ordinarily be paid for like services by like enterprises under like circumstances.

In determining reasonableness of compensation, nonprofits must be careful to consider all forms of compensation provided. These include, but are not limited to:

- Cash compensation, including salaries, bonuses, fees, severance payments, and salary deferrals
- Contributions to pension and profit-sharing plans
- Low-interest or no-interest loans
- Employer-paid insurance premiums, expense accounts
- Personal use of employer-provided automobiles
- Travel and entertainment expense reimbursements
- Club memberships, theater/sporting event tickets
- Vacations
- Bargain purchases or exchanges

Compensation arrangements should be approved by the nonprofit's board of directors, or a board committee, such as the audit committee. The members who participate in the approval process should not have any personal interest in the compensation arrangement. The board or board committee should obtain appropriate comparability data based on industry surveys, compensation studies, or other comparable data. The data should reflect the compensation of persons holding similar positions in similar organizations in similar communities.

The board or board committee should document the basis for its compensation determination. The documentation should include:

- The specific terms of the approved arrangement and the date approved
- The members of the board or board committee who are present during the approval process and their actual vote
- The comparability data relied upon and a description of its source

Section 6104

In April 1999, the IRS announced amendments to Section 6104, requiring public disclosure of certain nonprofit IRS forms and materials. In response to a written or in-person request, nonprofits must provide copies of their IRS exemption application (either Form 1023 or Form 1024) and annual information returns (Form 990 and its variants). Any written requests for copies of these documents must be responded to within 30 days of the request, and any in-person request should be filled promptly. In-person requests to merely inspect the documents should be met on that day.

The nonprofit must meet in-person requests to inspect the documents, but does not have to provide document copies if the documents are widely available through the Internet. The nonprofit meets the requirement of "widely available" if it publishes the documents on its own website or if it submits the documents to one of the online databases, such as GuideStar (www.guidestar.org) or the National Center for Charitable Statistics (http://nccsdataweb.urban.org/FAQ/index.php?category=31).

Similar to Section 4958, the fines imposed for violating Section 6104 are not imposed on the nonprofit, but rather on the "responsible" person at the nonprofit who fails to meet the request. Failure to allow public inspection or meet copy requests for the annual information returns has a penalty of $20 per day, until the request is met, up to a penalty of $10,000. Failure to allow public inspection or meet copy requests for the exemption application has a penalty of $20 per day, with no maximum. "Willfully" failing to meet the public inspection or copy requests for either the annual information returns or the exemption application imposes an additional fine of $5,000.

Form 990 and 501(c)(3) Nonprofits

Nonprofit status is primarily a state law concept. Nonprofit status may make an organization eligible for certain benefits, such as state sales, property, and income tax exemptions. Although most federal tax-exempt organizations are nonprofit organizations, organizing as a nonprofit at the state level does *not* automatically grant the organization exemption from federal income tax. To qualify as tax-exempt from federal income taxes, an organization must meet requirements set forth in the Internal Revenue Code.

A nonprofit's tax-exempt status is one of its most valuable assets. This tax-exempt status is not permanent and may be revoked for a number of reasons. If the nonprofit no longer meets the requirements of Internal Revenue Code 501(c)(3), its tax-exempt status can be revoked by the IRS. Complying with the requirement to file the annual information report with the IRS is one way for the nonprofit to demonstrate that it still fulfills the tax-exempt requirements.

Most nonprofits that are exempt from taxation under Internal Revenue Code 501(c)(3) are required to file a *Return of Organization Exempt from Income Tax* if their annual gross receipts are greater than $25,000. If the gross receipts are less than $100,000 and the total assets of the nonprofit are less than $250,000, the nonprofit may file either Form 990-EZ or Form 990. Nonprofits with annual gross receipts greater than $100,000 or whose total assets are greater than $250,000 file Form 990. Religious congregations are exempt from filing, regardless of annual gross receipts. Since Form 990-EZ is essentially a shorter version of Form 990, the words "Form 990" will be used in the rest of the chapter and also apply to Form 990-EZ.

Filing Deadlines and Penalties

The nonprofit must file Form 990 by the 15th day of the 5th month after its accounting period ends. For nonprofits not meeting the deadline, Form 8868 can be filed and it grants an automatic three-month extension for filing Form 990. If the three-month extension passes and the nonprofit still has not filed Form 990, it can again file Form 8868, requesting a three-month extension. In this case, however, the three-month extension is not automatically granted; the nonprofit must show reasonable cause for the request.

Nonprofits may receive penalties regarding the Form 990 for the following reasons:

- Late filing
- Incomplete form
- Incorrect information

For nonprofits with less than or equal to $1 million in annual gross receipts, the fine for late filing is $20 per day, not to exceed the smaller of 5% of the nonprofit's annual gross receipts or $10,000, unless the nonprofit can demonstrate a reasonable cause for the late filing. For nonprofits with annual gross receipts greater than $1 million, the fine for late filing is $100 per day, with a maximum penalty of $50,000.

For forms that are filed incomplete or with incorrect information, the IRS establishes a fixed time period for the nonprofit to submit the missing or corrected information.

If that deadline passes, the "responsible person" at the nonprofit will be fined $10 per day, with a maximum penalty of $5,000.

The IRS may impose fines and imprisonment for responsible persons who "willfully" do not file Form 990 or who "willfully" submit fraudulent forms.

The Urban Institute has also created 990 Online, which gives nonprofits a free way to prepare Form 990, Form 990-EZ, or Form 8868 completely online and to file the forms electronically with the IRS (http://efile.form990.org/). The IRS will accept electronic filings of forms for tax year 2003 and beyond. Having this free online preparation, verification, and electronic filing service makes it more difficult for a nonprofit to cite "reasonable cause" for late or inaccurate filings.

Primary Content of the Form 990

According to Peter Swords, the former Executive Director of the Nonprofit Coordinating Committee of New York (Sword, et al., 2003), Form 990 provides information in ten significant areas:

- Identity and tax status of the filer
- The amount and sources of income, including any unrelated business activity
- Breakdown of expenses among programming, management, and fundraising
- The composition of net assets
- The types of programs the filer offers and their costs
- The identity of the board of directors and salary information for top staff and managers
- Changes in activities or processes for governing and whether the filer engaged in excess benefits transactions
- Any self-dealing transactions
- Whether the filer is a private foundation
- Amount of lobbying activity

As can be seen in Exhibit 13.3, the top of Page 1 in the Form 990 contains the filer's name and address, the Employer Identification Number, the tax year, and the paragraph of Section 501(c) under which the filer is exempt.

Part I on Page 1 contains revenue, expenses, and changes in net assets. The revenue section is broken down among 11 sources of income (e.g., dividends, government contributions, direct public support, and sales). Knowing the sources of income for the filer gives information about the overall nature of the filer. Information regarding the type

EXHIBIT 13.3   FORM 990

Form 990

Return of Organization Exempt From Income Tax

Under section 501(c), 527, or 4947(a)(1) of the Internal Revenue Code (except black lung benefit trust or private foundation)

▶ The organization may have to use a copy of this return to satisfy state reporting requirements.

OMB No. 1545-0047

2004

Open to Public Inspection

Department of the Treasury
Internal Revenue Service

A   For the 2004 calendar year, or tax year beginning _____ , 2004, and ending _____ , 20 ____

B Check if applicable:	Please use IRS label or print or type. See Specific Instructions.	**C** Name of organization		**D** Employer identification number
☐ Address change		Number and street (or P.O. box if mail is not delivered to street address)	Room/suite	**E** Telephone number ( )
☐ Name change				
☐ Initial return		City or town, state or country, and ZIP + 4		**F** Accounting method: ☐ Cash ☐ Accrual ☐ Other (specify) ▶
☐ Final return				
☐ Amended return				
☐ Application pending				

● **Section 501(c)(3) organizations and 4947(a)(1) nonexempt charitable trusts must attach a completed Schedule A (Form 990 or 990-EZ).**

G   Website: ▶

J   Organization type (check only one) ▶ ☐ 501(c) ( ) ◀ (insert no.) ☐ 4947(a)(1) or ☐ 527

K   Check here ▶ ☐ if the organization's gross receipts are normally not more than $25,000. The organization need not file a return with the IRS; but if the organization received a Form 990 Package in the mail, it should file a return without financial data. **Some states require a complete return.**

L   Gross receipts: Add lines 6b, 8b, 9b, and 10b to line 12 ▶

H and **I** are not applicable to section 527 organizations.

H(a)   Is this a group return for affiliates? ☐ Yes ☐ No

H(b)   If "Yes," enter number of affiliates ▶ ....

H(c)   Are all affiliates included? ☐ Yes ☐ No
(If "No," attach a list. See instructions.)

H(d)   Is this a separate return filed by an organization covered by a group ruling? ☐ Yes ☐ No

I   Group Exemption Number ▶

M   Check ▶ ☐ if the organization is **not** required to attach Sch. B (Form 990, 990-EZ, or 990-PF).

Part I   **Revenue, Expenses, and Changes in Net Assets or Fund Balances** (See page 18 of the instructions.)

Revenue

1	Contributions, gifts, grants, and similar amounts received:		
a	Direct public support	**1a**	
b	Indirect public support	**1b**	
c	Government contributions (grants)	**1c**	
d	**Total** (add lines 1a through 1c) (cash $ _____ noncash $ _____) .	**1d**	
2	Program service revenue including government fees and contracts (from Part VII, line 93)	**2**	
3	Membership dues and assessments	**3**	
4	Interest on savings and temporary cash investments	**4**	
5	Dividends and interest from securities	**5**	
6a	Gross rents	**6a**	
b	Less: rental expenses	**6b**	
c	Net rental income or (loss) (subtract line 6b from line 6a)	**6c**	
7	Other investment income (describe ▶)	**7**	
8a	Gross amount from sales of assets other than inventory . . . . (A) Securities **8a** (B) Other		
b	Less: cost or other basis and sales expenses **8b**		
c	Gain or (loss) (attach schedule) **8c**		
d	Net gain or (loss) (combine line 8c, columns (A) and (B))	**8d**	
9	Special events and activities (attach schedule). If any amount is from **gaming,** check here ▶ ☐		
a	Gross revenue (not including $ _____ of contributions reported on line 1a) **9a**		
b	Less: direct expenses other than fundraising expenses . **9b**		
c	Net income or (loss) from special events (subtract line 9b from line 9a)	**9c**	
10a	Gross sales of inventory, less returns and allowances . . **10a**		
b	Less: cost of goods sold **10b**		
c	Gross profit or (loss) from sales of inventory (attach schedule) (subtract line 10b from line 10a).	**10c**	
11	Other revenue (from Part VII, line 103)	**11**	
12	**Total revenue** (add lines 1d, 2, 3, 4, 5, 6c, 7, 8d, 9c, 10c, and 11)	**12**	

Expenses

13	Program services (from line 44, column (B))	**13**	
14	Management and general (from line 44, column (C))	**14**	
15	Fundraising (from line 44, column (D))	**15**	
16	Payments to affiliates (attach schedule)	**16**	
17	**Total expenses** (add lines 16 and 44, column (A))	**17**	

Net Assets

18	Excess or (deficit) for the year (subtract line 17 from line 12)	**18**	
19	Net assets or fund balances at beginning of year (from line 73, column (A))	**19**	
20	Other changes in net assets or fund balances (attach explanation)	**20**	
21	Net assets or fund balances at end of year (combine lines 18, 19, and 20)	**21**	

For Privacy Act and Paperwork Reduction Act Notice, see the separate instructions.   Cat. No. 11282Y   Form **990** (2004)

(continues)

EXHIBIT 13.3   FORM 990 (CONTINUED)

Form 990 (2004)   Page **2**

Part II   Statement of Functional Expenses   All organizations must complete column (A). Columns (B), (C), and (D) are required for section 501(c)(3) and (4) organizations and section 4947(a)(1) nonexempt charitable trusts but optional for others. (See page 22 of the instructions.)

Do not include amounts reported on line 6b, 8b, 9b, 10b, or 16 of Part I.		**(A) Total**	**(B)** Program services	**(C)** Management and general	**(D)** Fundraising
22	Grants and allocations (attach schedule) . . (cash $ _____ noncash $ _____)	**22**			
23	Specific assistance to individuals (attach schedule)	**23**			
24	Benefits paid to or for members (attach schedule)	**24**			
25	Compensation of officers, directors, etc. . .	**25**			
26	Other salaries and wages	**26**			
27	Pension plan contributions	**27**			
28	Other employee benefits	**28**			
29	Payroll taxes	**29**			
30	Professional fundraising fees	**30**			
31	Accounting fees	**31**			
32	Legal fees	**32**			
33	Supplies	**33**			
34	Telephone	**34**			
35	Postage and shipping	**35**			
36	Occupancy	**36**			
37	Equipment rental and maintenance	**37**			
38	Printing and publications	**38**			
39	Travel	**39**			
40	Conferences, conventions, and meetings .	**40**			
41	Interest	**41**			
42	Depreciation, depletion, etc. (attach schedule)	**42**			
43	Other expenses not covered above (itemize): **a**	**43a**			
b	....	**43b**			
c	....	**43c**			
d	....	**43d**			
e	....	**43e**			
44	**Total functional expenses** (add lines 22 through 43). *Organizations completing columns (B)-(D), carry these totals to lines 13—15* .	**44**			

Joint Costs. Check ▶ ☐ if you are following SOP 98-2.
Are any joint costs from a combined educational campaign and fundraising solicitation reported in **(B)** Program services? . ▶ ☐ **Yes** ☐ **No**
If "Yes," enter **(i)** the aggregate amount of these joint costs $_____; **(ii)** the amount allocated to Program services $_____;
(iii) the amount allocated to Management and general $_____ ; and **(iv)** the amount allocated to Fundraising $_____

Part III   Statement of Program Service Accomplishments (See page 25 of the instructions.)

What is the organization's primary exempt purpose? ▶---

	Program Service Expenses (Required for 501(c)(3) and (4) orgs., and 4947(a)(1) trusts; but optional for others.)
All organizations must describe their exempt purpose achievements in a clear and concise manner. State the number of clients served, publications issued, etc. Discuss achievements that are not measurable. (Section 501(c)(3) and (4) organizations and 4947(a)(1) nonexempt charitable trusts must also enter the amount of grants and allocations to others.)	
a -- -- -- (Grants and allocations $)	
b -- -- -- (Grants and allocations $)	
c -- -- -- (Grants and allocations $)	
d -- -- -- (Grants and allocations $)	
e Other program services (attach schedule) (Grants and allocations $)	
f **Total of Program Service Expenses** (should equal line 44, column (B), Program services) . . . . . ▶	

Form **990** (2004)

EXHIBIT 13.3   FORM 990 (CONTINUED)

Form 990 (2004)   Page **3**

| Part IV | Balance Sheets (See page 25 of the instructions.) |

Note:	Where required, attached schedules and amounts within the description column should be for end-of-year amounts only.		**(A)** Beginning of year		**(B)** End of year

Assets

			(A)		(B)
45	Cash—non-interest-bearing			**45**	
46	Savings and temporary cash investments			**46**	
47a	Accounts receivable	**47a**			
b	Less: allowance for doubtful accounts .	**47b**		**47c**	
48a	Pledges receivable	**48a**			
b	Less: allowance for doubtful accounts .	**48b**		**48c**	
49	Grants receivable			**49**	
50	Receivables from officers, directors, trustees, and key employees (attach schedule)			**50**	
51a	Other notes and loans receivable (attach schedule)	**51a**			
b	Less: allowance for doubtful accounts .	**51b**		**51c**	
52	Inventories for sale or use			**52**	
53	Prepaid expenses and deferred charges			**53**	
54	Investments—securities (attach schedule) . . ▶ ☐ Cost ☐ FMV			**54**	
55a	Investments—land, buildings, and equipment: basis	**55a**			
b	Less: accumulated depreciation (attach schedule)	**55b**		**55c**	
56	Investments—other (attach schedule) . . .			**56**	
57a	Land, buildings, and equipment: basis .	**57a**			
b	Less: accumulated depreciation (attach schedule)	**57b**		**57c**	
58	Other assets (describe ▶ _____)			**58**	
59	**Total assets** (add lines 45 through 58) (must equal line 74) . . .			**59**	

Liabilities

60	Accounts payable and accrued expenses			**60**	
61	Grants payable			**61**	
62	Deferred revenue			**62**	
63	Loans from officers, directors, trustees, and key employees (attach schedule)			**63**	
64a	Tax-exempt bond liabilities (attach schedule)			**64a**	
b	Mortgages and other notes payable (attach schedule)			**64b**	
65	Other liabilities (describe ▶ _____)			**65**	
66	**Total liabilities** (add lines 60 through 65)			**66**	

Net Assets or Fund Balances

Organizations that follow SFAS 117, check here ▶ ☐ and complete lines 67 through 69 and lines 73 and 74.

67	Unrestricted			**67**	
68	Temporarily restricted			**68**	
69	Permanently restricted			**69**	

Organizations that do not follow SFAS 117, check here ▶ ☐ and complete lines 70 through 74.

70	Capital stock, trust principal, or current funds.			**70**	
71	Paid-in or capital surplus, or land, building, and equipment fund .			**71**	
72	Retained earnings, endowment, accumulated income, or other funds			**72**	
73	**Total net assets or fund balances** (add lines 67 through 69 **or** lines 70 through 72; column (A) **must** equal line 19; column (B) **must** equal line 21) . .			**73**	
74	**Total liabilities and net assets / fund balances** (add lines 66 and 73)			**74**	

Form 990 is available for public inspection and, for some people, serves as the primary or sole source of information about a particular organization. How the public perceives an organization in such cases may be determined by the information presented on its return. Therefore, please make sure the return is complete and accurate and fully describes, in Part III, the organization's programs and accomplishments.

(continues)

Exhibit 13.3　form 990 (continued)

Form 990 (2004) Page **4**

| **Part IV-A** Reconciliation of Revenue per Audited Financial Statements with Revenue per Return (See page 27 of the instructions.) | | **Part IV-B** Reconciliation of Expenses per Audited Financial Statements with Expenses per Return | |

a Total revenue, gains, and other support per audited financial statements . ▶ | **a**

b Amounts included on line **a** but not on line 12, Form 990:

  (1) Net unrealized gains on investments . . $

  (2) Donated services and use of facilities $

  (3) Recoveries of prior year grants . . . $

  (4) Other (specify):

  ....
  .... $

  Add amounts on lines **(1)** through **(4)** ▶ | **b**

c Line **a** minus line **b** . . . . . ▶ | **c**

d Amounts included on line 12, Form 990 but not on line **a:**

  (1) Investment expenses not included on line 6b, Form 990. . . $

  (2) Other (specify):

  ....
  .... $

  Add amounts on lines **(1)** and **(2)** ▶ | **d**

e Total revenue per line 12, Form 990 (line **c** plus line **d**). . . . . . ▶ | **e**

a Total expenses and losses per audited financial statements . . ▶ | **a**

b Amounts included on line **a** but not on line 17, Form 990:

  (1) Donated services and use of facilities $

  (2) Prior year adjustments reported on line 20, Form 990. . . . $

  (3) Losses reported on line 20, Form 990 . $

  (4) Other (specify):

  ....
  .... $

  Add amounts on lines **(1)** through **(4)**▶ | **b**

c Line **a** minus line **b** . . . . . ▶ | **c**

d Amounts included on line 17, Form 990 but not on line **a:**

  (1) Investment expenses not included on line 6b, Form 990 . . $

  (2) Other (specify):

  ....
  .... $

  Add amounts on lines **(1)** and **(2)** ▶ | **d**

e Total expenses per line 17, Form 990 (line **c** plus line **d**) . . . . . ▶ | **e**

Part V **List of Officers, Directors, Trustees, and Key Employees** (List each one even if not compensated; see page 27 of the instructions.)

(A) Name and address	**(B)** Title and average hours per week devoted to position	**(C)** Compensation (If not paid, enter -0-.)	**(D)** Contributions to employee benefit plans & deferred compensation	**(E)** Expense account and other allowances
---				

---				

75 Did any officer, director, trustee, or key employee receive aggregate compensation of more than $100,000 from your organization and all related organizations, of which more than $10,000 was provided by the related organizations? ▶ ☐ **Yes** ☐ **No** If "Yes," attach schedule—see page 28 of the instructions.

Form **990** (2004)

EXHIBIT 13.3   FORM 990 (CONTINUED)

Form 990 (2004)   Page **5**

Part VI	**Other Information** (See page 28 of the instructions.)		Yes	No

			Yes	No
76	Did the organization engage in any activity not previously reported to the IRS? If "Yes," attach a detailed description of each activity.	**76**		
77	Were any changes made in the organizing or governing documents but not reported to the IRS? . . .	**77**		
	If "Yes," attach a conformed copy of the changes.			
78a	Did the organization have unrelated business gross income of $1,000 or more during the year covered by this return?	**78a**		
b	If "Yes," has it filed a tax return on **Form 990-T** for this year?	**78b**		
79	Was there a liquidation, dissolution, termination, or substantial contraction during the year? If "Yes," attach a statement	**79**		
80a	Is the organization related (other than by association with a statewide or nationwide organization) through common membership, governing bodies, trustees, officers, etc., to any other exempt or nonexempt organization? . .	**80a**		
b	If "Yes," enter the name of the organization ▶ --			

-- and check whether it is ☐ exempt **or** ☐ nonexempt.

81a	Enter direct and indirect political expenditures. See line 81 instructions . .	**81a**		
b	Did the organization file **Form 1120-POL** for this year?	**81b**		
82a	Did the organization receive donated services or the use of materials, equipment, or facilities at no charge or at substantially less than fair rental value?	**82a**		
b	If "Yes," you may indicate the value of these items here. Do not include this amount as revenue in Part I or as an expense in Part II. (See instructions in Part III.). .	**82b**		
83a	Did the organization comply with the public inspection requirements for returns and exemption applications?	**83a**		
b	Did the organization comply with the disclosure requirements relating to quid pro quo contributions?. .	**83b**		
84a	Did the organization solicit any contributions or gifts that were not tax deductible?	**84a**		
b	If "Yes," did the organization include with every solicitation an express statement that such contributions or gifts were not tax deductible?	**84b**		
85	*501(c)(4), (5), or (6) organizations.* **a** Were substantially all dues nondeductible by members?	**85a**		
b	Did the organization make only in-house lobbying expenditures of $2,000 or less?	**85b**		
	If "Yes" was answered to either 85a or 85b, **do not** complete 85c through 85h below unless the organization received a waiver for proxy tax owed for the prior year.			
c	Dues, assessments, and similar amounts from members.	**85c**		
d	Section 162(e) lobbying and political expenditures	**85d**		
e	Aggregate nondeductible amount of section 6033(e)(1)(A) dues notices . . .	**85e**		
f	Taxable amount of lobbying and political expenditures (line 85d less 85e) . .	**85f**		
g	Does the organization elect to pay the section 6033(e) tax on the amount on line 85f?	**85g**		
h	If section 6033(e)(1)(A) dues notices were sent, does the organization agree to add the amount on line 85f to its reasonable estimate of dues allocable to nondeductible lobbying and political expenditures for the following tax year?	**85h**		
86	*501(c)(7) orgs.* Enter: **a** Initiation fees and capital contributions included on line 12 .	**86a**		
b	Gross receipts, included on line 12, for public use of club facilities	**86b**		
87	*501(c)(12) orgs.* Enter: **a** Gross income from members or shareholders . . .	**87a**		
b	Gross income from other sources. (Do not net amounts due or paid to other sources against amounts due or received from them.)	**87b**		
88	At any time during the year, did the organization own a 50% or greater interest in a taxable corporation or partnership, or an entity disregarded as separate from the organization under Regulations sections 301.7701-2 and 301.7701-3? If "Yes," complete Part IX	**88**		
89a	*501(c)(3) organizations.* Enter: Amount of tax imposed on the organization during the year under: section 4911 ▶_____ ; section 4912 ▶_____ ; section 4955 ▶_____			
b	*501(c)(3) and 501(c)(4) orgs.* Did the organization engage in any section 4958 excess benefit transaction during the year or did it become aware of an excess benefit transaction from a prior year? If "Yes," attach a statement explaining each transaction	**89b**		
c	Enter: Amount of tax imposed on the organization managers or disqualified persons during the year under sections 4912, 4955, and 4958 . . . . ▶ _____			
d	Enter: Amount of tax on line 89c, above, reimbursed by the organization . . . . ▶ _____			
90a	List the states with which a copy of this return is filed ▶ --			
b	Number of employees employed in the pay period that includes March 12, 2004 (See instructions.) **90b** _____			
91	The books are in care of ▶ ------------------------------ Telephone no. ▶ (_____)_____			
	Located at ▶ -- ZIP + 4 ▶ ------------------------------			
92	*Section 4947(a)(1) nonexempt charitable trusts filing Form 990 in lieu of **Form 1041**—Check here. . . . . . ▶* ☐ and enter the amount of tax-exempt interest received or accrued during the tax year . . . ▶ **92**			

Form **990** (2004)

(*continues*)

EXHIBIT 13.3   FORM 990 (CONTINUED)

Form 990 (2004)   Page **6**

Part VII   Analysis of Income-Producing Activities (See page 33 of the instructions.)

Note: Enter gross amounts unless otherwise indicated.

		Unrelated business income		Excluded by section 512, 513, or 514		(E) Related or exempt function income
		(A) Business code	**(B)** Amount	**(C)** Exclusion code	**(D)** Amount	
93	Program service revenue:					
a						
b						
c						
d						
e						
f	Medicare/Medicaid payments					
g	Fees and contracts from government agencies					
94	Membership dues and assessments . . .					
95	Interest on savings and temporary cash investments					
96	Dividends and interest from securities . .					
97	Net rental income or (loss) from real estate:					
a	debt-financed property					
b	not debt-financed property					
98	Net rental income or (loss) from personal property					
99	Other investment income					
100	Gain or (loss) from sales of assets other than inventory					
101	Net income or (loss) from special events .					
102	Gross profit or (loss) from sales of inventory					
103	Other revenue: a					
b						
c						
d						
e						
104	Subtotal (add columns (B), (D), and (E)) . .					
105	**Total** (add line 104, columns (B), (D), and (E)) . . . . ▶					

Note: Line 105 plus line 1d, Part I, should equal the amount on line 12, Part I.

Part VIII   Relationship of Activities to the Accomplishment of Exempt Purposes (See page 34 of the instructions.)

Line No. ▼	Explain how each activity for which income is reported in column (E) of Part VII contributed importantly to the accomplishment of the organization's exempt purposes (other than by providing funds for such purposes).

Part IX   Information Regarding Taxable Subsidiaries and Disregarded Entities (See page 34 of the instructions.)

(A) Name, address, and EIN of corporation, partnership, or disregarded entity	(B) Percentage of ownership interest	(C) Nature of activities	(D) Total income	(E) End-of-year assets
	%			
	%			
	%			
	%			

Part X   Information Regarding Transfers Associated with Personal Benefit Contracts (See page 34 of the instructions.)

(a) Did the organization, during the year, receive any funds, directly or indirectly, to pay premiums on a personal benefit contract?   .   ☐ Yes ☐ No

(b) Did the organization, during the year, pay premiums, directly or indirectly, on a personal benefit contract?   ☐ Yes ☐ No

Note: If "Yes" to (b), file Form 8870 and Form 4720 (see instructions).

Please Sign Here	Under penalties of perjury, I declare that I have examined this return, including accompanying schedules and statements, and to the best of my knowledge and belief, it is true, correct, and complete. Declaration of preparer (other than officer) is based on all information of which preparer has any knowledge.	
	▶ Signature of officer	Date
	▶ Type or print name and title.	

Paid Preparer's Use Only	Preparer's signature ▶		Date	Check if self-employed ▶ ☐	Preparer's SSN or PTIN (See Gen. Inst. W)
	Firm's name (or yours if self-employed), address, and ZIP + 4 ▶			EIN ▶	
				Phone no. ▶ ( )	

Form **990** (2004)

and amount of unrelated business activity is reported in Part VII, on Page 6. This section of the Form 990 can answer questions such as:

- From where does the nonprofit get its money?
- Does it have a variety of income sources, or is it dependent on one type of income?
- Did the nonprofit have a deficit?
- How large are the nonprofit's net assets?
- Did net assets increase or decrease over the last year?

Lines 13–17 in Part I contain the list of expenses, broken across programs, management, and fundraising. Lines 18–21 in Part I give a breakdown of the net assets, giving an indication of the level of resources the filer has to support its activities in the future. Part III on Page 2 describes each program the filer conducts, the purpose of each program, the number of services offered through each program, and the expenses for each program. This part of Form 990 can be used to answer the following questions:

- Did the nonprofit use any professional fundraisers?
- How did the nonprofit use its resources?
- Were fundraising and management expenses reasonable with regard to results?

Part V of the form contains the name and address of each board member and the amount of compensation, if any, each board member receives. Part V also contains information about the compensation level of key employees (such as the CFO and the Executive Director). Schedule A of Form 990 can be seen in Exhibit 13.4. Part I of Schedule A contains the compensation of the five highest paid employees who are paid more than $50,000. The compensation amount for the key employees and the top five is reported as the entire compensation package; that is salary, deferred compensation and employee benefits, bonuses, expense accounts, etc.

This part of Form 990 can be used to help answer the following questions:

- Are the members of the board reputable and well known in the nonprofit sector?
- Is this nonprofit paying excessively high compensation?
- How much are senior managers allowed for expense accounts?
- Does the amount of compensation match the duties and responsibilities of the employees?

Part VI of Form 990 reports whether the filer made any significant changes in the kind of activities it conducts (Line 76), if there have been any changes in the filer's governing documents (Line 77), or if there were any excess benefit transactions (Line 89).

Line 2 of Part III reports information about any transactions that might be considered "self-dealing," or which might be interpreted as excess benefits transactions. Part IV of

EXIHBIT 13.4   SCHEDULE A FOR FORM 990

SCHEDULE A (Form 990 or 990-EZ) Department of the Treasury Internal Revenue Service	**Organization Exempt Under Section 501(c)(3)** (Except Private Foundation) and Section 501(e), 501(f), 501(k), 501(n), or Section 4947(a)(1) Nonexempt Charitable Trust **Supplementary Information—(See separate instructions.)** ▶ **MUST be completed by the above organizations and attached to their Form 990 or 990-EZ**	OMB No. 1545-0047 20**04**

Name of the organization	Employer identification number

Part I   Compensation of the Five Highest Paid Employees Other Than Officers, Directors, and Trustees
(See page 1 of the instructions. List each one. If there are none, enter "None.")

(a) Name and address of each employee paid more than $50,000	(b) Title and average hours per week devoted to position	(c) Compensation	(d) Contributions to employee benefit plans & deferred compensation	(e) Expense account and other allowances

Total number of other employees paid over $50,000 . . . . ▶				

Part II   Compensation of the Five Highest Paid Independent Contractors for Professional Services
(See page 2 of the instructions. List each one (whether individuals or firms). If there are none, enter "None.")

(a) Name and address of each independent contractor paid more than $50,000	(b) Type of service	(c) Compensation

Total number of others receiving over $50,000 for professional services . . . . ▶		

For Paperwork Reduction Act Notice, see the Instructions for Form 990 and Form 990-EZ.   Cat. No. 11285F   **Schedule A (Form 990 or 990-EZ) 2004**

EXIHBIT I3.4   SCHEDULE A FOR FORM 990 (CONTINUED)

Schedule A (Form 990 or 990-EZ) 2004   Page **2**

Part III	**Statements About Activities** (See page 2 of the instructions.)	Yes	No

1 During the year, has the organization attempted to influence national, state, or local legislation, including any attempt to influence public opinion on a legislative matter or referendum? If "Yes," enter the total expenses paid or incurred in connection with the lobbying activities ▶ $ _____ (Must equal amounts on line 38, Part VI-A, or line **i** of Part VI-B.) **1**

Organizations that made an election under section 501(h) by filing Form 5768 must complete Part VI-A. Other organizations checking "Yes" must complete Part VI-B AND attach a statement giving a detailed description of the lobbying activities.

2 During the year, has the organization, either directly or indirectly, engaged in any of the following acts with any substantial contributors, trustees, directors, officers, creators, key employees, or members of their families, or with any taxable organization with which any such person is affiliated as an officer, director, trustee, majority owner, or principal beneficiary? *(If the answer to any question is "Yes," attach a detailed statement explaining the transactions.)*

a Sale, exchange, or leasing of property? **2a**

b Lending of money or other extension of credit? **2b**

c Furnishing of goods, services, or facilities? **2c**

d Payment of compensation (or payment or reimbursement of expenses if more than $1,000)? **2d**

e Transfer of any part of its income or assets? **2e**

3a Do you make grants for scholarships, fellowships, student loans, etc.? (If "Yes," attach an explanation of how you determine that recipients qualify to receive payments.) **3a**

b Do you have a section 403(b) annuity plan for your employees? **3b**

4a Did you maintain any separate account for participating donors where donors have the right to provide advice on the use or distribution of funds? **4a**

b Do you provide credit counseling, debt management, credit repair, or debt negotiation services? **4b**

Part IV	**Reason for Non-Private Foundation Status** (See pages 3 through 6 of the instructions.)

The organization is not a private foundation because it is: (Please check only **ONE** applicable box.)

5 ☐ A church, convention of churches, or association of churches. Section 170(b)(1)(A)(i).

6 ☐ A school. Section 170(b)(1)(A)(ii). (Also complete Part V.)

7 ☐ A hospital or a cooperative hospital service organization. Section 170(b)(1)(A)(iii).

8 ☐ A Federal, state, or local government or governmental unit. Section 170(b)(1)(A)(v).

9 ☐ A medical research organization operated in conjunction with a hospital. Section 170(b)(1)(A)(iii). **Enter the hospital's name, city, and state** ▶ ....

10 ☐ An organization operated for the benefit of a college or university owned or operated by a governmental unit. Section 170(b)(1)(A)(iv). (Also complete the **Support Schedule** in Part IV-A.)

11a ☐ An organization that normally receives a substantial part of its support from a governmental unit or from the general public. Section 170(b)(1)(A)(vi). (Also complete the **Support Schedule** in Part IV-A.)

11b ☐ A community trust. Section 170(b)(1)(A)(vi). (Also complete the **Support Schedule** in Part IV-A.)

12 ☐ An organization that normally receives: **(1)** more than 33⅓% of its support from contributions, membership fees, and gross receipts from activities related to its charitable, etc., functions—subject to certain exceptions, and **(2)** no more than 33⅓% of its support from gross investment income and unrelated business taxable income (less section 511 tax) from businesses acquired by the organization after June 30, 1975. See section 509(a)(2). (Also complete the **Support Schedule** in Part IV-A.)

13 ☐ An organization that is not controlled by any disqualified persons (other than foundation managers) and supports organizations described in: **(1)** lines 5 through 12 above; or **(2)** section 501(c)(4), (5), or (6), if they meet the test of section 509(a)(2). (See section 509(a)(3).)

Provide the following information about the supported organizations. (See page 5 of the instructions.)

(a) Name(s) of supported organization(s)	**(b)** Line number from above

14 ☐ An organization organized and operated to test for public safety. Section 509(a)(4). (See page 5 of the instructions.)

Schedule A (Form 990 or 990-EZ) 2004

(continues)

EXIHBIT 13.4   SCHEDULE A FOR FORM 990 (CONTINUED)

Schedule A (Form 990 or 990-EZ) 2004   Page **3**

Part IV-A   **Support Schedule** (Complete only if you checked a box on line 10, 11, or 12.) *Use cash method of accounting.*

Note: *You may use the worksheet in the instructions for converting from the accrual to the cash method of accounting.*

Calendar year (or fiscal year beginning in) ▶	(a) 2003	(b) 2002	(c) 2001	(d) 2000	(e) Total
15 Gifts, grants, and contributions received. (Do not include unusual grants. See line 28.) .					
16 Membership fees received					
17 Gross receipts from admissions, merchandise sold or services performed, or furnishing of facilities in any activity that is related to the organization's charitable, etc., purpose . .					
18 Gross income from interest, dividends, amounts received from payments on securities loans (section 512(a)(5)), rents, royalties, and unrelated business taxable income (less section 511 taxes) from businesses acquired by the organization after June 30, 1975 .					
19 Net income from unrelated business activities not included in line 18. . . .					
20 Tax revenues levied for the organization's benefit and either paid to it or expended on its behalf					
21 The value of services or facilities furnished to the organization by a governmental unit without charge. Do not include the value of services or facilities generally furnished to the public without charge					
22 Other income. Attach a schedule. Do not include gain or (loss) from sale of capital assets					
23 Total of lines 15 through 22					
24 Line 23 minus line 17					
25 Enter 1% of line 23					

26 **Organizations described on lines 10 or 11:** **a** Enter 2% of amount in column (e), line 24 . . . . ▶ | **26a** |

  b Prepare a list for your records to show the name of and amount contributed by each person (other than a governmental unit or publicly supported organization) whose total gifts for 2000 through 2003 exceeded the amount shown in line 26a. **Do not file this list with your return.** Enter the total of all these excess amounts ▶ | **26b** |

  c Total support for section 509(a)(1) test: Enter line 24, column (e) . . . . ▶ | **26c** |

  d Add: Amounts from column (e) for lines: 18 _____   19 _____
                                                22 _____   26b _____ . . . . ▶ | **26d** |

  e Public support (line 26c minus line 26d total) . . . . ▶ | **26e** |

  f **Public support percentage (line 26e (numerator) divided by line 26c (denominator))** . . . . . ▶ | **26f** | % |

27 **Organizations described on line 12:** **a** For amounts included in lines 15, 16, and 17 that were received from a "disqualified person," prepare a list for your records to show the name of, and total amounts received in each year from, each "disqualified person." **Do not file this list with your return.** Enter the sum of such amounts for each year:

  (2003) .... (2002) .... (2001) .... (2000) ....

  b For any amount included in line 17 that was received from each person (other than "disqualified persons"), prepare a list for your records to show the name of, and amount received for each year, that was more than the **larger** of **(1)** the amount on line 25 for the year or **(2)** $5,000. (Include in the list organizations described in lines 5 through 11, as well as individuals.) **Do not file this list with your return.** After computing the difference between the amount received and the larger amount described in **(1)** or **(2)**, enter the sum of these differences (the excess amounts) for each year:

  (2003) .... (2002) .... (2001) .... (2000) ....

  c Add: Amounts from column (e) for lines: 15 _____   16 _____
                                                17 _____   20 _____   21 _____ . . . . . ▶ | **27c** |

  d Add: Line 27a total. _____ and line 27b total . _____ . . . . . . ▶ | **27d** |

  e Public support (line 27c total minus line 27d total). . . . . ▶ | **27e** |

  f Total support for section 509(a)(2) test: Enter amount from line 23, column (e) . ▶ | **27f** |

  g **Public support percentage (line 27e (numerator) divided by line 27f (denominator))** . . . . . ▶ | **27g** | % |

  h **Investment income percentage (line 18, column (e) (numerator) divided by line 27f (denominator)).** ▶ | **27h** | % |

28 **Unusual Grants:** For an organization described in line 10, 11, or 12 that received any unusual grants during 2000 through 2003, prepare a list for your records to show, for each year, the name of the contributor, the date and amount of the grant, and a brief description of the nature of the grant. **Do not file this list with your return.** Do not include these grants in line 15.

Schedule A (Form 990 or 990-EZ) 2004

EXIHBIT 13.4   SCHEDULE A FOR FORM 990 (CONTINUED)

Schedule A (Form 990 or 990-EZ) 2004   Page **4**

Part V	**Private School Questionnaire** (See page 7 of the instructions.) (To be completed ONLY by schools that checked the box on line 6 in Part IV)		Yes	No

			Yes	No
29	Does the organization have a racially nondiscriminatory policy toward students by statement in its charter, bylaws, other governing instrument, or in a resolution of its governing body?	29		
30	Does the organization include a statement of its racially nondiscriminatory policy toward students in all its brochures, catalogues, and other written communications with the public dealing with student admissions, programs, and scholarships?	30		
31	Has the organization publicized its racially nondiscriminatory policy through newspaper or broadcast media during the period of solicitation for students, or during the registration period if it has no solicitation program, in a way that makes the policy known to all parts of the general community it serves?	31		

If "Yes," please describe; if "No," please explain. (If you need more space, attach a separate statement.)

32	Does the organization maintain the following:			
a	Records indicating the racial composition of the student body, faculty, and administrative staff?	32a		
b	Records documenting that scholarships and other financial assistance are awarded on a racially nondiscriminatory basis?	32b		
c	Copies of all catalogues, brochures, announcements, and other written communications to the public dealing with student admissions, programs, and scholarships?	32c		
d	Copies of all material used by the organization or on its behalf to solicit contributions?	32d		

If you answered "No" to any of the above, please explain. (If you need more space, attach a separate statement.)

33	Does the organization discriminate by race in any way with respect to:			
a	Students' rights or privileges?	33a		
b	Admissions policies?	33b		
c	Employment of faculty or administrative staff?	33c		
d	Scholarships or other financial assistance?	33d		
e	Educational policies?	33e		
f	Use of facilities?	33f		
g	Athletic programs?	33g		
h	Other extracurricular activities?	33h		

If you answered "Yes" to any of the above, please explain. (If you need more space, attach a separate statement.)

34a	Does the organization receive any financial aid or assistance from a governmental agency?	34a		
b	Has the organization's right to such aid ever been revoked or suspended?	34b		

If you answered "Yes" to either 34a or b, please explain using an attached statement.

35	Does the organization certify that it has complied with the applicable requirements of sections 4.01 through 4.05 of Rev. Proc. 75-50, 1975-2 C.B. 587, covering racial nondiscrimination? If "No," attach an explanation	35		

Schedule A (Form 990 or 990-EZ) 2004

(continues)

EXIHBIT 13.4   SCHEDULE A FOR FORM 990 (CONTINUED)

Schedule A (Form 990 or 990-EZ) 2004   Page **5**

Part VI-A   **Lobbying Expenditures by Electing Public Charities** (See page 9 of the instructions.)
(To be completed **ONLY** by an eligible organization that filed Form 5768)

Check ▶ **a** ☐ if the organization belongs to an affiliated group.   Check ▶ **b** ☐ if you checked "**a**" and "limited control" provisions apply.

	Limits on Lobbying Expenditures (The term "expenditures" means amounts paid or incurred.)		**(a)** Affiliated group totals	**(b)** To be completed for ALL electing organizations
36	Total lobbying expenditures to influence public opinion (grassroots lobbying)	36		
37	Total lobbying expenditures to influence a legislative body (direct lobbying).	37		
38	Total lobbying expenditures (add lines 36 and 37)	38		
39	Other exempt purpose expenditures	39		
40	Total exempt purpose expenditures (add lines 38 and 39)	40		
41	Lobbying nontaxable amount. Enter the amount from the following table—			

If the amount on line 40 is—	**The lobbying nontaxable amount is—**			
Not over $500,000	20% of the amount on line 40			
Over $500,000 but not over $1,000,000 .	$100,000 plus 15% of the excess over $500,000			
Over $1,000,000 but not over $1,500,000 .	$175,000 plus 10% of the excess over $1,000,000	41		
Over $1,500,000 but not over $17,000,000.	$225,000 plus 5% of the excess over $1,500,000			
Over $17,000,000.	$1,000,000			

42	Grassroots nontaxable amount (enter 25% of line 41).	42		
43	Subtract line 42 from line 36. Enter -0- if line 42 is more than line 36.	43		
44	Subtract line 41 from line 38. Enter -0- if line 41 is more than line 38.	44		

Caution: *If there is an amount on either line 43 or line 44, you must file Form 4720.*

4-Year Averaging Period Under Section 501(h)
(Some organizations that made a section 501(h) election do not have to complete all of the five columns below.
See the instructions for lines 45 through 50 on page 11 of the instructions.)

	Calendar year (or fiscal year beginning in) ▶	Lobbying Expenditures During 4-Year Averaging Period				
		(a) 2004	**(b)** 2003	**(c)** 2002	**(d)** 2001	**(e)** Total
45	Lobbying nontaxable amount					
46	Lobbying ceiling amount (150% of line 45(e))					
47	Total lobbying expenditures					
48	Grassroots nontaxable amount					
49	Grassroots ceiling amount (150% of line 48(e))					
50	Grassroots lobbying expenditures					

Part VI-B   **Lobbying Activity by Nonelecting Public Charities**
(For reporting only by organizations that did not complete Part VI-A) (See page 11 of the instructions.)

During the year, did the organization attempt to influence national, state or local legislation, including any
attempt to influence public opinion on a legislative matter or referendum, through the use of:

		Yes	No	Amount
a	Volunteers			
b	Paid staff or management (Include compensation in expenses reported on lines **c** through **h.**) . . .			
c	Media advertisements			
d	Mailings to members, legislators, or the public			
e	Publications, or published or broadcast statements			
f	Grants to other organizations for lobbying purposes			
g	Direct contact with legislators, their staffs, government officials, or a legislative body.			
h	Rallies, demonstrations, seminars, conventions, speeches, lectures, or any other means			
i	Total lobbying expenditures (Add lines **c** through **h.**)			
	If "Yes" to any of the above, also attach a statement giving a detailed description of the lobbying activities.			

Schedule A (Form 990 or 990-EZ) 2004

EXIHBIT 13.4   SCHEDULE A FOR FORM 990 (CONTINUED)

Schedule A (Form 990 or 990-EZ) 2004

Page **6**

Part VII	Information Regarding Transfers To and Transactions and Relationships With Noncharitable Exempt **Organizations** (See page 11 of the instructions.)

51 Did the reporting organization directly or indirectly engage in any of the following with any other organization described in section 501(c) of the Code (other than section 501(c)(3) organizations) or in section 527, relating to political organizations?

			Yes	No
a Transfers from the reporting organization to a noncharitable exempt organization of:				
(i) Cash	**51a(i)**			
(ii) Other assets	**a(ii)**			
b Other transactions:				
(i) Sales or exchanges of assets with a noncharitable exempt organization	**b(i)**			
(ii) Purchases of assets from a noncharitable exempt organization	**b(ii)**			
(iii) Rental of facilities, equipment, or other assets	**b(iii)**			
(iv) Reimbursement arrangements	**b(iv)**			
(v) Loans or loan guarantees	**b(v)**			
(vi) Performance of services or membership or fundraising solicitations	**b(vi)**			
c Sharing of facilities, equipment, mailing lists, other assets, or paid employees	**c**			

d If the answer to any of the above is "Yes," complete the following schedule. Column (b) should always show the fair market value of the goods, other assets, or services given by the reporting organization. If the organization received less than fair market value in any transaction or sharing arrangement, show in column (d) the value of the goods, other assets, or services received:

(a) Line no.	(b) Amount involved	(c) Name of noncharitable exempt organization	(d) Description of transfers, transactions, and sharing arrangements

52a Is the organization directly or indirectly affiliated with, or related to, one or more tax-exempt organizations described in section 501(c) of the Code (other than section 501(c)(3)) or in section 527? . . . . ▶ ☐ **Yes** ☐ **No**

b If "Yes," complete the following schedule:

(a) Name of organization	(b) Type of organization	(c) Description of relationship

Schedule A (Form 990 or 990-EZ) 2004

Schedule A reports whether the filer is a private foundation, and Part III of Schedule A reports any lobbying activities.

This part of Form 990 helps to answer questions such as:

- How much lobbying is this nonprofit conducting?
- Is lobbying a major objective of this nonprofit?
- Are any of the nonprofit's transactions resulting in excess benefit?

The IRS has a number of rules and regulations for nonprofits related to lobbying and political activities, but they are not included in this chapter. These requirements are covered in Chapter 14.

It is easy to see why the IRS requests the information on Form 990; it is among the primary ways the IRS verifies that the nonprofit still merits its tax-exempt status.

Importance of Filing a Timely and Accurate Form

In addition to the disincentives posed by the fines, a nonprofit has another reason for filing a timely and accurate Form 990. As mentioned in the discussion of Section 6104, Form 990 and other IRS materials are open for public inspection. Since 1998, Forms 990 received by the IRS have been scanned and their images posted on the National Center for Charitable Statistics website (http://nccsdataweb.urban.org/FAQ/index.php?category=31), a program of the Center on Nonprofits and Philanthropy at the Urban Institute. Form 990 information is also available at GuideStar.org (www.guidestar.org). The availability of a nonprofit's Form 990 could result in a public relations problem if the Form 990 is sloppily prepared, contains misleading information, or gives the impression that the nonprofit is misusing funds. On the other hand, if the nonprofit uses Form 990 to present the nonprofit in an accurate and positive way, potential donors and grant makers may make a positive contribution or funding decision.

Relationship between Timely and Accurate Form 990 Filing and the Internal Control System

As discussed in Chapters 11 and 12, the board of directors and senior management are responsible for creating, implementing, and evaluating the nonprofit's internal control system. Internal controls are basically just good business practices, and a nonprofit has an effective system if the board of directors and management have reasonable assurance that:

- They have an evidence-based and accurate understanding regarding the extent to which the nonprofit's operational objectives are being met.
- The financial statements and all other financial data reported publicly are prepared reliably and properly within GAAP.
- The nonprofit is complying with all applicable laws and regulations at the federal, state, and local level.

The timely and accurate reporting of Form 990 would be a direct result of an effective internal control system. Management and the board would have reasonable assurance that operational objectives of the nonprofit were being met and that the nonprofit's behavior does not threaten its tax-exempt status; would have reasonable assurance that all of the financial information and data required for the Form 990 are prepared reliably and properly within GAAP; and would have reasonable assurance that the filing of the Form 990 complied with the IRS rules and regulations. A properly completed and filed Form 990 would be the direct result of the set of internal controls in place in the nonprofit.

WORKING WITH ATTORNEYS

As discussed in Chapter 1, SOX Section 307 establishes "minimum standards of professional conduct" for attorneys who provide legal services and who are in an attorney-client relationship with a public company. The provision requires the attorney to follow an "up-the-ladder" reporting path if the attorney becomes reasonably aware of evidence of a material violation. While this provision of SOX does not currently apply to non-public companies, it can be viewed as one of the "best practices" that nonprofits should adopt. The core concept of Section 307 is that the attorney does not represent the board of directors or the senior managers, but rather the attorney represents the company as an entity. This provision is akin to Title II in SOX, which seeks to establish auditor independence. Section 307 seeks to establish a type of "attorney independence."

Up-the-Ladder Reporting Path

The up-the-ladder reporting path required under Section 307 has the following steps:

1. The attorney becomes aware of evidence of a material violation.

2. The attorney reports the problem to senior management, the chief legal officer or chief operating officer.

3. If the attorney receives an appropriate response, that ends the attorney's obligation; if there is no appropriate response, the attorney would report the problem to the audit committee.

4. If the attorney receives an appropriate response, that ends the attorney's obligation; if there is no appropriate response, the attorney would report the problem to the full board.

5. If the attorney received an appropriate response, that ends the attorney's obligation; if there is no appropriate response, the attorney would make a "noisy withdrawal," leaving evidence of his or her belief of a material violation and that he or she had taken appropriate steps to report the violation.

In addition to making evidence of suspected wrongdoing more likely to be reported to management and the board, formalizing this type of reporting path adds strength to the control environment of the nonprofit. It becomes more apparent that the full disclosure of suspected wrongdoing is the norm, and that "covering up" wrongdoing is not condoned.

Conclusion

Complying with legal requirements is important for any nonprofit that wishes to maintain its tax-exempt status and wishes to continue its mission. Having an effective audit committee will help the nonprofit meet many of its financial reporting obligations, as will having an effective internal control system such as the one described in Chapter 11. The responsibility of legal compliance rests with both the board and the management. For the board of directors, legal compliance is the heart of the duty of obedience.

Worksheet: Legal Compliance Review

Since legal compliance with all applicable rules, regulations, and laws is such a critical issue for nonprofits that wish to protect their tax-exempt status, conducting a legal compliance review can be a valuable exercise. A nonprofit cannot begin to correct any "holes" in its legal compliance processes if it doesn't know the status of those processes. What are we missing? What is in good shape? What correction do we need to make first? How long will it take and who will be responsible?

Similar to conducting an internal control system review, the first step in a legal compliance review is to convey to all members of the nonprofit the importance of legal compliance and the very real threat of loss of tax-exempt status. Senior management will be critical in "setting the tone" of the review, and must demonstrate strong leadership in the review process. If it appears that management thinks the review is a waste of time, then staff will not effectively participate in the review.

The next steps include the following:

1. Using the Legal Compliance Review Worksheet in Exhibit 13.5, evaluate the nonprofit's compliance with the list of activities that are commonly required by various federal, state, and local rules, regulations, and laws.

2. Determine which activities are in place and working well, which are in place but need additional work, which are missing and thus need work, and which are not applicable for the specific nonprofit.

3. Determine the priority level of each activity that needs work, based on the "doability" of the corrective work and the importance of the activity to the nonprofit's compliance.

4. For each activity that needs work, assign it to the person who will be responsible for developing the needed corrective actions.

5. Create a reasonable timeline for developing the needed corrective actions.

EXHIBIT 13.5   LEGAL COMPLIANCE REVIEW WORKSHEET

Priority Level	Indicator	Needs Work	N/A	Timeline
	All relevant filings to the Secretary of State are current. These filings might include: annual registration, articles of incorporation with all amendments, change of corporate name, change of corporate address (the particular state office that processes these filings depends on the state in which the nonprofit resides).			
	The nonprofit has furnished each director and officer a copy of the nonprofit's articles of incorporation and bylaws.			
	The organization is registered with and has filed its annual report with the Attorney General's Office (the particular state office that processes these filings depends on the state in which the nonprofit resides).			
	The nonprofit complies with the reporting requirements for periodic wage reports along with the payment of unemployment insurance tax.			
	The nonprofit complies with the IRS rules governing the status of independent contractors, prepares proper documentation of all independent contractor agreements, and reports compensation to independent contractors on IRS Form 1099 MISC.			
	The nonprofit has adopted an updated personnel policy manual and complies with the personnel policies and procedures contained in the manual.			
	The nonprofit complies with its employee benefit plan requirements.			
	The nonprofit complies with wage and hours laws, workplace safety laws, and nondiscrimination laws, including the Americans with Disabilities Act.			
	The nonprofit posts or provides to its employees the required employment notices, such as EEOC, OSHA, U.S. Department of Labor, and Workers' Compensation.			
	The nonprofit obtains a completed IRS Form I-9 and Form W-4 from all new employees.			
	The nonprofit has applied for and been assigned a federal identification number by the IRS.			
	The board or a board committee regularly determines that all filing and reporting requirements have been met in a timely manner, or that appropriate and timely corrective action has been taken.			

(continues)

EXHIBIT 13.5   LEGAL COMPLIANCE REVIEW WORKSHEET
(CONTINUED)

Priority Level	Indicator	Needs Work	N/A	Timeline
	The nonprofit has assigned the responsibility for meeting all filing and reporting requirements to appropriate directors and staff.			
	The nonprofit files quarter wage reports (IRS Form 941) with the IRS.			
	The nonprofit withholds federal income taxes and federal social security and Medicare taxes from taxable wages paid to employees, pays the employer share of taxes, and deposits all such funds in a timely manner and with the appropriate IRS forms.			
	The nonprofit maintains personnel records for the required period of time.			
	The nonprofit furnishes each employee with a completed IRS Form W-2 by January 31 for the previous year.			
	The nonprofit provides to each employee from whom the corporation did not withhold any income tax a notice about the Earned Income Tax Credit, by providing the employee with IRS Notice 797.			
	The nonprofit files annual tax information returns (IRS Form 990 or 990-EZ).			
	If the nonprofit has unrelated business income, it files IRS Form 990-T.			
	The nonprofit obtains an annual financial audit from an independent auditor and, if required by federal funding sources, the corporation obtains an A-133 audit.			
	The nonprofit engages legal counsel to conduct an annual review of its past year's operations and coming year's proposed operations to identify any conflicts and inconsistencies with the information previously provided to the IRS, and for an opinion on whether the nonprofit is or will be engaged in unrelated business activity.			
	The nonprofit complies with IRS disclosure, substantiation, and reporting requirements for charitable contributions received.			
	The nonprofit observes the IRS prohibition on political campaign activities.			

Priority Level	Indicator	Needs Work	N/A	Timeline
	For nonprofits within the IRS advance ruling period, the corporation conducts an annual review to determine its compliance with public charity status requirements and obtains a final ruling on its public charity status from the IRS in a timely manner.			
	The nonprofit observes the limitations on lobbying activities and maintains appropriate records to document its lobbying expenditures and activities.			
	If the nonprofit lobbies and utilizes the 501(h) election, it makes appropriate filings with the IRS to comply with lobbying registration, disclosure, and reporting requirements.			
	If the nonprofit has an employee benefit plan, the nonprofit makes annual benefit plan filings (IRS Form 5500) as required.			
	The nonprofit has applied for and maintains the appropriate property tax exemptions with the county assessor.			
	The nonprofit has obtained a nonprofit mailing permit to use special bulk postal rates.			
	The nonprofit has selected a bank after comparing and negotiating rates and fees.			
	The nonprofit has authorized at least two persons as check signers.			
	The nonprofit appropriately invests its assets that are held for investment.			
	The nonprofit maintains an up-to-date copy of its articles of incorporation, bylaws, 501(c)(3) tax exemption application and determination letter, and franchise tax exemption letter and keeps a copy at its principal office.			
	The nonprofit maintains a seller's permit for any items it sells.			
	The nonprofit maintains on record a current name and address for its registered agent.			
	The nonprofit has obtained a sales tax exemption.			
	The nonprofit has obtained other federal, state, or local licenses as required for its activities.			
	The nonprofit prepares and maintains for at least three years adequate and correct books and records of account, including records relating to all income and expenditures, and prepares or approves an annual report of financial activity.			

(continues)

Exhibit 13.5   Legal Compliance Review Worksheet (Continued)

Priority Level	Indicator	Needs Work	N/A	Timeline
	The nonprofit makes all of its financial records available to members of the public for inspection.			
	The nonprofit prepares and maintains minutes of board, committee, and member meetings for a minimum of three calendar years following the end of the fiscal year.			
	The nonprofit maintains copies of notices of board and member meetings, written waivers of notice, consents to votes taken without a meeting, and approvals of all minutes.			
	The nonprofit maintains copies of written director and officer resignations, proxies, and similar documents.			
	The nonprofit makes available for public inspection a copy of its federal tax exemption application, IRS tax exemption determination letter, and IRS Forms 990 from the previous three years, and provides a copy on request.			
	The nonprofit complies with its bylaws, including the provisions on the terms of directors, election of officers, quorums, and obtaining approval for certain actions.			
	The nonprofit holds all meetings it is required to hold and provides proper notice of meetings.			
	The nonprofit maintains a procurement policy to ensure that purchases are at a fair market value or are otherwise favorable to the corporation and, if applicable, the nonprofit complies with federal procurement standards.			
	The nonprofit maintains a financial system that requires receipt of written invoices prior to payment for any services or goods.			
	The nonprofit conducts appropriate investigations to ascertain that loans, leases, and other transactions are at fair market value or are otherwise favorable to the nonprofit.			
	The nonprofit prepares appropriate documentation in support of all transactions with directors, officers, or other insiders, and to demonstrate the reasonableness of all compensation.			
	The nonprofit has adopted a conflict of interest policy for transactions and meets all requirements for approval of transactions involving a conflict of interest, including transactions with corporations under its control.			

Priority Level	Indicator	Needs Work	N/A	Timeline
	The nonprofit engages legal counsel to review proposed contracts and agreements, corporate obligations to perform acts that might jeopardize its tax-exempt status, and whether there are appropriate safeguards to assure that corporate funds granted to other organizations are being used for tax-exempt purposes.			
	The nonprofit receives the benefits of, and meets its obligations under, all leases, loans, contracts, partnerships, joint ventures, and similar agreements.			
	If the nonprofit is the fiscal agent for another organization, it monitors the other organization's performance and compliance with all formalities.			
	If the nonprofit has qualified employee health and welfare and retirement benefit plans, they meet with all the federal laws, including: COBRA, initial IRS registration, plan documents, annuals filings of the 5500 C/R with copies available to employees.			
	If the nonprofit has employees represented by a union, it must maintain copies of the union contracts on file.			
	The nonprofit understands the policy limits of insurance policies, including: the events covered, exclusions, amount of coverage, deductibles, whether policies are "occurrence" or "claims made" policies, and any gaps in coverage.			
	The nonprofit maintains appropriate bonding for those persons who handle its funds, with reasonable limitations and exclusions.			
	The nonprofit maintains appropriate commercial general liability insurance, with reasonable exclusions and limitations, with coverage for the acts and omissions of the organization and its employees and volunteers in the appropriate amounts.			
	The nonprofit maintains, as applicable, errors and omissions or other professional liability insurance, with reasonable exclusions and limitations.			
	The nonprofit maintains appropriate director's and officer's liability insurance, with reasonable exclusions and limitations, or annually reviews the affordability of such insurance.			
	The nonprofit maintains appropriate property and automobile insurance, with reasonable limitations and exclusions.			
	The nonprofit maintains appropriate workers' compensation insurance, with reasonable limitations and exclusions.			

(continues)

EXHIBIT 13.5   LEGAL COMPLIANCE REVIEW WORKSHEET
(CONTINUED)

Priority Level	Indicator	Needs Work	N/A	Timeline
	The nonprofit maintains appropriate employment practices liability coverage, with reasonable limitations and exclusions.			
	The nonprofit has copies of executed waivers of liability for volunteers and clients.			
	The nonprofit has adopted policies and procedures to modify risks and monitors their implementation.			
	The nonprofit promptly advises insurance companies of facts that could give rise to claims in accordance with notice provisions of the policies.			

6. Evaluate the proposed corrective actions for "doability" and completeness, and make revisions if necessary.

7. Establish a realistic timeline for implementing the corrective actions for each of the activities.

8. Implement the corrective actions for each activity, according to the timeline.

9. Establish a realistic timeline for evaluating the effectiveness of the implemented corrective actions for each activity.

10. Evaluate the effectiveness of the implemented corrective actions for each activity, according to the timeline.

11. Write a report for senior management and the board of directors.

12. Senior management and the board of directors respond to the report, suggesting areas of improvement, reconsiderations of priority levels, and suggested corrective actions.

13. Establish a realistic timeline to implement the recommendations of senior management and the board of directors.

14. Implement the recommendations, according to the timeline.

15. Establish a realistic timeline for evaluating the effectiveness of the implemented recommendations.

16. Evaluate the effectiveness of the implemented recommendations.

17. Write a report for senior management and the board of directors.

18. Begin again.

As with the internal control system review in Chapter 11, the legal compliance review is not a "quick fix," and, as evidenced by the last step, it is an ongoing process. The legal compliance review process must become a part of the nonprofit's culture, with continuous improvement of legal compliance being the norm.

Not every nonprofit will have the resources necessary to complete every step in the review, and provide corrective actions for all of the activities that need them. That is why establishing the priority level for each activity is important. In addition, establishing realistic timelines should take organizational resources into account and avoid "organizational overload." The important key to improving legal compliance is simply to start.

CHAPTER 14

SOX Best Practices and Political Competence

Padmaja is the Executive Director of a small nonprofit. She and the Chair of the Board, Sophie, are discussing the agenda for the next Board meeting. "I'm really concerned about some of the proposals the IRS is considering for nonprofits," Padmaja said worriedly. We don't have the money to apply for our tax-exempt status every five years and pay a processing fee. And if Form 990 becomes any more complicated than it already is, I don't know if we'll be able to get it in on time. We're not a big nonprofit; we don't have the kind of resources it would take to meet these proposals if the IRS adopts them. Maybe discussing these IRS proposals should be on the agenda for the next meeting." "Well," said Sophie, "I don't see why we should waste time during the meeting talking about what the IRS might do. There isn't really a lot we can do to make the IRS change anything they decide to do. We'll just have to wait and see what happens. Let's just keep our fingers crossed and hope for the best. That's about all we can do."

CHAPTER OVERVIEW

In the near future, it is doubtful that SOX's influence on nonprofits is going away. As discussed in Chapter 1, two provisions in SOX, whistleblower protection and document preservation, already apply to nonprofits. It appears, based on the reports and statements from the U.S. Finance Committee, the IRS, and the Panel on the Non-profit Sector discussed in Chapter 1 and other chapters, that a number of parties are pushing for SOX-influenced legislation and regulations in the nonprofit sector. Some states, such as California with its Nonprofit Integrity Act, have already started the process of requiring changes for nonprofits that mirror some of the requirements of SOX. To better understand how nonprofits can better monitor and affect their regulatory environment, this chapter introduces the concept of "political competence," the ability to effectively analyze the environment, and influence the policymaking process.

The chapter will review the U.S. policymaking process, describe the development of a strategic plan to develop competence, and identifies organizations and websites nonprofits should monitor to stay informed about policies that may affect them.

CHAPTER OBJECTIVES

By the end of this chapter, you should be able to:

- Outline the U.S. policymaking process.
- Describe the steps in rulemaking.
- Discuss the concept of political competence and its implications for nonprofits.
- Identify the components of the strategic planning process.
- Define influence.
- Apply the strategic planning process to develop political competence.
- Describe the five-step process for environmental analysis.
- Evaluate organizations for potential alignments.
- Discuss the resources needed to develop political competence.

DEVELOPING POLITICAL COMPETENCE

As discussed in previous chapters, even if no additional SOX-influenced legislation or regulations were instituted for the nonprofit sector, many nonprofits could benefit operationally from adopting some of the SOX rules as best practices. This could give the nonprofits better credibility and ability to recruit high-quality board members, and attract the favorable attention of major donor, foundations, and other funding sources. There is a difference, however, between nonprofits voluntarily adopting SOX and having formal legislation and regulations enacted and imposed on them. In many areas, but particularly in the area of SOX, nonprofits must develop political competence to help shape their regulatory world. Otherwise, nonprofits may find themselves being adversely affected by regulations. In the case of SOX, for example, a relatively wholesale adoption of SOX onto nonprofits may affect nonprofits adversely because rules designed for publicly held companies may not be a "good fit" with nonprofits. Nonprofits have different goals and needs than public companies do; complying with the rules may divert the nonprofit's attention from its mission; or compliance may too onerous, expensive, or time-consuming for nonprofits, especially the smaller and asset-poor ones.

Definition of Political Competence

Fundamentally, political competence is the ability to effectively analyze the environment, and influence the policymaking process (Longest, 2002). It involves being aware of one's own interests, understanding how the political system and policymaking process work, knowing how to obtain relevant information and anticipate policy issues, and how and when to apply pressure to the system. To productively engage in the political process, nonprofits need to understand the context, the process, and the people involved in each particular decision. It is also important for a nonprofit to understand its role in the policy market, specifically where, how, and when the nonprofit can play a role, or influence the process.

U.S. Policymaking Process

One step in developing political competence is having a general understanding of the U.S. policymaking process. In this context, policy is defined as laws and enacted legislation, the rules and regulations developed by the agencies to implement legislation or operate the government or its programs, and the legal decisions made at the judicial level regarding laws, rules, or regulations.

The policymaking process can be, and has been, conceptualized in a number of models that describe the components of the process and the relationships among the components. One conceptual model includes five stages: problem definition, agenda setting, policy adoption, policy implementation, and policy evaluation (Eyestone, 1978). Although the use of the word *stage* may imply that the process is an orderly one, moving in a linear fashion, that is not necessarily the case in many instances. The process is a circular process, not a linear one, with "later" stages occurring before "earlier" ones. For example, policy evaluation is the "fifth" stage in the model, and "problem definition" is the "first." In some cases, evaluation of an existing policy may stimulate redefinition of the problem the policy was supposed to address (Jenkins-Smith, 1993). Nonprofits can be involved or influence activity anywhere along the policymaking spectrum, from problem definition to modifying policy.

Problem Definition

In the problem definition stage in the policymaking process, the goal is to "define" the problem—to describe its salient features and characteristics. However, individuals or groups may look at a problem or issue and define it in substantially different ways. Some may not even view the issue as a "problem" requiring solving. How one defines the problem has implications for how one solves a problem, and controlling problem definition is one of the ways to control the problem solution.

Agenda Setting

In the agenda setting stage in the policymaking process, a particular problem or issue emerges out of the almost unlimited number of existing issues as one of the problems that policymakers will focus on, or will try to solve. If an issue or problem never comes to the attention of the policymakers, however, it will not be able to proceed through the next stages in the process. Having the problem placed on the policymaking agenda is thus a critical stage in the policymaking process.

Policy Adoption

Once a problem makes its way onto the policymakers' agenda, a solution for the problem must be developed. In many, if not most, cases, a number of potential solutions, each with its own supporters and opponents, compete for adoption. At this stage, legislation is drafted, debated, passed, or not passed at the legislative level, and approved or not approved at the executive level. A comprehensive description of the policy adoption process is not possible here due to the limitations of the book; what follows is a general description that outlines the main events in the process at the federal level. For those who want a more detailed description of the process, please refer to the brochure "How Laws Are Made" (Johnson, 2003), available at http://thomas.loc.gov/home/lawsmade.toc.html.

Role of Congress

At the federal level, legislative law originates as a written bill or resolution. The bill or resolution is then introduced—independently, jointly, or concurrently—in the House of Representatives and/or the Senate. Only a member of Congress may introduce a bill. When the bill is introduced, it is read into the *Congressional Record*, the daily transcript of Congressional floor action.

After introduction, the bill is placed on the Congressional Calendar and referred to Committee. The Committee may edit the language of the bill and may hold hearings to gather information from experts. After the hearings are concluded, if there are any, the Committee votes whether to revise the language, send the bill to another Committee for review, or send a report back to whichever chamber of Congress the bill was introduced. If the Committee reports back to Congress, the report is scheduled for floor debate and then a vote. At this time, amendments and riders to the bill may be added. If the bill is passed, it is sent to the other chamber and the process begins again. Any number of bills on the same topic may be introduced into each chamber with different text, and each chamber may alter each text of a bill originally introduced for consideration.

A bill passed in the House may differ from the version passed in the Senate. When differences arise, they are resolved through the negotiations of a joint committee. Both chambers must agree on an identical form of the bill before it can go to the President for further action.

Role of the President

Once the President has received the bill, he or she may sign the bill, veto the bill, or do nothing. If the President signs the bill, it becomes public law. If the President vetoes the bill, it is returned to whichever chamber in Congress originated the bill, along with the Presidents objections. The chamber may do nothing or try to override the veto; two-thirds of the chamber must vote in the affirmative to override the veto. If the override attempt is not successful, the bill dies. If the attempt is successful, the bill is passed to the other Congressional chamber that exercises the same process. If there is an override attempt and it is successful in the second chamber, the bill becomes public law.

If a bill is presented to the President and he or she does not sign the bill or return the bill to the originating chamber with the President's objections within ten days, the effect of the action on the bill depends upon the number of days remaining in session. If there are more than ten days left in the session and the President does nothing, the bill is enacted and becomes public law. If Congress adjourns before the ten-day period passes, the bill is not enacted and does not become public law. This action is called the pocket veto.

At the State Level

The enactment process at the state level varies from state to state, but in general is similar to the federal process, meaning that legislation is drafted, debated, passed, or not passed at the legislative level, and approved or not approved at the executive level. At the state level, the executive is the governor, and he or she has options similar to those of the President.

Policy Implementation

Once legislation is passed, it must be implemented, or "brought to life." A comprehensive description of the policy implementation process is not possible here due to the limitations of the book; what follows is a general description that outlines the main events in the process at the federal level. For those who want a more detailed description of the process, please refer to the "Federal Register Tutorial," at the National Archives and Records Administration (NARA): http://www.archives.gov/federal_register/tutorial/tutorial.html.

Rulemaking

At the federal level, Congress delegates implementation authority to the relevant executive departments and agencies. The Food and Drug Administration (FDA), for example, would generally be the implementing agency for legislation regarding the pharmaceutical industry. The primary activity during the implementation process is rulemaking, which is the creation of the formal rules and regulations necessary to operationalize the legislative intent. Congress relies on the implementing agency and rulemaking to add more detailed scientific, economic, or industry expertise to the implementation of the legislation, in effect "fleshing" out the Congressional intent.

Advanced Notice

The first step in the rulemaking process is optional. The implementing agency may or may not publish an advanced notice in the Federal Register. An advanced notice contains the agency's initial analysis of the regulatory matter and may solicit early public comment. Published by NARA, the *Federal Register* is the official daily publication for rules, proposed rules, and notices of federal agencies and organizations, as well as executive orders and other presidential documents. It is updated daily by 6 a.m. and is published Monday through Friday, excluding federal holidays.

Notice of Proposed Rulemaking

If the implementing agency does not publish an advanced notice, the first step is the notice of proposed rulemaking (NPRM). The NPRM is the agency's proposed set of rules and regulations, a justification and analysis of the proposal, and the agency's response to any public comment if there had been an advanced notice. The NPRM also solicits public commentary, and provides information for filing comments and the deadline for filing. The NPRM provides the public an opportunity to participate in the rulemaking process.

Final Rule

If the agency's response to the public commentary results in modifications to the proposed rule that are substantial, the agency may publish another draft proposed rule and seek comments on it. Substantial modification is not typical, and many times the second draft proposed rule step is skipped. The next step is then for the agency to publish the final rule, which may or may not differ from the proposed rule. In this step, the agency publishes a full response to all of the public comments and provides an updated analysis and justification for the rule, addressing any data that was submitted during the public comment period. Once there is a final rule, the rule is published in the Code of Federal Regulations (CFR), which is easily available to the public.

Policy Modification

Policy modification can occur at almost any stage of the policymaking process. The problem definition may be changed; the importance or lack of importance of a problem or issue to the policymakers' agenda may vary, bills frequently undergo substantial modification before they are enacted, legislation passed previously may be amended, and the rules and regulations are frequently revised. Several factors may drive policy modification. At the rulemaking stage, for example, interested parties who object to the implementing agency's final rule may seek judicial review of the rulemaking process. The interested parties may claim that the final rule is arbitrary and capricious, in that there is a substantial gap between the agency's data and its analysis. Alternatively, they may claim that the rule exceeds statutory authority, meaning that they are too strict or too lax. Another claim that may be made is that some of the provisions in the rule were not available to the public for commentary. If the claim is found to have merit during the judicial review, the implementing agency may have to modify the rule or begin the rulemaking process again.

ROLE OF NONPROFITS

What is the role of nonprofit organizations in the policymaking process and how do they develop the skills to play their role well? Nonprofit organizations can, and do, participate in the policymaking process in much the same way that interest groups and private companies do. To develop their political competence, nonprofit organizations need to first be aware of the skills required and steps involved in influencing the political process. In addition, they need a strategic plan on how to develop their own competence, and a strategy to approach individual policy issues. While nonprofit organizations individually have a broad range of resources (both financial and human), and issues, collectively they are quite a large contingent with the potential to have significant impact.

Nonprofit organizations, which may also be called voluntary, nongovernmental, or independent (Hrebenar, 1998), collectively comprise a large group with 1,140,000 organizations in the U.S. These break down into 400,000 member-serving organizations (e.g., social clubs, business associations, labor unions, cooperatives, political parties) and 740,000 public serving organizations (e.g., service providers, churches, political action committees, funding intermediaries) (Salamon, 1992). In 1997, the nonprofit sector accounted for 8% of the U.S. gross domestic product and 10% of the U.S. workforce (Economist, 1998). According to Giving USA, Americans gave $241 billion to nonprofits in 2003. Of the total, $179 billion came from individuals, $13 billion from corporations, $22 billion from bequests, and $26 billion from foundations. Donations went to a variety of types of organizations, including religious (36%), education (13%), foundations (9%), health (9%), human services (8%), art, culture, and humanities (5%), public society benefit (5%), environmental/animals (3%), and international affairs (2%) (Giving USA, 2004).

Given the size and scope of this sector of the market, nonprofit organizations, if armed with the right tactics and strategy, have the potential to make a significant impact on policy issues.

TWO COMPONENTS IN POLITICAL COMPETENCE

According to Longest (2002), there are two major components in political competence: analyzing the environment and influencing the policymaking process. Environmental analysis would allow nonprofits to be involved in the political marketplace in a proactive rather than reactive way. By understanding the history and context of an issue, as well as current activities and debates, a nonprofit would be able to anticipate potential policy issues well in advance of political action. If a nonprofit has effectively looked at the environment and anticipated potential issues, that nonprofit is well positioned to use its influence to affect the course of political action very early in the process (i.e., agenda setting or rulemaking).

Environmental Analysis

This part of political competence allows an organization to increase awareness of opportunities and threats by clearly identifying, tracking, anticipating, and planning for changes related to strategic policy issues. It is a key step in preparing an organization to effectively exert influence on the policymaking process. Ginter, Duncan, and Swayne outline a five-step process for analyzing public policy environments: scanning, monitoring, forecasting, assessing, and diffusing (Ginter, Duncan, and Swayne, 2002).

Scanning

The first step, scanning, involves identifying strategic public policy issues for the organization, issues that may have an impact on the future, decision-making, or operations of the organization. The scan includes identification of current policy, and the problems, potential solutions, and political circumstances that might eventually lead to new policy or policy modification. The process of identifying these issues can be very complex, involving many internal/external experts, and ultimately requires agreement by the organization's leadership. It is a critical step in an organization to become aware of its own critical political issues, those that will require attention and tracking on an ongoing basis.

Monitoring

The second step, monitoring, has a narrower focus than scanning. Monitoring entails collecting specific information about the strategic policy issues identified during scanning (or through previous monitoring). Because policy is so frequently affected through policy modification (as opposed to new policy), many of a nonprofit's strategic policy issues are likely to have long histories that tie back to a relatively small number of actual policies. Keeping pace with modifications to those policies, chronicling the history, and identifying the sometimes subtle indications that a strategic issue is looming are all key components of monitoring.

Forecasting

Scanning and monitoring provide the background information required to effectively execute the third step in environmental analysis, forecasting. Forecasting involves predicting future conditions. Once future conditions are predicted, an organization can use a variety of methods to develop a plan of action. Trend extrapolation and scenario development are two of the most common techniques used for forecasting. Trend extrapolation basically involves tracking information regarding a particular issue (monitoring), and predicting future changes based on the historical patterns. This technique is used most effectively in relatively stable environments without significant policy change (Klein and Linneman, 1984). Scenario development is perhaps a better tool for a less stable, more uncertain environment. It involves the development of a variety of alternatives of what the future might look like (Leemhuis, 1985). The idea is to develop plans for how the organization will react to each scenario, or combination of scenarios. It is in essence an elaborate "if . . . then . . ." exercise.

Assessment and Diffusion

The last two steps of environmental analysis are assessment and diffusion. Assessment involves a strategic evaluation of the importance and implications of policy issues. This step allows an organization to prioritize issues and activities. The assessment may be based on judgment, past experiences (own or others), and/or any modeling/quantification possible. Diffusion entails sharing information with all individuals within an organization, especially those who have responsibilities to carry out some part of the decision/activities.

Using the Environmental Analysis for Strategic Planning

If the environmental analysis is done well, the plan of action will include proactive activities to influence the policy outcome prior to official action even being put in motion. Based on the environmental analysis, an organization knows what its key issues are, what is/has been going on with those issues, has projected likely future conditions, and assessed the importance of issues and shared information with those who need to know. It has not, however, developed a strategic plan or an action plan regarding the approach to influencing the policy. A classic strategic planning process (QuickMBA, 2005), as outlined later in the chapter, can help an organization think through this aspect of political competence and influence.

Mission and Objectives

While the organization's mission and vision stays constant regardless of the issue, the objectives certainly change. What does the organization want to see as the outcome for each of its strategic policy issues? Ideally, the objectives are measurable. In the case of policy, an objective may be to get a certain bill passed, get a certain issue on the agenda, or just the opposite.

Environmental Scanning

Similar to the environmental scanning process discussed earlier, in general, this phase of the strategic planning process entails assessing internal and external factors to identify strengths, weaknesses, opportunities, and threats (SWOT). One can also use the PEST analysis, which calls for the assessment of political, economic, social, and technological factors in the external environment.

Strategy Formulation and Action Planning

Developing the strategy and action plan relies on the two prior steps: Using the identified internal strengths to capitalize on opportunities, and having a mitigation plan for the identified threats and internal weaknesses. In the context of political competence, what is the desired outcome? What is the organization's current ability to exert influence and what needs improvement? What will the organization do to influence policy? Who will represent the organization? What will they communicate? At what point in the process? When, how, where, and to whom will they communicate?

Strategy Implementation

Strategy implementation involves mobilizing the resources of the organization to execute the designed strategy. For them to execute the strategy successfully, individuals accountable for acting will need information regarding the strategy itself and the background information. The step of diffusion, described earlier, is critical in ensuring effective implementation. The specific actions outlined are those that most likely comprise the step of influencing the process, to be discussed in the next section.

Evaluation

The nonprofit must always evaluate the outcomes of the strategy. The organization needs to evaluate how it did in meeting its defined objectives. If it was successful, what made it so? If not, where did the effort break down?

The strategic planning process is clearly intermingled with both the environmental assessment and influencing the policy process, but it adds in the key steps of outlining objectives, developing a strategy and action plan, implementing a strategy (in a more comprehensive way than diffusion or influence), and on-going evaluation. In terms of political competence, much of the strategy implementation comes in the form of influencing the process.

Influencing the Process

The second component of political competence is influencing the policymaking process. By definition, influence is "simply the process by which people successfully persuade others to follow their advice, suggestion or order" (Keys and Case, 1990). In the context of the policymaking process, organizations and individuals have the opportunity to exert influence at virtually any point along the process.

For example, one might influence the problem definition and agenda-setting stages by helping to define and/or document problems, or by changing political circumstances through lobbying efforts or litigation. An organization or individual can influence the policy development stage by participating in drafting legislation and/or by testifying at legislative hearings.

Within the policy implementation phase, there are also many opportunities for individuals or organizations to exert influence. Perhaps one of the most powerful ways is by participating in the rulemaking process. One can participate in public hearings, or provide comment through the *Federal Register*, either on draft rules or in response to advanced notices of proposed rulemaking. Another way individuals or groups can participate is by serving on or providing input to rulemaking advisory bodies, or by influencing those who sit on those bodies. Individuals and organizations can also exert influence by building a case for modification based on operational experience and formal evaluations.

The Influencing Role

With all of these opportunities to exert influence, how exactly does a nonprofit go about doing this? Who is sending key messages, and how can the nonprofit be structured to support all of these activities? Typically, the influencing is done by the individuals at the "strategic apex" of an organization (Mintzberg, 1983). This is often the CEO or other senior leader. A CEO or other senior leader may be able to effectively use his or her power (positional, reward, coercive, or expert) to apply pressure at any one of the points discussed previously. The CEO or other senior leader can establish and/or oversee the activities of a department or division dedicated to political competence. In many private companies, there may be a Public Affairs or Government Relations department that is accountable for all of the behind-the-scenes activities involved with environmental scanning and laying the groundwork for high-level influence. In some cases, organizations have special units specifically to perform environmental analysis, with varying degrees of success (Lenz and Engledow, 1986).

Strategic Plan to Develop Political Competence

Just as organizations need to develop strategic plans to address individual policy issues, a nonprofit organization wishing to enhance its political competence needs to establish a plan to do so. Following the strategic planning process outlined earlier (QuickMBA, 2005), nonprofit organizations should consider the issues discussed next.

Mission and Objectives   The mission in this case may be to develop or improve the organization's political competence to better support the overall vision of the organization. Specific objectives might include identifying organizations for potential alignment, acquiring the skills, and establishing the infrastructure needed to influence the outcome of strategic policy issues.

Environmental Scanning   Environmental scanning is essential for the nonprofit to assess its current position, identifying its internal strengths and weaknesses and external opportunities and threats. What is the organization's current position? How politically competent is it? What skills and resources does it have? How influential are its leaders? What are other nonprofits doing in this area? What resources are they dedicating to political competence and what results are they getting? What groups or individuals do they hold influence over, and how did they get to be in that position? Are there other groups with a similar stance on key issues? What groups out there have an opposing viewpoint, how politically competent are they, what are they doing, and what are their results?

Strategy Formulation   Using information from the two previous steps, the nonprofit needs to develop a political competence strategy. What will the organization do? How will the needed skills and knowledge be acquired (hire an expert or develop skills internally)? How will environmental assessment and influence be made a reality? What entities and individuals will it try to align with both initially and on an ongoing basis? What policy-related "trading" can and will it engage in? What will the structure be? Who will do the work? What resources will they need? What needs to be done to improve the organization's influence?

Strategy Implementation   After answering the questions related to strategy formulation, the organization then needs to implement the designed strategy. Implementing the plan may include activities such as personnel recruitment, skill building, budget allocation, and relationship building.

Evaluation   On an ongoing basis, the nonprofit needs to know its progress toward the objectives. Has it been successful in establishing the requisite infrastructure and developing the needed skills and knowledge? Does it have the leaders in place who can successfully influence the right individuals and entities? And ultimately, is it successful in terms of the legislative and policy outcomes achieved?

ALIGNMENT WITH OTHERS

Once an organization has considered these issues in the context of developing political competence, it will need to continually address the same topics on an ongoing, issue-specific basis. In terms of strategy formulation, organizations need to consider their position in the political marketplace and develop a strategic approach to their alignment with other organizations around specific issues. For nonprofits with few resources, alignment with other groups may be especially important, especially if those organizations have a high level of resources and a high interest in the issue. Even if neither organization has a high level of resources, if they share a high interest in the issue, alignment may be beneficial. Figuerido (2000) provides a simple but helpful theoretical model for considering potential alignments.

As can be seen in Exhibit 14.1, nonprofit resources, characterized as either low or high, are represented on the Y-axis. Interest in a particular issue, characterized as either

---

EXHIBIT 14.1   POTENTIAL ALIGNMENTS

Resources

A: High Resources Low Interest	B: High Resources High Interest
C: Low Resources Low Interest	D: High Interest Low Resources

Interest in Issue

---

low or high is represented on the X-axis. Nonprofits in Quadrant B are in the best position to influence policies due to their high resources and strong interest, and a nonprofit with a strong interest and high resources or strong issues and low resources might find an alignment beneficial. Nonprofits in Quadrant C would not be attractive alignment partners, as they are essentially "out of the game"—they have little or no interest in the issue and are not well resourced. Nonprofits in Quadrant A have the resources required, but have low interest in the issue, and an alignment with them may bring little benefit. A Quadrant A organization may be interested in aligning with Quadrant B or D companies if they can find some common ground, or if the issue is secondary on their political agenda and they might use the alignment to enhance their position on a different strategic policy issue. Nonprofits in Quadrant D offer some alignment benefit, even though they are not well resourced due to their high interest in the issue. Organizations in Quadrant D could be well served in aligning with organizations in either Quadrants A or B.

ARGUMENTS AGAINST EXERCISING POLITICAL COMPETENCE

As discussed previously, fundamentally, political competence is the ability to effectively analyze the environment, and influence the policymaking process (Longest, 2002). Because of their tax-exempt status, nonprofits must be prudent in how, when, and where they try to influence the process. It is critical that nonprofits balance the exertion of their political competence with existing and proposed prohibitions on nonprofit political activities and lobbying. For example, if a 501(c)(3) nonprofit has an article in its newsletter supporting or opposing the election of a particular federal candidate, participates in voter registration or get-out-the-vote activities, or is perceived as having supporting or opposing particular federal political candidates as its primary goal, that nonprofit may be categorized as a "political committee" and must register as such with the Federal Election Commission (FEC) and be subject to FEC regulation (OMB Watch, 2000; Alliance for Justice, 2005).

The IRS has specified the amount and type of lobbying and political activities in which a 501(c)(3) nonprofit may engage. The IRS has created a publication, "Political and Lobbying Activities," which was adapted from IRS Publication 1828, *Tax Guide for Churches and Religious Organizations* (IRS, 2004). The publication states the following issues.

Lobbying Activity

In general, no organization may qualify for Section 501(c)(3) status if a substantial part of its activities is attempting to influence legislation (commonly known as lobbying). A 501(c)(3) organization may engage in some lobbying, but too much lobbying activity risks loss of tax-exempt status.

Legislation includes action by Congress, any state legislature, any local council, or similar governing body, with respect to acts, bills, resolutions, or similar items (such as legislative confirmation of appointive office), or by the public in referendum, ballot initiative, constitutional amendment, or similar procedure. It does not include actions by executive, judicial, or administrative bodies.

An organization will be regarded as attempting to influence legislation if it contacts, or urges the public to contact, members or employees of a legislative body for the purpose of proposing, supporting, or opposing legislation, or if the organization advocates the adoption or rejection of legislation.

Organizations may, however, involve themselves in issues of public policy without the activity being considered as lobbying. For example, organizations may conduct educational meetings, prepare and distribute educational materials, or otherwise consider public policy issues in an educational manner without jeopardizing their tax-exempt status.

Measuring Lobbying Activity: Substantial Part Test

Whether an organization's attempts to influence legislation constitute a substantial part of its overall activities is determined on the basis of all the pertinent facts and circumstances in each case. The IRS considers a variety of factors, including the time devoted (by both compensated and volunteer workers) and the expenditures devoted by the organization to the activity, when determining whether the lobbying activity is substantial.

Under the substantial part test, an organization that conducts excessive lobbying activity in any taxable year may lose its tax-exempt status, resulting in all of its income being subject to tax. In addition, a religious organization is subject to an excise tax equal to 5% of its lobbying expenditures for the year in which it ceases to qualify for exemption.

Further, a tax equal to 5% of the lobbying expenditures for the year may be imposed against organization managers, jointly and separately, who agree to the making of such expenditures knowing that the expenditures would likely result in the loss of tax-exempt status.

Measuring Lobbying Activity: Expenditure Test

Organizations other than churches and private foundations may elect the expenditure test under Section 501(h) as an alternative method for measuring lobbying activity. Under the expenditure test, the extent of an organization's lobbying activity will not jeopardize its tax-exempt status, provided its expenditures, related to such activity, do not normally exceed an amount specified in Section 4911. This limit is generally based on the size of the organization and may not exceed $1,000,000.

Organizations electing to use the expenditure test must file Form 5767, *Election/Revocation of Election by an Eligible IRC Section 501(c)(3) Organization to Make Expenditures to Influence Legislation*, at any time during the tax year for which it is to be effective. The election remains in effect for succeeding years unless it is revoked by the organization. Revocation of the election is effective beginning with the year following the year in which the revocation is filed.

Under the expenditure test, an organization that engages in excessive lobbying activity over a four-year period may lose its tax-exempt status, making all of its income for that period subject to tax. Should the organization exceed its lobbying expenditure dollar limit in a particular year, it must pay an excise tax equal to 25% of the excess.

Political Campaign Activity

Under the Internal Revenue Code, all Section 501(c)(3) organizations are absolutely prohibited from directly or indirectly participating in, or intervening in, any political campaign on behalf of (or in opposition to) any candidate for elective public office. Contributions to political campaign funds or public statements of position (verbal or written) made on behalf of the organization in favor of or in opposition to any candidate for public office clearly violate the prohibition against political campaign activity. Violation of this prohibition may result in denial or revocation of tax-exempt status and the imposition of certain excise tax.

Certain activities or expenditures may not be prohibited depending on the facts and circumstances. For example, certain voter education activities (including the presentation of public forums and the publication of voter education guides) conducted in a non-partisan manner do not constitute prohibited political campaign activity.

In addition, other activities intended to encourage people to participate in the electoral process, such as voter registration and get-out-the-vote drives, would not constitute prohibited political campaign activity if conducted in a non-partisan manner. On the other hand, voter education or registration activities with evidence of bias that: (a) would favor one candidate over another; (b) oppose a candidate in some manner; or (c) have the effect of favoring a candidate or group of candidates, will constitute prohibited participation or intervention.

Individual Activity by Organization Leaders

The political campaign activity prohibition is not intended to restrict free expression on political matters by leaders of organizations speaking for themselves, as individuals. Nor are leaders prohibited from speaking about important issues of public policy. However, for their organizations to remain tax-exempt under Section 501(c)(3), leaders cannot make partisan comments in official organization publications or at official functions.

To avoid potential attribution of their comments outside of organization functions and publications, organization leaders who speak or write in their individual capacity are encouraged to clearly indicate that their comments are personal and not intended to represent the views of the organization.

Inviting a Candidate to Speak

Depending on the facts and circumstances, an organization may invite political candidates to speak at its events without jeopardizing its tax-exempt status. Political candidates may be invited in their capacity as candidates, or individually (not as a candidate).

Speaking as a Candidate

When a candidate is invited to speak at an organization event as a political candidate, the organization must take steps to ensure that:

- It provides an equal opportunity to the political candidates seeking the same office.
- It does not indicate any support of or opposition to the candidate (this should be stated explicitly when the candidate is introduced and in communications concerning the candidate's attendance).
- No political fundraising occurs.

Equal Opportunity to Participate

In determining whether candidates are given an equal opportunity to participate, an organization should consider the nature of the event to which each candidate is invited, in addition to the manner of presentation.

For example, an organization that invites one candidate to speak at its well-attended annual banquet, but invites the opposing candidate to speak at a sparsely attended general meeting, will likely be found to have violated the political campaign prohibition, even if the manner of presentation for both speakers is otherwise neutral.

Depending on the facts and circumstances, an organization may invite political candidates to speak at its events without jeopardizing its tax-exempt status. Political candidates may be invited in their capacity as candidates, or individually (not as a candidate).

Public Forum

Sometimes, an organization invites several candidates to speak at a public forum. A public forum involving several candidates for public office may qualify as an exempt educational activity. However, if the forum is operated to show a bias for or against any candidate, then the forum would be a prohibited campaign activity, as it would be considered intervention or participation in a political campaign.

When an organization invites several candidates to speak at a forum, it should consider the following factors:

- Whether questions for the candidate are prepared and presented by an independent nonpartisan panel.
- Whether the topics discussed by the candidates cover a broad range of issues that the candidates would address if elected to the office sought and are of interest to the public.
- Whether each candidate is given an equal opportunity to present his or her views on the issues discussed.
- Whether the candidates are asked to agree or disagree with positions, agendas, platforms, or statements of the organization.
- Whether a moderator comments on the questions or otherwise implies approval or disapproval of the candidates.

Speaking as a Noncandidate

An organization may invite political candidates to speak in a noncandidate capacity. For instance, a political candidate may be a public figure because he or she: (a) currently holds, or formerly held, public office; (b) is considered an expert in a nonpolitical field; or (c) is a celebrity or has led a distinguished military, legal, or public service career. When a candidate is invited to speak at an event in a noncandidate capacity, it is not necessary for the organization to provide equal access to all political candidates.

However, the organization must ensure that:

- The individual speaks only in a noncandidate capacity.
- Neither the individual nor any representative of the organization makes any mention of his or her candidacy or the election.
- No campaign activity occurs in connection with the candidate's attendance.

In addition, the organization should clearly indicate the capacity in which the candidate is appearing and should not mention the individual's political candidacy or the upcoming election in the communications announcing the candidate's attendance at the event.

Voter Guides

Organizations undertake voter education activities by distributing voter guides. Voter guides, generally, are distributed during an election campaign and provide information on how all candidates stand on various issues. These guides may be distributed with the purpose of educating voters; however, they may not be used to attempt to favor or oppose candidates for public elected office.

Since its tax-exempt status is one of a nonprofit's most valuable assets, it must be careful not to endanger that status by exercising its political competence. The strategic plan for developing and exercising influence must include an analysis of the impact of any action on the nonprofit's tax-exempt status. Being fully aware of changes or proposed changes in IRS rules or regulations is critical for the politically competent nonprofit.

HELPFUL WEBSITES FOR THE NONPROFIT DEVELOPING ITS POLITICAL COMPETENCE

FirstGov

FirstGov is the official web portal for the U.S. government. It is a free-access website that provides a centralized location to find information from the U.S. local, state, and federal government websites. The following URL links to a wealth of information for nonprofits, including laws, regulations, and rulemaking: http://www.firstgov.gov/Business/Nonprofit.

Regulations.gov

Regulations.gov is the U.S. Government website that allows the public to more easily participate in federal rulemaking. From the site, one can find, review, and submit comments on federal documents that are open for comment and published in the *Federal Register*. The URL is http://www.regulations.gov/.

Code of Federal Regulations

This website allows one to search the Code of Federal Regulations, which contains the final rules developed by the executive departments and agencies of the U.S. Federal government. The URL is: http://www.archives.gov/federal_register/code_of_federal_regulations/code_of_federal_regulations.html.

The Federal Register: What It Is and How to Use It

This site provides a tutorial on using the *Federal Register*. The URL is http://www
.archives.gov/federal_register/tutorial/about_tutorial.html.

OMB Watch

OMB Watch is a nonprofit research and advocacy organization that monitors the Office of Management and Budget (OMB), particularly for policies and information regarding the nonprofit sector. The URL is http://www.ombwatch.org/.

U.S. Senate

The U.S. Senate's website provides information regarding individual Senators, Senate Committees' composition and activities, enacted and proposed legislation, and the Senate calendar. The URL is http://www.senate.gov/.

U.S. House of Representatives

The U.S. House of Representatives' website provides information regarding individual members of the House, House Committees' composition and activities, enacted and proposed legislation, and the House calendar. The URL is http://www.house.gov/.

Independent Sector

The Independent Sector is a national network of nonprofits, charities, foundations, and corporate giving programs. The Independent Sector, at the request of the U.S. Senate Finance Committee, formed the Panel on the Nonprofit Sector. The Panel on the Nonprofit Sector was formed to make recommendations to Congress geared toward improving the oversight and governance of nonprofits. As such, the work performed by the Panel on the Nonprofit Network Sector and the Independent Sector should be monitored by nonprofits who wish to exercise political competence. The URL is http://www.independentsector.org/.

CONCLUSION

Political competence involves a complex slate of knowledge, skills, and talent. A nonprofit needs to understand its own strategic policy issues, be able to complete an effective assessment of the environment (including projections of the future), lay out a strategic approach (including influencing the process and others in it), and execute on the strategic vision through influence. Nonprofit organizations need to think of themselves as interest groups or private companies in their endeavor to be more politically competent. They need to leverage their resources (financial, membership, and employees), and ensure that they have the appropriate talent to lead the organization and to execute on the specific tasks that make up the components of political competence. In addition, they need to work to find common ground and align with other entities, even those with completely different overall missions. They must, however, exercise prudence in exercising their political competence or they may risk losing their tax-exempt status.

WORKSHEET: PRESSURES FOR NONPROFIT REFORM

As discussed in Chapter 1, nonprofits are experiencing pressure for reform from a number of sources: the U.S. Senate Finance Committee, the IRS, the Panel on the Nonprofit Sector, and others. Each of these sources has made proposals for reform or has provided testimony regarding the apparent lack of accountability in the nonprofit sector. These proposals, suggestions, and testimonies all have implications for nonprofits and how they are to operate. Exhibit 14.2 contains the URLs to relevant statements, reports, and testimony regarding nonprofit reform. In this chapter, we discussed the importance of political competence and the necessity of nonprofits to understand the internal and external environments in which they operate. To begin your external environmental scan, visit each URL, read the materials, and reflect on the implications for nonprofits. What do these pressures portend for nonprofits? What actions should a nonprofit take to lessen or better control the impact of these pressures? How can a nonprofit use this information to increase its political competence?

Source of Pressure	Implications and Possible Responses
Panel on the Nonprofit Sector Final Report of the Panel *http://www.nonprofitpanel.org/final/*	
Senate Finance Committee Staff Discussion Draft White Paper June 22, 2004 Exempt Status Reforms *http://finance.senate.gov/hearings/testimony/2004test/062204stfdis.pdf*	
Mark Everson Commissioner, Internal Revenue Service Senate Hearing Statement Charity Oversight and Reform: Keeping Bad Things from Happening to Good Charities *http://finance.senate.gov/hearings/testimony/2004test/062204metest.pdf*	
Senator Charles Grassley Chair, Senate Finance Committee Senate Hearing Opening and Closing Remarks Charities and Charitable Giving: Proposals for Reform April 5, 2005 *http://finance.senate.gov/hearings/statements/040505cg.pdf*	
Mark Everson Commissioner, Internal Revenue Service	

(continues)

Source of Pressure	Implications and Possible Responses
Senate Hearing Statement Charities and Charitable Giving: Proposal for Reform April 5, 2005 *http://finance.senate.gov/hearings/testimony/2005test/metesto40505.pdf*	
Diana Aviv President and CEO—Independent Sector Executive Director—Panel on the Nonprofit Sector Senate Hearing Statement Charities and Charitable Giving: Proposal for Reform April 5, 2005 *http://finance.senate.gov/hearings/testimony/2005test/datesto40505.pdf*	
Brian A. Gallagher President and CEO—United Way of America Senate Hearing Statement Charities and Charitable Giving: Proposal for Reform April 5, 2005 *http://finance.senate.gov/hearings/testimony/2005test/bgtesto40505.pdf*	
Attorney General Mike Hatch, Minnesota Senate Hearing Statement Charities and Charitable Giving: Proposal for Reform April 5, 2005 *http://finance.senate.gov/hearings/testimony/2005test/mhtesto40505.pdf*	

Chapter Questions

Chapter 1

1. Chapter 1 discusses a number of factors in the private sector that drove the passage of SOX. Of these factors, which do you think was the most influential? Why?

2. Title III of SOX imposes new obligations on the senior management team, the audit committee, and the attorneys of companies registered with the SEC. Do you think these obligations should be imposed in the nonprofit sector? Why or why not?

3. Title II of SOX tries to establish the independence of auditors for public companies. Why is auditor independence desirable? What barriers do you see to creating auditor independence?

4. Some have complained that the cost to public companies to implement the SOX requirements is excessive and exceeds the benefits of SOX. Do you agree that the costs outweigh the benefits? Why or why not?

5. In part, SOX was passed to restore investor confidence in the stock market and increase the reliability of the financial statements of public companies. Do you think SOX will achieve these goals? Why or why not?

6. To achieve the two goals of SOX—increased investor confidence and reliable financial statements—what additional provisions should have been included in the legislation?

7. Currently, only two provisions in SOX—whistleblower protection and document preservation—apply to nonprofits. Why do you think that nonprofits were included in these provisions? What other provisions do you think should have applied to nonprofits? Why?

Chapter 2

1. Chapter 2 discusses some of the sources of increased pressure for the adoption of SOX-like rules and regulations in the nonprofit sector. For example, the Panel on the Nonprofit Sector is calling for increases in nonprofit oversight. Of the sources discussed in the chapter, which do you think will be the most influential? Why?

2. There are benefits and costs to nonprofits that adopt the "best practices" from SOX. Do the benefits outweigh the costs? Why or why not?

3. Of all of the proposals in the White Paper from the Senate Finance Committee, which do you think is most likely to be adopted? Why?

4. One of the proposed changes in board composition restricts the number of board members, no more than 15 and no fewer than 3. What are the advantages of this size restriction? What are the disadvantages?

5. The Panel on the Nonprofit Sector had a number of recommendations directed at the nonprofit sector and the IRS. Of the recommendations, which do you think is most likely to be adopted? Why?

6. Given the recent scandals in the nonprofit sector, do you think that self-regulation is ineffective? Why or why not?

7. Do you think it is likely that other states will pass legislation similar to California's Nonprofit Integrity Act? Why or why not?

Chapter 3

1. What is organizational culture, and how can it contribute to dysfunction in nonprofits?

2. What are some of the costs of organizational dysfunction?

3. A dysfunctional belief system is sometimes at the root of organizational dysfunction. What is a dysfunctional belief system, and how does it become embedded in the organization?

4. What does the statement "the Executive Director is the Board of Directors' only employee" mean? If a board believed that statement and acted accordingly, how would the board act?

5. If the organizational culture of a nonprofit were adversely affecting its performance, what steps could management and the board take to create change?

6. The chapter discussed eight symptoms of board dysfunction. Which symptoms do you think are most common in nonprofits, and which do you think is most detrimental? Why?

7. Have you ever been employed by, consulted with, served on the board, or worked as a volunteer for a dysfunctional nonprofit? How did it affect the non-profit's performance and your interactions with it?

Chapter 4

1. What aspects in the organizational culture of the American Red Cross contributed to the Liberty Fund crisis? How did the culture affect organizational functioning?

2. What aspects of board governance at the United Way of National Capital Area contributed to the criminal behavior of the Executive Director? What could the board have done to avoid the crisis?

3. What were the primary causes of the crisis at the James Beard Foundation? How could the crisis have been avoided?

4. What were the events, allegations, or criminal behavior that triggered the Liberty Fund crisis at the American Red Cross?

5. What role did whistleblowers play in each of the three crises discussed in the chapter? How could an effective Whistleblower Protection policy have mitigated some of the fallout from each crisis?

6. What are some of the negative results for a nonprofit once it experiences a crisis at the level of the ones discussed in Chapter 4? How can these impacts be mitigated?

7. What tactics could Dr. Healy have used with the American Red Cross board to avert the Liberty Fund crisis and her subsequent "resignation?" What would you have done if faced with the same situation?

Chapter 5

1. If the board at the United Way of National Capital Area had included an audit committee, do you think the nonprofit would have experienced the crisis that occurred? Why or why not?

2. If the recommendations from the Panel on the Nonprofit Sector had been in place, do you think they would have lessened or significantly reduced the likelihood of the three nonprofit crises discussed in Chapters 4 and 5? Why or why not?

3. What are internal controls and what value do they have for nonprofits? What are the barriers to adopting effective internal controls?

4. What does it mean for a board of directors to be independent? How does it affect board behavior and governance?

5. Assuming there are advantages to having an independent board of directors, how can board independence be achieved in a nonprofit?

6. Could an effective Document Preservation policy have averted any of the three crises discussed in Chapters 4 and 5? How? Why do you think these nonprofits did *not* have this type of policy?

7. If any or all of the three nonprofits discussed in Chapters 4 and 5 had prepared complete and accurate Form 990s with the IRS, would the crises have been averted? Why or why not?

Chapter 6

1. What are the legal and ethical standards for board members? How do they influence board behavior?

2. What are the duties and the responsibilities of the executive committee? How can the executive committee best meet its duties?

3. Compare and contrast the nonprofit board of today with that of the past. What are the primary differences?

4. How can a board develop and implement an effective decision-making model? What are the barriers to doing so?

5. What are the board's fiduciary responsibilities and how are they met? What are the barriers that hold boards back from meeting these responsibilities?

6. How could an orientation for board members increase the overall functioning of the board? What topics should be covered in the orientation? Why?

7. What role does the Nominating Committee play in developing board competence? How could this committee play a more effective role?

Chapter 7

1. What steps should the Executive Team take to develop and implement an effective crisis communication plan? What priority level should implementing a crisis communication plan have? Why?

2. How have recent state and federal legislation and proposals, such as the Panel on the Nonprofit Sector's Final Report and the California Nonprofit Integrity Act, changed the public's expectations of nonprofit senior managers? Are these expectations realistic? Why or why not?

3. What role does the Executive Team have in developing and implementing SOX best practices? How can the Executive Team ensure compliance throughout the nonprofit?

4. If the supporting factors within a nonprofit facilitate fraud, which factor would be the easiest to correct and why? Which would be the most difficult and why? Which should be the first factor the Executive Team tackles and why?

5. What tools can the Executive Team use to bring about changes in organizational culture? Of the tools, which are the least and most effective? Why?

6. What steps should be taken in responding to an emergency or crisis? What should the nonprofit do first? Why?

7. Why is having a Technology Policy important for a nonprofit? What topics should the policy cover and why?

Chapter 8

1. What are the benefits of having a Document Management and Preservation policy? What topics should be addressed in the policy and why?

2. What are the steps in developing a document preservation system that is in compliance with SOX best practices?

3. The Technology policy discussed in the chapter addressed three talking points. What are these points and how should the Technology policy address them?

4. How can a nonprofit use its website to show its compliance with SOX best practices? Why would a nonprofit want to do this?

5. How can the board and management convey the "tone at the top" in regard to implementing policies such as a Technology policy or a Document Preservation policy? Is conveying the tone necessary or helpful in ensuring compliance? How?

6. What role does evaluation and continuous quality improvement play in the development and implementation of nonprofit policies?

7. What are some of the challenges that nonprofits have in terms of website and computer network security? What steps can be taken to increase the level of security?

Chapter 9

1. What is the function of a Whistleblower Protection policy? What features should the policy include to be in compliance with SOX?

2. Compare and contrast independent contractors with employees. How do the legal requirements differ between contractors and employees?

3. Why should a nonprofit develop protocols for exit interviews? What issues should be addressed in the protocols?

4. Why should a nonprofit develop protocols for travel expenses, credit cards, and other credit accounts? What issues should be addressed in the protocols? How can these protocols be implemented?

5. Why is having a confidential reporting system advantageous for a nonprofit? What type of systems can be used and which would be most effective?

6. Once an employee or manager has reported suspected inappropriate activity, such as fraud or waste, what steps should be taken to investigate the claim? If the claim is borne out, what should the next steps be?

7. What steps should a nonprofit take to ensure the privacy of its employees, donors, clients, and volunteers? Why are these steps necessary?

Chapter 10

1. What impact has the changing federal and state legislative environment had on nonprofit fundraising practices? Are these impacts negative or positive? Why?

2. What are the roles of the board and management in providing oversight and guidance to the nonprofit's fundraising activities? How can these roles be met?

3. What is the role of an internal control system in combating fraud in nonprofit fundraising? How can this role be met?

4. What are some of the common red flags for fundraising fraud? How should these red flags be addressed?

5. What steps can a nonprofit take to ensure the security of donor records and other confidential information? Why is this important?

6. What flaws are present in the current system of nonprofit car donations? What role do fundraising vendors play in these flaws and how can these flaws be addressed?

7. What were the key findings from the Wise Giving Alliance survey? Which of these findings is most problematic? How can these findings be addressed?

Chapter 11

1. What is the function of an internal control system? What are the benefits to a nonprofit for having an effective system in place?

2. What are the five components of an effective internal control system? Give two examples for each of the five components.

3. What roles did the Committee of Sponsoring Organizations (COSO) and the Committee on Fraudulent Financial Reporting play in the development of some of the requirements of SOX? What roles did COSO play in establishing a standard internal control framework?

4. What are the roles of the board, management, and staff in developing and implementing an internal control system?

5. What is the relationship between financial controls and the internal control system? Provide examples of financial controls.

6. What were the primary findings of the National Commission of Fraudulent Financial Reporting? Although the report only included public companies, which of the findings do you think would hold true for nonprofits?

7. Of the key areas of financial controls discussed in the chapter, which do you think the majority of nonprofits have in place? Which do you think are not in place? What steps could a nonprofit take to increase the effectiveness of its financial controls?

Chapter 12

1. Why is it important for a nonprofit's board to be financially literate? What attributes should a board have to be considered financially literate?

2. What are the major differences between adult learners and "traditional" learners? How should board training incorporate those differences?

3. Why should training programs take learning styles into account? What are the different types of learning styles and what tactics can be used to address them?

4. What role does the board have with developing, implementing, and evaluating the budget? What methods can the board use to evaluate budget performance?

5. What are the methods the board can use to analyze financial statements for red flags? What are some of the common red flags and how can they be addressed?

6. What are the functions and duties of an audit committee? What is the benefit to a nonprofit for having an audit committee?

7. Compare and contrast the cash basis of accounting with the accrual basis of accounting. Which type is preferable and why?

Chapter 13

1. What factors should an audit committee use to evaluate the suitability of potential external auditors? Which is the most important factor? Why?

2. What are the three duties of the nonprofit board? How are those duties exercised?

3. What is the audit plan? Why is having an effective audit plan key to an effective audit? Who participates in developing the audit plan?

4. What is the value of having an external audit? What are the different audit opinions and how do they pertain to the reliability of the financial statements?

5. What duties and responsibilities does the audit committee have regarding the external audit?

6. What are the salient features of Internal Revenue Code Section 4958? What are implications of Section 4958 for nonprofits and management?

7. What are the salient features of Internal Revenue Code Section 6104? What are implications of Section 6104 for nonprofits and management?

Chapter 14

1. What is political competence? Is political competence a desirable attribute for a nonprofit? Why or why not?

2. What steps should a nonprofit take to develop its political competence?

3. What are the steps in the U.S. policymaking process? At what point will a nonprofit be more likely to exert influence?

4. What is environmental analysis? What is the five-step process for environmental analysis? What is the value of performing environmental analysis?

5. What resources does a nonprofit need to develop political competence?

6. What are the steps in rulemaking? What are the sources of information regarding new and proposed rules?

7. Why should a nonprofit use caution when developing and exerting political competence? What are the IRS regulations regarding political activities and lobbying for nonprofits?

Bibliography

Abernathy, K.Q. (2002). Special alert: What WorldCom bankruptcy means to consumers. *Focus on Consumer Concerns*, vol. 2(5). Retrieved on August 15, 2004 from http://www.fcc.gov/commissioners/abernathy/news/worldcom.html.

About the Great Depression. (n.d.). Retrieved on September 24, 2004 from http://www.english.uiuc.edu/maps/depression/about.htm.

AICPA. (n.d.). Sarbanes-Oxley Act/PCAOB implementation central. Retrieved on June 25, 2004 from http://www.aicpa.org/sarbanes/index.asp.

AICPA (2005). "*Summary of Sarbanes-Oxley Act of 2002*," American Institute of Certified Public Accountants, retrieved on April 2, 2005 from http://www.aicpa.org/info/sarbanes_oxley_summary.htm.

All Business.Com: The Advisor, *Know the Difference Between Regular and Contract Workers, SF Gate*, San Francisco, CA, June 1, 2005.

Alliance for Justice (2005). "*The Facts on the FEC's Proposed Rules Regarding Political Committees that Could Adversely Affect Nonprofit Advocacy*", retrieved on April 10, 2005 from http://www.afj.org/nonprofit/public_policy/campaign_finance_reform/FEC_Prop527.pdf.

American Red Cross, Chapter Audits FY 2001, Washington, DC.

Anderson, Christopher B., *Form 990: More Than Just a Tax Return, The Tax Advisor*, April 2004, v.35, i4, p. 200 (2).

Arthur Andersen LLP v. United States. (2005), No. 04-368, retrieved on July 21, 2005 from http://caselaw.lp.findlaw.com/scripts/getcase.pl?court=US&vol=000&invol=04-368&friend=usatoday#opinion1.

Association of Certified Fraud Examiners. (1996) *Report to the Nation, 1996*, retrieved on July 1, 2005 from www.cfenet.com/pdfs/Report_to_the_Nation.pdf.

Babcock, Charles R. and Havemann, Judith. *Managing an Agency and Image, The Washington Post*, Washington, DC, February 16, 1999.

Barstow, David. *In Congress, Harsh Words for Red Cross, New York Times*, New York, NY, November 7, 2001.

Beattie, A. (2003). Why it's all our fault: How investors often cause the market's problems. Retrieved on June 17, 2004 from http://www.investopedia.com/articles/basics/03/062003.asp.

Beltran, L. (2002). "*Waksal Indicted in ImClone Scandal*," *CNN/Money*, retrieved on March 16, 2005 from http://money.cnn.com/2002/08/07/news/waksal_indictment/.

Better Business Bureau Wise Giving Alliance *Standards for Charity Accountability*, Arlington, VA, Spring 2003.

BoardSource and Independent Sector. (2003). "*The Sarbanes-Oxley Act and Implications for Non-profit Organizations*," retrieved on March 14, 2004 from http://www.boardsource.org/clientfiles/Sarbanes-Oxley.pdf.

Bonello, F.J. (2004). Stock exchange. *Microsoft Encarta Online Encyclopedia*. Retrieved on May 23, 2004 from http://encarta.msn.com/encyclopedia_761560145_2/Stock_Exchange.html #p67.

Borenstein, E.R. (1998). Legal need relative to non-profit and/or tax-exempt status of new organizations. Retrieved on June 27, 2004 from http://www.muridae.com/nporegulation/.

Bothwell, R.O. (2002). "Trends in Self-Regulation and Transparency of Nonprofit Organizations in the U.S.," *Journal of Not-for-Profit Law*, Vol. 4, Issue 1, retrieved on February, 2005 from http://www.icnl.org/journal/vol4iss1/bothwell2.htm.

Bumgardner, L.J. (2003). How does the Sarbanes-Oxley Act impact American business? *Journal of Contemporary Business Practice*, vol. 6(1). Retrieved on July 19, 2004 from http://gbr.pepperdine.edu/031/sarbanesoxley.html.

Chronicle of Philanthropy. (2004). "Ex-United Way CEO Gets Jail Sentence," retrieved May 23, 2005 from http://www.unitedwaynca.org/website/content/media/pdf/chronphil5-27-04.pdf.

Clark, D. (2000). "Learning Styles," ISD-Development, retrieved on April 25, 2005 from http://www.nwlink.com/~donclark/hrd/learning/styles.html.

CNN.com (1998). The market "circuit breakers": How they work. Retrieved on July 17, 2004 from http://www.cnn.com/US/9809/01/market.circuit.breakers/.

Cohen, Jay, *Protecting Privacy in an Exposed Business Environment*, IDA/Kahn Conference proceedings, San Jose, CA, May 2004.

Corporate and Auditing Accountability, Responsibility, and Transparency Act of 2002, H.R. 3763, 107th Congress, retrieved on January 28, 2004 from http://thomas.loc.gov/cgi-bin/query/D?c107:1:./temp/~c107GaX96X.

COSO (1999). *Fraudulent Financial Reporting: 1987–1997—An Analysis of U.S. Public Companies—Executive Summary and Introduction*, retrieved on April 29, 2005 from http://www.coso.org/publications/executive_summary_fraudulent_financial_reporting.htm.

COSO (1992). *Internal Control—Integrated Framework: Executive Summary*, retrieved on April 29, 2005 from http://www.coso.org/publications/executive_summary_integrated_framework.htm.

COSO (1987). *Report of the National Commission of Fraudulent Financial Reporting*, retrieved on April 29, 2005 from http://www.coso.org/publications/NCFFR_Part_1.htm.

CSBC (2002). "Executive Summary of the Sarbanes-Oxley Act of 2002: P.L. 107–204", Conference of State Bank Supervisors, retrieved on January 3, 2005 from http://www.csbs.org/government/legislative/misc/2002_sarbanes-oxley_summary.htm.

Davis, Linda J. "Compliance Programs in 2005: What is Good Enough?" (IDC/Kahn Conference, May 12, 2005).

Davis, R.R. (2004, April). Using disclaimers in audit reports: Discerning between shades of opinion. *The CPA Journal, Online*. Retrieved on August 3, 2004 from http://www.nysscpa.org/cpajournal/2004/404/essentials/p26.htm.

DeBare, Ilana, *Determining Whether Worker is a Contractor or an Employee*, SF Gate, San Francisco, CA, June 1, 2005.

Decker, Harold, *Letter to Senator Charles E. Grassley*, Washington, DC, June 14, 2002.

Deloitte, *Corporate Responsibility: The Impact of Sarbanes-Oxley on Not-for-Profit Health Care*, Presentation at the Healthcare Financial Management Association ANI 2004.

Deloitte Development LLC. (2004). *Corporate Responsibility: The Impact of Sarbanes-Oxley on Not-For-Profit Health Care*, retrieved on July 2, 2005 from http://www.deloitte.com/dtt/cda/doc/content/us_healthcare_BigalkeHFMASarbanes%20_0604.pdf.

Economist (1998). "Philanthropy in America: The Gospel of Wealth." *Economist*: May 30. pp. 19–21.

Editors of Career Press. (1998). *Business Finance for the Numerically Challenged*. Career Press: New Jersey.

Eichenwald, Kurt. (2002). Arthur Andersen convicted of obstruction of justice. *New York Times*, New York, NY, June 15.

Emert, Carol, *Financial Irregularities Prompt Shakeups at Beard Foundation*, San Francisco Chronicle, September 15, 2004.

Estrada, Heron Marquez, *Theft at Paper Exposes Vulnerability of Nonprofits*, Minneapolis Star Tribune, Minneapolis, MN, October 4, 2004.

Evergreen State Society. (2003). What is Form 990? How is it used? Retrieved on June 16, 2004 from http://www.nonprofits.org/npofaq/19/06.html.

Everson, Mark W., Commissioner of the Internal Revenue Service, Testimony before the U.S. Senate Finance Committee hearings on *Charities and Charitable Giving: Proposals for Reform*, Washington, DC, April 2005.

Everson, Mark W., Commissioner of the Internal Revenue Service, Testimony before the U.S. Senate Finance Committee hearings on *Charity Oversight and Reform: Keeping Bad Things from Happening to Good Charities*, Washington, DC, June 2004.

Eyestone, R. (1978). *From Social Issues to Public Policy*. New York: John Wiley & Sons Inc.

Fabrizius, Michael P. and Sarafini, Richard M., *Learning to Love the Scrutiny: Initiating a Quality Assessment Can Help an Internal Audit Group Come Out on Top*, Internal Auditor, February 2004, v61, i1, p. 38(7).

Farrell, G. (2002). Anderson staffer says phrase was a hint to shred. *USA Today*, May 21.

Flaherty, Mary Pat. *Red Cross Defends Use of Donations*, The Washington Post, Washington, DC, November 7, 2001.

Flynn, D.M. (2004). "New IRS Tax Exempt Compensation Enforcement Project," *duane morris.com*, retrieved June 21, 2005 from http://www.duanemorris.com/alerts/static/A_IRSProject082004.pdf.

France, David and Noonan, David, *Blood + Money*, Newsweek, New York, New York, December 17, 2001, Vol. 138; Iss. 25.

Francis-Smithy, Janice, *Sarbanes-Oxley Holds Big Implications for Nonprofits*, Journal Record, Oklahoma City, OK, January 8, 2004, pg. 1.

Gallegher, Brian, Testimony before the U.S. Senate Finance Committee hearings on *Charities and Charitable Giving: Proposals for Reform*, Washington, DC, April 2005.

Gallegos, Frederick, CISA, CGFM, CDE, *Sarbanes-Oxley Act of 2002 and Impact on the IT Auditor*, Auerbach Publications, 2003.

Gaul, Gilbert M. and Flaherty, Mary Pat, *Red Cross Collected Unneeded Blood; Resources Lacking to Freeze Surplus*, *The Washington Post*, Washington, DC, November 11, 2001.

Gately, E. (2005). "Some Say New SEC Regulations Waste Company Time and Money," East Valley Tribune.com retrieved on July 9, 2005 from http://www.eastvalleytribune.com/index.php?sty=44045.

Ginter, P.M., W.J. Duncan and L.E. Swayne (2002). *Strategic Management of Health Care Organizations*, 4th ed. Malden, MA: Blackwell Publishers.

Giving USA Foundation (2005). "AAFRC Trust for Philanthropy/Giving USA 2004." Retrieved on March 23, 2005 from http://www.givingusa.org/gusa/.

Glaser, M. (2004). "Net Changes Game of Political Advocacy for Groups on the Right and Left," USC Annenberg Online Journalism Review, retrieved on July 10, 2005 from http://www.ojr.org/ojr/glaser/1073429305.php.

Gottlieb, H. (2003). "The Dirty Little Secret of Nonprofit Boards," ReSolve, Inc. retrieved on May 26, 2005 from http://www.help4nonprofits.com/NP_Bd_DirtyLittleSecrets_Art.htm.

Grassley, Charles, *Letter to Marsha Evans*, Washington DC. August 12, 2002.

Greenberg, Daniel S. *Blood, Politics, and the American Red Cross*, *The Lancet*, November 24, 2001, v358 i9295.

Healy, Bernadine M.D., *Letter to Kathryn Forbes and Norman Augustine*, Washington DC, April 3, 2001.

Healy, Bernadine M.D., *Memorandum to Ron Lund*, Washington, DC, April 16, 2001.

Herman, M.L., Head, G.L., Jackson, P.M., & Fogarty, T.E. (2004). *Managing Risk in Nonprofit Organizations: A Comprehensive Guide*. Hoboken, New Jersey: John Wiley & Sons, Inc.

Hopkins, Bruce, *Sarbanes-Oxley Act of 2002: What It Means For Nonprofit Organizations*, Nonprofit Counsel, Vol. XIX, No. 10, October 2002.

Herbenar, R. (1998). "The Influence of Nongovernmental Organizations and Nonprofit Organizations on Government Relations in the United States." National Academy of Public Administration, retrieved on June 5, 2005 from www.napawash.org/aa_federal_system/98_national_influence.html.

Huffstutter, P.J. and Gold, Scott, *Red Cross Chief Quits Amid Policy Disputes*, *Los Angeles Times*, Los Angeles, CA, October 27, 2001.

Independent Sector, *Learning from Sarbanes-Oxley: A Checklist for Nonprofits and Foundations*, Washington, DC, 2004.

Independent Sector, Panel on the Nonprofit Sector, *Report to Congress and the Nonprofit Sector on Governance, Transparency and Accountability*, Washington, DC, June 2005.

Internal Revenue Service—Ann. 2002-87,37 *"Corporate Responsibility."*

Internal Revenue Service—Publication. 463, Travel, Entertainment, Gift and Car Expenses, 2004.

IRS. (1999) "Internal Revenue Bulletin," IR Bulletin 1999-17, retrieved April 28, 2005 from http://www.irs.gov/pub/irs-irbs/irb99-17.pdf.

IRS.gov (2004). "Political Lobbying and Political Activities," Internal Revenue Service, retrieved on July 6 from http://www.irs.gov/charities/charitable/article/0,,id=120703,00.html.

Jacobs, Jerald, *Conflict of Interest Policies—Address Them Now* Association Management. Washington, DC, May 2003. Vol. 55, Iss 5; p. 17 (2).

Johnson, C.W. (2003). "How Our Laws Are Made," Thomas, retrieved on May 7, 2005 from http://thomas.loc.gov/home/lawsmade.toc.html.

Johnston, D.C. (2004). "Former Head of United Way in the Washington Area Pleads Guilty to Theft," *Nytimes.com*, retrieved on February 27, 2005 from http://www.unitedwaynca.org/website/content/media/pdf/newyork3.5.04.pdf.

Jones, Ashby, *Nonprofits on Alert*, *New York Law Journal*, American Lawyer Media L.P. January 27, 2005.

Jones, J. (2005). "Panel on the Nonprofit Sector Issues Report," *The NonProfit Times*, retrieved on June 28, 2005 from http://www.nptimes.com/Apr05/npt1.html.

Jones, Jeff, *Special Report: The Year in Review. The Nonprofit Times*, December 2004.

Karass, E.A. and Brann T.E. (2005). *Office of the State Controller*, retrieved on July 2, 2005 from http://www.state.me.us/bac/internal_control/steps.htm.

Kastl, Melanie A., Avitablile, Louis and Kleiner, Brian H. *How to Assess Credibility in Workplace Investigations, Nonprofit World*, Madison, WI Jan/Feb 2005, Vol. 23(1).

Keys, B. and T. Case (1990). "How to Become an Influential Manager," *The Executive* 4 (November): pp. 38–51.

Klein, H.E. and R.E. Linneman (1984). "Environmental Assessment: An International Study of Corporate Practices," *Journal of Business Strategy* 5: pp. 66–77.

Knowles, M. S. (1984). *The Adult Learner: A Neglected Species* (3rd. ed.), Houston, TX: Gulf Publishing Company.

Knowles, M. S. (1995). *Designs For Adult Learning: Practical Resources, Exercises, And Course Outlines From The Father Of Adult Learning*. Alexandria, VA: ASTD.

Kohn, S.M. (2004). "The Sarbanes-Oxley Act Legal Protections for Corporate Whistleblowers," National Whistleblower Center, retrieved on February 17, 2005 from http://jobsearchtech.about.com/gi/dynamic/offsite.htm?zi=1/XJ&sdn=jobsearchtech&zu=http%3A%2F%2Fwww.whistleblowers.org%2F.

Kolb, D.A. (1984). *Experiential Learning*. Englewood Cliff, NJ: Prentice Hall.

Kolb, D.A. (1985). *Learning Style Inventory and Technical Manual*. Boston, MA: McBer.

Kosinski, Gregory, and Cohen, Jay M. *Fundamentals of Compliance*, IDA/Kahn Conference proceedings, San Jose, CA, May 2004.

Lambert, Joyce, *Reduce Your Losses From Errors and Fraud*, Nonprofit World, Madison, WI, Sept/Oct 1998, Vol. 16, Iss 5: pp. 46–49.

Kuhn, N.O. (2001). "Intermediate Sanctions on NPO Executives," *Journal of Accountancy*, retrieved May 6, 2005 from http://www.aicpa.org/pubs/jofa/nov2001/kuhn.htm.

Lange, Michele, C.S. Keeping Your Head: New Sarbanes-Oxley Rules Make Document Retention Dizzying. *Corporate Counsel Magazine*, April 2003.

Larsen, K. (2004). "Summary: SB1262 'The Nonprofit Integrity Act,' " California Association of Nonprofits, retrieved on March 1, 2005 from http://www2.niac.org/Documents/DocumentRetrieve.cfm?q_DocumentID=147&UploadDocClass=DynamicContent.

Levine, Samantha, Red Crossroads: The Nation's Best-Known Charity Is Under Fire For How It Spends September 11th Disaster Funds, *U.S. News & World Report*, Washington, DC, November 19, 2001. Vol. 131, Iss. 21.

Leemhuis, J.P. (1985). "Using Scenarios to Develop Strategies." *Long Range Planning* 18: pp. 30–37.

Lenz, R.T. and J.L. Engledow (1986). "Environmental Analysis Units and Strategic Decision-Making: A Field Study of Selected 'Leading Edge' Corporations," *Strategic Management Journal* 7 (1): pp. 69–89.

Light, Paul C. Fact Sheet on the Continued Crisis in Charitable Confidence, Brookings Institution, Washington, DC, September 13, 2004.

Lindbloom, E.E. (1969). "The Sciences of 'Muddling Through'." In *Readings in Modern Organizations*, edited by A. Etzioni, pp. 154–65, Englewood Cliffs, NJ: Prentice Hall.

Longest, B. (2002). *Health Policymaking in the United States*, 3rd ed. Chicago, IL: Health Administration Press.

Longest, Jr. Beaufort B. *Eight Questions Every Board Needs to Answer*, Nonprofit World, Madison, WI, May/June 2004, Vol. 22, Iss. 3.

Markon, Jerry, *Ex-Chief of Local United Way Sentenced*, Washington Post, Washington, DC, May 15, 2004.

Markon, Jerry and Salmon, Jacqueline L., *Ex-United Way Official Rejects Court Deal*, Washington Post, Washington, DC, March 4, 2004.

Maryland Association of Nonprofit Organizations, *Standards for Excellence: An Ethics and Accountability Code for the Nonprofit Sector*, Baltimore, MD, 2004.

Mayer, C.E. (2005). "IRS Revokes Tax-Exempt Status of 4 Credit-Counseling Agencies," *washingpost.com*, retrieved July 27, 2005 from http://www.washingtonpost.com/wp-dyn/content/article/2005/07/16/AR2005071601040.html.

McDonough, Siobhan, *Survey: Charity CEO Raises Nearly Double Inflation Rate*, Advocate, Baton Rouge, LA, September 27, 2004, p. 12.A.

McNab, J.J. Testimony before the U.S. Senate Finance Committee hearings on *Charity Oversight and Reform: Keeping Bad Things from Happening to Good Charities*, Washington, DC, June 2004.

MacRae, C. (2004). "Learning Styles," BBC Skillswise, retrieved on April 25, 2005 from http://www.bbc.co.uk/skillswise/tutors/expertcolumn/learningstyles/.

Minnis, William C. *Four Steps to Evaluation Success*, Nonprofit World, Madison, WI Mar/April 2005 Vol. 23, Iss 2.

Mintzberg, H. (1983). *Structure in Fives: Designing Effective Organizations*. Englewood Cliffs, NJ: Prentice Hall.

Moerschbaecher, L.S. (2004). "Nonprofit Integrity Act Comes to California: Will Nation Follow?" Planning Design Center, retrieved on February 12, 2005 from http://www.pgdc.com/usa/item/?itemID=246141.

Mollison, Andrew. *Red Cross Chief Got $1.9 Million Gold Parachute*, The Atlanta Journal–Constitution, Atlanta, GA, April 19, 2003.

Mondaq Business Briefing, Governance and Nonprofit Corporations: Requirements and Expectations in a Post-Sarbanes-Oxley World, May 20, 2004.

Mondaq Business Briefing, *Nonprofit Governance Reforms: Five Steps Toward Improved Accountability*, May 25, 2004.

Moore, Geoffrey, *Managing Electronic Records is No Longer Optional*, White Paper published by Information Managers, Edison, NJ, March 2003.

Moskin, Julia, *Thousands Missing in Revenue Records of Culinary Charity*, New York Times, New York, NY, September 6, 2004, p. A.1.

"Mr. Car" (Confidential Witness) Testimony before the U.S. Senate Finance Committee hearings on *Charity Oversight and Reform: Keeping Bad Things from Happening to Good Charities*, Washington, DC, June 2004.

National Council of Nonprofit Associations Advocacy Rights. (2004). "Advocacy Rights," retrieved on July 3, 2005 from http://www.ncna.org/index.cfm?fuseaction=Page.viewPage&pageId=247.

Nation's Restaurant News Daily, *All Members of the Board of Trustees of the Troubled James Beard Foundation are Expected to Resign January 6, 2005*, News Fax, December 23, 2004.

Nonprofit Integrity Act (2004), State of California, State Senate Bill 1262, September 2004.

Office of the Attorney General, State of California, *Attorney General Lockyer Unveils Reforms to Toughen Nonprofit Accountability, Fundraiser Controls*, Sacramento, CA, February 12, 2004.

Office of the Attorney General, State of California, *FAQ on Nonprofit Integrity Act of 2004*, Sacramento, CA, January 2005.

Office of the Attorney General, State of California, *Summary of Key Provisions of the Nonprofit Integrity Act of 2004*, Sacramento, CA, October 2004.

Office of the Press Secretary. (2002). "Executive Order Establishment of the Corporate Fraud Task Force," retrieved on February 17, from http://www.whitehouse.gov/news/releases/2002/07/20020709-2.html.

Office of the Press Secretary. (2002). "President Bush Signs Corporate Corruption Bill," retrieved on February 21, 2005 from http://www.whitehouse.gov/news/releases/2002/07/20020730.html.

OMB Watch (2000). "Statement on Disclosure of Nonprofit Political Activity", retrieved on July 10, 2005 from http://www.ombwatch.org/npadv/2000/campfinstatement.html.

OMB Watch. (2004). "Senate Finance Committee Staff Proposals for Nonprofits," retrieved on July 1, 2005 from http://www.ombwatch.org/article/articleview/2248/1/49?TopicID=1.

O'Reilly-Allen, Margaret, "How to have an Audit Without Breaking the Bank," *Nonprofit World*, Madison, WI, July/August 2002. Vol. 20, Iss 4; p. 26(3).

Panel on the Nonprofit Sector. (2005). "Final Report of the Panel," Independent Sector, retrieved on July 1, 2005 from http://www.nonprofitpanel.org/final/.

Panetta, Leon, Testimony before the U.S. Senate Finance Committee hearings on *Charities and Charitable Giving: Proposals for Reform*, Washington, DC, April 2005.

Patsuris, P. (2002). "The Corporate Scandal Sheet," Forbes.com, retrieved on June 2, 2005 from http://www.forbes.com/2002/07/25/accountingtracker.html.

Payroll Manager's Letter, *Employee or Independent Contractor? Points to Consider in Worker Classification*. Aspen Publishers, Inc. March 7, 2005, v21 i5.

Planning Design Center. (2005). "Panel on the Nonprofit Sector Testifies on Charitable Giving Reform," retrieved on May 17, 2005 from http://www.pgdc.com/usa/item/?itemID=269232.

Peregrine, Michael W. and Schwartz, James R., *Taking the Prudent path: Best Practices for Not-for-Profit Boards*, Trustee, Nov/Dec 2003, Vol. 56, Iss. 10, p. 24. Chicago.

Perry, Phillip M. *Employee or Independent Contractor? The IRS Wants to Know*, Rural Telecommunications, National Telephone Cooperative Association Sept–Oct 2004, v21, i5.

Pogrebin, R. (2004). "2 Whitney Museum Employees Arrested in Embezzlement Case," NYTimes.com, retrieved on June 17, 2005 from http://www.nytimes.com/2004/07/30/nyregion/30museum.html?ex=1120968000&en=798392c88bf70bef&ei=5070.

Price Waterhouse Coopers LLP, *United Way of the National Capital Area Forensic Accounting Investigation*, Washington, DC, August 7, 2003.

PR Newswire, *Statement by the American Red Cross on Blood Donations*, Washington, DC, November 12, 2001.

Public Company Accounting Oversight Board (2003). "Accounting Support Fees," retrieved on June 17, 2005 from http://www.pcaobus.org/Support_Fees/index.asp.

Public Company Accounting Oversight Board (2003). "About PCAOB," retrieved on June 17, 2005 from http://www.pcaobus.org/About_Us/index.asp.

Public Company Accounting Oversight Board (2005). "Board Revokes Firm's Registration, Disciplines Three Accountants for Failure to Cooperate," Public Affairs 202-207-9227, retrieved on June 7, 2005 from http://www.pcaobus.org/News_and_Events/News/2005/05-24.asp.

Public Company Accounting Oversight Board (2005). "Bylaws and Rules of the Public company Accounting Oversight Board," retrieved on June 17, 2005 from http://www.pcaobus.org/Rules_of_the_Board/Documents/Rules_of_the_Board/all.pdf.

Public Company Accounting Oversight Board (2003). "Frequently Asked Questions Regarding Registration with the Board," PCAOB Release 2003-011A, retrieved on June 17, 2005 from http://www.pcaobus.org/Rules_of_the_Board/Documents/Release2003-011A.pdf.

Public Company Accounting Oversight Board (2005). "Frequently Asked Questions: The Accounting Support Fee and the Funding Process," retrieved on June 20, 2005 from http://www.pcaob.org/Support_Fees/SupportFeeFAQ.pdf.

Public Company Accounting Oversight Board (2005). "Order Instituting Disciplinary Proceedings, Making Findings and Imposing Sanctions in the Matter of Alan J. Goldberger, CPA and William A. Postelnick, CPA," PCAOB Release No. 2005-011, retrieved on June 18, 2005 from http://www.pcaobus.org/Enforcement/Disciplinary_Proceedings/2005/05-24_Goldberger_and_Postelnik.pdf.

Public Company Accounting Oversight Board (2005). "Order Instituting Disciplinary Proceedings, Making Findings and Imposing Sanctions in the Matter of Goldstein and Morris, CPAs, P.C. and Edward B. Morris, CPA," PCAOB Release No. 2005-010, retrieved on June 18, 2005 from http://www.pcaobus.org/Enforcement/Disciplinary_Proceedings/2005/05-24_Goldstein_and_Morris.pdf.

Public Company Accounting Oversight Board (2003). "PCAOB Center for Enforcement Tips, Complaints and Other Information," retrieved on June 17, 2005 from http://www.pcaobus.org/Enforcement/Tips/index.asp.

Public Company Accounting Oversight Board (2004). "PCAOB 2004 Budget", retrieved on June 17, 2005 from http://www.pcaobus.org/About_Us/Budget_Presentations/2004.pdf.

Public Company Accounting Oversight Board (2005). "PCAOB 2005 Budget (Revised)," retrieved on June 17, 2005 from http://www.pcaobus.org/About_Us/Budget_Presentations/2005.pdf.

Public Company Accounting Oversight Board (2004). "Statement Concerning the Issuance of Inspection Reports," PCAOB Release No. 104-2004-001, retrieved on June 17, 2005 from http://www.pcaobus.org/Inspections/Statement_Concerning_Inspection_Reports.pdf.

Public Company Accounting Reform and Investor Protection Act of 2002, S. 2673, 107th Congress, retrieved on January 28, 2004 from http://thomas.loc.gov/cgi-bin/query/z?c107:S.2673.

Public Company Accounting Reform and Investor Protection Act of 2002, H.R. 3763, 107th Congress, P.L. 107-204, retrieved on January 28, 2004 from http://frwebgate.access.gpo.gov/cgi-bin/getdoc.cgi?dbname=107_cong_public_laws&docid=f:publ204.107.

QuickMBA.com (2005). "Strategic Planning Process," retrieved on May 3, 2005 from http://www.quickmba.com/strategy/strategic-planning/.

Ramos, Michael, *Auditors' Responsibility for Fraud Detection*, Adapted from Fraud Detection in a GAAS Audit—SAS 99 Implementation Guide, www.aicap.org/pubs/jofa/jan2003/ramos.htm.

Reaves, Cynthia F. *The Impact of Sarbanes-Oxley Act of 2002 on Nonprofit Entities*, *Michigan Business Law Journal*, Summer 2003.

RevenueRecognition.com (2005). "The Compliance Chasm," retrieved on July 3, 2005 from http://www.softrax.com/pdf/ComplianceChasm_PPC2.pdf.

Revised Model Nonprofit Corporation Act (1987) defines "duty of care" in section 8:30.

Rouse, Robert, Ph.D. *Impact of Corporate Financial Scandals on Nonprofit Organizations*, Nonprofit Fiscal Fitness http://bbwebdev/solutions/eNewsletters/FiscalFitnessOctober.htm.

Salmon, Jacqueline L. *American Red Cross to Cut 231 Jobs*, *The Washington Post*, Washington, DC, June 6, 2003.

Salmon, Jacqueline L. *Area United Way Late on Payments*, *The Washington Post*, Washington, DC, July 24, 2004.

Salmon, Jacqueline L. *D.C Area United Way Pays $114,000 to Settle With Ex-Chief*, *The Washington Post*, Washington, DC, June 17, 2004.

Salmon, Jacqueline L. *Finances Questioned at Regional United Way; Ex-Board Member Raises Concerns*, *The Washington Post*, Washington, DC, January 23, 2002.

Salmon, Jacqueline L. *Red Cross President Resigns Amid Conflict*. *The Washington Post*, Washington, DC, October 27, 2001.

Salmon, Jacqueline L. *United Way Chief Toils to Resuscitate Charity*, *The Washington Post*, Washington, DC, November 1, 2004.

Salmon, Jacqueline L. *United Way Role in Federal Drive Is Questioned*, *The Washington Post*, Washington, DC, September 14, 2002.

Salmon, Jacqueline L. *United Way Rejected for U.S. Drive: Area Federal Workers Choose Another Group*, *The Washington Post*, Washington, DC, April 16, 2003.

Salmon, Jacqueline L. and Whorisky, Peter, *Audit Excoriates United Way Leadership*, *The Washington Post*, Washington, DC, August 12, 2003.

Salamon, L. (1992). *America's Nonprofit Sector: A Primer*. Baltimore, MD: The Johns Hopkins University Foundation Center.

Securities and Exchange Commission v. HealthSouth Corporation and Richard M. Scrushy. (2003). Civil Action No.CV-03-J-0615-S, retrieved on March 26, 2005 from http://www.sec.gov/litigation/complaints/comphealths.htm.

Securities and Exchange Commission v. Richard A. Causey, Jeffery K.

Securities Exchange Commission v. Time Warner.

Securities and Exchange Commission v. Timothy A. DeSpain (2005). Litigation Release No. 19067, retrieved on June 17, 2005 from http://www.sec.gov/litigation/litreleases/lr19067.htm

Securities and Exchange Commission v. WorldCom (2002). Civil Action No. COMPLAINT (Securities Fraud) retrieved on March 26, 2005 from http://www.sec.gov/litigation/complaints/complr17588.htm.

Securities and Exchange Commission v. Xerox Corporation. (2002). Civil Action No. 02-272789 (DLC), retrieved on February 21, 2005 from http://www.sec.gov/litigation/complaints/complr17465.htm.

Schein, Edgar, *Organizational Culture and Leadership*, 2nd Ed. Jossey-Bass Publishers, San Francisco, CA. 1992.

Schroeder, Mike, *Is It Time to Rethink Your Board's Structure?*, Nonprofit World, Madison, WI, November/December 2003. Vol. 21, Iss. 6; p. 9.

Schweitzer, Carole, *The Board Balancing Act: Achieving Board Accountability Without Micromanaging*, Association Management, January 2004, Vol. 56, i1 p. 34(7).

Schwinn, Elizabeth, and Williams, Grant, IRS Outlines Audit Plans for Nonprofit Organizations, *Chronicle of Philanthropy*, October 16, 2003, Vol. 16 Issue 1, p. 33.

Siegel, J. (2005). "*Avoiding Trouble While Doing Good, A Guide for the Non-Profit Director and Officer*", Charity Governance: Internal Controls, retrieved on June 21, 2005 from http://www.charitygovernance.blogs.com/charity_governance/internal_controls/.

Silk, Thomas, *Corporate Scandals and the Governance of Nonprofit Organizations*, The Exempt Organization Tax Review, December 2002, Vol. 38, No 3.

Silk, Thomas, *Ten Emerging Principles of Governance of Nonprofit Corporations*, The Exempt Organization Tax Review, January 2004, Vol. 43, No. 1, p. 35 (4).

Silverman, Rachel Emma, *Charities to Start to Grade Themselves*, Wall Street Journal, New York City, NY, August 18, 2004.

Skilling and Kenneth L. Lay. (2004). Litigation Release No. 18776, retrieved on June 29, 2005 from http://www.sec.gov/litigation/litreleases/lr18776.htm.

SmartPros, LTD (2005). "Investors Support Pre-Sox Rollback," retrieved on July 2, 2005 from http://accounting.smartpros.com/x48762.xml.

Smith, A. (2001). *Accelerated Learning in Practice*. Stafford: Network Educational Press, LTD.

Snyder, Gary, *Boards Must Change the Way They Do Business*, Nonprofit World, Madison, WI, Jul/Aug 2003. Vol. 21, Iss. 4; p. 14.

Sontag, Deborah, *Who Brought Bernadine Healy Down? New York Times Magazine*, New York, NY, December 23, 2001.

Stamer, C.M. (2004). "IRS Plans to Put Tax-Exempt Organizations Under Microscope," *Houston Business Journal*, retrieved June 14, 2005 from http://www.bizjournals.com/houston/stories/2004/09/06/focus2.html.

Strom, Stephanie, *Public Confidence in Charities Stays Flat*, New York Times, New York, NY, September 13, 2004, p. A.17.

Strom, Stephanie, *Questions About Some Charities' Activities Lead to a Push for Tighter Regulation*, New York Times, New York, NY, March 21, 2004, p. 1.23.

Strom, Stephanie, *Senator Questions Finances of United Way*, New York Times, New York, NY, August 22, 2002.

Strom, Stephanie, *Washington United Way to Select New Board*, New York Times, New York, NY, October 4, 2002.

Stroot, S., Keil, V., Stedman, P., Lohr, L., Faust, R., Schincariol-Randall, L., Sullivan, A., Czerniak, G., Kuchcinski, J., Orel, N., and Richter, M. (1998). *Peer Assistance and Review Guidebook*. Columbus, OH: Ohio Department of Education.

Sun, Lena H. *Red Cross to Give All Funds To Victims*, The Washington Post, Washington, DC, November 15, 2001.

Swards, P.; Bjorklund, V. and Small, J. (2003). "How to Read the IRS Form 990 & Find Out What It Means," Nonprofit Coordinating Committee of New York, retrieved on January 12, 2005 from http://www.npccny.org/Form_990/990.htm.

Tyler, J. Larry, Biggs, Errol. L. *Conflict of Interest: Strategies for Remaining "Purer Than Caesar's Wife,"* Trustee, Chicago, IL, March 2004. Vol. 57, Iss. 3; p. 22(5).

United States Senate Finance Committee, Staff Discussion Paper released in conjunction with June 2004 hearings on *Charity Oversight and Reform: Keeping Bad Things from Happening to Good Charities*, Washington, DC, June 2004.

United Way of the National Capital Area, *United Way of the National Capital Area Moves DC Office*, Press Release, Washington, DC, July 18, 2005.

Van Derbeken, Jaxon, *Free Clinics' Ex-Exec Accused Of Fraud, San Francisco Chronicle*, San Francisco, CA, June 25, 2004.

Ventures, G. (2005). *For Entrepreneurs: Financial Controls for Start Ups*, retrieved on June 30, 2005 from www.gaebler.com/Small-Business-Financial-Controls.htm.

Vishneski, John S. III, *New Liabilities Created by Sarbanes-Oxley: Are Your Directors, Officers Covered?* National Underwriter, December 1, 2003, Vol. 107, Iss. 48, p. 36.

Wallack, Todd, *Charity Settles in Pipevine Fiasco, San Francisco Chronicle*, San Francisco, CA, February 19, 2004.

Wallack, Todd, *Nonprofit Advisory Group in Crisis, Management Center Helped Local Agencies, San Francisco Chronicle*, San Francisco, CA, January 22, 2004.

Wallack, Todd, *SF Nonprofit to shut down, San Francisco Chronicle*, San Francisco, CA, May 19, 2004.

Wallack, Todd, *Nonprofits Fight Tougher Disclosure* Rules, *San Francisco Chronicle*, San Francisco, CA, June 24, 2004.

Wallack, Todd, *Breast Cancer Charity Is Probed/Big Bam's Use of Funds Questioned, San Francisco Chronicle*, San Francisco, CA, November 9, 2004.

Walters, Brent R. Nonprofits are Corporations too: Now It's time for Iowa to Treat Them That Way, *Journal of Corporation Law*, Iowa City, IA, Fall 2002, Vol. 28, Iss. 1; p.179, (25).

Weidenfeld, Edward L. *Sarbanes-Oxley and Fiduciary Best Practices for Officers and Directors of Nonprofit Organizations, Tax Management Estates, Gifts and Trusts Journal*, Washington, DC, March 11, 2004, Vol. 29, Iss 2, p. 104 (4).

Weiss, Mike, *James Beard President Sentenced for Swiping $1 million From Charity. San Francisco Chronicle*, San Francisco, CA June 14, 2005.

Weiss, Mike, *Recipe for Scandal, San Francisco Chronicle*, San Francisco, CA May 4, 5 and 6, 2005.

Whatcom Council of Nonprofits *Best Practices for Executive Directors and Boards of Nonprofit Organizations*, Bellingham, WA 2004.

Whitehouse, Sheldon, *The Sarbanes-Oxley Act and Nonprofits, Nonprofit World*, Madison, WI, Sep/Oct 2004, Vol. 22, Iss. 5.

Whoriskey, Peter and Salmon, Jacqueline L. *United Way Fires Fifth Key Official in a Year, The Washington Post*, Washington, DC, September 5, 2002.

Whoriskey, Peter and Salmon, Jacqueline L. *United Way CEO Quits as Charity is Recast, The Washington Post*, Washington, DC, September 6, 2002.

Wilhide, Kathleen F. and DeWald, Terrace, *Compliance and Technology: Lessons Learned in the Financial Services Sector*, IDC/Kahn Conference proceedings, San Jose, CA May 2004.

Wolverton, Brad, *What Went Wrong? Board Actions at Issue At Troubled D.C. United Way*, Chronicle of Philanthropy, September 4, 2003, Vol. 15, Issue 22, p. 27(4).

Wolverton, Brad, *Fighting Nonprofit Abuses, Chronicle of Philanthropy*, June 9, 2005, p. 35(4).

Zurick, John, *Reengineering the (Cultural Nonprofit) Organization*, ZQI, Inc. 2004.

About the Authors

Peggy M. Jackson, DPA, CPCU (San Francisco, CA) is a founding partner of the Fogarty, Jackson & Associates Consulting Group, which provides consulting services in the areas of risk management, business continuity planning, injury and illness prevention programs, and distance education and training. Dr. Jackson has coauthored five books on risk management in nonprofit organizations: *Managing Risk in Nonprofit Organization*; *Mission Accomplished: A Practical Guide to Risk Management for Nonprofits*; *Mission Accomplished: The Workbook*; *No Surprises: Harmonizing Risk & Reward in Volunteer Management*; and *Risk Management for Schools*. Dr. Jackson is a frequent speaker on risk management and business continuity planning.

Toni E. Fogarty, Ph.D. (San Francisco, CA) is an associate professor in the Department of Public Affairs and Administration at California State University, East Bay. Dr. Fogarty serves as the graduate coordinator for the Master of Science in Health Care Administration program, and teaches courses in health care management, finance and budgeting, research methods, data analysis, quality assessment and improvement, and the legal and ethical aspects of health care. Dr. Fogarty is a founding partner and the CFO of the Fogarty, Jackson & Associates Consulting Group, which provides consulting services in the areas of risk management, business continuity planning, injury and illness prevention programs, and distance education and training. Dr. Fogarty has been published in several professional and academic journals and has made a number of presentations and invited lectures at professional conferences. She has served as a principal investigator, project manager, and consultant on major research grants funded by the National Institute on Aging, the California Healthcare Foundation, the David and Lucile Packard Foundation, the National Institute of Nursing Research, and the Archstone Foundation. In addition, she coauthored the textbook *Managing Risk in Nonprofit Organizations*.

Peggy Jackson and Toni Fogarty are also the coauthors of *Sarbanes-Oxley for Nonprofits: A Guide to Building Competitive Advantage*, published in April 2005 by John Wiley & Sons, Inc.

Index